I'LL SAMBA SOMEPLACE ELSE

I'LL SAMBA SOMEPLACE ELSE

A SPATIAL HISTORY OF RACE, ETHNICITY, AND DISPLACEMENT IN SÃO PAULO

Andrew G. Britt

DUKE UNIVERSITY PRESS *Durham and London* 2026

Project Editor: Ihsan Taylor
Designed by Matthew Tauch
Typeset in Warnock Pro and Comma Base by Westchester Publishing Services

Library of Congress Cataloging-in-Publication Data
Names: Britt, Andrew G., [date] author
Title: I'll samba someplace else : a spatial history of race, ethnicity, and displacement in São Paulo / Andrew G. Britt.
Other titles: Spatial history of race, ethnicity, and displacement in São Paulo
Description: Durham : Duke University Press, 2026. | Includes bibliographical references and index.
Identifiers: LCCN 2025022902 (print)
LCCN 2025022903 (ebook)
ISBN 9781478032816 paperback
ISBN 9781478029373 hardcover
ISBN 9781478061571 ebook
Subjects: LCSH: Sociology, Urban—Brazil—São Paulo | Urban minorities—Brazil—São Paulo | Ethnicity—Brazil—São Paulo | Racism—Brazil—São Paulo | Cities and towns—Brazil—São Paulo—Sociological aspects | Urban geography—Brazil—São Paulo | São Paulo (Brazil)—Race relations
Classification: LCC HT129.B7 B758 2026 (print) | LCC HT129.B7 (ebook) | DDC 307.760981/6—dc23/eng/20251126
LC record available at https://lccn.loc.gov/2025022902
LC ebook record available at https://lccn.loc.gov/2025022903

Cover art: Maps: (*top*) Mappa topographico do Municipio de São Paulo, parte principal da cidade, Folha 36/24, ca. 1930 (Museu Paulista); (*inset*) Mappa topographico do Municipio de São Paulo, Folha 36, ca. 1930 (Museu Paulista). Wikimedia Commons. Photo: "Stretch of Parapuã Street." Photo archive of Célio Pires.

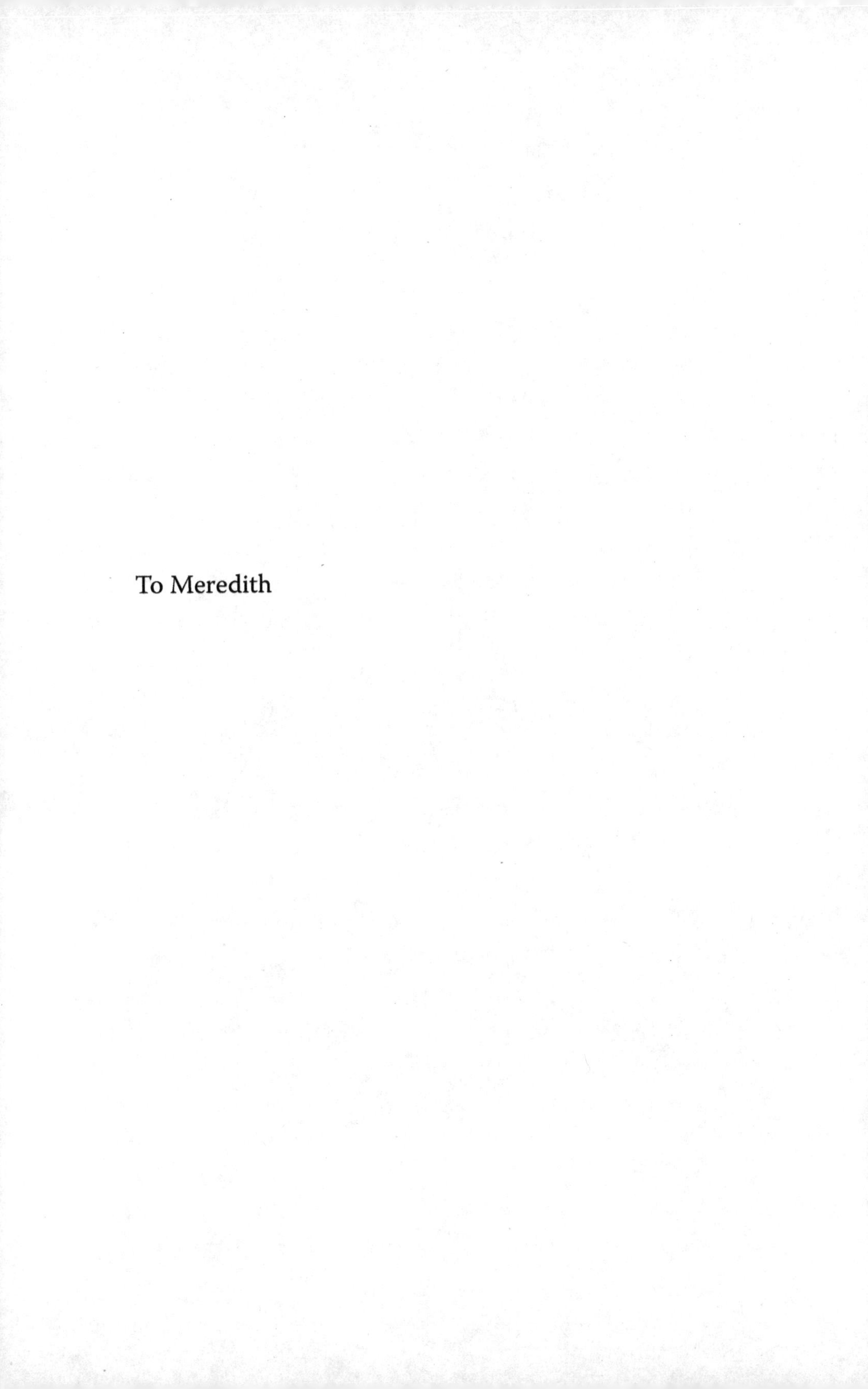

To Meredith

Contents

Acknowledgments

This book is the outcome of fourteen years of research and writing. That sum sounds substantial, particularly when calculating its share of my life (one-third). At each phase of this project, however, I have grown more cognizant of the generations of contributors to the histories collected and narrated in this book. I am thankful to have engaged with the work of the historians (very broadly defined) invested in these pasts across generations and to have formed direct and meaningful relationships with multiple of those still living. I hope *I'll Samba Someplace Else* contributes to this collective body of work and the broad project of advancing reparative relationships between the present and our individual and collective pasts.

I feel fortunate to have pursued this project first at Emory University under the advisement of Jeffrey Lesser and Thomas D. Rogers. Lesser introduced me to the frenetic, magnetic city of São Paulo in 2013 at his Charme office. From then through the early research and into the present, he has helped to shepherd this project with an uncompromising commitment to unconventional thinking, uncovering original histories, and developing inventive methods of examining them. Thomas D. Rogers was the first to see this project in the form of a seminar paper. His perspicacious, meticulous, and appreciative approach to historical inquiry guided the project from its earliest stage through the present. Thank you for your mentorship, collaboration, and friendship.

Many other faculty and staff at Emory, including Yanna Yannakakis, Phil McLeod, Ana Catarina Teixeira, Katherine Ostrom, James Melton,

Clifton Crais, Kristin Mann, Katie Wilson, Kelly Yates, Marcy Alexander, and Becky Herring, offered critical contributions and varied support throughout the graduate-school phase of this project. I was fortunate to work alongside sharp, amiable, and imaginative colleagues and friends at Emory. I would like to thank Jonathan Earl Coulis, Clint Fluker, María de los Ángeles Picone, Xanda Lemos, Danielle Wiggins, Melissa Creary, Lena Suk, Leonard Marques, Christopher David Brown, Ariel Svarch, Benjamin J. Nobbs-Thiessen, Jennifer L. Schaefer, Glen Goodman, and Audrey Fals Henderson, in particular, for their keen observations about, and contributions to, this project.

I am exceptionally grateful for the support of collaborators, research partners, and friends in Brazil, without whom this project would not have been possible. Brasilândia journalist and historian Célio Pires responded to a cold message from me in fieldwork and then warmly invited me into the headquarters of his local newspaper, *Freguesia News*, in my first months in Brazil. Pires had produced and curated an archive about Brasilândia's past throughout his career, a critical corpus of information about the history of the region. Pires generously connected me to other residents of Brasilândia, including the cofounder and leader of Samba do Congo, composer and musician Fernando Ripol. Ripol welcomed me at regular gatherings of Samba do Congo, first at the Brasilândia Community Center and later at the group's new headquarters in Morro Grande.

Through Pires and Ripol I met an ever-expanding network of people, many of whom went out of their way to support this project. Among them are André, Cicero, Dicá, Francisco, Gilberto, Joel, Luz, Maria Helena, Nicole, Suzete, Mug, Pulquéira, Rafa, Ricardo, Sara, and Waldir. I thank all the members of Samba do Congo, the Terreiro Santa Bárbara, and the other groups throughout São Paulo who invited me to events, gatherings, and intimate conversations. I am especially thankful for the time and stories of residents from Brasilândia, Liberdade, and Bela Vista who participated in recorded oral histories or informal conversations. I have learned—and continue to learn—much from these collaborators and friends about São Paulo, Brazil, and beyond. To Célio, Mug, and Luz: *descanse em paz.*

Luis Ferla and Fernando Atique of the Federal University of São Paulo have contributed to and collaborated on various aspects of this project since its earliest stages. During fieldwork, they invited me to participate in their research groups at the Federal University of São

Paulo: Cidade, Arquitetura e Preservação em Perspectiva Histórica (CAPPH) and História, Mapas e Computadores (Hímaco). Atique, Ferla, and undergraduate and graduate students in their research groups shared illuminating insights about the history of the city of São Paulo, digital methodologies, and multiple iterations of my project. I thank the archivists at São Paulo's historical archives, especially the Arquivo Público do Estado de São Paulo and the Arquivo Histórico da Cidade de São Paulo, for their support. I also express my gratitude to officials from urban planning and development institutions in the city, especially the Coordenadoria de Gestão de Documentos Públicos (CGDP) and the Departamento de Desapropriações. They provided vital access to source material about the development of the city of São Paulo broadly and the neighborhoods of Brasilândia, Liberdade, and Bela Vista, specifically.

Over the life of this project I have also been fortunate to count on the support and collaboration of Brazilianists across the globe, including Jerry Dávila, Bryan McCann, Jake Blanc, Frederico Freitas, Daryl Williams, Gladys Mitchell-Walthour, Gillian A. McGillivray, Michael Amoruso, Nate Millington, Manuel Rosaldo, Rebecca Tarlau, Graham Denyer Willis, James Green, Daria Jaremtchuk, Benito Schmidt, and César Braga-Pinto. Thank you also to mentors, colleagues, students, and friends at Wake Forest University, Northwestern University, and the University of North Carolina School of the Arts (UNCSA), including Pete Dunlap, Nate Plagemann, Michele Gillespie, David Lubin, Keith Woodhouse, Harris Feinsod, Rachel Williams, Hans Gabriel, Reagan Mitchell, Mike Wakeford, Anson Koch-Rein, Joe Mills, Marina Zurita, and Luca Kevorkian. In ways small and large, direct and indirect, you have all made significant contributions to this work.

I arrived at the University of Texas at Austin in the late stage of the book's production and to a warm welcome from new colleagues within African and African Diaspora Studies (ADDS) and across the campus. The support, rich conversations, and intellectual community made an immediate and positive impact on the final revisions.

Multiple institutions provided pivotal financial support for this project at all stages. The Social Science Research Council's Mellon International Dissertation Research Fellowship and Fulbright-Hays Doctoral Dissertation Research Abroad fellowship program financed eighteen months of fieldwork in Brazil over 2015–2016. A Project Development Grant from the American Council of Learned Societies generously supported my hiring a caregiver during the summer of 2022, which enabled me to complete late-stage manuscript revisions. The Thomas S. Kenan Institute for the Arts, the Division of Liberal Arts at UNCSA, and the Office of the Provost at UNCSA supported a book subvention to facilitate the publication of *I'll Samba Someplace Else* in the open access format. Thank you to the staff and faculty colleagues within these institutions for their investment in this project, including those who continue to support the new branches growing from it.

Thank you to the Duke University Press staff, external readers, and editorial board—especially Gisela Fosado, Alejandra Mejía, and Ihsan Taylor—for their stellar work on the revisions to and production of this book. The third section of chapter 2, focused on the demolition of the Church of Our Lady of the Remedies in São Paulo, appeared as an article in the *Journal of Latin American Studies* under the title "Spatial Projects of Forgetting: Razing the Remedies Church and Museum to the Enslaved in São Paulo's 'Black Zone,' 1930s–1940s." I thank the external readers and *JLAS* editor Graham Denyer Willis for their comments, which strengthened my narration of the Remedies history in critical ways.

I hope this book serves as a tribute to the memory of my dad, Mike, who was an expert at telling stories that moved people, and my father-in-law, Mark, whose supreme love made so many people (myself included) feel alive and at home in the world. To the Frazier, Britt, Hubert, Dunlap, and Niblock families: Thank you for your care and encouragement over these fourteen years and beyond.

Meredith Frazier Britt decided to study abroad during college in Curitiba in 2006 and is, therefore, responsible for introducing me to Brazil. After her summer in Paraná, she told me, on somewhat of a whim, she thought we might live in Brazil in the future. Neither of us anticipated the incredible ways that Brazil would become a deep and meaningful part of our lives and those of our young children, Alex and Zannah (who loves making up words in "Por-ga-tcheez"), in the years since. Meredith and I realized her 2006 intuition in 2015–2016 by living in São Paulo and collaborating—formally and informally—on nearly all aspects of this project. Her partnership, support, and sacrifices made this book possible; her curiosity, knowledge, empathy, and sense of justice made it so much better. Thank you for twenty-three years of friendship, family, and love.

INTRODUCTION

The Paradoxes of Ethnoracial Space

1958 Eu vou-me embora / Vou sambar n'outro lugar
(I'm out of here / I'll samba someplace else)

Composer Geraldo Filme repeated the same lines six times in succession: "I'm out of here / I'll samba someplace else."[1] Blending resignation and resolve, the lyrics concluded Filme's elegy to a place razed by municipal authorities in 1958 for the building of an asphalted avenue and concrete overpass in São Paulo's Barra Funda neighborhood. The full second verse of his composition, titled "I'll Samba Someplace Else," ran:

An overpass rises, it's progress
I can't protest
Goodbye, to the cradle of samba
I'm out of here
I'll samba someplace else[2]

Known popularly as the Largo da Banana (Banana Square) and named for the commerce in fruit that took place here, this site is commonly remembered among African descendants in São Paulo as a center of samba, capoeira, and labor linked to the adjacent railway line.[3] Filme frequented the Largo da Banana throughout his childhood in the 1930s and 1940s, a formative experience that would lead to a career as one of São Paulo's most influential samba composers and performers. Known affectionately as "Big Geraldo of Barra Funda," he would describe Barra Funda, along with São Paulo's Liberdade and Bexiga neighborhoods, as the city's "Black zone" (*zona do negro*).[4]

The second stanza of "I'll Samba Someplace Else" encapsulates the histories exhumed throughout this book. Indeed, while Filme's lyrics focused on the demolition of the Largo da Banana specifically, the destruction of that place was only one episode in a more expansive spatial history of burying and rebuilding São Paulo's "Black zone" throughout the mid-twentieth century. As Filme's lyrics imply, paved roadways dislocating a site significant to African descendants symbolized São Paulo–style progress in this era. From the 1930s to the 1980s, this type of redevelopment led to the asphalting of the city's early twentieth-century Black zone and paved the way—literally and figuratively—for the remaking of the neighborhoods of Liberdade and Bexiga into non-Black, immigrant enclaves. Residents displaced by this redevelopment, meanwhile, would reproduce that zone in the form of a "Little Africa" *someplace else.* Though seldom chronicled and sometimes altogether unacknowledged (particularly in academic literature), this spatial history sheds illuminating light on Brazil's most populous metropolis along with other ethnoracially diverse, highly stratified cities worldwide. And in key, perhaps unexpected, ways, the dynamics at play in São Paulo's mid-twentieth-century spatial history persist into the present.

THE PARADOXES

The temptation to characterize Brazilian social reality as defined by contradictions has captured the imaginations of many observers analyzing the country's distant and recent pasts. Some of the most prominent contradictions in analyses of contemporary Brazil include stark rates of social inequality, vast regional disparities, a political culture torn between authoritarianism and democracy, and urban landscapes divided between formal and informal cities.[5] Journalist and urbanist Tuca Vieira captured multiple of these contrasts in a now-iconic 2004 photo juxtaposing part of one of São Paulo's largest favelas, Paraísopo-

FIGURE I.1 · Tuca Vieira, *Paraisópolis*, 2004.

lis, and a luxury condominium complex in the Morumbi neighborhood (figure I.1). Initially printed on the front page of one of Brazil's most influential newspapers, *Folha de São Paulo*, the image circulated globally in the years following. Vieira found that some foreign observers did not believe the photo was real.[6] The "unbelievable" picture epitomized the contradictions at the core of Brazilian society, and the irresolvable—or at least perpetually unresolved—nature of those contradictions seemed to explain Brazil's persistent underdevelopment. Such contrasts were and are commonly seen as why, in other words, Brazil has failed to fulfill its potential as the so-called country of the future.[7]

Like others before it, this book also engages with contrasts in Brazil, specifically through the lens of that most intractable of contradictions, the paradox. I do not aim to show how contradictions have arrested Brazil's development, however. Instead, I advance a novel argument about the paradoxical nature of race/ethnicity and space that helps us to understand better the endurance of seemingly incompatible, yet stubbornly coeval, social realities. I develop this argument through the interwoven histories of three of São Paulo's most iconic ethnoracialized neighborhoods: "Japanese" Liberdade, "Italian" Bexiga, and "African" Brasilândia (map I.1). From the mid-nineteenth century through the 1930s, Liberdade and Bexiga had two of the largest concentrations of residents of African descent in the city of São Paulo. They also possessed significant, in some cases sacred, sites linked to slavery, racial violence, the abolitionist movement, and Black self-determination. As noted above, samba composer and musician Geraldo Filme described these neighborhoods as key sites in São Paulo's early twentieth-century "Black zone."

An ambitious urban redevelopment scheme, led by urban planner-turned-mayor Francisco Prestes Maia, began reshaping the material and social geographies of Liberdade and Bexiga in the 1930s. Prestes Maia's project, known as the Avenues Plan, propelled extensive demolitions, higher property values, and the displacement of many local residents of African descent through the 1960s. Some dislocated residents migrated from the city center to the north of the Tietê River to a rural parish in the Cantareira Forest. There, they partnered with regional migrants to produce the neighborhood of Brasilândia, oftentimes independent of official city planners and other state authorities.

By the 1980s, Brasilândia had one of the highest concentrations of African descendants in the city and had become a locus of Black self-determination: a "Little Africa" or "Black territory," as some observers would describe it.[8] Meanwhile, in the same era, governmental authorities partnered with non-Black residents of Liberdade and Bexiga to transform the built environments of these neighborhoods to index Japanese and Italian ethnoracial identities. Bankrolled by state institutions and produced in part through the labor of ordinary residents, these twin ethnoracialization projects would fix the ethnoracial-spatial identities of "Japanese" Liberdade and "Italian" Bexiga in material space as well as popular and official discourse by the early 1980s.

The interwoven histories of Liberdade, Bexiga, and Brasilândia mirror the interlaced histories of populations of Japanese, Italian, and African descent in São Paulo and Brazil more broadly from the late nineteenth century through the present. Beginning in the nineteenth century, officials and powerful economic agents in São Paulo promoted Italian and then Japanese immigration as the means for a profitable transition from enslaved to wage labor. Newcomers from the Italian peninsula and Japan would replace Africans and African descendants on plantations in the province and later state of São Paulo, where a

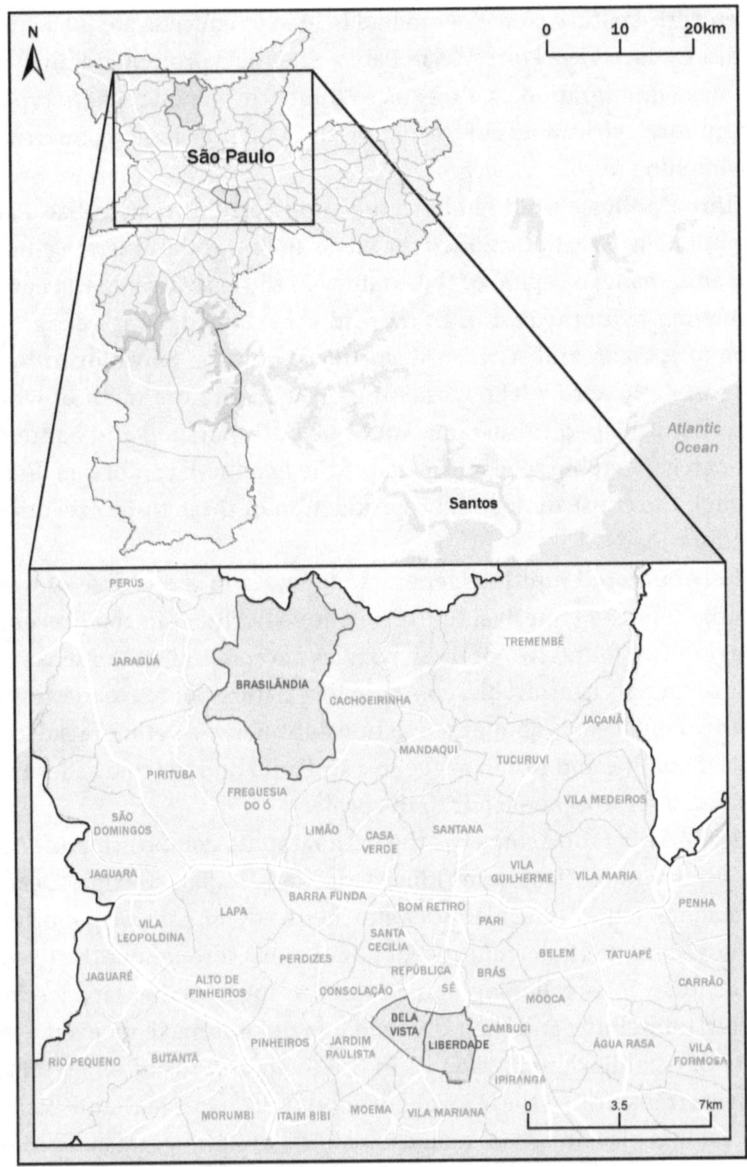

MAP I.1 · City of São Paulo by district with Brasilândia, Liberdade, and Bela Vista highlighted, 2024. Data sources: GeoSampa; OpenStreetMap (Light Gray Canvas) © OpenStreetMap contributors, Microsoft, Facebook, Google, Esri Community Maps contributors, map layer by Esri. Map by Andrew G. Britt.

nineteenth-century coffee boom had helped to concentrate the nation's largest enslaved workforce.[9] São Paulo elites also promoted Italian and Japanese immigration as a means to dilute the genetic, phenotypical, and cultural Africanness of the nation through policies they referred to as whitening (*branqueamento*).[10]

Those policies would help to fuel a powerful thread of São Paulo exceptionalism that positioned the city, which was the emerging industrial and financial capital of the country in the early twentieth century, as distinct from the rest of Brazil and especially its long-recognized hubs of African and African-descendent culture, Salvador in Bahia and Rio de Janeiro.[11] The whitening project, and the myth of whiteness that it helped to sustain, would be both pursued and contested through geographic space throughout the twentieth century, including through the construction and reproduction of these three exceptional neighborhoods.

I encountered multiple generative puzzles in the course of weaving together the cohesive, linear narrative outlined in the preceding paragraphs. I found two of these puzzles paradoxical, in the sense that their seemingly irresolvable, contradictory nature points, to me, toward broader conclusions about the relationships between ethnoracial identity, inequality, and urban space in São Paulo and beyond. These two paradoxes serve as bookends to the project.

The first paradox concerns the demographic composition of "African" Brasilândia, "Japanese" Liberdade, and "Italian" Bexiga. Despite the singular ethnoracial identities attached to them, each neighborhood possessed multiethnic, multiracial populations throughout the twentieth century. In fact, demographic evidence suggests that Japanese and Italian immigrants and their descendants did not make up even a majority of neighborhood residents in the 1970s and 1980s, when official projects transformed these neighborhoods into "Japanese" and "Italian" spaces. It is plausible that Japanese and Italian immigrants and immigrant descendants did not, in fact, constitute a majority of the neighborhoods' populations *at any point* in the twentieth century. Brasilândia, similarly, has had nearly as many non-Black as Black residents since its formal establishment in 1947. If the ethnoracial-spatial constructions associated with each neighborhood correlated only loosely to the ethnoracial composition of neighborhood residents, then how—and, crucially, *why*—did these specific, singular ethnoracial identities become attached to these urban spaces? Answering this question animated much of the research for this project and ultimately led to the second paradox, which forms the central argument of the book.

The second paradox engages one of the most significant and enduring contradictions in contemporary Brazil: the coexistence of a postracial ideology that emphasizes interracial harmony, mixture, and equality alongside a racialized social structure of endemic inequality, anti-Black violence, and anti-Blackness. Generations of researchers, as well as activists and organizers, have puzzled over the coexistence of these competing, constitutive elements of Brazilian social reality.[12] Some of the most influential work in this century has advanced precise social scientific analyses that detail high rates of racialized inequalities and violence in multiple social domains, from health and housing to education and employment.[13] Following in the footsteps of earlier generations of researchers and activists, such studies have cast convincing and quantified doubt on the discourse of racial harmony in Brazil, famously articulated as the ideology of "racial democracy."[14] These studies have also served as support for novel federal programs designed to promote racial equality in the twenty-first century. Postracialism, nonetheless, remains a powerful, consequential ideological force in the twenty-first century in Brazil and other highly stratified societies shaped by slavery and its afterlives, including the United States.

THE ARGUMENTS

I'll Samba Someplace Else contributes to this multigenerational body of work by arguing that the reproduction of urban space in mid-twentieth-century São Paulo helped to reproduce ethnoracialized social inequalities while, simultaneously and paradoxically, also structuring postracialist discourses. I advance this argument through three principal points that weave throughout the book.

First, anti-Black violence shaped spatial change in São Paulo through dispossession, demolitions, displacement, and disinvestment during a pivotal period of the city's development and amid the ascendance and increasing contestation of the ideology of "racial democracy." For some readers, this argument may seem unsurprising, perhaps even banal. Indeed, African descendants in São Paulo have long made this critique and in myriad forms, from scholarly work and creative nonfiction to popular music. Readers will find many examples of their critiques chronicled throughout this book. Nonetheless, this critical position has largely remained on the margins of mainstream academic and official discourses about the spatial history of São Paulo, especially, though not exclusively, in texts written in English.[15] One central objective of this project, therefore, has been to analyze the significance of anti-Blackness and urban space by locating evidence and employing methods considered authoritative in mainstream academic and official discourse.

I offer, for instance, granular though revealing archival evidence that anti-Blackness influenced the planning and execution of São Paulo's seminal twentieth-century redevelopment program, the Avenues Plan. I employ historical mapping methods to show how urban redevelopment negatively impacted neighborhoods with some of the largest populations of African descent in the city. Through oral histories I document the circulation of a racist neighborhood nickname that structured popular prejudices against Brasilândia, which by the 1980s had both one of the highest concentrations of African descendants and one of the largest populations of any district in São Paulo. I show, relatedly, that Brasilândia was among the São Paulo neighborhoods hardest hit by municipal disinvestment in the twentieth century. Such histories illuminate how anti-Blackness shaped the spatial development of twentieth-century São Paulo in consequential and enduring ways. This research thus confirms and builds on critiques about the salience of anti-Blackness in São Paulo's spatial history. The broad contours of those critiques, again, did not originate with me.

Second, some African descendants in São Paulo confronted an environment of racialized inequality and anti-Black violence, along with an official ideology of postracialism, through a distinctive set of practices that reproduced space and that were informed by a distinctive set of conceptions of space. Embodied, material practices in physical space and theoretical conceptions of space exist in a dialectical relationship and therefore constitute a spatial praxis. I term the distinctive spatial praxis developed by some African descendants in São Paulo as the *spatial praxis of belonging-as-being.*[16]

This particular spatial praxis was shaped by the racialized social and spatial dynamics of the city of São Paulo from the early twentieth century to the present. For Black residents of São Paulo, avoiding violent and unnatural corporeal death has been, as anthropologist Jaime Alves has persuasively chronicled, an ever-present struggle.[17] Their spatial praxis in what Alves has termed "the anti-Black city," however, transcended base survival alone. Some African descendants linked survival—the ontological condition of being—to belonging *in* and *to* place. This spatial praxis secured the material foundations for survival and, at times, Black self-determination, while also asserting a claim of belonging and being in a city where officials had communicated anti-Black nonbelonging and nonbeing in multiple ways. While the context of São Paulo helped to shape the unique contours of this praxis, the praxis also drew on epistemologies of space perhaps particular to, and seemingly particularly prominent among, African descendants in Brazil. I develop this point further in the remainder of this section and the one that follows about leading Black theorist Beatriz Nascimento, who, I argue, articulated key aspects of the spatial praxis of belonging-as-being before me.

Repossession and rebuilding—discernible in Geraldo Filme's declaration, "I'm out of here / I'll samba someplace else"—lay at the core of this praxis. The vast spatial transformations in the city of São Paulo at midcentury, changes in part unleashed by the Avenues Plan, made repossession and rebuilding a necessity for many Paulistanos, especially those African descendants in neighborhoods that had been hard hit by dispossession and demolition. To echo the argument from the first point above: Dispossession and demolition were not indiscriminate. Through officials' choices of where to concentrate redevelopment, along with their rhetoric about those projects, spaces, and the bodies within them, officials sometimes asserted that Black Paulistanos did not belong in the city (anti-Blackness). The extension of that argument was that Black Paulistanos did not exist in the city: São Paulo was, in other words, a non-Black, ethnically immigrant metropolis (non-Blackness). Brasilândia was one particularly significant, though not singular, "someplace else" that African descendants in São Paulo rebuilt in the wake of the dislocations caused by this marginalizing, anti-Black urban redevelopment.

The maintenance of ties to ancestors and the ancestral also figured centrally in the spatial praxis of belonging-as-being. I show in chapter 1, for instance, that dislocated residents of African descent likely chose Brasilândia for repossession and rebuilding because the surrounding parish had deep ties to enslaved and freed African descendants in the nineteenth century. Those ties manifested notably in the toponym, or place-name, of the main road through the region: Congo Road. Popularly given in the early nineteenth century if not before, Congo Road would endure until 1960, when São Paulo's mayor agreed to requests from non-Black residents of the region to replace the name. Memory of Congo Road would persist, however, including among the founders of a roots samba group in Brasilândia (established in 2011) who named their new collective Samba do Congo after the roadway. Earlier and later generations of African descendants similarly sought to sustain or forge ancestral ties through place-names as a part of this spatial praxis.

The final principal element of this praxis was ethnoracial inclusion. While some African descendants in São Paulo contested anti-Blackness through claims of belonging and being specific to their lived experiences, the vision that many advanced of who had the *right* to belong—at the scale of local institutions, neighborhoods, or the city as a whole—often included those not of African descent. This inclusive vision reflected, and likely was influenced by, the ethnoracial diversity of the city's neighborhoods, including Brasilândia, which, again, despite having one of the largest concentrations of African descendants in the city of São Paulo in the 1980s, still had upward of a 45 percent non-Black population.[18] One of the complicated results of this inclusive posture, I surmise, was that it helped to sustain the sociospatial foundations and ideological consonance of postracial discourses.

Third, the production of "Japanese" Liberdade and "Italian" Bexiga established what I term an *ethnoracialized infrastructure* that, paradoxically, both bolstered postracial discourses and deepened racialized inequalities. Produced through official and grassroots spatial practices, the publicly funded construction of this infrastructure transformed the built environments of Liberdade and Bexiga from the 1960s to 1980s. The changes introduced an array of features designed to index Japanese and Italian ethnoracial identities, such as cherry blossom lanterns, lampposts colored in the Italian flag, and Samurai-themed sidewalks. The resulting neighborhoods appeared as seemingly natural and timeless ethnic enclaves: material manifestations of supposedly organic settlement patterns among Japanese and Italian immigrants and their descendants that reflected high-prestige, non-Black immigrant identities. The ethnoracialized neighborhoods thus served as a concrete representation of the city's supposedly unique capacity for harmonious—though, crucially, non-Black—ethnoracial mixture. The ethnoracialization projects left few material remains from the neighborhoods' central position in São Paulo's "Black zone" in prior generations. In doing so, they contributed to rendering African descendants less visible in the city of São Paulo: neither belonging nor being in its past, present, or future.

While these ethnoracialization projects established a material foundation of support for postracial discourses, they also participated in the reproduction of racialized inequalities in the city. That inequality was not just symbolic—about the valorization, again, of high-prestige immigrant identities over Black identity, for instance—though such racial hierarchies were and remain, of course, significant. Instead, the inequalities created through these projects were concrete, tactile, and visible: public funds supporting an ethnoracialized infrastructure of urban services and amenities—public illumination, sidewalks, parks, libraries, and more—rare in most São Paulo neighborhoods through much of the mid-twentieth century and *least* prevalent in places like Brasilândia. The ethnoracialized infrastructure created in these neighborhoods thus served to reproduce racialized spatial inequalities between neighborhoods and displace the bodies and material histories of African descendants while, simultaneously, serving as tactile support for popular, enduring discourses about São Paulo's racialized particularity specifically and Brazil's supposedly unique brand of harmonious ethnoracial mixture more broadly.

Together, these arguments offer insights into a few pivotal questions from São Paulo's past and present, including how the provincial capital of one of racialized chattel slavery's final frontiers in the Americas in the late nineteenth century became commonly and, to some, convincingly represented as a non-Black, immigrant metropolis by the mid-twentieth.[19] I show that the reproduction of space, particularly though, again, not exclusively in these three neighborhoods, helped to engender this transformation. The reproduction of Liberdade as "Japanese" and Bexiga as "Italian" from the 1930s to the 1980s helped to demarcate São Paulo in material form as a non-Black, ethnically immigrant metropolis: (seemingly) racially egalitarian yet also fundamentally distinct from the (supposed) true urban hearts of Africa in Brazil, Salvador, and Rio de Janeiro.

The displacement of African descendants to São Paulo's geographic margins deepened racialized inequalities and further excluded Black Paulistanos from certain spaces in the city. Official ethnoracialization projects in the years following exacerbated those inequalities by furnishing a substantial public investment in the creation of non-Black, ethnically immigrant neighborhoods and continuing disinvestment in places like Brasilândia. *I'll Samba Someplace Else* thus challenges representations of São Paulo as a non-Black city by detailing how spatialized anti-Blackness contributed to the construction and concretization of this mythic representation itself.

The book also challenges representations of São Paulo as a non-Black city by recentering African descendants in the city's spatial history in the mid-twentieth century. A rich body of work has chronicled the lives of Black Paulistanos from earlier in the century, especially from the 1910s to 1937, when the Black press and associative life flourished and Black intellectuals founded seminal organizations, such as Brazil's first Black political party, the Brazilian Black Front (Frente Negra Brasileira, FNB). Headquartered in Liberdade, the FNB was forced to close after the declaration of the New State in 1937 and the outlawing of all political parties. The Unified Black Movement (MNU), founded in São Paulo in 1978 in the midst of Brazil's military dictatorship (1964–85), would help to reignite organized antiracist activism and mobilization throughout the country.[20]

I'll Samba Someplace Else contributes to our understanding of the years between the two eras of formal Black movement organizing and advances an expansive conception of the term *movement* itself.[21] Attending carefully to geographic space, this conception foregrounds the displacement of African descendants spurred by urban redevelopment in between the two seminal periods of antiracist organizing (1910s–1930s and 1978 onward) as well as the African-descendent migrants who moved to, settled in, and produced places like Brasilândia. Following their migrations and the someplace(s) else they created helps to recenter African descendants, particularly those outside the Black middle class or elite, in a period when antiracist critique and expressions of Black identity were challenged by powerful, at times repressive, promotion of ideologies of postracialism.[22] Foregrounding this history of displacement and resettlement also invites greater attention to Black self-determination as a spatial praxis, in São Paulo and beyond.

The history of producing Brasilândia is emblematic of this spatial praxis. Little published research about Brasilândia exists in English or Portuguese.[23] Several factors have obscured the recording of Brasilândia's past. A hub of informality since its settlement, Brasilândia was founded, and largely grew, off the map. The neighborhood concentrated some of the city of São Paulo's first favelas, the informal urban settlement common throughout Brazil. By the 1970s, Brasilândia would have the largest number of favelas in the city. Because Brasilândia was settled informally, written sources about its development are not readily accessible in São Paulo's historical archives. The textual documentation I located about Brasilândia, combined with other ethnographic sources and spatial history methodologies, provides revealing insights into the neighborhood's past. Popular stigma has also kept the history of Brasilândia largely unwritten. When the name of the place appears in São Paulo's popular press, commentators frequently depict it as a hub of poverty, violence, and crime.[24] That stigma is discernibly racialized, a fact that I first discerned in warnings from strangers that my whiteness would make me unsafe in the neighborhood. Chapter 4 details the construction of this racialized stigma—which ran parallel to, and was contested by, the "Little Africa" ascription—in the late 1960s and early 1970s. The individuals and narratives I follow throughout the book aim to disrupt the popular misconceptions about this place and its residents. Those misconceptions continue to structure racial prejudices and inequalities through the present.

While *I'll Samba Someplace Else* centers on the spatialization of African, Japanese, and Italian ethnoracial identities specifically, the population of the city of São Paulo has long included, of course, many ethnoracial groups. Among these varied groups, the experiences of Indigenous peoples have closely paralleled and, in some cases, directly intersected with the same of African descendants. Readers will note those parallels and intersections at multiple instances throughout the book, including in the context of historical practices of enslavement and contemporary practices of dispossession (many of which affected Indigenous and African-descendent peoples in these three neighborhoods).

Some readers will also recognize that the construction of the myth of São Paulo as a non-Black, immigrant metropolis mirrors misrepresentations of São Paulo as a non-Indigenous city. Researchers and activists, including prominent Indigenous leaders, have worked to contest this process of erasure.[25] Their arguments build on the precolonial and early colonial Indigenous origins of the settlement of São Paulo, whose first official designation, São Paulo dos Campos de Piratininga, retained the Indigenous toponym for the region. Their arguments also commonly contest the enduring misconceptions that Indigenous populations were entirely disappeared in the colonial period through genocide or assimilation and that all Indigenous people live only in rural villages or other nonurban contexts. Demographic data provides quantified support for these observations. On federal censuses since 1991, the city of São Paulo has consistently had one of the largest Indigenous populations (in absolute terms) of any city in Brazil.[26] The city also has multiple federally designated Indigenous territories, including one in the Jaraguá district, which sits adjacent to Brasilândia.

One of the leading academic voices to counter representations of São Paulo as a non-Black *and* non-Indigenous city has been Casé Angatu (also known as Carlos José Ferreira dos Santos), an Indigenous scholar with specializations in history, architecture, and urbanism. In 1998 Angatu published *Not Everything Was Italian: São Paulo and Poverty, 1890–1915*, a seminal work tracking the quotidian lives, livelihoods, and cultural practices of non-White Brazilian populations, especially African descendants, in the city at the turn of the twentieth century.[27] By foregrounding these groups, Angatu's book counters the supremacy of ethnically immigrant, and especially Italian, populations and culture in popular and academic narratives about the city. Angatu's recent works have more even directly illuminated the presence of Indigenous people, past and present, in São Paulo and beyond.[28]

I'll Samba Someplace Else builds on works like *Not Everything Was Italian* by showing how the transformation of the city's ethnoracialized geography in the middle of the twentieth century intersected with Indigenous peoples and places. This book does not, however, offer a comprehensive analysis of Indigenous peoples and spaces in contemporary São Paulo or those groups' sociospatial relationships with African descendants. Historians of Latin America have made recent and significant contributions on these topics, including Brazilianists writing about both the nineteenth and twentieth centuries. I expect other researchers will continue to advance this scholarship, including, hopefully, in the context of the city of São Paulo itself.[29]

1989 Onde estou, eu sou
(Where I am [in space], I am [I exist])

A scene late in the 1989 film *Orí*—a collaboration between African descendant historian, philosopher, activist, and poet Beatriz Nascimento and film director Raquel Gerber—opens with an aerial shot of São Paulo's urban landscape.[30] A text overlay reads, "Saracura Valley, Bixiga,

São Paulo." The camera begins to rotate around one street corner below, anchored by the headquarters of the Vai-Vai samba school but also encompassing buzzing traffic on the nearby July 9 Avenue. Nascimento narrates this view, her voice crisp above the helicopter's hum:

> Quilombo is a history. This word has a history. It also has a typology according to region and according to chronology. Your relationship to your territory. It is important to see that today the quilombo is for us no longer a geographic territory, but a territory at the level of a symbology. We are people, we have the right to the territory, to the land. Many parts of my history tell me that I have the right to the space that I occupy in the nation. This is what Palmares was telling us. I have the right to the space that I occupy within this system, within this nation, within this geographic limit that is the captaincy of Pernambuco. The land is my quilombo, my space is my quilombo. Where I am (*estou*), I am (*estou*). Where I am (*estou*), I am (*sou*).[31]

Here Nascimento draws on her research on *quilombos*, or communities created by enslaved people fleeing from captivity, in Brazil and Angola in the 1970s and 1980s. She theorized the *quilombo* as more than a material place or settlement. In Nascimento's conception, Christen Smith explains, *quilombo* was "also a verb—the ideological practice of encampment against the oppression of slavery." Nascimento defined slavery broadly as a condition encompassing "racialized poverty, the disparagement of Black aesthetics, urban segregation, and the erasure of history," or what more recent scholars have termed the "afterlives of slavery."[32] She argued that favelas were a contemporary manifestation of *quilombos*, and through historical mapping she aimed to document how favelas in the twentieth century sat in the same geographical locations as historical *quilombos*.[33]

Of all the potential places throughout Brazil (or beyond) that Nascimento and Gerber might have chosen for this shot in *Orí*, why did they select Bexiga and the Saracura valley, in particular? Would not another, more well-known site—remnants of the Palmares kingdom in the state of Alagoas, the Pelourinho neighborhood in Salvador, or the "Little Africa" region of Rio de Janeiro, to choose three iconic examples—better represent the sociospatial critique and interwoven claims of African-descendent belonging and being that Nascimento articulates? What spatial histories of *this* place compelled them to anchor this shot in this corner of Bexiga? The answer lay, in part, beneath that buzzing traffic on July 9 Avenue in a demolished place called Saracura.

Founded as a *quilombo* in the nineteenth century, Saracura was, by the early twentieth century, considered a neighborhood. At that time, Saracura likely had the largest concentration of African descendants in the city of São Paulo. The execution of the Avenues Plan in the 1930s, specifically the construction of July 9 Avenue, involved the demolition of Saracura and displacement of residents. Not unlike the Largo da Banana, this corner of the Saracura Valley thus symbolized the demolitions, dispossession, dislocation, and asphalting of spaces significant to African descendants throughout twentieth-century São Paulo.[34] Such erasure was perhaps especially acute at the time of *Orí's* release, coming on the heels of a state-sponsored Italianization campaign to transform the ethnoracial identity associated with the neighborhood. At the same time, the endurance of the headquarters of Vai-Vai, which remained at this site through the early 2020s, symbolized Black self-determination and the preservation of the histories and identities of African descendants in São Paulo and beyond.[35] The shot therefore captured, in short, some of the core paradoxes that structure ethnoracialized inequality in Brazil and that necessitated the spatial praxis of belonging-as-being that Nascimento here conveys.

MAPPING ETHNORACIAL SPACE IN "POSTRACIAL" SOCIETIES

This book analyzes the intersection of two discrete, though often related, processes: the production of space and the construction of ethnoracialized social difference.[36] I see the product of those intersecting processes—ethnoracial space—as a discursive and material spatial-identity construct that structures unequal social relationships. I examine ethnoracial space most commonly at the scale of the neighborhood, though similar constructions at both more localized and broader geographic frames also factor into my analysis.[37]

Prior work on urban space and race/ethnicity, much of it also often focused on the neighborhood scale, has frequently centered on North American and European cities and detailed how ethnoracial spaces result from either racist segregation or immigrant networks in so-called ethnic enclaves. The former paradigm, centered on a Black/White conception of racialized difference, often privileges the role of institutional and state actors in enacting racist spatial programs that typically result in Black or White neighborhoods.[38] The latter, "ethnic enclaves" approach often focuses on immigrant ethnicity and deemphasizes the role of the state in favor of nonstate actors such as "ethnic entrepreneurs," whose principally economic activities (the framework holds) help to form seemingly homogenous and naturally occurring immigrant enclaves.[39]

The creation of ethnoracial space at the neighborhood scale in mid-twentieth-century São Paulo calls for an approach that integrates and transcends these frameworks. This approach holds ethnoracial space as neither naturally occurring nor the incidental byproduct of more significant, first-order factors such as immigrant and migrant settlement patterns.[40] From regions to neighborhoods, ethnoracial space was reproduced over time through specific, identifiable spatial practices and projects in contingent processes that involved contested negotiations between, perhaps most prominently, local residents and officials.[41] These practices and projects had a markedly relational character. As I elucidate in chapter 5, for example, "Japanese" Liberdade was constructed from the 1960s to the 1980s in relation and even direct opposition to representations of Liberdade as part of São Paulo's "Black zone" from earlier in the century as well as the then-contemporary migration of non-White Northeasterners into the neighborhood. Such dynamics require us to analyze the development of "Japanese" Liberdade and comparable ethnoracialized places as relational constructs produced in contact with and, quite often, in contrast to (in this case) non-Japanese social identities as well as spaces outside of Liberdade.

As noted in my discussion of the first paradox above, ethnoracialized spaces representing a singular group were also produced in spite of ethnoracially diverse resident populations. To be sure, the ethnoracial identities of local residents in ethnoracialized spaces bore some relationship to the identity commonly associated with a space. I have yet to encounter, for instance, a "Little Italy" that did not have at least some history of settlement by Italian immigrants and their descendants. However, the link between the demographic composition of a place and the identity attached to it is rarely clear-cut. Stated differently: The settlement of Italian immigrants and their descendants in a neighborhood accounts for only part of the explanation for the ethnoracialization of that neighborhood as "Italian."

My understanding of ethnoracial space encompasses both discursive and physical constructions. The former includes how ordinary residents and, at times, officials describe ethnoracialized neighborhoods, including by designating them as "Japanese" Liberdade, "Italian" Bexiga, and "African" Brasilândia. Physical constructions representative of such ethnoracial identities also figure centrally in the production of ethnoracial spaces. Sometimes the architects of ethnoracial spaces designed them with the explicit intent to index a certain ethnoracial group, such as in the Samurai-themed sidewalks that line Liberdade. At other times, seemingly mundane features of a city's built environment—ones that, on their surface, have no readily apparent relationship to race/ethnicity—can acquire a meaningful and widely held ethnoracialized significance apart from their planners' original intent.

Attending to ethnoracialized physical constructions asks us to take seriously how social identities can become fixed—even if momentarily and impermanently—in material space. This approach, in other words, invites us to pay closer attention to the tactile significance of "construction" in our understanding of ethnoracial identities as social constructions.[42] While social identities are, of course, produced through regimes of classification and performance (to take two examples), they can also be tangibly constructed—and, in the process, disembodied—through material features of the built environment. Though neither permanent nor unmovable, such constructions are stable, durable, and, at times, structural. These qualities enable ethnoracial space—and, more specifically, what I term an ethnoracialized infrastructure—to do consequential work reshaping material conditions, ideologies, and social relationships.

This conception of ethnoracial space and its significance has particular relevance to (supposedly) postracial societies. Researchers Brooke Neely and Michelle Samura make this case when they write: "At a time when the term 'post-racial' is used to signal a supposed decline in the significance of race, a spatial perspective can provide a particularly useful lens and language for locating and understanding persistent racial processes."[43] Neely and Samura focus on the twenty-first-century United States in their work, specifically the rise of postracial discourses following the 2008 election of Barack Obama to the US presidency. While such discourses have gone mainstream in the United States in the late twentieth and especially early twenty-first centuries, Brazilian state officials, academics, and ordinary citizens alike have asserted and contested representations of Brazil as a postracial society for nearly a century. Thus, while Neely and Samura's perspective has clear relevance for our analysis of contemporary geographic landscapes in places like the United States, we can also find instructive antecedents in the socio-spatial histories of mid-twentieth-century Brazil.

The substance of and rationale supporting discourses of Brazil as a postracial society have varied across time and space. All have emphasized the relative insignificance of racialized social difference in Brazil in comparison with social class and, quite often, in contrast to the other former major slave society of the hemisphere, the United States.[44] Other prominent elements in discourses of postracialism in Brazil have included: a celebration of proximity between racial groups, racial mixture (through miscegenation and/or culture), and, at times, an imagined meta-Brazilian race; assertions about the lack of racial animus, anti-Black prejudice, and discrimination in Brazilian society; and arguments about equality between different racialized groups.[45] The prominence of these discursive threads in mid-twentieth-century Brazil, and especially São Paulo, lead me to describe the country as a "postracial" society. By doing so, I do not imply that Brazil was an actually existing postracial society in the mid-twentieth century, before, or since. Instead, I employ this term to describe a context in which individuals in an array of social positions took postracial discourses seriously, including by advancing policies designed to realize postracial ideals or taking actions under the assumption that Brazil was indeed already a postracial society.

Space has occupied a central, though somewhat ambiguous, role in analyses of racial inequity in Brazil. In one of the most influential works on twentieth-century São Paulo, anthropologist Teresa Caldeira has argued that, by the 1970s and 1980s, São Paulo had become a highly segregated "city of walls." Caldeira attends to the racialized nature of this phenomena in her analysis, though social class forms the basis of the segregation she deftly charts.[46] Caldeira's analysis indeed aligns with conclusions from common measurements of racial segregation in contemporary Brazilian cities. One of the most common methods used to measure racial segregation, the Dissimilarity Index, compares the ethnoracial composition of a single census tract with the entire city. The discrepancy between these measurements generates a value between 0 and 100, with values closer to 100 indicating a higher degree of racial segregation. In 1980, São Paulo had a value of 37 for Black-White segregation based on the Dissimilarity Index.[47] This value positioned São Paulo in a four-way tie with Rio de

Janeiro, Porto Alegre, and Belém for *least segregated* among the ten most populous metropolitan regions in Brazil. Aside from Salvador in Bahia, which had a value of 48, the range among the other nine most populous metropolitan regions was only four points (37–41).[48] These data indicate that, aside from Salvador, Brazil's most populous cities exhibited a similar degree of residential segregation in 1980.

Such conditions contrast sharply with the eight most populous metropolitan regions in the United States in 1980. None of the eight fell below 73 (the value in Detroit), three ranked above 80 (Los Angeles, Baltimore, and Philadelphia), and Chicago led the ranking at 92.[49] Such comparisons seem to indicate that racial segregation in Brazil is comparatively mild and not a determinative factor in structuring ethnoracial inequalities. Space, in other words, seems to be one of the arenas in which Brazil appears closest to an actually existing postracial society. An extension of this conclusion might be that if we want to understand racialized social inequality in Brazil, we should concentrate our analysis on more determinative factors, such as access to education, employment opportunities, health, etc.

I do not, unsurprisingly, adopt this position. I present it, nonetheless, in order to illustrate how sophisticated analyses of space, informed by racial demographic data rare throughout most of twentieth-century Brazil, can support a view of Brazil as a postracial society. The production of space is, I argue, one of the most significant and convincing ways through which the myth of postracialism is supported. At the same time, I document how space has played a determinative role in structuring social inequalities in urban Brazil as in societies like the United States.[50] Those patterns might appear less obvious because spatialized racial inequality can manifest differently across space and time. This point echoes the assertion of sociologist Edward Telles that "racial segregation in Brazil is not self-apparent and requires systematic measurement." Telles proceeds to prescribe an analysis that "neither imposes assumptions from systems of legalized black-white segregation like the United States and South Africa, nor embraces the racial democracy ideology, which obscures a true understanding of how race and class operate in Brazil."[51]

I provide examples of how spatialized racial inequalities manifest differently in Brazil compared to other contexts, including in the three neighborhoods at the core of this study. Though distinct from patterns in cities in the United States, these alternative geographies and topographies of segregation still structure racialized social inequalities.

I also suggest that residential segregation and racialized displacement are not the only means through which race and space manifest or produce inequality. Ethnoracialized space, which, again, does not hinge in Brazil on ethnoracial uniformity at the neighborhood level, also plays a significant role in structuring racialized inequalities. Though framed by the history of São Paulo, the insights gleaned from the histories of these neighborhoods speak directly to highly stratified, ethnoracially diverse cities beyond Brazil. They shed particular light on the consequential, thorny relationships between space and race in (supposedly) postracial urban contexts across the globe.

MEASURING SPACE AND RACE

There is a crucial distinction between the categories of *neighborhood*, *subdistrict*, and *district* in São Paulo. The primary subjects of this book are neighborhoods, yet neighborhoods in the city of São Paulo possess no official definition by the municipal government.[52] They are, instead, fluid sociospatial constructs produced through everyday spatial practices, large-scale projects, and much more. In the twentieth century, São Paulo was officially organized by districts and subdistricts, which often shared the same names as neighborhoods. For example, the neighborhoods of Brasilândia, Liberdade, and Bexiga are distinct from, but located within, the districts of Brasilândia, Liberdade, and Bela Vista (map I.1 and table I.1). To confuse matters further, these classifications change over time. Liberdade and Bela Vista have been districts since the early twentieth century. Brasilândia, by contrast, changed from a neighborhood into a subdistrict and ultimately a district during the mid-twentieth century. Given that neighborhoods are the central subjects of my analysis, I often omit the word *neighborhood* itself when discussing Brasilândia, Liberdade, or Bexiga. I include the word *district* when I refer to that category of official space instead of the neighborhood. Readers will note, in addition, that throughout the book I use quotations when describing the ethnoracialized identities of these neighborhoods, as in: "African" Brasilândia, "Japanese" Liberdade, and "Italian" Bexiga. I do so in order to emphasize that these are sociospatial constructs and to avoid reifying them as natural, essential, or timeless.

Above, I argue that the demographic composition of a neighborhood plays only a part in determining the ethnoracial identity attached

TABLE I.1 · Population Change by District and Subdistrict

	POPULATION BY YEAR							
	1934	1940	1950	1960	1970	1980	1991	2000
Liberdade	39,726	43,795	55,523	68,210	71,503	82,472	76,245	61,875
Bela Vista	43,861	47,440	46,340	57,364	64,704	85,416	71,825	63,190
Nossa Senhora do Ó	7,866	13,436	17,487	45,002	103,908	150,578	152,672	144,923
Brasilândia	-	-	19,329*	49,743*	114,855*	166,441*	201,591	247,328

Sources:
IBGE, *Censos Demográficos* (1940–2000); Azevedo, *A Cidade*, vol. II (1934), 232; *População e taxas anuais de crescimento: Município de São Paulo, subprefeituras e distritos municipais, 1950–2022*, elaborado por SMUL/GEOINFO com dados do Censo Demográfico do IBGE, Prefeitura Municipal de São Paulo, https://drive.prefeitura.sp.gov.br/cidade/secretarias/upload/chamadas/314-02_censo_r5-sub-distr_pop-abs_var-rel_1950-2022_final_1715805137.htm (accessed January 16, 2026).
*Brasilândia was a subdistrict in these years and part of the Nossa Senhora do Ó district.

to that space. However, a key facet of mapping ethnoracial space is to establish *some* understanding of how residents in a neighborhood self-identify according to categories such as race and ethnicity. The force of postracial ideologies in twentieth-century Brazil, combined with the fluidity of neighborhood boundaries and other archival challenges, make this aspect of mapping ethnoracial space a complicated endeavor. Demographic data about the ethnoracial composition of districts in mid-twentieth-century São Paulo is quite challenging to locate or to generate. These challenges owe both to the methods by which race has been measured in Brazil's federal censuses throughout the twentieth century and the small scale of the district level.

Brazil's censuses do not track race on the universal questionnaire, which collects data on all citizens, but instead on the complementary questionnaire, which samples only a segment of the population. Access to the source data—not just the summary conclusions—from the complementary questionnaire is necessary to calculate demographic data on race at the district level. For censuses before 1960, the source data from the complementary questionnaires has been lost. For the

1960 census, the source data is available; however, census authorities sampled only 5 percent of the population for the complementary questionnaire. That small of a sample size prevents us from computing ethnoracial identification at the district level with a sufficient degree of statistical confidence. In 1970, authorities expanded the scope of the complementary questionnaire, applying it to 25 percent of the population. However, Brazil's military regime in 1970 omitted race from the census based on the logic that Brazil was a postracial society and thus did not require such data collection.[53]

Race was reinstated in the 1980 census, and the complementary questionnaire from that year sampled 25 percent of the population. The source data from the complementary questionnaire is still available, and researchers from the University of São Paulo's Centro de Estudos das Metrópoles (CEM) have conducted the harmonization of the 1980 census data, a key step in demographic research. The 1980 census provides the earliest dataset, therefore, with information both usable and directly relevant to this book. That information figures centrally into chapter 5, which tracks the official ethnoracialization projects for Liberdade and Bexiga. Ideally, we would have data from prior censuses to capture a longitudinal view of how the ethnoracial composition of these neighborhoods has changed over time. The challenges outlined above, however, prevent us from gleaning such a view through the federal census. To address this limitation, throughout the book I draw on other sources of qualitative and quantitative information that illustrate the ethnoracial characteristics of a neighborhood's population. I foreground these sources throughout the text so that the reader can track the evidentiary and methodological basis for the narratives and arguments I advance.

METHODS OF SPATIAL HISTORY

This project draws from eighteen months of research in São Paulo between 2015 and 2016, along with shorter research trips from 2012 to 2023, that concentrated on archival research, oral histories, and digital historical mapping. Influenced by critical theorists of the production of space, I organized my research on these ethnoracialized neighborhoods into three categories: *material constructions*, such as "Japanese"-themed streetscapes in Liberdade; *representations*, such as an annotated map from São Paulo's Department of Urbanism; and *lived experiences*, such as a musician's memories of founding a samba school in Brasilândia. Sources from these three categories enabled me to chart how officials and local residents planned and reproduced "African" Brasilândia, "Japanese" Liberdade, and "Italian" Bexiga over time.

Throughout the book I analyze these spatial histories with a theory of planning praxis that brings together the two major drivers of the city of São Paulo's urbanization: official city planning and the production of informal settlements. Scholars have produced extensive studies on both in Brazil, especially high modernist planning in Brasília and favelas in Rio de Janeiro.[54] São Paulo's sprawling mix of the formally planned and seemingly improvised invites an analysis that includes the range of individuals—located in an array of institutional and social positions—who contributed to sociospatial change. That analysis has precedence in the work of urban anthropologists and planning theorists who have argued that planning theory should encompass social actors beyond state-employed technocrats and private developers. James Holston, Ranier Randolph, and Faranak Miraftab, for example, have written about "subversive" or "insurgent" planning through land occupation as a means through which residents contest deeply rooted social inequality and political exclusion.[55]

I attend both to state and nonstate planning and see popular participation in the production of space as a sometimes, but not always, counterhegemonic practice. My examination of this array of planners in one frame privileges the interrelatedness between local residents and municipal officials (along with the spaces each produced). Recalling my discussion of dominant approaches to ethnoracial space above, detailing those connections calibrates the emphasis on institutional and state actors in the Black-White segregation paradigm and the privileging of nonstate actors in the ethnic-enclaves framework. This approach thus helps to integrate what are often treated as discrete and juxtaposed places—recall the Vieira image (figure I.1)—and proves necessary to chart the reproduction of ethnoracial space contingently and over time.

A range of textual and visual source material support this analysis and narrative. This material includes an extensive collection of maps of the city (with highly detailed citywide maps from 1930, 1954, and 1973); large-scale official planning projects; municipal legislation and decrees; property and real estate records; and internal documentation from urban development institutions. Of particular value from the last category are blueprints relating to over three hundred urban development or redevelopment projects extending from the 1930s to the 1980s, most within the boundaries of the contemporary Brasilândia district, as well as case files from a selection of those three hundred. This array of source material helps to shed light on how city planning and urban redevelopment occurred in practice and shaped these ethnoracialized neighborhoods over time.

Another valuable collection of source material consisted of the expropriation records for the construction of the most significant avenues involved in the remaking of Liberdade and Bela Vista from the 1930s to the 1960s. These records come from São Paulo's Department of Expropriations, today located, perhaps tellingly, in the Liberdade district. This material helped me to identify or gather further information about significant spaces razed in the course of executing redevelopment through Prestes Maia's Avenues Plan. I also highlight patterns of expropriation and demolition in these records that show how official planners remade these historic centers of African-descendent settlement, thereby helping clear the way for the construction of "Japanese" Liberdade and "Italian" Bexiga in decades following.

I'll Samba Someplace Else also draws on in-depth oral histories, informal conversations, and regular participation in public events and gatherings within Brasilândia, Liberdade, and Bexiga. Interviewees included neighborhood residents who participated directly in projects of ethnoracialization, were involved in practices or organizations related to those processes, or who possessed valuable insights into the neighborhoods' histories. While most recorded interviews took place within homes or public spaces, several interviewees participated in an experimental method of collaborative mapping using printed maps or a tablet-based application that contained three layers of large-scale historical maps of the city of São Paulo (figure I.2). This experimental methodology yielded some novel insights. Interviewees highlighted, for example, how nonstate actors participated in the reproduction of Brasilândia, Liberdade, and Bexiga and provided further context for histories seldom registered in official documentation, like displacement. They also helped to illuminate further the ethnoracial composition of certain neighborhood spaces, whose distinctive characteristics were not easily discernable owing to the demographic limitations discussed in the prior section.

I also employed digital historical mapping methodologies (or HGIS) to chart the reproduction of these ethnoracialized neighborhoods

FIGURE I.2 · Screenshot of collaborative mapping application showing the Liberdade and Bela Vista districts with swipe feature activated. Users can employ the feature to visualize changes between the two layers, 1954 (left) and 1973 (right), in real time. Data sources: "Mapeamento 1954—Vasp Cruzeiro," GeoSampa, accessed June 12, 2018, https://www.geosampa.prefeitura.sp.gov.br; and "São Paulo—GEGRAN," 1973, Acervo Técnico Gegran/EMPLASA. Assembled in ArcGIS Online, Esri.

over time.[56] This methodological approach furnished an ever-growing layered digital map that I could consult in the course of reconstructing the spatial histories of these places, constructing this narrative, and, ultimately, devising the core arguments I outline above. The approach proved especially useful in developing the first point about the significance of anti-Black racism in shaping the redevelopment of Liberdade and Bexiga. Mapping sites with ties to slavery, racial violence, the abolitionist campaign, and Black self-determination—and then comparing the locations of those sites with proposed or executed demolitions for redevelopment—yielded valuable insights about the influence of anti-Blackness in the spatial management of São Paulo at midcentury.

Much of this digital spatial analysis required substantial technical training, which hinged on substantial resources of time and, in some cases, funding. This approach was especially productive for this project, where the mapping of demolitions, for example, was pivotal to documenting how powerful discourses of both anti-Blackness and non-Blackness produced erasure through space. Platforms that offer lower barriers to entry, including pioneering Brazilian spatial history platforms like Pauliceia 2.0 and imagineRio, will, I expect, make such methodological approaches increasingly accessible to an array of researchers and enhance their interpretative, in addition to descriptive, utility.[57]

CHAPTER OUTLINE

In the first chapter, "Avenues and the Afterlives of Slavery," I chart São Paulo's position as a provincial capital of slavery in Southeast Brazil with a focus on the Nossa Senhora do Ó parish: a hub of enslavement, settlements of people fleeing captivity, and later the region where Brasilândia would be produced. I elucidate the ties that connected slavery in the nineteenth century to urban redevelopment projects initiated in the 1930s, especially Prestes Maia's Avenues Plan, which remade neighborhoods prominently associated with African descendants through asphalted avenues.

In chapter 2, "Spatial Projects of Forgetting," I excavate three significant sites demolished in Liberdade and Bela Vista. This excavation reveals how the authors of the Avenues Plan razed and remade local spaces with deep ties to slavery, racial violence, the abolitionist campaign, and Black self-determination, along with high concentrations of African-descendent populations. Through what I term spatial projects of forgetting, official city planners endeavored to render African descendants invisible in the city, thus reproducing the metropolis in a whitened image of modern progress.

In chapter 3, "Neighborhoods of Mixture and Massacre," I tell the stories of residents who migrated to and produced Vila Brasilândia beginning in the late 1940s in the wake of the displacement spurred by the Avenues Plan. I track how, throughout the 1940s and 1950s, local residents and officials negotiated the transformation of this former hub of both slavery and Black self-determination into a microcosmic "Brazil-land." That transformation aimed both to reflect and engender a nationalist ideal of harmonious ethnoracial mixture. That celebration of mixture, however, quite often entailed the threat or practice of anti-Black violence—massacre—both in Brasilândia and beyond. While centered on Brasilândia, this chapter also details how the context of World War II and its aftermath, particularly anti-Japanese sentiment, also influenced popular ideas about ethnoracial mixture and massacre in geographic space throughout the city of São Paulo.

Chapter 4, "Belonging-as-Being: Brasilândia as 'Little Africa,'" details the ethnoracialization of Brasilândia as a "Little Africa" with a focus on the 1960s and 1970s. I foreground three processes that contributed to this ethnoracialization: a shift in dominant approaches to official urban planning in metropolitan São Paulo, the founding of a championship samba school in Brasilândia named Rosas de Ouro, and the application of a racist nickname to the region through a widely popular reality radio program. While introducing continued, novel, and significant instances of anti-Black violence, this chapter also highlights how and why Brasilândia became a privileged site through the spatial praxis of belonging-as-being among African descendants in São Paulo in these years.

In chapter 5, "Producing Ethnoracial Infrastructures: Making 'Japanese' Liberdade and 'Italian' Bexiga," I follow the actions of neighborhood residents who partnered with city officials on campaigns to ethnoracialize Liberdade and Bela Vista from the 1960s to the 1980s. Tourism-oriented economic development drove public funding for the project to make Liberdade "Japanese," while the official rationale behind producing "Italian" Bexiga centered on historic preservation. I show how these projects were conceived of and pursued in relation to earlier ethnoracial identities prominent in these spaces as well as in-migration from other regions of Brazil, especially the Northeast. These ethnoracialization projects would reinforce the social prestige of populations of Japanese and Italian descent in São Paulo, transforming places previously associated with African descendants into seemingly timeless, naturally occurring, and non-Black immigrant enclaves.

2013 Não vou me mudar da Brasilândia
(I'm not leaving Brasilândia)

Behind graffitied partitions that line one of Brasilândia's oldest streets, the buildings continue to disappear (figure I.3). Most locals need no explanation for the impetus of the demolitions, but the orange stripes on every other barrier remind them anyway. The metro is coming, with Brasilândia the planned northern terminus of the city's new Orange Line. Similar white and orange barriers enclose razed spaces on the southern end of this new line at the penultimate station in the district of Bela Vista (map I.2). Eight decades earlier, demolitions linked to avenues projects in Liberdade and Bexiga began spurring displacement that would pave the way for the creation of Brasilândia. Some of those displaced residents likely built some of the structures being leveled for the metro in Brasilândia today. I did not meet the residents of these homes, however, and I have heard that most have acquiesced to expropriation for the metro and moved—perhaps once again—to new frontiers on São Paulo's periphery. Echoes from the earlier era of transportation schemes resound in the present, even as the crumbling bricks from demolitions conspire to conceal the continuities. I ask myself: Are the dynamics of the Avenues Plan unfolding once again? Has nothing changed?

It is tempting, in fact, to see the arrival of the metro in Brasilândia as a moment of fundamental rupture in the neighborhood's history. Since the settlement of Brasilândia in 1947 and through the first decades of the twenty-first century, geographic marginality and a *lack* of integration within the city of São Paulo have largely defined narratives about this place. In the words of one local resident, Brasilândia has long been "the periphery of the periphery."[58] The arrival of the metro will, no doubt, alter this spatial dynamic, providing residents who remain with an alternative means of transportation to the clogged buses and congested roads that strain daily commutes. The unprecedented connectivity between Brasilândia and center-city districts like Bela Vista will also, of course, generate other changes whose repercussions extend beyond commute conditions and durations. The Orange Line will spur growth in local land values, new real estate development, and the installation of a more robust infrastructure of urban services long absent in the region. The metro, in other words, portends progress, with all its prices and costs.

A block north of these demolitions for the future metro station, musician Luz Nascimento regularly leads fellow members of the group Samba do Congo in a composition titled "Metrô da Brasilândia" (Brasilândia's metro).[59] Nascimento lived in the Bela Vista district as a child before moving to Brasilândia in the 1960s. She coauthored this

FIGURE I.3 · Construction partitions and half-demolished buildings in Brasilândia, November 2016. Intersection of Estrada do Sabão and R. Prof. Viveiros Raposo. The building was subsequently fully demolished. Photo by Andrew G. Britt.

samba in 2013 with Luiz do Pandeiro, an official ambassador of São Paulo samba (a distinction awarded by the governing organization of local samba schools) and a photojournalist for the regional newspaper. In the latter capacity, Luiz has snapped hundreds of photos of structures demolished for the metro. He even considered filming a music video of "Metrô da Brasilândia" in a half-razed building. Their song opens:

> I'm going to call
> Mato Grosso and Joca
> My real friends
> Who already went through this drama
>
> The people are saying
> That the metro will come soon
> And because of it
> We'll have to move

Mato Gross and Joca were the two protagonists in one of São Paulo's most iconic sambas, "Saudosa Maloca" (My beloved ruin). Adoniran Barbosa, the White child of Italian immigrants and a much revered

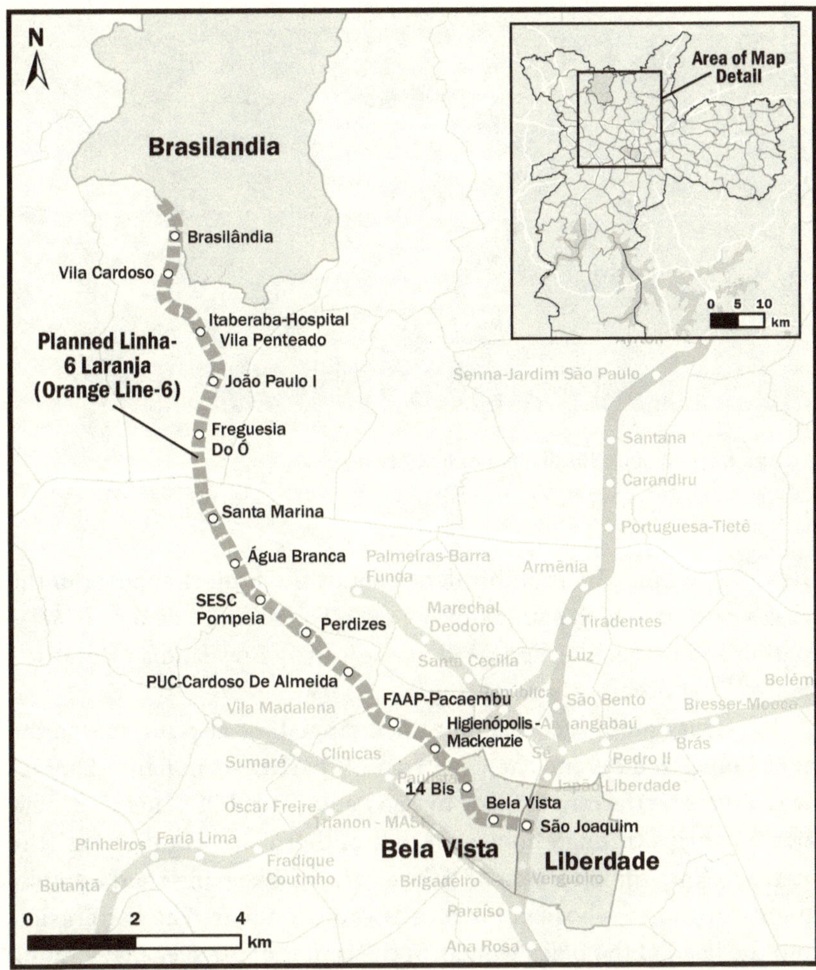

MAP I.2 · Map of the planned Orange Line-6 route and stations (circa 2024), connecting Brasilândia to Bela Vista, along with existing metro lines in São Paulo. Data sources: GeoSampa; OpenStreetMap (Light Gray Canvas) © OpenStreetMap contributors, Microsoft, Facebook, Google, Esri Community Maps contributors, map layer by Esri. Map by Andrew G. Britt.

musician throughout São Paulo (especially in "Italian" Bexiga), penned "Saudosa Maloca" in 1955.[60] His song chronicles the demolition of a center-city building occupied by the fictitious figures Mato Grosso and Joca.[61] In their song, Nascimento and Pandeiro summon the memory of Mato Grosso and Joca for wisdom in a contemporary moment clouded by the certainty of demolitions and prospect of displacement linked to

FIGURE I.4 · Mural in Brasilândia by JOKS, 2018.

the Orange Line. Their ambivalence about the project appears in the song's refrain, which sounds to my ears like a mix of defiant proclamation and beseeching appeal: "I'm not leaving Brasilândia / Because I know / That progress is on its way."

Residents' ambivalence about the Orange Line also surfaces in the mural obscured behind the construction partitions in figure I.3. Figure I.4 displays the mural, made by São Paulo artist JOKS, in full. A fiery metro car rips through homes on the southern side of the street. The metro follows the direction of White, wizard-like hands and a smoky green substance whose color recalls the US dollar. The car crashes into the head of the Black woman at the center of the scene. The mural presents the woman, her son, and her daughter as threatened by the Orange Line. While the metro enters the composition from the south, the woman gazes to the northern side of the street, where a skull implies impending doom and death. This family has no expectation of benefiting from the Orange Line. The composition traps their bodies, though their gazes transcend the threatened space to *someplace else* on the horizon. JOKS's mural presents progress in the form of the metro as a whitening and dislocating force for African descendants, including those who helped to build this "Little Africa" in the wake of an earlier era of displacement. The metro is not so different, the mural implies, from the asphalted avenues of years past.

Is he right? Is this, indeed, just another chapter in that same old story of "I'm out of here / I'll samba someplace else"? Or will Luz and

Luiz's cautious optimism of a new dawn—"I'm not leaving Brasilândia / Because I know / That progress is on its way"—ultimately prevail? The following pages, full of the interlaced ruptures and continuities that got us to this moment, elucidate both possible resolutions and enduring paradoxes relevant to these questions.

ONE

Avenues and the Afterlives of Slavery

I follow Fernando toward the abandoned, graffitied shell of a church in Morro Grande (Large Hill). With dusk fading to night, he points to the valley-filled horizon behind the structure and traces the dim line we came here to see: the former Congo Road (Estrada do Congo). Fernando grew up a few blocks away in a more populated area of the surrounding district, Brasilândia. A public administrator by day and samba musician otherwise, he commemorated this road's former name in 2011 when he cofounded the musical group Samba do Congo. I look at the tablet I have carted along to compare the contemporary space with historical maps of the region, and the pulsing cobalt mark reveals our location a few hundred feet east of the road. I zoom in on a map layer from 1954: the former Congo Road is now Elísio Teixeira Leite Avenue.[1] The change raises multiple, generative questions: What are the origins of this road? What led to its renaming? Why do roadways, pavement, and asphalt continually surface in conversations about neighborhood and identity with residents of Brasilândia? What is the relationship between this "Congo" place-name and descriptions of Brasilândia as São Paulo's "Little Africa"?

The earliest references I have found to Brasilândia as a "Little Africa" date from the 1980s. The history of Congo Road, however, points to substantially earlier and significant histories of African descendants in São Paulo. Those earlier histories began in the parish of Nossa Senhora do Ó, the site of (the formerly named) Congo Road and the place where real estate developers and residents would create Vila Brasilândia in the late 1940s. One of São Paulo's oldest parishes, Nossa Senhora do Ó was a hub of enslavement for centuries and, at the same time, home to settlements of people fleeing captivity. The parish was also the last place in São Paulo where slaveholders acceded to formal abolition in the 1880s. In providing an overview of these aspects of Nossa Senhora do Ó's past, the first two sections in this chapter contribute to the broader project of destabilizing representations of São Paulo as a non-Black city whose development had little to do with enslavement.[2] This analysis also provides pivotal context for understanding why African-descendent residents dislocated from the city center likely chose this parish, specifically, for repossession and rebuilding in the wake of dislocation from the Avenues Plan in the mid-twentieth century (the subject of chapter 3).

In the third and fourth sections of the chapter, I introduce the urban redevelopment project that, through asphalted avenues, would demolish and dislocate sites populated by, and sacred among, many African descendants in São Paulo from the 1930s forward. The publication of city planner and later mayor Francisco Prestes Maia's *A Study for a Plan of Avenues for the City of São Paulo* (1930) signaled the beginning of this era of urban transformation, which attempted to modernize São Paulo after a period of meteoric growth over sixty years. From just thirty thousand residents in 1870, the city's population increased to one million by 1930. It would grow nearly another million in the following decade. The seminal redevelopment project of twentieth-century São Paulo, the Avenues Plan would guide the spatial development of the city from the 1930s through the mid-1960s.

While much of the literature about the Avenues Plan has either eulogized or demonized its author, Prestes Maia, my analysis draws on novel source materials from São Paulo's Department of Expropriations, oral histories, and music to detail how this plan was put into practice. That analysis proves critical in developing an informed narrative about both the possible motivations behind and effects of this consequential redevelopment scheme. The final section of this chapter discusses how samba in the city and state of São Paulo—samba paulista—has served as a crucial register of demolitions, dispossession, and dislocation connected to African descendants in the city. This audible archive recorded key chapters from the history of São Paulo's "Black zone," including its demolition in the context of the Avenues Plan.

Chapter 1 does substantial stage-setting for the four subsequent chapters, including by addressing prominent misconceptions that have long clouded both popular and academic understandings of the city's past. Such misconceptions include representations of São Paulo as a non-Black city, whose growth had little to do with racial chattel slavery; uncritically positive *and* negative assessments of São Paulo's seminal twentieth-century modernization program, the Avenues Plan; and the nonexistence (or, at best, inferiority) of samba in São Paulo compared with the more celebrated manifestations of the cultural form in cities like Rio de Janeiro. At first glance, these three skewed representations of São Paulo seem to have little to do with each other. This chapter, however, shows meaningful connections between them, offering an interpretative perspective that, in turn, helps to reframe dominant understandings of change and continuity in the spatial history of São Paulo as well as the history of racial inequality and violence in the city before and after 1888.

This interpretative perspective is distilled in the title of the chapter: "Avenues and the Afterlives of Slavery." Critical theorist Saidiya Hartman has defined the afterlives of slavery as "skewed life chances, limited access to health and education, premature death, incarceration, and impoverishment" among people of African descent, all structured by a centuries-old "racial calculus and a political arithmetic."[3] The construction of avenues in mid-twentieth-century São Paulo—a process that hinged on dispossession, demolition, and dislocation—served, in the words of Hartman, to "imperil and devalue" the lives of African descendants in the city and to reproduce the underlying ontological precondition of enslavement from before formal abolition in 1888 in the post-emancipation period. That precondition was "social death," one of the fundamental characteristics of slavery offered by sociologist Orlando Patterson in which an enslaved person's status was equivalent to a fundamental state of nonbelonging.[4]

In the late nineteenth century, elite and official projects of whitening (*branqueamento*) in Brazil, premised on the nonbelonging of African descendants, also envisioned the ultimate nonexistence of African descendants through annihilating absorption and disappearance.[5] This dominant epistemology would shape the design and execution of the Avenues Plan, thereby contributing to (adapting Patterson) a socio*spa-*

tial death for the African descendants to whom the city's "Black zone" was a fundamental place of belonging. Why did roadways, pavement, and asphalt keep surfacing, then, in conversations about the city's mid-twentieth-century development? Because paved avenues played a central role not only in reshaping the infrastructure of the city but also in reproducing the epistemologies that structured racialized inequality and anti-Black violence. Avenues were, in other words, an afterlife of slavery.

A SOCIOSPATIAL SKETCH OF NOSSA SENHORA DO Ó

The parish of Nossa Senhora do Ó (N. S. do Ó) was an early hub of slavery in the city of São Paulo. Enslaved populations in N. S. do Ó grew sugarcane and produced a blend of cachaça named the "little cane of Ó." By the middle of the nineteenth century, Caninha do Ó was a prestige product in the city of São Paulo, and its production relied on widespread slaveholding in the parish until the very eve of slavery's formal abolition in 1888.[6] On the near margins of this local slave society, enslaved people created fugitive communities, or *quilombos*, that preoccupied slaveholders and administrative officials in São Paulo. The following two sections illuminate these sociospatial histories of N. S. do Ó with a focus on the nineteenth century, when the slave trade and enslavement intensified in the then-province of São Paulo and Southeast Brazil more broadly.

The parish of N. S. do Ó originated in the mid-sixteenth century with campaigns of enslavement and settler colonialism led by an infamous *bandeirante* Manuel Preto. *Bandeirantes* commanded expeditions to enslave native populations and collect precious metals in the interior of South America from the sixteenth to eighteenth centuries. Launched from the captaincy of São Vicente (later São Paulo), their campaigns secured captive laborers, expanded the geographic reach of the colony, and funneled wealth to the Portuguese Crown.[7] That wealth also funded colonial settlements in places like N. S. do Ó. In 1610 Manuel Preto submitted a request to construct a church on the northern banks of the Tietê River, about twelve kilometers north of the geographical center of São Paulo. The distance between N. S. do Ó and the city center, along with the precarious conditions of the roadways and the passage across the Tietê River, made travel for worship in São Paulo's center onerous. A new chapel, Preto argued, would alleviate these challenges and give the Catholic Church a foothold on the northern margins of the city.[8]

The chapel erected shortly thereafter constituted one among multiple foundations that Preto laid in the establishment of N. S. do Ó.

Slavery was also fundamental to the settlement that Preto carved from the northern, hilly banks of the Tietê River. Preto led a campaign in 1607 to Villa Rica del Guayra in Paraguay, where he enslaved an estimated one thousand indigenous people and transferred them back to the city of São Paulo. He would lead subsequent expeditions throughout the 1610s and 1620s.[9] Historian John Manuel Monteiro records that, following a 1628 raid that enslaved Guaraní people, Jesuits described Preto as one of the "principle and worst assailants." A Guaraní cacique interviewed three decades later identified Preto as responsible for the destruction of his community.[10] This violent extraction would enable Preto to develop large-scale agriculture that included the production of sugar cane. While Preto likely died in the 1630s, memory of him as one of São Paulo's pioneering figures has persisted into the twentieth and twenty-first centuries, including through an elementary school named for him in the parish today. The slavery-based agriculture that Preto established would persist in N. S. do Ó after his death and continue to support ties between the parish and more centrally located regions of the city.[11] Wealthy families owned properties in N. S. do Ó, planters from the region supplied agricultural goods to residents in the center, and the provincial government and church included N. S. do Ó as part of São Paulo's official geography. Despite its geographic marginality, N. S. do Ó formed part of the city of São Paulo since the colonial settlement's earliest days.

Demographic sources provide a picture of the social composition of N. S. do Ó beginning in the late eighteenth century. This picture comes from the *maços da população*, annual census-style records from 1765 to 1851. Organized by household, these tables included demographic information such as name, age, free or enslaved status, marital condition, color, and occupation. For the eighty-six years between 1765 and 1851, there are twenty-five years of *maço* records for N. S. do Ó housed at the State Archive of São Paulo.[12] The level of detail in these rolls, down to the name of each household member, and their availability over time supply a rich record of the social history of the region.

Maço records depict N. S. do Ó as a slave society that rivaled, when it did not surpass, other parishes in the city of São Paulo in terms of the pervasiveness of slaveholding (table 1.1). Slaveholding grew in direct proportion to N. S. do Ó's population from the late eighteenth to early nineteenth centuries. Between 1779 and 1832 the parish's population grew from 1,023 to 1,644. The portion of the population that was enslaved remained relatively steady, averaging 34 percent for five years sampled during this period. In 1802 nearly half of all households in N. S. do Ó held slaves, a proportion that surpassed all other parishes in the city.[13] Other demographic trends indicate characteristics typical of a slave society. *Maço* rolls included three color classifications: White (*branco*), Brown (*pardo*), and Black (*preto*). Among White and Brown adults, a sex imbalance favored women, while the inverse was true among Black adults. Such an imbalance was typical among sugar-producing regions elsewhere in the province of São Paulo. The sex imbalance favoring men differed from patterns in the center of the city of São Paulo, however, where single women predominated as heads of households.[14]

In the early nineteenth century, Black individuals made up an increasing portion of the enslaved population in N. S. do Ó, and both Black and Brown enslaved people had relatively little mobility to become free. Between 1804 and 1834, the proportion of Black people among the enslaved population averaged 72 percent. In the same period, the proportion of enslaved Brown people decreased 8 percent, while averaging 28 percent. The percentage of Brown individuals among the total free population remained steady, remaining at 31 percent for the entire period. Their proportion in N. S. do Ó well exceeded the 19 percent average gleaned from a survey of forty-one counties throughout the province of São Paulo between 1829 and 1831.[15] Free Blacks decreased from the already-low 4 percent to 2 percent of the total free population in the first three decades of the nineteenth century. As economist Francisco Vidal Luna and historian Herbert S. Klein have shown, the disparity between Brown and Black captives among the freed population was consistent throughout the province of São Paulo.[16] Few descendants of the natives that Manoel Preto enslaved in the seventeenth century appear in these official records: The 1832 *maço* includes a category for Indigenous (*índios*), and in that year just six individuals were counted as such in N. S. do Ó. These figures should be viewed with caution, however, as they may have captured only a portion of the Indigenous population that lived in the region.

While enslaved people were ubiquitous in the city of São Paulo, N. S. do Ó stood out among the city's parishes for the high proportion of non-White and enslaved populations. In 1836, 31 percent of the N. S. do Ó population was enslaved. In Penha, a similarly remote,

TABLE 1.1 · Captive and Free Population in Freguesia da Nossa Senhora do Ó, 1799–1832

YEAR	CAPTIVE POPULATION				FREE POPULATION					N. S. DO Ó TOTAL
	GROSS TOTAL	% BLACK	% BROWN	% OF N. S. DO Ó POPULATION	GROSS TOTAL	% BROWN	% BLACK	% WHITE	% OF N. S. DO Ó POPULATION	GROSS TOTAL
1799	327	-	-	32%	696	-	-	-	68%	**1,023**
1804	519	69%	31%	36%	935	32%	4%	64%	64%	**1,454**
1817	449	71%	29%	37%	750	29%	2%	69%	63%	**1,199**
1825	373	71%	29%	33%	760	31%	3%	66%	67%	**1,133**
1832	515	76%	23%	31%	1,129	31%	2%	67%	69%	**1,644**
Avg.	437	72%	28%	34%	854	31%	3%	66%	66%	1,291

Source: *Maços*, Arquivo Público do Estado de São Paulo.
Note: Racial categories in *maços* were *preto* (Black), *pardo* (Brown), and *branco* (White).

agricultural parish situated on the eastern margins of the city, the figure sat at 22 percent.[17] In the 1820s and 1830s, the intensification of slavery also corresponded to an increasing population of African-born individuals in N. S. do Ó. In 1832, a new category for African-born was introduced into the *maço* rolls and methodology. The adult Black population born in Brazil was 262, compared to 130 people born in Africa. Through the 1820s and 1830s the names *Africanus* and *Congo*, terms of origin and ethnic identity, began to appear more frequently in *maços* for N. S. do Ó.[18] While the sex ratio was relatively balanced among the native-born Black population, for those born in Africa the ratio favored males by nearly three to one.

The increased presence of enslaved Africans among N. S. do Ó's enslaved population corresponded to the expansion of enslavement and large-scale plantation agriculture throughout the province of São Paulo, including in the Paraíba Valley to the northeast and the West Paulista region in the west.[19] The development of sugar, initially, and then coffee plantations in these regions would make São Paulo one of the final frontiers of what historians have termed "second slavery." This period encompassed the intensification of slavery following the abolition of the slave trade by Britain in 1807 and, through the middle of the nineteenth century, offical enslavement itself throughout the Americas. As the capital of the province and a center in regional webs of commerce and communication, the city of São Paulo's nineteenth-century growth was intimately linked to second slavery in the city and the surrounding province.

N. S. do Ó sits adjacent to the Jaraguá Peak, the highest point surrounding the city of São Paulo. The panoramic view, combined with the region's location along the principal route into the interior of the province, made the area a popular stop for visitors in the early nineteenth century. Those visitors included one of the first people from the United States to publish an account of travels through Brazil, Methodist missionary Daniel Kidder. In his 1845 *Sketches of Residence and Travels in Brazil*, Kidder recounted a brief stay on the plantation of one Donna Gertrudes, who owned six properties throughout São Paulo. Kidder describes her plantation as named Jaraguá, meaning it was likely closer to the peak itself, though he may have also visited N. S. do Ó. Other members of São Paulo's elite also possessed plantations in the area. A survey map from the 1890s shows that Dona Veridiana da Silva Prado, for example, from one of São Paulo's wealthiest and most politically powerful families, owned a tract in N. S. do Ó.[20] Elite landowners with properties throughout São Paulo may have hosted foreign guests to the parish as a rural retreat proximate in comparison to their plantations further into the interior of the province.[21]

Foreign travelers filled their pages with observations of local agriculture and plantation life. Kidder described Gertrudes's plantation as follows: "Around the farm-house as a centre, were situated numerous out-houses, such as quarters for negros, store-houses for the staple vegetables, and fixtures for reducing them to a marketable form."[22] Kidder included a sketch of African-descendent slaves processing *mandioca* (manioc), perhaps one of the earliest images of people of African descent from this northern region of the city of São Paulo (figure 1.1).

Among other crops grown locally, sugar occupied a privileged place in the productive activity of the region, particularly for the production of cachaça. Portuguese traveler Luiz D'Allincourt wrote in the 1830s that the "residents of this Freguesia [parish] cultivate sugar cane to make cane alcohol, which forms the principal branch of their business."[23] Kidder elaborated that "on most of the sugar estates there exist distilleries, which convert the treacle drained from the sugar into a species of

FIGURE 1.1 · Enslaved African descendants producing manioc in the northern region of São Paulo. Daniel P. Kidder, *Sketches of Residence and Travels in Brazil, Embracing Historical and Geographical Notices of the Empire and Its Several Provinces*, vol. 1 (Philadelphia: Sorin and Ball; London: Wiley and Putnam, 1845), 243.

alcohol called cachassa; but on this, either from its proximity to market, or from some other cause connected with profit, nothing but cachassa was manufactured."[24] Historian Maria Odila Silva Dias also found records of sugar production among women small holders in N. S. do Ó: "A few of the women rural workers in Penha and Freguesia do Ó had small sugar mills, where they made brandy to sell retail."[25] Luna and Klein's findings for sugar production in the West Paulista region suggest that N. S. do Ó was typical in that sugarcane was primarily for local consumption and not the export market. The region differed from other regions in the state of São Paulo, however, as cane was grown for the exclusive production of cachaça and not unrefined brown sugar and molasses.[26]

FUGITIVITY AND CONGO ROAD IN N. S. DO Ó

Africans and African descendants resisted enslavement in N. S. do Ó, and fugitive communities in the parish concerned provincial officials in the late eighteenth and early nineteenth centuries.[27] The provincial governor wrote in 1777 to the police captain of N. S. do Ó praising him for ordering *capitães de mato*, or headhunters contracted to capture enslaved people who had fled, to disarm any Black person seen with a stick or knife at the parish's central church.[28] A subsequent governor issued a decree, in 1807:

> The disturbances, thefts, and offenses committed by fugitive Blacks, *aquilombados* [settled in *quilombos*] in the outskirts around the capital . . . must be curtailed and punished: I therefore order you to bring together all of the officials in your ordinance . . . to send them to surround and strike the forests, and in deserted regions where the said *negros* are hiding, and this not just in the part of your district, but in all suspected places nearby . . . capture not just all the Blacks that are found in hiding, but also all suspicious individuals (*pessoas de desconfiança*) found in such foreign parts, so that all should be brought, accompanied by the appropriate security, and collected in the prison to be questioned and punished.[29]

The decree indicates the settlement of *quilombos*, or fugitive settlements of people who fled captivity, on São Paulo's geographical margins. Though not noted explicitly here, N. S. do Ó's dense Atlantic Forest environment was likely auspicious for escape and the creation of such settlements. The governor's apprehension about fugitives accompanied a concern about those aiding them, described as "*pessoas de desconfiança*," and indicated the possibility of networks that included free-born, those freed through manumission, and those who fled.

As elsewhere throughout the province of São Paulo, newspapers delivered announcements about fugitives in N. S. do Ó to reading publics. In 1867, *Diário de São Paulo* published a story about Domingos, identified as the "Brown . . . slave of dr. Martinho da Silva Prado," who was apprehended in N. S. do Ó on suspicion of having killed a man named João Martin. The murder occurred in Mogy-Mirim, a city more than 150 kilometers north of the city of São Paulo, where Martin had suspected Domingos of being a fugitive and attempted to apprehend him. Domingos resisted the apprehension and was accused of killing the attempted captor.[30] An 1869 announcement in the same paper by João Baptista Alves de Siqueira sought assistance in capturing José, identified as of "black color, regular height, ugly figure; his most evident defect are small toes, nearly closed."[31] In 1877, Vicente José de Campos posted an announcement in *O Estado de S. Paulo* for Manoel, a man last seen in N. S. do Ó who had previously fled from Limeira, a city more than 175 kilometers northwest of São Paulo. Manoel was described as "black, average height, no beard, he has some signs of punishment on his back: handsome figure. This slave was seen in Freguesia do Ó, and was dressed in a black alpaca jacket, dark pants, boots cut in the shape of slippers, a vinegar-colored hat, and is said to be carrying a large knife and a linen sack with clothes."[32] A postscript noted that "Matheus and Cesario were captured in Ó, on the fourteenth of this month, and on this same day Manoel was seen passing."[33] These announcements support the supposition gleaned from official government sources that enslaved people sought refuge in N. S. do Ó.[34] Examining similar conditions for Rio Claro, a comparable place founded on sugar agriculture in the West Paulista region, historian Warren Dean writes: "The frequent advertisements in newspapers for escaped slaves suggest that they ran away often, but it is difficult to determine the rate of permanent desertions."[35]

For enslaved people fleeing, N. S. do Ó seems to have had a particular appeal: The road to Juqueri or Jundiaí, one of the city's main passages to the interior of the province, ran through the middle of the parish. Through the 1860s this thoroughfare was crucial to the exchange of agricultural goods and livestock, even functioning as an entry point for foodstuffs into the city.[36] When necessary, that commerce supplied a means of sustenance for freed slave communities. Historian Emilia Viotti da Costa finds that fugitive communities often concentrated around roadways: "Reunited in groups, fugitive slaves held up farms and roads, making the passages dangerous. Concealed in forests, they planted lots, most times insufficient, for their sustenance. Cornered, they survived by theft."[37] Along the main roadway of N. S. do Ó, attacks attributed to fugitives generated "abundant" complaints from "traveling traders (*estradeiros*), principally of cattle, who threaten[ed] to cut off the village's food supply if the incursions of *quilombolas* are not curbed."[38]

Through the grievances of commercial travelers, fugitive settlements in N. S. do Ó became well-known among municipal officials. In his study of the parish's history, historian Máximo Barro found N. S. do Ó "cited repeated times in the city council for having become one of the most favorable sanctuaries" in the city for fugitives.[39] The natural environment of the road, described by Kidder on his way north out of town in 1839, indeed sounded auspicious for escape: "The route was greatly diversified, between hill and dale . . . each successive turn of our winding way, seemed to take us deeper into a vast labyrinth of vegetable beauty, only here and there touched by the hand of cultivation."[40] Lacking more systematic records of *quilombo* settlements, such records serve as the best indication of the frequency—seemingly high—of fugitive settlements in N. S. do Ó and especially along what was commonly referred to in official documentation as the road to Juqueri or Jundiaí.

In the nineteenth century the construction and material condition of such roadways were major concerns for provincial officials in São Paulo.[41] An 1866 report described roads as "the primary necessity of modern industry; today it is the dogma of civilization." The condition of the province's roads was rarely deemed sufficient. The same report lamented the "unfortunate" state of roads to the interior, which, rather than efficient means for the transfer of agricultural goods, were cause for the admiration of the "preservation, the indominable energy" of the population that had to traverse them.[42] N. S. do Ó received special attention in an 1861 report, as winter flooding had left "the roads most deadly."[43] The railroad system would expand only in the last third of the nineteenth century, making roads the principal mode of transportation and communication.

While provincial officials in the nineteenth century described N. S. do Ó's main thoroughfare as the road to Juqueri or Jundiaí, some of the residents in the parish likely used an alternative name: Estrada do Congo, or Congo Road. Until the late nineteenth century, the naming of São Paulo's roads was not conducted through a centralized process. Even afterwards, into the twentieth century, local residents often named roads without official approval.[44] Congo Road existed well before its first appearance on an official map of the city in the late 1920s, when cartographers mapped for the first time at a detailed scale the northern region of the N. S. do Ó parish. On that map they used the name "Congo Road," cementing the seemingly popularly given ascription in the official space of the city for perhaps the first time.

Though not common as an official place-name in São Paulo, the name "Congo" did appear as an enslaved African's so-called *nação* (nation) in census-type registers and fugitive announcements. In such registers from N. S. do Ó in 1825 and 1842, for instance, Congo appeared as the *nação* of enslaved individuals and surfaced as the last name of free Black men.[45] In 1825, there were only two free Black adult males in N. S. do Ó, with one of the families headed by Anna Maria, born in Brazil, and Pedro de Jesus Maria, identified as "Congo."[46] A later *maço* from 1842 included one man, João Congo. Given that the record lists him as the head of a household, he was likely also a freed person. These figures counting freed people only included those who let themselves be counted. The frequency of fugitives in N. S. do Ó makes it likely that other Africans and African descendants resided in the region yet were excluded from these tabulations. The prevalence of the Congo identifier was not unique to Africans and African descendants in N. S. do Ó.[47] However, the paucity of free people in the parish overall and prevalence of Congo among them suggests a potential correlation between manumitted individuals or those who had escaped and the name.

Lacking sources that detail the origin of Congo Road, we must speculate about the possibilities. The road may have referenced a specific person, such as a freedman like Pedro Congo from the *maço* of 1825 or João Congo from 1842. One of them might have owned land along the road, and their neighbors could have taken to describing the name by the property owner who lived along it. An alternative interpretation would suggest a broader ascription: The roadway referred to a critical mass of people identified as from the *nação* Congo. These people could have been enslaved at a nearby plantation or, as the previous records suggest, a group of freed people who had established a *quilombo* alongside or near the roadway. A final interpretation could place the responsibility for naming on fearful travelers (the *estradeiros* referenced earlier), who named the place "Congo" as a warning to others about the (perceived) threat of attack. All of these explanations could have some degree of accuracy: an individual identified as "Congo" might have resided near the road and may have played an important role in providing assistance—if not helping to settle originally—the fugitive collective. As fugitives took advantage of commerce along the roadway to Juqueri or Jundiaí, the place could have gained infamy among nonlocal passersby.

Amid these plausible scenarios, I find it reasonable to think that Africans and their descendants were responsible for the naming of Congo Road and that they had a particular motivation in doing so. As noted in the announcements above, fugitive notices that mentioned N. S. do Ó frequently described enslaved people from outside of the parish. To an extent, this frequency aligned with broader patterns of movement in the years immediately preceding formal abolition in 1888, when the city of São Paulo became a destination for flight.[48] However, as indicated above, announcements from decades prior to the 1880s reveal a notable presence of fugitives in N. S. do Ó, pointing to the region as a destination for enslaved persons fleeing from elsewhere well before formal abolition. The places of origin were, in some cases, quite far from N. S. do Ó, such as the cities Limeira (175+ km) and Mogy-Mirim (150+ km). In other cases, enslaved residents from the center of the city of São Paulo itself seemed to have fled north to N. S. do Ó. Historian Lilia Moritz Schwarcz prints, for instance, the following announcement from 1879: "*Fugitive slave*: From house n. 2 on Rua das Flores in the capital, the slave Maria fled, with the following appearance: tall, thin, born in Brazil, 40 or 50 years old. . . . She was seen having a conversation, headed in the direction of Juquery [Juqueri] or [N. S. do] Ó."[49] These sources lead me to understand the name *Congo* as originating with those who escaped in order to signal to other captive Africans and their descendants throughout the province that Congo Road was a place of possible freedom. This interpretation would help to explain the frequency of fugitivity in this region, as enslaved Africans and their descendants learned of the place, through its name, and fled from enslavement to this seeming site of refuge. The increase of enslaved Africans in the early 1800s points to the early to mid-nineteenth century as a likely period of origin for the naming of Congo Road.

Roadways have loomed large in interpretations of society and geographic space in Brazil. Anthropologist Roberto DaMatta has argued famously that two basic "social domains" structure Brazilian social reality: the house and the street. The house functions as an ordered, hierarchical, and authoritarian space of calm, respect, and rest. The street, by contrast, signifies a relative lack of control: a place of unclear, undefined, or inverted social hierarchies, where individuals compete among themselves and with official institutions that claim authority over "public" spaces and bodies therein.[50] For marginalized Africans and their descendants, streets such as Congo Road functioned as places of potential self-determination and mobility in the midst of hostile and violent slave societies like nineteenth-century São Paulo.

Roads afforded opportunities for trade and the accumulation of resources that could allow an enslaved person to secure their freedom. Theft of food or goods from passersby could provide means for subsistence. In addition to the reports of theft and *quilombos*, observers in N. S. do Ó noted commercial activities along Congo Road. Silva Dias notes: "In 1854, Ferreira de Rezende noticed countrywomen going past his house on the road to Ó, selling eggs, vegetables and fresh fish 'for next to nothing.' In 1839, Kidder described the women sellers [who] carry jays on their heads, full of sugar cane brandy from Ó." Ultimately, the street also held the possibility of escape to "someplace else."[51]

Congo Road in N. S. do Ó had significant parallels elsewhere in the Atlantic world. One of the most well-known is New Orleans's Congo Square, which served as a site of public gatherings that included exchanging goods, spiritual practices, dance, and music. Historian Rashauna Johnson writes that in Congo Square "people of African descent reclaimed their bodies and created communities even as free, predominately white spectators gazed on them with a mixture of desire and repulsion." While Congo Road did not occupy such a public, geographically central place in São Paulo, both that roadway and Congo Square existed well before they appeared in government records (with the latter officialized in the 1810s).[52] Though representing distinct forms of the built environment, these sites were tied together as places with the name *Congo* that held prospects of autonomy and varied degrees of self-determination for African descendants in the midst of slave societies.

Through the end of the nineteenth century, N. S. do Ó maintained high proportions of enslaved Africans and African descendants.[53] In 1872, 15.6 percent of N. S. do Ó's population was enslaved (315 of 1,708). The region ranked second to the parish Sé, where 1,909 enslaved people made up just over a fifth of the total. N. S. do Ó had the highest proportion of African-born enslaved people with 34. That number amounted to nearly 60 percent of the nonnative residents in N. S. do Ó and far exceeded the same for the next-highest region: 35 percent in S. João Batista (the contemporary Consolação neighborhood). Viotti da Costa finds that plantation owners had long preferred African-born captives, as they considered them less likely to spark insurrection or rebellions than enslaved people born in Brazil.[54] Though smaller in comparison to the 1830s, the proportion of African-born among the population in N. S. do Ó remained comparatively high well after 1850.

Enslavers in N. S. do Ó acceded to the formal abolition of slavery later than anywhere else in the city of São Paulo. In 1944 historian Nuto Sant'Anna published *Historical São Paulo: Traits, Legends, and Customs*. In a section titled "Slaves," he wrote that "the neighborhood Nossa Senhora do Ó was the last to liberate its slaves. And this was well before May 13, 1888. Because already long before that date the hour of liberty had sounded in our land."[55] Sant'Anna's rhetoric echoed the self-image that São Paulo elites cultivated in the later nineteenth century as part of intertwined campaigns to modernize Brazil through abolition, republicanism, and non-Black immigrant wage labor.[56] Sant'Anna's interpretation overstated the actual timeline of abolition in N. S. do Ó along with the coffee-intensive regions in the West Paulista region, whose plantations depended on slavery until the very eve of formal abolition despite playing a prominent role in promoting immigrant labor as its substitute.[57]

Slaveholders in N. S. do Ó may have acquiesced to formal abolition later than anywhere else in the city of São Paulo, but this was not well before 1888. A provincial statistical report in 1886 provides data on the total number of enslaved individuals at the municipal level; however, it includes tables with deaths (averaged per year) at the more local parish level. In that year, only two São Paulo parishes reported deaths of enslaved people: Sé and N. S. do Ó. The former counted five deaths of enslaved people, or 1.3 percent of the total deaths that year. N. S. do Ó also had five deaths of enslaved people, though this accounted for 9.1 percent of all deaths in the district. A subsequent report from 1887 indicated that the city of São Paulo had just 493 enslaved people. This evidence further suggests that N. S. do Ó had a sizable portion of the enslaved population in the city on the eve of formal abolition.[58]

In contrast to the growth in the first half of the century, the overall population of N. S. do Ó decreased slightly between 1855 and 1872.[59] This trend owed in part to the expansion of railways in the province of São Paulo. In 1865 a train line was laid between the port of Santos and the city of São Paulo, and three years later it expanded to Jundiaí.[60] The new line (named Santos–Jundiaí) offered an alternative means of transportation that did not require travel along Congo Road—the road to Juquerí and Jundiaí. Historian Richard Morse writes that, with the expansion of the railway, "the outlying nuclei, Penha and Ó, once lively way stations for mule teams, were now left in quiescence by trains that changed without loitering into the city's expanding heart."[61] In his 1914 memoir, São Paulo author Bernardo Guimarães offered a more detailed depiction of quiescence, describing the landscape of Nossa Senhora do Ó as characterized by "ownerless estates, surrounded by old, ruined walls, abandoned to the ants and the pigs."[62]

As abolition came late to N. S. do Ó, so too did the parish's place in cartographic representations of the city. The parish had comprised part of the city's institutional geography since the late eighteenth century. Only in 1897, however, did N. S. do Ó appear on a citywide map (*planta geral*) of São Paulo.[63] Its presence on the 1897 planta owed in part to changes in the geographic extent of São Paulo as represented in official cartography in the 1890s. An 1893 *planta* had displayed a smaller, more densely settled territory.[64] Likely inspired by São Paulo's population growth and the imminent dawn of the new century, cartographers in the middle of the 1890s expanded their frame of the city to encompass pockets of settlement surrounding São Paulo along with large, empty swaths of territory represented as prime for the city's seemingly inevitable and swift growth.

In the census of 1890, the population of African descent in the city of São Paulo amounted to 15.6 percent of the total. In N. S. do Ó, however, the figure exceeded 40 percent.[65] What's more, the marginal geographic position that had allowed for the late persistence of slavery also supported the continuation of the place-name *Congo* in N. S. do Ó. Congo Road would ultimately be incorporated into the official linguistic landscape of the city, appearing on maps of São Paulo for thirty years in the middle of the twentieth century. After scanning maps of nineteenth- and twentieth-century São Paulo, I have found no major artery whose name so directly referenced African descendants. While the extant sources permit only a sketchy understanding of that road's origins, its history nonetheless illuminates the uniqueness of the N. S. do Ó parish for African descendants in the city of São Paulo and highlights the significance of toponyms in what I describe as the spatial praxis of belonging-as-being (which I discuss further in chapters 3 and 4).

In the first three decades of the twentieth century, the city of São Paulo underwent a population and geographic boom that would earn it the nickname "the city that cannot stop."[66] Meanwhile, in the parish of N. S. do Ó, little seemed to change, a stark contrast to the concrete modernity and frenzied urbanization in areas closer to the geographic center of the city. Beginning in the late 1920s, redevelopment projects would begin to reshape N. S. do Ó's place in the city. Center-city avenues projects would entail extensive demolitions and spur the dislocation of residents seeking new homes. The city's expanded transportation network, including a concrete bridge over the Tietê River, would carry those residents to relatively remote places like the northern limits of the N. S. do Ó parish. There, in the late 1940s, newcomers would construct the neighborhood of Vila Brasilândia.

"SAINDO DO PAPEL" UNDER PRESTES MAIA, 1920S–1960S

Architects and historians of the city of São Paulo have variously described Francisco Prestes Maia as the "inventor" of the metropolis, a "great urbanist, engineer, architect and probably the most significant mayor in the history of São Paulo," and an artist in concrete who "installed modernity in the city."[67] The outsized praise has some basis in historical fact. Spanning his early work as an urbanist in the 1920s through his terms as mayor (1938–1945 and 1961–1965), the city of São Paulo grew to a global metropolis among the most important urban centers in the Americas.[68] Prestes Maia played a prominent role in realizing that trajectory. Popular and academic appraisals of Prestes Maia's legacy are not, however, uniformly positive. A former resident of and business owner in São Paulo's Liberdade district described Prestes Maia to me as the mayor who unfolded a map of the city and drew new avenues wherever he felt like it.[69] Historian Joel Outtes appraised him as a "conservative" planner.[70] Historian Richard Morse recorded that São Paulo architects sarcastically renamed Prestes Maia's famous works, *Study for a Plan of Avenues in São Paulo* (1930) and *Improvements in São Paulo* (1945), as "The Divine Comedy" and "Purgatory."[71] Beyond this excessive praise and biting criticism, much remains to be understood about the remaking of São Paulo at the hands of Prestes Maia.

Prestes Maia's legacy has tended toward praise or polemic in part because observers have emphasized the grandeur of his plans on paper or the destructive nature of those plans when put into practice. The urbanist-mayor understood well that the reality fell somewhere in between. He wrote, for instance, in the Avenues Plan that "master plans are frequently very beautiful but destined to remain on paper (*permanecer no papel*)."[72] Here he drew the distinction between the conception and elaboration of planning projects, on the one hand, and their execution, on the other. A neat, rationalized, and "beautiful" plan is put into practice—*sai do papel*, or "leaves paper"—in unexpected, messier form. Prestes Maia would, over the course of his career, become intimately acquainted with the scope of administrative, legal, and financial heavy lifting required for the realization of the ambitious schemes like the Avenues Plan. Much of that heavy lifting would occur well before the first meters of asphalt were laid and revolve around the seizure and razing of buildings that stood in the way of projected avenues.

Like many urban redevelopment proposals, the success of Prestes Maia's scheme depended on securing the expropriation and demolition of structures he deemed necessary for the project. Demolitions for avenues projects in São Paulo began during the mayoral administration of Pires do Rio in the 1920s, and in the first pages of the Avenues Plan Prestes Maia touted the progress on those projects. The three prime areas for expropriations in the 1920s were São João Avenue, the city center, and Anhangabaú Avenue.[73] The geographic focus of expropriation would shift following the 1930 Avenues Plan and into Prestes Maia's mayoral terms to Itororó Avenue and the ring road. The construction of three of the key roadways under Prestes Maia's leadership, Anhangabaú Avenue, Itororó Avenue, and a ring road circling the city center, would require extensive expropriations and demolitions. Anhangabaú Avenue bordered the Bela Vista district on its western edge. In the east, Itororó Avenue split Bela Vista from the Liberdade district. The ring road ran through the northern sections of both neighborhoods. The completion of these three roadways would reshape the districts of Bela Vista and Liberdade from the 1920s through the 1960s.

Prestes Maia authored the Avenues Plan as the head of the Department of Traffic and Public Works of the City of São Paulo from 1926 to 1930. The project outlined a redevelopment of the roadway network from the city center and extending outward. As shown in Prestes Maia's "Theoretical Scheme" (figure 1.2) the plan consisted of a ring road with radial avenues. The ring road had five main aims, as Prestes Maia explained: "Decentralize commercial activity and, in doing so, expand the city center; deflect traffic flows through thoroughfares; distribute circulation to secondary roads; integrate segregated sectors within the city center; [and] maintain the local appearance (culture), to the extent possible."[74] Three principal radial avenues overlay the ring road, stretching north and south in the shape of an inverted Y. The avenues Anhangabaú and Itororó were the two southern legs of that Y.

While roadways were the means by which Prestes Maia aimed to modernize São Paulo, the products of that modernization went beyond the confines of transportation planning and included the redevelopment of neighborhoods. Prestes Maia himself described the construction of Anhangabaú and Itororó as a means for the "exploitation of extensive central areas, the correction of poorly formed neighborhoods, [and] the possibility of rapid traffic circulation in the very heart of the city."[75] An additional goal for the urbanist, the quote reveals, was the "correction"

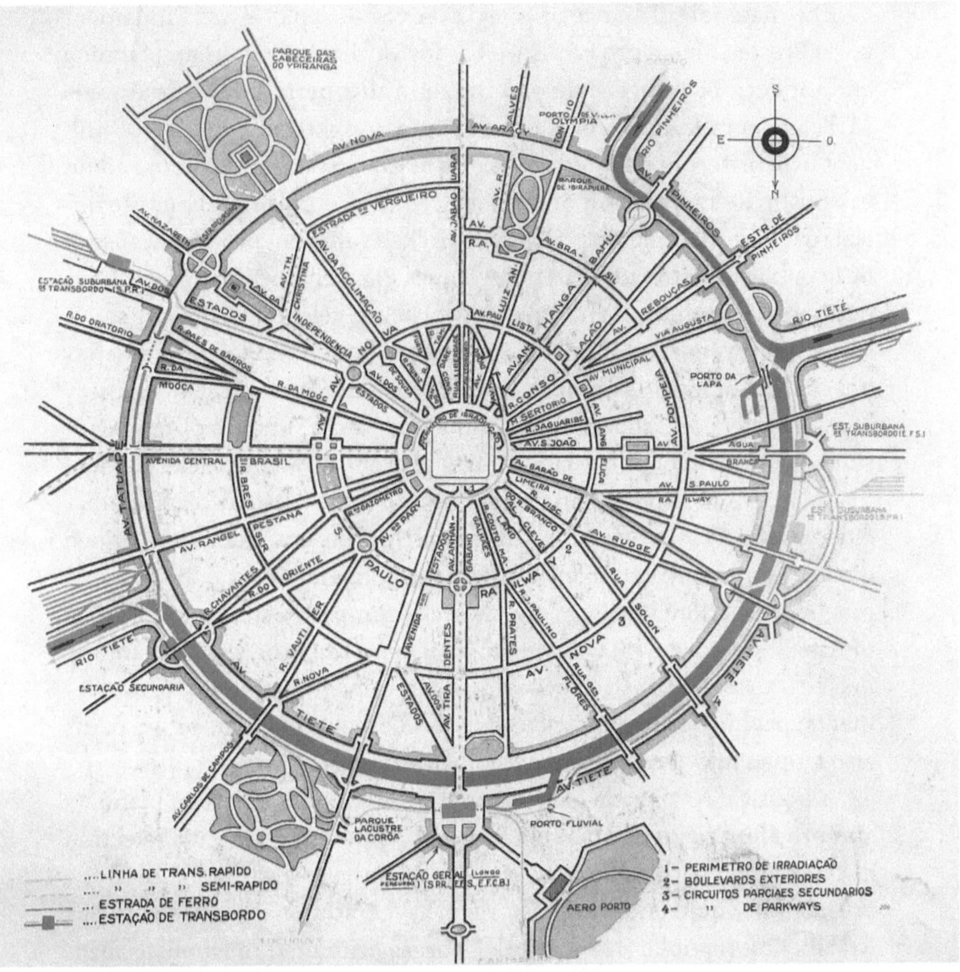

FIGURE 1.2 · Francisco Prestes Maia's "Theoretical Scheme" for São Paulo from *Estudo do um plano de avenidas para a cidade de São Paulo* (São Paulo: Companhia Melhoramentos de São Paulo, 1930).

of "poorly formed" neighborhoods. Such descriptors likely referenced environmental challenges such as the sharp topography that led to flooding problems in the region, which leveling for the new system of avenues would ostensibly improve. At the same time, representing two of the three most significant spaces in São Paulo's "Black zone" with such terms raises questions about the racialized dimensions of this modernization program.

The material substance of paved avenues—asphalt—was fundamental to Prestes Maia's project as well as forward-thinking urban planning and modern city governance in Brazil in this period. Luiz de Anhaia Mello, mayor of the city of São Paulo in 1930–1931 and himself a prominent urbanist, concentrated on paving in the first article he wrote about urbanism. Reminiscent of nineteenth-century complaints about provincial roads, he asserted that "São Paulo lacked sufficient paving because of little public investment."[76] In the Avenues Plan, engineer Arthur Saboya (author of the preface) and Prestes Maia both celebrated the city's new stone quarry, named Pires do Rio after the then-mayor, which (they boasted) had South America's largest crusher. Shots of the machinery and an excavated landscape accompanied "after" images of newly installed pavement on Liberdade Street.[77] Pavement was a crucial element for collective transportation and connected Prestes Maia's plan to other cities redesigned around the automobile in this era. Planners imbued concrete and asphalted roadways with meanings far beyond their strictly practical function, however. The material comprised the building block of urban improvements, as a 1942 article on the progress of planning projects explained: "In São Paulo, when one speaks of city improvements, paving quickly comes to mind."[78] Discourses about paved paths also tapped into the Paulista mythologization of the *bandeirantes*.

A political revolution gave new autonomy to official urban planners and private developers in 1930s Brazil. A disputed presidential election in 1930 ended with a coup led by Getúlio Vargas, whose seizure of the presidency would end what historians have traditionally categorized as Brazil's first republic (1889–1930).[79] Vargas promoted the industrialization and urbanization of Brazil through a populist authoritarianism that would, in 1937, climax in the dissolution of the national congress and the declaration of the fascist-inspired Estado Novo (new state). Vargas reshaped local politics, as well, through such measures as the suspension of São Paulo's city council. In the vacuum, a group of São Paulo elites formed the Society of Friends of the City, or SAC. Former mayor Antonio Prado Jr. assumed the presidency of SAC at its founding in 1934, though Prestes Maia would be elevated to the post by the second meeting. The organization produced studies and publications about urban issues and took charge of responsibilities typical of a municipal planning institution. Some members held an ambitious view of the organization's reach. In an article explaining the purpose of SAC, for example, Luiz de Anhaia Mello wrote that the organization "shall teach the paulistas the symphony of modern life, for us to be tuned with the epoch and, like diligent spiders, build a bit of ourselves, through the golden web of the city of our dreams."[80] For Mello and like-minded urbanists, the construction of identities—"a bit of ourselves"—and the production of space constituted a singular process.

Lofty rhetoric accompanied the mundane but consequential administration of urban space by SAC authorities. The organization fielded complaints from local residents "on simple issues like the improvement of a plaza or in protest to the change of the name of a street."[81] As a private organization with no public accountability but in charge of public spatial regulation, the planners and municipal administrators who composed SAC had seemingly unchecked latitude.[82] SAC's capacity to make decisions about the spatial management and development of the city—already impressive—would expand further when its president became the head of the municipal administration itself.

In 1938 Vargas nominated Prestes Maia to be the mayor of the city of São Paulo. Historian José Alfredo O. Vidigal Pontes writes that Prestes Maia was chosen "by the personal imposition of Getúlio Vargas, who admired him as an urbanist."[83] Vargas's rise and the initial period of his rule were characterized by tensions between power brokers on the regional and federal scales. Those tensions included armed civil conflict in 1932, when Paulistas, chafing at their diminished influence under Vargas, led a revolt called the Constitutionalist Revolution.[84] Federal troops suppressed the rebellion in a matter of months. In the wake of the 1932 civil war, Vargas aimed to concentrate power at the federal level and curb local and regional resistance by personally selecting state and municipal administrators. Many of his picks included urbanists and engineers, and, as a result, writes Cristina Peixoto-Mehrtens, the position of mayor "came to be a place in politics for engineers" as well as urbanists.[85]

Officials during the Vargas era promoted social unity and economic development through a celebratory discourse of Brazilianness (*brasilidade*).[86] Urbanists- and engineers-turned-mayors played significant roles in enacting that project through concrete changes on the local scale. We can see, for instance, how the five objectives of the all-important ring road outlined in the Avenues Plan would also help to advance key aspects of the *brasilidade* project. "Circulation," for example, foresaw the freer flow of capital and the easier transit of the labor force from marginal areas to industrial and commercial jobs elsewhere in the city. The integration of "segregated sectors," within and between neighborhoods, especially in the central part of the city with high populations of African descendants, mirrored the premium that Vargas placed on social unity. Describing the links between infrastructure and Vargas's vision for unification, historian Joel Wolfe writes that "the physical movement of people, through advanced transportation networks, would be required to complement the more ethereal components of Vargas's state making."[87]

São Paulo's urbanists, however, appropriated the *brasilidade* project in a distinctly Paulista manner. This appropriation surfaced in an article written by Victor da Silva Freire, an engineer who spent nearly forty years as director of the city's Department of Works (1888–1926). Reviewing a 1942 speech that Prestes Maia delivered about progress on the Avenues Plan, Freire exclaimed: "I will say, at this point in time, that engineering, in São Paulo, represents a historical vocation. The *bandeirantes* were engineers."[88] As historian Barbara Weinstein has shown, the celebration of *bandeirantes* in constructions of Paulista and Paulistano identity following the Constitutionalist Revolution of 1932 was intertwined with the ideology that equated modernity and progress with whiteness.[89] Seen in this light, Freire's comments represented Paulistano urbanists like Prestes Maia as the leaders responsible for constructing an imagined and material city that reflected a racialized ideal of modernity and progress. The realization of this aspiration depended on the transformation of places that planners understood as barriers to progress.

Prestes Maia arrived in his new post well prepared and eager to enact his ambitious redevelopment vision. "To establish great guiding lines is the principal responsibility, and the most elemental, of municipal administrations—and to establish them courageously, with a wide and assured vision, eyes to the future."[90] Empowered by the authoritarian Estado Novo regime, he would have substantial latitude to execute the plan as head of the city from 1938 to 1945. Already in 1925, he had articulated his lofty ambitions for city officials, and presumably planners in particular. Articles like this 1939 piece from *Correio Paulistano* celebrated his work after a year in office: "Prestes Maia, in a magnificent plan of urbanism . . . continues reforms in an urgent manner. . . . Expropriating, rending new avenues, acquiring parks and great swaths of lands, soon the Mayor of São Paulo, [will] realize his objectives, bringing to the population that comfort that has long been promised."[91] The full-page article proceeded through an alphabetized list of ongoing projects that amounted to an updated version of the Avenues Plan itself. Other articles tried to anticipate readers' concerns and impatience with the pace of progress. One argued, for instance, that Prestes Maia was committed to carrying out expropriations and demolitions in the "shortest possible time frame."[92] Another piece from the same year touted Prestes Maia's program as "one of the greatest urbanistic works carried out in South America."[93]

Expropriation has long been a critical element of city planning practice.[94] Urbanists in São Paulo saw expropriation as a necessary and unavoidable aspect of the reproduction of urban space in response to territorial expansion, population growth, and the deterioration of infrastructure.[95] Yet much remained to be determined and negotiated in the fine print, including decisions about which places would be razed, the precise terms of expropriation (including sums paid to owners), and the justification for certain sites instead of others. In these decisions we can discern some of the ideological dimensions of planners' decision-making. Doing so follows in the footsteps of some contemporary observers in Brazil, such as Roland Corbisier, an intellectual and chief architect of nationalist-developmentalist programs. Corbisier questioned the justification of expropriation in the name of the "social good" (*interesse social*) in 1949: "And what should one understand exactly as social good? Will it not be the interest of the majority that prevails over those particular concerns of groups or classes?"[96]

Expropriations preoccupied Prestes Maia. He dedicated the first section after the introduction of the Avenues Plan to questions, norms, and international practices of expropriation, opening the chapter with the declaration that expropriation "is the great source of expenditures and difficulties in the execution of any plan." In the same era, engineer Anhaia Mello argued that a law of expropriation was "the initial landmark on the road of urbanism."[97] During Prestes Maia's administration federal authorities established a new tool for municipal administrators—again, many of them urbanists—throughout the country. Enacted in June of 1941, Decreto-Lei n. 3.365 created at the federal level a standard process for the state to seize land for public utility or interest. The first federal law granting expropriation rights, the policy was a product of the authoritarian climate of the Estado Novo. The law would be cited in the many decrees that Prestes Maia issued to seize structures for the construction of new avenues.[98]

Demolitions for grand avenues took place amid meteoric growth in the city of São Paulo during Prestes Maia's first two terms. During the 1940s alone, the city's population expanded from 1.3 to 2.2 million. This influx would strain the already-insufficient housing stock, with demolitions of housing units for avenues exacerbating the situation further. Urbanist Nabil Bonduki writes that the "demographic increase created the additional necessity of, at the least, 12,000 new housing units, without counting the already-existing deficit and the considerable number of buildings demolished in function of the real estate boom and expropriations for transportation projects." Though the shortage in São Paulo was perhaps more acute than elsewhere, these dynamics were seen throughout urban Brazil. Comparable redevelopment projects by Vargas-appointed officials (on state and municipal levels) generated similar problems for low-income residents seeking housing in other cities across the country.[99]

In parallel to expropriations and demolitions, the 1930s and 1940s in São Paulo saw real estate prices increase alongside new government programs aimed at regulating the housing sector. Between 1941 and 1946 a real estate boom took off in the city, as land became an investment opportunity for industrial, agricultural, and commercial profits. Speculation generated record land prices, with median prices in 1946 up 70 percent from 1930.[100] Vargas's 1942 Tenancy Law, which froze rents throughout the entire country, would further complicate matters. Multiple factors motivated this unprecedented state intervention in housing, which remained in effect until 1964. The law represented a populist, paternalistic effort to assist the urban masses. It also had a developmentalist side, as Vargas sought to curb rental income as a primary source of capital accumulation in favor of investment in industrial development.[101] The ceiling on rental income, however, likely disincentivized the construction of new housing stock. The already existing and quickly increasing shortage of rentable units limited the socially minded goals of the measure in the city of São Paulo, where landlords also found other ways to extract income from tenants.[102]

Its intended aims notwithstanding, the Tenancy Law helped to reshape the pattern of urban settlement in São Paulo. The housing shortage led residents to seek cheap housing on new frontiers of the city's geographic periphery, where they would purchase and build their own homes instead of renting. Private developers would capitalize on this demand by selling lots in often bare-bones housing developments in regions remote from the city's historic center. São Paulo's expanding network of asphalted avenues, designed to facilitate automobile and bus transportation, would further encourage this local migration. Real estate developers made out especially well sponsoring this sprawl, which, in São Paulo's natural geography, encountered almost no natural barriers. The "fix" for the 1930s–1940s housing crisis—the production of low-cost housing developments on the city's geographic margins—served to hasten the advancement of industrial capitalism in São Paulo and would have profound effects for the sociospatial reconfiguration of the city in the years ahead.[103]

Some observers expressed concern at these patterns of spatial change in São Paulo. Anhaia Mello, for example, criticized Prestes Maia in a 1945 article about São Paulo's housing problem in the journal *Engenharia.* Historian Joel Outtes summarized the article: "Mello criticized Maia again, saying that the planning being practised was twenty years too late, and claimed that the City Hall should have an organized service of research in order to avoid the present situation in which 150,000 people were *sem teto* [homeless]."[104] While some historians have described Prestes Maia's first administration as characterized by "consensus," these critiques indicate a more nuanced landscape where other influential observers contested how planning projects in this era were "leaving paper."[105]

The overthrow of Getúlio Vargas and end of the Estado Novo in 1945 also spelled the departure of Prestes Maia from São Paulo's municipal administration. In 1945 he published *Improvements of São Paulo,* which amounted to a retrospective of the range of projects coordinated over the seven preceding years. Progress on the two southern legs of the all-important "Y system" of avenues remained front and center, with Prestes Maia celebrating the completion of Anhangabaú Avenue: "It is extremely original for its topographical conditions. . . . The first expropriations date to the Pires do Rio administration; that administration began the work, that we continued and concluded, with notable modifications."[106]

Despite this success, much of the work of the Avenues Plan had not yet left paper. In contrast to the completion of Anhangabaú Avenue was its "twin" Itororó, which Prestes Maia admitted, in 1945, had "only begun."[107] Officials would later rename this avenue, replacing the original Indigenous place-name with May 23 Avenue. The roadway remained incomplete through 1960, when Prestes Maia mounted a competitive campaign for a third term as mayor. Successive delays, including challenges with expropriations, had halted the work. While unopened to traffic, some local residents hosted soccer matches on the completed (but unopened) sections of May 23 Avenue.[108] In his 1960 campaign, Prestes Maia promised to finish, once and for all, the avenues first outlined more than three decades prior. Construction would only be completed, however, under his successor, engineer-turned-mayor José Vicente Faria Lima (1965–1969). The messy saga of making May 23 Avenue reveals the long lifespan of the Avenues Plan and the continuities that bound the late 1920s to the late 1960s.[109]

During Prestes Maia's 1960 mayoral campaign, the pro–Prestes Maia team distributed a series of pamphlets—almost on the scale of the Avenues Plan itself—with examples exalting the great successes of the urbanist. Pamphlets like "Prestes Maia Did It—Prestes Maia Will Do It" cast the former mayor as the only person capable of returning São Paulo to its former glory. The campaign appropriated the image of a pothole in political advertisements, referencing the supposedly ubiquitous dilapidated asphalt in the city and serving as a metaphor for the decay into which the city had allegedly fallen without Prestes Maia's leadership. Interspersed with the political rhetoric was a revealing explanation for what had hindered Prestes Maia's work in earlier terms: "If the mayor, who foresaw the growth of the city, did not fulfill a promise . . . it was because of the impossibility of a greater number of expropriations."[110] The pamphlet concluded with the lamentation: "If it had been possible he would have completed a greater number of expropriations and achieved the desired areas."[111] The statements further highlight expropriation as the critical factor through which planning projects left paper and determined the realization of Prestes Maia's vision for a transformed São Paulo.

CORTIÇOS "NAVIOS"

Standing at the meeting point of the former Anhangabaú (now July 9) Avenue and Itororó (now May 23) Avenue—the fulcrum of the inverted Y—the products of Prestes Maia's Avenues Plan dominate my view of São Paulo's center-city urban landscape. The structures cleared to make way for those avenues, however, are not nearly as discernible. One way to surface them involves layering (often within a mapping application)

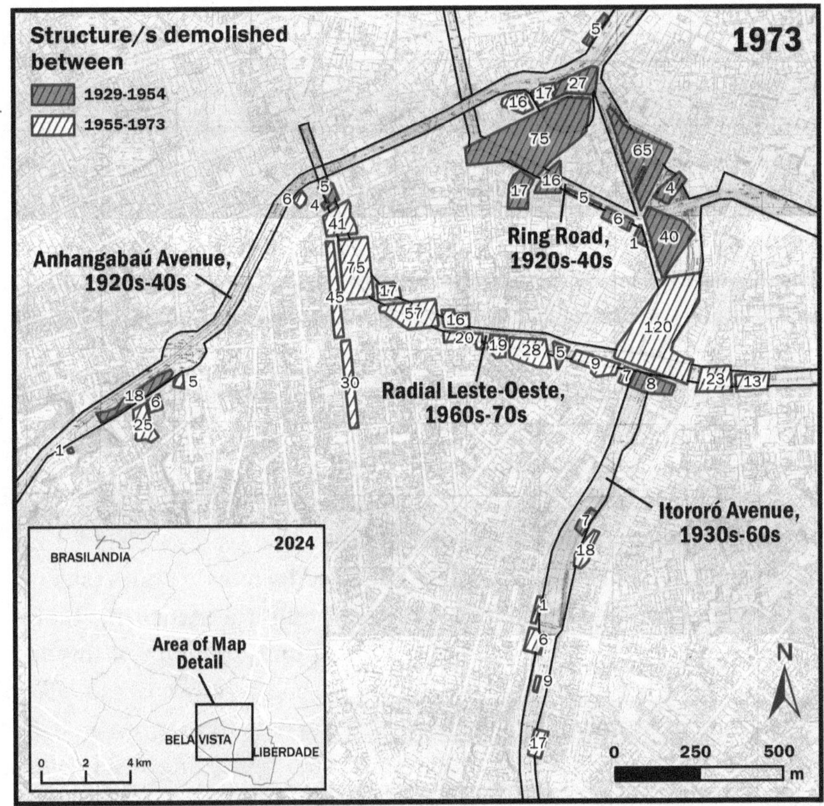

MAP 1.1 · Demolitions carried out in the Bela Vista and Liberdade districts linked to roadways projects from the late 1920s to the 1970s. Polygons display the location, size, and approximate number of demolished structures. Layer crated by comparing changes across large-scale maps from 1930 (SARA), 1954 (VASP), and 1973 (GEGRAN). Georeferenced map is "São Paulo—GEGRAN," 1973, Acervo Técnico Gegran/EMPLASA. Other map data sources: GeoSampa; OpenStreetMap (Light Gray Canvas) © OpenStreetMap contributors, Microsoft, Facebook, Google, Esri Community Maps contributors, map layer by Esri. Map by Andrew G. Britt.

maps produced at different moments in time, searching for changes and continuities in the urban built environment, and identifying structures demolished over time. Map 1.1 displays demolitions linked to the construction of the Ring Road, Anhangabaú Avenue, Itororó Avenue, Radial Leste-Oeste, and a few other major arteries in Bela Vista and Liberdade, stretching from the late 1920s through the 1970s. The map includes approximate numbers of structures demolished. Such maps offer a starting and continuous reference point in reconstructing the sociospatial history of these neighborhoods before and after projects like the Avenues Plan.

That practice of reconstruction also provides insights into the residents who participated in the planning and development of urban spaces independent of, yet in dialogue with, official city planners. In the face of official planning projects motivated by a desire for rupture, such residents likely drew on generations of knowledge about normative sociospatial relations in Brazil and pursued a spatial praxis that sought to maintain continuities of everyday life in areas like housing.[112] In the process of highlighting the interplay between official planners and local residents in center-city São Paulo, I show how the Avenues Plan was about both the construction of modern roadways and the transformation of spaces and inhabitants deemed undesirable.

Cortiços—literally, "beehives"—were one of the most common types of structures demolished in the realization of the Avenues Plan.[113] *Cortiços* were tenement-style complexes peopled by mostly poor residents who rented, occupied, and, in some cases, built the structures themselves. A degree of precarity in terms of the built structure is implicit in the term, as is a blurriness between public and private spaces.[114] *Cortiços* were commonly seen as undesirable barriers to progress in early twentieth-century São Paulo, and not just among city officials. In 1929, the article "Cortiços: Favellas paulistanas" ran in *Progresso*, one of the journals in São Paulo's flourishing Black press in the late 1920s and early 1930s.[115] As hinted by the title, the piece drew a parallel between São Paulo's tenements and favelas, the stigmatized housing form prominent especially in Rio de Janeiro in the early twentieth century and relatively uncommon in São Paulo at the time. The article explained that "São Paulo conserves in the midst of the rapid development of its new urbanist expansion . . . barbarous . . . almost savage nuclei." Identifying the nuclei as *cortiços*, the unnamed author wrote that they are an "anachronism to the progress of the Paulista capital.'" The piece highlighted one *cortiço*, named "Trezentos" (three hundred), that stood along São João Avenue. Lauding the demolition of the *cortiço* and the avenue expansion, the *Progresso* article continued: "Now for the opening of São João Avenue, the City Government demolished Trezentos, the most infamous '*cortiço*' of the capital, finishing, therefore, with the ugliest stain that stands out from the progress of the beauty of modern S. Paulo."[116] Given the probability that many residents of *cortiços*, including Trezentos, were of African descent, this article points toward divisions of social class between African descendants in São Paulo. I elaborate on those divisions in subsequent chapters, especially in the context of Brasilândia's history.

Prestes Maia addressed *cortiços* in a section on housing in the Avenues Plan. He included a sketch of a *cortiço* similar to the ones being demolished in the Pires do Rio administration, along with the caption "Popular Housing . . . Bexiga."[117] The accompanying text did not directly reference a specific corollary to the drawing. Prestes Maia drew an implicit contrast, however, in explaining the desired type of housing: "The ideal housing is naturally the individual."[118] He placed a premium on single-family housing, a valorization that would anticipate the move toward individual families owning their own lots and homes in the expanding periphery in the wake of the Avenues Plan. Prestes Maia's caption also reveals the centrality of Bexiga as emblematic of stigmatized *cortiços*, a feature that would make it prime for remaking through the construction of Anhangabaú and Itororó Avenues along with the ring road.

One of the most infamous *cortiços* demolished during this era, following Trezentos, was popularly known as the "Navio Parado," or "stationary ship," and located in the northern area of the Bela Vista district (figure 1.3). This structure formed part of a larger complex, known as Vila Barros, that included other *cortiços* named Vaticano, Geladeira, and Pombal. Among the multiple *cortiços* located between Jacarehy Street, Japurá Street, and Santo Antônio Street, Navio Parado was considered the oldest.[119] Bonduki writes that Vila Barros was condemned by "the elite and by the press as a territory of promiscuity and lack of hygiene."[120] Observations in Nádia Marzola's City-sponsored neighborhood history of Bela Vista suggest a more specific stigma attached to the *cortiços* in Vila Barros:

> The glory days of Bexiga run parallel to the life of the *cortiço* Vaticano or Navio Parado. They were formed by dozens of houses of a wall-and-a-half (*parede-e-meia*) where hundreds of families lived together. . . . The majority of the residents of *cortiços* were not immigrants, but domestics, factory workers without training, and principally Blacks. "In old Bexiga, the whitest Black was the color of the telephone," says Paulo Vanzolini, poet for whom Bexiga was his inspirational muse.[121]

FIGURE 1.3 · Navio Parado *cortiço*, 1942, Vale do Bexiga, by Benedito J. Duarte and Antônio R. Muller. Acervo Fotográfico do Museu da Cidade de São Paulo.

In her in-depth study of *cortiços* in Bela Vista, historian Sheila Schneck has shown that in the 1920s and 1930s these complexes had multiethnic compositions, with a population comprised of non-White residents as well as a multiethnic composition of European immigrants and their descendants.[122] Despite their diverse populations, *cortiços* like the Navio Parado would sometimes be represented in Marzola's description and others as centers of Black populations.[123] This dynamic reflects the first paradox of ethnoracial space I outline in the introduction of a multiethnic place (in this case a housing complex, not a neighborhood) being reduced to a singular ethnoracial identity.

Prestes Maia slated the Navio Parado for demolition in the 1930 Avenues Plan, but delays prevented demolition past the end of his term in 1945. He had secured the demolition of other *cortiços* in Vila Barros, as indicated in his 1945 *Improvements of São Paulo*. In that volume he touted the completion of Jacareí Bridge, which sat adjacent to the complex of *cortiços*.[124] Leading up to celebrations for the four-hundred-year anniversary of São Paulo in 1954, a fresh round of urbanistic projects would lead to the demolition of the Navio Parado. A 1951 article in *Jornal de Notícias* explained: "Whole roads will be widened, old blocks destroyed as well, such as various cortiços that remain standing in the very center of the city, like the 'Navio Parado,' the *cortiço*-favela of the Jacareí Bridge."[125] The article continued, revealing the role the *cortiço*'s residents played in the daily life of the city: "This *cortiço* houses some five hundred people and is known as the headquarters of São Paulo's laundrywomen, and for a while it has been threatened by demolition, since it constitutes a terrible urban stain on the progress of our city."[126] The term "stain" mirrored the language used to describe the Trezentos *cortiço* decades earlier and, given the complex's comparatively high non-White population, had a decidedly racialized valence.

Navio Parado was the hub of São Paulo's dirty (and clean) laundry, where many of the complex's female residents performed domestic labor for families in nearby wealthy neighborhoods. A 1948 piece in the satirical journal *A Marmita* (The lunchbox),[127] based on a visit to Navio Parado, described the place in an absurdist piece critiquing sociospatial inequities and public disinvestment in São Paulo:

> This is another magnificent housing complex of our capital. It's there on Japurá Street. It occupies an immense valley. The "valley of promise." 2,000 people reside there in a beautiful example of civility and human fraternity. From the height of the Jacareí Bridge we had the opportunity to appreciate the panorama. Beautiful. Enchanting. As one admires a beautiful woman from behind, we appreciated this work of modern engineering, also from behind. Tall houses, slender, of solid construction. . . . There are even doors and windows, sometimes. Great columns lift up from some of these houses, reminiscent of those in the old and marvelous Oriental legends. . . . It is a paradise. The children, to justify such a characterization, walk nude until we don't know how old.[128]

A photo of the complex showing sprawling laundry accompanied the article and was captioned "The Valley of Promise, with its flags of peace." While the article critiqued the social conditions in which the residents lived, the satire also drew a parallel between skilled, degreed engineers and the builders of the *cortiço*. The authors of the *A Marmita* piece recounted a visit to another, tellingly named settlement nearby in the Liberdade district. With typical sarcasm, they wrote: "We drove ourselves to one of the aristocratic neighborhoods of the city, a peaceful and tranquil neighborhood, where the poor can die of hunger without worrying that the government will bother them with help: Jardim

Glicério, also known as Prestes Maia City."[129] The article noted that the municipal government itself constructed the "30 or more wooden shacks" in Prestes Maia City. Officials may have named the neighborhood after the urbanist-mayor. Alternatively, the name may have come from residents themselves, perhaps some of them dislocated from demolitions, to identify Prestes Maia explicitly as responsible for the stark sociospatial inequalities exacerbated during his administration.

Amid the demolition of various *cortiços* in the execution of Prestes Maia's Avenues Plan, Navio Parado and its longer trajectory bring into high relief the interconnectedness of the production of space by officials and nonstate actors. An earlier round of urban redevelopment, in fact, triggered the construction of the complex. From the 1951 article about its demolition, we learn that history: "The *cortiço* has existed since 1921, when it was built by old material taken from the demolitions and widening of São João Avenue."[130] The 1910s–1920s expansion of São João Avenue involved the demolitions of *cortiços* like Trezentos and the associated dislocation of resident populations. Some of those residents seem to have carried their belongings along with rubble from that demolition blocks away, where they constructed, in the early 1920s, the expansive new housing complex (map 1.2). Less than a decade later, Prestes Maia projected the Anhangabaú Avenue through this new place. Following the demolition of Navio Parado, residents would then have to migrate someplace else and rebuild once more. Such examples of repeated displacement recur throughout this book.

The links between Trezentos and Navio Parado suggest that the expropriation and demolition of *cortiços* was not necessarily an aberration for local residents. These individuals saw, lived, and constructed spatial continuities of housing despite formal planners' projects that caused rupture. The example reveals the multigenerational process of negotiated, official planning and popular production of space that reproduced the city in this era and beyond. The process that led to the migration of residents from São João Avenue to the Navio Parado in the north of Bela Vista is a clear example of displacement triggered by official urban planning. The precision of this example of dislocation linked to demolitions is rather exceptional. The infamy of *cortiços* like Trezentos and Navio Parado pushed them into the spotlight at the moment of their demolition, prompting journalists to pen articles rich with information that reveals a specific process of movement. Dislocations caused by the demolition of Navio Parado, however, prove more challenging to chart as precisely, as I discuss at length in chapter 3.

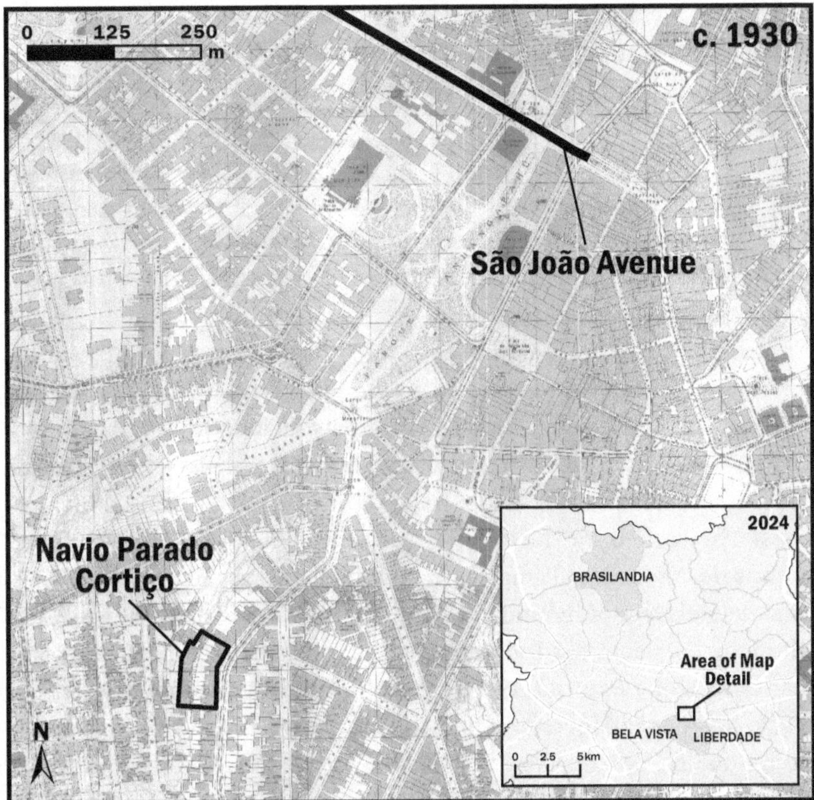

MAP 1.2 · Cycles of formal and informal urban development: from Trezentos to Navio Parado. Georeferenced map is "Mapeamento 1930—SARA," GeoSampa, accessed June 12, 2018, https://www.geosampa.prefeitura.sp.gov.br. Other map data sources: GeoSampa; OpenStreetMap (Light Gray Canvas) © OpenStreetMap contributors, Microsoft, Facebook, Google, Esri Community Maps contributors, map layer by Esri. Map by Andrew G. Britt.

The headquarters of São Paulo's Expropriation Department, or DESAP, sits today in the district of Liberdade, just a short stroll from the avenues that occupied so much of its time in the twentieth century. The records within this department would seem to hold valuable information about the social history of expropriation, such as the dislocations spurred by demolitions. DESAP documents are organized by roadways, capturing the lifespan of the former Anhangabaú Avenue, for example, from inception through completion. These spatial histories of avenues are situated at the moment when planning on paper met practice, providing an inside look at details such as the names of property owners, dimensions of the structures identified for demolition, and the amounts paid by the municipal government for the lots and structures to be demolished. DESAP maps served as the key documents to align a planned construction with the material space and to sort out the financial and legal terms of expropriation.[131]

Expropriation, as these documents reveal, sometimes involved the demolition of an entire city block. One of the largest sections demolished in the early 1930s sat at the very beginning of the projected Anhangabaú Avenue, adjacent to the Largo do Riachuelo. Among the thirty-five lots to be expropriated on this site, fourteen belonged to one woman: Maria Adelaide Rossi. Her complex included a building identified on the expropriation blueprint as a "villa." Rossi was likely of Italian descent and was married to the Italian-born Domiziano (or Domenico) Rossi. He worked for thirty-one years with famed São Paulo architect Ramos de Azevedo, ultimately becoming a partner in this firm. Rossi was the architect of monumental buildings in São Paulo like the Teatro Municipal, Palácio das Indústrias, Liceu de Artes e Ofícios, and some mansions along Paulista Avenue.[132] Following the expropriation of the block, Rossi would invest in a new urban subdivision (*loteamento*) in São Bernardo do Campo, where a name and school today bear her name.[133]

A nearby settlement along Saracura Pequena Street would meet a similar fate as this block in the late 1930s and early 1940s. A December 1925 article from the widely circulated and mainstream paper *A Gazeta* recounted an argument on Saracura Pequena Street between a Black tenant, Aldemiro Benedicto Corrêa, and his Portuguese landlord, Sebastião Bernardo. Corrêa was a month behind on his rent, prompting a "violent dispute" with Bernardo wherein the landlord threatened him. Later that night Corrêa attacked and gravely injured Bernardo.[134] By the time DESAP expropriated the lot, Sebastião's property had passed to his widow, Emilia, who accepted the city government's offer for the land and home.

Despite the details about the processes of expropriation, the DESAP records offer only a partial picture of the social composition of these demolished structures. The sources include the names of individuals who lived at demolished sites; however, these lists include only the property owners themselves. Unnoticed and unrecorded in the official record was the tenant population. Landlords and renters were not segregated, as property owners often lived at the same site they were renting. Scarlato explains the pattern in the formation of *cortiços* in Bexiga:

> In the process of building the neighborhood, houses did not occupy an entire lot. As long as the demand for housing increased . . . the property owners began to expand the built sections of the lots, constructing additional rooms. . . . Besides incorporating new constructed areas, they began to rent, as well, the basements of buildings transformed into rooms. The possibility to live from rental income, through tenants, fascinated the property owners. . . . In this manner *cortiços* surged.[135]

In 1942, sociologist Donald Pierson published a study about popular housing in three neighborhoods, including Bela Vista. Conducted among families who lived along Manoel Dutra Street, the article also emphasized the centrality of renting in Bela Vista.[136]

Sociologist Florestan Fernandes offered further commentary on this housing pattern in Bela Vista that also revealed its relationship to racialized inequalities.[137] Fernandes drew on his research about race relations in São Paulo, through firsthand observations from having himself grown up in the district also likely shaped his interpretation: "In the USA, segregation exists. Here (in Brazil), segregation, along with prejudice, is not systematic. . . . Segregation is invisible. You could say: In the 1930s, in a neighborhood like Bela Vista, Blacks and Whites lived beside each other. But the black person lived in the basement and the white person lived upstairs."[138] Francisco Lucrécio, a leader in the FNB, offered a similar interpretation: "Black people lived in the majority in *cortiços*, and Italians had their own houses, they lived above and rented the *cortiços* to the Black residents. There all the mansions had basements and *cortiços*."[139] In her study of Black intellectuals, including Bexiga resident, journalist, and FNB leader José Correia Leite, historian Paulina Alberto expands on these dynamics in Bela Vista, observing that "people of color frequently interacted (and clashed) with immigrants as neighbors, tenants, or customers."[140]

These authors illuminate a geometry of ethnoracial segregation that distinguishes a place like Bela Vista from other exemplary contexts for urban segregation, such as the United States. Instead of a horizontal division, where segregated spaces sit adjacently on a plane (typical of cities in the United States), these authors highlight racialized sociospatial separation along a vertical axis. The apparent lack of segregation in a district like 1930s Bela Vista, therefore, did not indicate the lack of segregation or racialized sociospatial inequalities. Instead, racialized sociospatial inequalities manifested differently. I expand my analysis of the prevalence of those inequalities throughout the following chapters. The observations of Ferndandes, Lucrécio, and Alberto complement the limitations of the DESAP records in capturing a more complete understanding of the social history, and especially the ethnoracial composition of tenant populations, in the residences slated for demolition.

DESAP records also do not contain information about the tenant population because state officials and private developers likely had little interest in documenting the social effects of the Avenues Plan. A more socially oriented planning ethos would begin to change planning practices in São Paulo in the late 1960s and early 1970s. That shift would lead officials to observe and ultimately record residents into similar kinds of institutional records. Official planners during this earlier era, however, did not register the dislocation caused by redevelopment projects.

By the early 1940s, expropriations and demolitions left a sizable tenant population in the city of São Paulo without housing amid a severe housing shortage and real estate boom. These residents had to move somewhere. Written sources from institutions such as DESAP offer frustratingly little evidence of dislocation stemming from demolitions. Residents' memories—spoken and sung—provide a prime source for charting dislocation triggered by avenues development. A 2002 interview with Cacilda, a Black resident of Casa Verde (the neighborhood adjacent to Freguesia do Ó and Brasilândia to the east), proves illustrative:

> 1950, it was fifty years ago when I came to live here. Before that I lived in Bela Vista, there in those *cortiços*, and they were being demolished, demolished for new constructions, they were expelling everyone, and then my spouse came and found this house to rent, and a friend told him: Here you do not rent, you buy. When he bought this house, it was one room, a bathroom and a kitchen. From the kitchen I made the living room, the kid's room, the pantry, and I continued constructing, you know that I am still building even today.[141]

The timeline of demolition and Cacilda's migration make it probable that she lived in one of the *cortiços* in Vila Barros, such as the Navio Parado. While multiple factors contributed to the exodus of renters

FIGURE 1.4 · Navio Negreiro in Bela Vista district. Sits along May 13 Street, May 2017. Photo by Andrew G. Britt.

from *cortiços*, Cacilda's language—"they were expelling everyone"—suggests that she, at least, indeed understood the process as one of forced removal.

Over decades, the popular housing complexes where residents like Cacilda lived had also served in the construction and mediation of ethnoracialized social difference. The popularly constructed and designated Navio Parado shared the "*navio*" ascription with another well-known complex a few blocks away. Navio Negreiro (figure 1.4), or "slave ship," sat at 750–772 on May 13 Street, a street named for the date of the formal abolition of slavery. Like Navio Parado, Navio Negreiro appears infrequently in official records, and, when it does so, the popular name is not used.

Both White and non-White long-term residents of Bela Vista today associate Navio Negreiro with African descendants. One afternoon while standing next to the *cortiço*, an older, White resident asked me if I knew the name of the place. Before I could respond, he interjected in a whisper-like tone: "Navio Negreiro . . . it's where the Blacks lived." On a separate afternoon, a long-term Black resident asked me the same question and cited the long presence of the Black resident population at the *cortiço*. To prove her point, she compelled me to visit a nearby pizza joint (founded and still owned by Italian immigrants), where an enlarged historic photo across one wall shows a Black family sitting in front of the *cortiço*. Sometimes stigmatized, other times a space of pride and autonomy, Navio Negreiro persists among long-term residents as a space prominently associated with African descendants.[142]

On the surface, the popularly given "*navio*" part of these names referenced the design of the structures: horizontally expansive, multistory buildings whose shape, symmetry, and breadth resembled that of a ship. The meanings of the names, however, also transcended their physical appearance. With high populations of African-descendent and immigrant-descendent families in Bela Vista, the "ship" name also captured the related, though discrete, diasporic experiences that brought families of disparate origins together under one roof and likely provided some measure of social cohesion for residents of such complexes. The proximity between distinct ethnoracial groups did not prevent outsiders from essentializing the "*navio*" *cortiços*: reducing them to ethnoracialized "stains" on the city's landscape. Despite the ethnoracial associations attached to it, Navio Negreiro—a much smaller complex in comparison to Navio Parado—would survive the urban reform program of Prestes Maia. Its location, far removed from any major avenue project, likely helped to spare it from demolition.

SOUNDS OF DEMOLITION AND DISLOCATION: SAMBA PAULISTA/NO

While planners coordinated the demolition of *cortiços* and construction of avenues in Liberdade and Bela Vista, an organized samba scene flourished in this same era and in these districts. This local expansion paralleled the consecration of samba as a staple of Brazilian national identity in the same period. Beginning in the late 1920s, a diverse collection of intellectuals, musicians, and politicians promoted samba as a sacred symbol of Brazilianness. Disseminated on an unprecedented national scale in the 1930s and 1940s, samba articulated the supposedly unique and harmonious ethnoracial mixture at the heart of the nation.[143] The celebration of a genre developed by African-descendent enslaved people also challenged the ideology that held African descendent culture and people should be transformed through *branqueamento*. This section centers on samba in the state and city of São Paulo, or what musicians describe as samba paulista (encompassing the state as a whole) and samba paulistano (referring to the city specifically). I do not see samba as a reflection of an authentic, essential, or singular African descendant identity.[144] Instead, I am interested in how popular musicians used samba as a register of the demolitions, dislocations, and resettlement that especially (though not exclusively) affected African descendants in São Paulo during the 1930s and 1940s. Samba furnishes, in other words, a window into the sociospatial histories of African descendants in the city rendered invisible by the Avenues Plan. Passed down over multiple generations in the city's redevelopment, samba paulista/no thus serves as a precious record of both popular memory and sociospatial histories.

The city of São Paulo seldom appears in academic or popular histories of Brazilian samba.[145] Famous Rio de Janeiro sambista and poet Vinicius de Moraes once declared São Paulo the "tomb of samba."[146] Samba in São Paulo had a history, geography, and sound distinct from the more celebrated compositions of Rio de Janeiro. The development of samba in Rio de Janeiro took place within the city, despite debates about whether it emerged in the *cidade* (urban center) or in favelas on the *morro* (hillside).[147] The more expansive geography of São Paulo's samba stretched over a large swath of territory deep into the agricultural interior of the state on plantations and in towns along the Tietê River, such as Tietê, Pirapora do Bom Jesus, and Piracicaba. The roots of samba paulista on coffee plantations in the rural interior created a sound that distinguished the style from the more melodic rhythms of Rio de Janeiro.[148] The move to waged immigrant labor on coffee plantations, the construction of an extensive railroad network, and the urbanization of the city of São Paulo in the late nineteenth and early twentieth centuries brought the creators of these sounds into the city.

An organized samba scene flourished in the city of São Paulo between 1914 and 1937 in three primary regions: Liberdade, Bela Vista, and Barra Funda. These regions corresponded to what Geraldo Filme characterized as the city's "Black zone."[149] The city's first *cordão*, Camisa Verde e Branco, a samba group that played and marched during Carnival parades, was founded in Barra Funda in 1914. The *cordão* Vai-Vai would follow in Bela Vista in 1930. The city's oldest surviving and the first samba school (different from a *cordão*), Lavapés, was founded in Liberdade in 1937 by Deolinda Madre, known as Madrinha Eunice.[150] Eunice was born in the São Paulo interior in 1909 and migrated to São Paulo in the early 1920s, settling on Tamandaré Street in Liberdade. In 1936 she cofounded a samba group comprised of twenty women, named

Baianas Paulistas, with her husband Francisco Papa (known as "Chico Pinga"), who was the White child of Italian immigrants.[151]

The year following, they founded Lavapés, which went on to win championships in Carnival competitions eighteen years in a row, from 1941 to 1958.[152] The migration trajectory of Eunice, one of the few prominent female figures from São Paulo's samba scene remembered today, represents the migration pattern of samba from the Paulista interior into the city of São Paulo. The founding of Lavapés, in addition, highlights Liberdade as a locus for African descendants as well as samba in the first half of the twentieth century. The significance that African descendants in São Paulo attached to Liberdade did not exclude White populations, however, as the mixed-race couple at the heart of Lavapés's founding demonstrates.

While organized samba began to thrive within the city of São Paulo, strong connections remained to the rural interior. Musicians reestablished those connections each year through events like the festival at Pirapora do Bom Jesus on the Tietê River. As the head of São Paulo's Department of Culture in the 1930s, Mário de Andrade traveled to Pirapora to document the rural origins of São Paulo samba and the annual festivities. Narrating his experience from 1934 in an article published in 1937 for the *Revista do Arquivo Municipal*, Andrade expressed disappointment when he learned that one of the leaders of the event in Pirapora was, in fact, a resident of the city of São Paulo. Andrade described the leader, Gustavo Leite, as a sambista and mason "of 60 years or more" who lived on Santana do Paraiso Street in the low-lying valley between Bela Vista and Liberdade.[153] The year that Andrade published his profile about samba in Pirapora, the City would begin demolitions to clear the way for Itororó Avenue. The site of Leite's home would ultimately be buried beneath the asphalt of that avenue.

The Avenues Plan reshaped the geography of samba in the city of São Paulo. That transformation included the demolition of the Largo da Banana, the subject of Geraldo Filme's composition "I'll Samba Someplace Else." Located adjacent to the São Paulo railway, the square provided labor for African-descendent migrants from the interior of the state of São Paulo. Historian Márcio Sampaio writes that loading bales in the area surrounding the terminal near the Largo da Banana amounted to "one of the rare occupations allowed to the man recently freed from the yoke of slavery."[154] In parallel to wage-earning opportunities was space for cultural practices like capoeira and samba. As folklorist Plinio Marcos explained, "The Largo da Banana, in Barra Funda, was where the rail cars unloaded and, naturally, the people came together and, between one rail car and another, played samba, which gradually spread throughout the city."[155] The Largo da Banana was a site where urban samba—samba paulistano—was forged. In 1986, author and journalist João Antônio criticized Mário de Andrade—who himself lived in Barra Funda—for overlooking the Largo da Banana in his writing. "There is a lacuna in the work of Mário de Andrade," he wrote. "I don't understand how he did not note even a single line about the warehouses around the station at the junction of the railroad, of the wagons pulled by oxen in the largo da Banana, that round and unforgettable fountain, the popular dances (*gafieiras*) of Barra Funda Street, of the Black and mixed population." Antônio concluded by highlighting the significance of the street as a locus of cultural practices of African descendants: "It's a shame that our intellectuals know so little of the street, of their city."[156]

Prestes Maia planned an extension of the Pacaembu Avenue, including an overpass above the São Paulo railway, that entailed the razing of the Largo da Banana (map 1.3). The extended avenue would connect the Perdizes and Barra Funda neighborhoods to the avenues projected along the edges of the soon-to-be-canalized Tietê River. In doing so, the avenue would provide improved access to the northern region of the city, paving the way in years following for the construction of neighborhoods like Vila Brasilândia. A 1942 article praised the "work of beautification" that made up part of the "Magnificent Urbanistic Plan" to transform this area—previously "swampy"—into one of the "most beautiful points of the capital."[157] The overpass was completed in 1958.

Sambista Geraldo Filme grew up frequenting the Largo da Banana, with Barra Funda "the neighborhood of his infancy and adolescence." The neighborhood composed part of his identity, as he became known popularly as "Big Geraldo of Barra Funda."[158] In the early 1970s, a decade after the completion of the overpass, Filme recorded "Vou samba n'outro lugar," whose full lyrics were:

> I've lost the territory of the samba school
> Already I can't samba anymore
> Sambista without the Largo da Banana
> Barra Funda will be finished

MAP 1.3 · Demolition of the Largo da Banana for the extension of Pacaembu Avenue. Note the proximity to the São Paulo railway and station. Georeferenced map is "Mapeamento 1930—SARA," GeoSampa, accessed June 12, 2018, https://www.geosampa.prefeitura.sp.gov.br. Other map data sources: GeoSampa; OpenStreetMap (Light Gray Canvas) © OpenStreetMap contributors, Microsoft, Facebook, Google, Esri Community Maps contributors, map layer by Esri. Map by Andrew G. Britt.

> An overpass rises, it's progress
> I can't protest
> Goodbye, to the cradle of samba
> I'm out of here
> I'll samba someplace else[159]

The song responded directly to the expansion of the Pacaembu Avenue and the construction of the overpass. "Barra Funda is finished" implied that, to Filme, the roadway project had dislocated a sacred space for African descendants. With a brief description of the ideology that the bridge symbolized ("it's progress")—juxtaposed with his melancholic resignation to the place's removal—he suggested that these were typical sociospatial dynamics in the city. In other words, he articulated a continuity similar to that of people across town dislocated in the course of *cortiço* demolitions with a mournful but resolute response to dislocation.

In another, likely earlier, composition, "The Last Sambista" (recorded in 1968 by the group Demônios da Garoa), Filme offered a more detailed and direct critique:

> Goodbye, the hour is arriving
> The Samba is finished, goodbye Barra Funda, I am out of here
> Progress came, and made the neighborhood into the city
> It took our happiness, and also our simplicity
>
> I carry *saudade* from the Banana Square
> Where we would samba every night of the week
> I leave behind this samba I made with so much care
> I carry the *saudade* in my chest, in my hands I carry my *cavaquinho*
> Goodbye, Barra Funda[160]

The dirge covers similar ground as "Vou samba n'outro lugar," with the exception of the addition about neighborhoods: "Progress came, and made the city from the neighborhoods." Filme depicts the type of progress-oriented city planning being practiced in São Paulo as a dislocating force for local neighborhood spaces where samba flourished.

The demolition of housing complexes emerged as a prominent theme in samba paulistano during this era. Italian-Brazilian sambista João Rubinato, known popularly as Adoniran Barbosa, dealt with the subject in multiple compositions. Perhaps the most emblematic was "Saudosa Maloca" (1951), which was set up as a dialogue between two former housemates, Mato Grosso and Joca.[161] Similar to *cortiços*, malocas were old, often decaying mansions built and occupied by low-income residents. The song opened:

> If the gentleman doesn't recall, please let me retell
> That here, where now there's this tall building
> There once was an old house, an abandoned palace

It was here, my sir, that I, Mato Grosso and Joca
We constructed our maloca
But one day, I don't even want to remind myself
Came the fellas with the tools, the owner sent them to destroy it
We got all our stuff
And went to the middle of the street to appreciate the demolition

Mato Gross and Joca here recount one chapter in the spatial history of demolitions in the city. Whereas Filme expressed melancholy at the demolition, Barbosa's Mato Gross and Joca sing a mournful but almost festive elegy to *their* "beloved maloca, maloca dearest" ("*saudosa maloca, maloca querida*"). Both Filme and Barbosa's Mato Gross and Joca share a sentiment of resignation, discernible in the exchange between the latter two (later in the samba): "Mato Gross wanted to cry out, but over him I yelled / The guys are right to do it, we'll find another place.'" Barbosa would return to the theme in subsequent sambas, and even a similar storyline in his 1969 "Eviction of the Favela."[162]

Sambistas like Geraldo Filme and Adoniran Barbosa composed lyrics about experiences of demolition and dislocation spurred by redevelopment. The geography of dispersion was not only discernible in their lyrics. In the years following Prestes Maia's first mayoral terms, only a handful of samba groups would maintain their headquarters in the city center. Vai-Vai in the Bela Vista district was among the most notable, though those headquarters would be relocated in the early 2020s. New samba schools would take root on the expanding margins of the city, including in Vila Brasilândia, in a process that paralleled the reconstruction of neighborhoods on the city's periphery.[163] Similar to other regions on São Paulo's geographic margins, Vila Brasilândia would receive a sizable influx of people from center-city neighborhoods along with regional migrants, with samba musicians well represented in this population. As a result, in the 1960s and 1970s, samba would occupy a central place in the construction of Vila Brasilândia as both a material place and African-descendent neighborhood identity. That history—itself replete with songs of asphalted avenues, progress, demolitions, and displacement—will come to the center of the frame in chapters 3 and 4.

The afterlives-of-slavery framework privileges continuities from before and after the official abolition of racialized chattel slavery. Often, celebratory discourses of emancipatory change have obscured those continuities. Saidiya Hartman's concise articulation of the persistence of racialized inequalities, violence, and prejudice after abolition in the United States follows generations of scholars who have advanced similar arguments, including in the context of Brazil. Indeed, scholars of and organizers in Brazil have long argued that formal abolition in 1888 changed little: Many freed people remained on or near former plantations, nineteenth-century land and labor patterns persisted, the threat and practices of racial violence endured, and anti-Blackness remained virulent if not, in some cases, more tenacious.[164] Such work reveals the particular resonance of the afterlives-of-slavery framework in Brazil, where the absence of brief, yet significant, projects like Reconstruction in the United States arguably made pre- and postabolition continuities stronger.

Those continuities endured in the city and state of São Paulo, one of the most prominent hubs of racialized chattel slavery in the Western Hemisphere in the nineteenth century and a principal site for the elaboration of *branqueamento* policies into the early twentieth. While the city of São Paulo experienced rapid growth in terms of population, territory, and verticality from 1870 to 1930, the spatial fabric of the city at the end of this period remained fundamentally linked to years before abolition. Indeed, while architects and engineers pursued urban interventions in the rapidly growing city throughout the first decades of the twentieth century, Prestes Maia's 1930 avenues study was the first plan to outline a comprehensive, citywide transformation of the core urban infrastructure. Prestes Maia's ambitious modernization project aimed to turn the page, once and for all, from a colonial city toward a modern metropolis of unfettered progress. Asphalted avenues would serve as the means to achieve this transformation.

Elucidating this history of planning in São Paulo helps to counter perceptions of the city as a place without planning, or what historian Richard J. Williams once characterized as "urbanistic megalomania."[165] The chapter illuminates how official planners put their plans into practice over time, including by foregrounding the demolitions that marked the moment when plans "left paper." Following demolitions has also helped to reveal popular participation in the production of space. That participation is exemplified, in this chapter, by the history of residents of the Trezentos *cortiço* on Avenida São João, who carried the rubble from their demolished tenement and rebuilt the Navio Parado housing complex a few blocks away in the Bela Vista district. This example demonstrates how São Paulo residents—many of them African descendants—navigated official spatial projects in a pivotal period of the city's redevelopment. This episode also lifts up the contested negotiations between official urban planners and informal spatial actors, two groups commonly analyzed in isolation in studies of urban Brazil.

This chapter sets the stage for, and serves as a pair to, chapter 2. Relying on the context painted here, chapter 2 outlines with precision the argument that anti-Black violence shaped the spatial history of São Paulo in the course of the decades-long execution of the Avenues Plan. I advance that argument by detailing the expropriation and demolition of three specific and significant sites within the neighborhoods of Bela Vista and Liberdade. In what I term "spatial projects of forgetting," official planners demolished these spaces with the aim of reproducing undesirable neighborhoods and, by extension, the city more broadly in a whitened image of modern progress. Those planners were not uniformly successful in putting this project into practice. However, the following chapter reveals forgotten episodes and episodes of forgetting where they planned and executed new spatial pasts and futures through the remaking of significant neighborhood spaces in São Paulo's "Black zone."

TWO

Spatial Projects of Forgetting

While repairing Rio de Janeiro's sewer network in advance of the 2016 Olympic Games, construction workers came upon an unexpected past: the remains of the port that received approximately 900,000 captives in the transatlantic slave trade. The rediscovery of the Valongo Wharf prompted Rio de Janeiro's then-mayor, Eduardo Paes, to exclaim, "When I saw the place, I was absolutely shocked. I am going to build a plaza there like in Rome. Those are our Roman ruins."[1] That plaza has yet to materialize, though in July 2017 officials from the United Nations Educational, Scientific and Cultural Organization (UNESCO) did add the site to its World Heritage list. Drawing comparisons to Hiroshima and Auschwitz, UNESCO's press release described Valongo as the "most important physical trace" of the transatlantic trade in enslaved Africans in the Americas.[2]

Both Paes's and UNESCO's recognition of the port aligns with a recent expansion in public, official sponsorship for the excavation and preservation of the material remains of the transatlantic slave trade, slavery, and racialized violence throughout the Atlantic basin. In what historian Ana Lucia Araujo has termed the "memorialization phenomenon," reais, euros, and dollars have funded an array of projects far beyond Valongo, from the International Slavery Museum in

Liverpool (opened in 2007) to the Whitney Plantation Museum in Louisiana (opened in 2015).[3] The *New York Times Magazine* billed the Louisiana site as the first museum dedicated to slavery "*in America*."[4]

The city of São Paulo has, to date, seldom appeared on the map of these myriad memorialization projects. Readers would be right to ask: Why should it? Dominant popular and academic representations have long cast the city of São Paulo as a non-Black, immigrant metropolis whose growth had little to do with slavery, the slave trade, and African descendants, particularly in comparison with the supposed true urban hearts of Africa in Brazil, the cities of Rio de Janeiro and Salvador in Bahia. The myth of São Paulo as a non-Black, immigrant metropolis obscures much of the actual history of the city and province of São Paulo, including the city's role as the provincial capital of one of racial chattel slavery's final frontiers in the Americas, or what historians have termed "second slavery."[5]

In this chapter I examine how the destruction and reproduction of geographic space served in the construction of the myth of São Paulo as a non-Black, ethnically immigrant metropolis in the middle of the twentieth century.[6] From the 1920s to the 1960s, São Paulo's urban planning and political elite transformed the geographic and historic center of the city through an ambitious modernization plan structured by asphalted avenues. The roadways that the plan's authors considered most vital—from functional as well as symbolic perspectives—cut through the districts of Liberdade and Bela Vista. Through the 1940s, these districts had the first and third highest proportions of populations of African descent in the city.[7] In addition, they possessed significant sites linked to histories of formal slavery, racial violence, abolition, and struggles for Black liberation. São Paulo musician Geraldo Filme described these places as two of the three neighborhoods comprising the city's early twentieth-century *zona do negro*, or "Black zone."[8]

Beginning in the 1930s, expropriations, demolitions, and roadway construction transformed the material and social composition of Bela Vista and Liberdade, pushing many African descendent residents to the city's margins and razing some of the sites they considered significant. For example, in the 1930s and 1940s, São Paulo planning officials carried out the expropriation and demolition of a museum to the enslaved established in the Liberdade neighborhood in the 1880s at the Church of the Remedies. Abolitionists based at the Remedies had coordinated mass flight from plantations in the provincial interior and relocation to *quilombos* (freed settlements) throughout the province of São Paulo.

They also published an influential antislavery journal, *A Redempção* (The redemption).

For five decades following the formal abolition of slavery in 1888, the church then housed the museum to the enslaved—perhaps, contrary to the *New York Times Magazine* appraisal of the Whitney Plantation Museum, the actual "first in [the] America[s]"—replete with objects like shackles and instruments of torture that freed people had carried with them into Liberdade. It would not be wrong to say that the Remedies church and museum were largely forgotten over the twentieth century, but such a characterization presents forgetting as a passive process: a seemingly inevitable result of palimpsestic urban change in former slave societies. Forgetting, however, can also take place through deliberate effort and an organized set of practices. In other words, forgetting can also amount to a project.[9]

The previous chapter outlined central aspects of, and generalizable patterns in, the history that connected racial chattel slavery in the nineteenth-century to avenues projects in the city of São Paulo in the twentieth century. While a complement to the first chapter, chapter 2 centers on decidedly uncommon and unordinary spatial histories: the silencing of singular, exceptional local sites where city planners razed materialized pasts associated with African descendants and reshaped their social composition in the present. I detail how avenues projects razed and remade three key sites in São Paulo's "Black zone": Saracura (a neighborhood), the Largo do Bexiga (Bexiga Square), and the Igreja dos Remédios (Church of the Remedies). These sites had meaningful ties to formal slavery, racialized violence, abolition, and movements for Black self-determination, along with significant populations of African descendants. The architect of the forgetting project, I conclude, saw the demolition and dislocation of the city's "Black zone" as a welcome byproduct, if not indeed desired outcome, of urban redevelopment.

These demolitions contributed to the enduring transformation of the ethnoracialized geography of Bela Vista and Liberdade. Constructing asphalted avenues in these districts paved the way—literally and figuratively—for their transformation in the following decades into two of the city's iconic "Japanese" and "Italian" spaces. While the spatial project of forgetting contributed to this transformation, that project did not produce a total erasure of São Paulo's "Black zone" in popular memory. In this chapter I also bring forth the stories of individuals, from the long-forgotten African-descendent author Gabriel Marques to famed modernist Mario de Andrade, who questioned the racialized erasure they saw taking place in São Paulo's center city through Prestes Maia's Avenues Plan. In some cases, these observers contested the erasure directly though, ultimately, unsuccessfully; in other cases, they recorded the significant histories being disappeared in prose, song, and more. Their actions helped to ensure the incompleteness of the spatial project of forgetting and the preservation of recollections of places like Saracura, Bexiga Square, and the Remedies church and museum into the present.

UNMAPPING SARACURA AND PAVING SÃO PAULO'S "PIECE OF AFRICA"

I frogger my way across São Paulo's busy July 9 Avenue, dodging articulated buses and chirping motorcycles (São Paulo's ubiquitous "motoboys") to begin the ascent from the asphalted base of the Anhangabaú Valley. I am headed into the place that, on official maps, is the district of Bela Vista. Unofficially, it is known commonly as Bexiga, Bixiga, or Saracura, depending on who and when you ask. I had never seen this last place, Saracura, on a city map, but at a recent gathering featuring one of São Paulo's Black female samba composers, I met someone from this unmapped place. I try to recall a string from one of her compositions as I climb May 13 Street, the road named for the date of the formal abolition of slavery in 1888 and that stretches through the center of Bela Vista. A few blocks north of the Navio Negreiro *cortiço*, discussed in chapter 1, I pass by an elementary school and notice a colorful mural spanning three sides of a wall (figure 2.1). In the mural, Black children splash in a fish-filled creek on the bottom half of the wall, with one woman laundering clothes and another walking with a basket on her head toward modest houses and a verdant forest in the background. The title stretching above the landscape reads: "Memories I have of Saracura." I wonder: "Is *this* Saracura?" I realize later that the mural is a popular memorial to a place that was disappeared from the urban landscape yet endures in the memories of local residents. The disappearance of Saracura did not take place through a passive process. Instead, it was a spatial project—meaningful in terms of its material effects yet incomplete—that dated to

FIGURE 2.1 · Map mural on May 13 Street, at corner with Manoel Dutra Street, May 2017. The text at the top reads, "Memories I have of Saracura." The bottom reads, "Bexiga, yesterday, today, and always!" Photo by Andrew G. Britt.

early twentieth-century avenue construction and efforts to remake the surrounding neighborhood in a whitened image of modern progress.

Eighty-two years before my walk past this mural on May 13 Avenue—on July 9, 1935—São Paulo's engineer-turned-mayor Fábio da Silva Prado (1934–1938) inaugurated July 9 Avenue in Bela Vista. The consecration was, in fact, a rechristening: July 9 was replacing the roadway's former name, Anhangabaú, the Indigenous place-name that would remain attached to the valley and creek through which the avenue stretched. São Paulo urbanists and political elites had dreamed of building this roadway well before Prestes Maia's 1930 Avenues Plan, with São Paulo Department of Works head Arthur Saboya terming this project the "old aspiration of Paulistanos."[10] The 1935 name change to "July 9" reflected the dramatic changes that had upended Brazilian and Paulista politics in the years prior. "July 9" commemorated a separatist rebellion and, ultimately, civil war launched by forces in São Paulo against the federal government on July 9, 1932. The Constitutionalist Revolution, as the conflict would come to be known, was stymied by the federal forces of Getúlio Vargas after three months.

Despite defeat, as historian Barbara Weinstein has persuasively shown, the experience of 1932 and its memory in decades following contributed to the consolidation of a "particular racialized construction of paulista identity—and Brazilian modernity."[11] Urban spaces within the city of São Paulo that had served as battlegrounds of the 1932 war served as significant sites for the construction and expression of this identity after arms had been laid down. Political and urban planning elites cemented the links between July 9 and Paulista identity by attaching it to urban spaces like the former Anhangabaú Avenue. For those elites, the July 9 Avenue served both constructive and destructive ends.[12] The roadway would extend through, and by consequence help to remake, an undesirable neighborhood space in the whitened image of modern São Paulo. This space was Saracura: a *quilombo*-turned-neighborhood with long ties to slavery and Black self-determination, along with an exceptionally high contemporary population of African descendants.

The urbanist-mayors who authored the July 9 Avenue project went far beyond technical matters when describing avenues. "This commemoration has a significance much deeper than the opening of a new road," explained Prado at the 1935 inauguration. "It is more significant than a war that lasted the short span of three months. It represents much more, so much more, than the reaction of a people for the reestablishment of a legal regime. It synthesizes the very spirit of São Paulo." This equation would recur over the decades following, as elite and nonelite individuals alike conflated the essence of São Paulo—here articulated as its "very spirit"—with roadways. Prado's comments, in fact, presented this conflation as a customary practice in São Paulo. He explained that the "great obsession of the paulista has always been opening roads that take him further on." He then referenced the *bandeirantes*, colonial settlers who departed from their base in São Paulo on expeditions to enslave Indigenous people in the continental interior.[13] Prado equated the construction of roadways to the formation of São Paulo's distinct ethnoracialized identity. As a result of the trailblazing expeditions of the *bandeirantes*, he explained, "Native blood dispersed itself in the veins of a people, as a substantial element in the formation of a race today about to enter its adolescence."[14] He cast here the population of São Paulo as a distinct race whose formation and progress depended on the production of roadways.

Prado, not surprisingly, depicted *bandeirantes* as the principal protagonists of this history, with Indigenous populations from territories far from the city of São Paulo making only modest and passive contributions.[15] This representation is rife with omissions and distortions, including the significant local presence of Indigenous populations before, during, and after the sixteenth-century founding of the city of São Paulo, whose original name, São Paulo dos Campos de Piratininga, retained the Indigenous place-name Piratininga. Prado's discourse also (again, not unexpectedly) neglects to specify that the dispersion of "native blood" took place through violent processes of kidnapping and enslavement committed against Indigenous people. Perhaps less obviously, however—and, perhaps, unbeknownst to Prado—was the fact that Indigenous populations in what became São Paulo had, for centuries, served as protagonists in the construction of roadways on both local and transcontinental scales. The most famous of these, the Caminho de Peabiru, extended from the Atlantic coast of the province of São Vicente (São Paulo), ran directly through what became the city of São Paulo, and stretched all the way to the Incan settlements of Potosí and Cuzco in contemporary Bolivia and Peru. Historian and archivist Eudes Campos has identified the likely trajectory of the Peabiru and other Indigenous trails through the city of São Paulo, concluding that "the basic structure of São Paulo's road network originated . . . from the structuring axes represented by old Indigenous trails."[16] Historian Júlia Mergulhão Estronioli used Campos's research to produce a map of these Indigenous trails, which, overlaid on the contemporary road network of São Paulo (map 2.1), illustrates the Indigenous roots of this most Paulistano of urban forms.

Despite Prado's skewed history lesson on roadway- and race-making in São Paulo, he ultimately concluded that the inauguration of the new avenue was most meaningful as a forward-looking event. Shifting abruptly from the tales of bygone *bandeirantes*, he explained:

> But all of this is history. It is behind us. In front of us is today. And, today, what is seen is what we see: a new civilization for which there will be no stumbles. The marshes and swamps flourish in culture or are cleared away through roads. The sludge of the wetlands is transformed on the asphalt of new avenues. And the conjuncture of all of this is São Paulo.[17]

The vivid imagery cast asphalted avenues as the civilizing force that would lead São Paulo, positioned at the crossroads of a colonial past and modern future, down the path of progress. Implied within that civi-

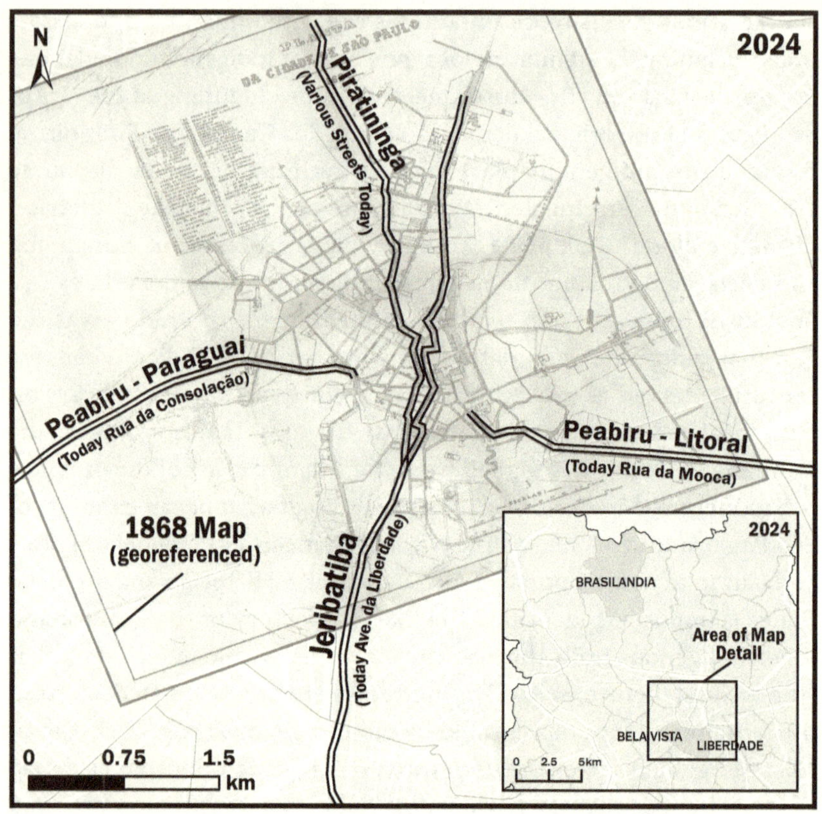

MAP 2.1 · Indigenous routes in contemporary São Paulo. Routes created by Júlia Mergulhão Estronioli, "Caminhos indígenas que originaram ruas de São Paulo," May 6, 2019, Plataforma Pauliceia 2.0: Mapeamento Colaborativo da História de São Paulo (1870–1940), accessed November 20, 2024, http://www.pauliceia.dpi.inpe.br. Georeferenced map from 1868 by Carlos Frederico Rath, "Planta da Cidade de São Paulo," Arquivo Histórico Municipal, accessed November 20, 2024, http://www.arquiamigos.org.br/info/info20/img/1868-download.jpg. Other map data sources: GeoSampa; OpenStreetMap (Light Gray Canvas) © OpenStreetMap contributors, Microsoft, Facebook, Google, Esri Community Maps contributors, map layer by Esri. Map by Andrew G. Britt.

lizing trajectory was a materialized temporality that held fluid, mixed, and "cultural" sludge as the stuff of history, located "behind us." The material manifestation of the future, by contrast, was the stability and fixity of asphalt, by which modern avenues were paved.

In Prado's rhetoric, substances like marshy sludge or asphalt did not passively reflect more significant factors on the actual front line of civilization-making. Instead, these tactile materials served as the agents of a project to achieve a desired future. That project implied the remaking of people and spaces together, and the rate of asphalt and concrete ran in direct proportion to the supposed successes of the effort. Prado's cherished view of roads was not exceptional. Washington Luis, a former mayor of the city and later president of Brazil, declared in 1928 at the inauguration of the first asphalted roadway in the country that "to govern is to open roads."[18] The end of Luis's term in 1930 ignited the disputed presidential election that concluded with Getúlio Vargas's coup. Asphalted roadways would remain, however, foundational to political and city planning projects in and beyond São Paulo.

In his speech, Prado represented the Anhangabaú Valley as unoccupied. Despite omitting them from his speech about "what is seen is what we see," he likely had individuals, families, and their homes in eyeshot when looking southwest down the Anhangabaú Valley in 1935. He characterized the local environment, nonetheless, as a vacant frontier, prime for development:

> The Anhangabahú Valley symbolizes well the final frontier of São Paulo. On that side is the civilization of the park, which converges here, at the opening of a new route. On this side everything is still in disorder. The recently excavated land seems like a trench. The severed hills are somewhat reminiscent of the crags and the torments (*sangras*) of [author Euclides da] Cunha or the Paraíba Valley.[19]

This representation of the local landscape had an ethnoracialized valence, articulated through the references to Cunha and the Paraíba Valley. In his 1902 work *Os sertões* (The backlands), journalist Euclides da Cunha presented Brazil's Northeast in the context of a regional uprising and federal attempts to quell it as a backward, uncivilized place peopled by an inferior, mixed-race population.[20] The Paraíba Valley, extending from the state of São Paulo to Rio de Janeiro, likely signified plantation agriculture and African descendent, enslaved labor: in other words, features of the nation's past, not São Paulo's future.[21] Invoking these spatial histories, Prado depicted the area to be paved as July 9 Avenue as a space of disorder, inferiority, and the colonial past that lacked the materiality or population purportedly necessary for modern civilization.

In Prado's field of vision, but absent by name in his rhetoric, sat Saracura. Few records survive about this place, which persists today predominately in memories of some long-term residents, especially residents of African descent, in the Bela Vista district. Early twentieth-century maps and chronicles of the city of São Paulo help to reconstruct the spatial and social composition of Saracura. Similar to regions elsewhere in São Paulo, numerous creeks and small rivers cut through this area. The two most prominent waterways were the Small Saracura Creek (Saracurinha) and Big Saracura Creek (Saracura Grande). They began southwest of Bela Vista along the ridge of Paulista Avenue and ran northeast through the district toward the historic center of the city. The creeks and topography made Saracura an aqueous environment, a fact implied by the name itself: Saracura is a bird common to swampy regions surrounding waterways, especially in Brazil's Atlantic Forest biome.

Settled originally as a *quilombo* in the nineteenth century, if not before, Saracura appeared briefly in São Paulo's official cartography as a neighborhood in the early twentieth century. A 1907 map of the city (map 2.2) shows the trajectory of the two Saracura creeks with almost no urban settlement (defined on these maps by roadways) between them. A planned but incomplete Saracura Street is the only discernible road on the map. The mapmaker depicted the area as mostly empty space. A subsequent map from 1913 displayed a modicum of development, with Saracura Path (Caminho Saracura, perhaps an informal roadway), Rocha Street, and the label Saracura positioned between the two creeks (map 2.3). This labeling identified Saracura as a neighborhood within the district of Bela Vista. The typographic hierarchy of the map positioned Saracura as on par with the nearby neighborhoods like Vila Buarque or Tabatinguera.[22]

Saracura appeared as a neighborhood only this once on an official city map. Following 1913, Bela Vista and/or Bexiga would replace it. From 1916 through the 1920s, in fact, mapmakers positioned the label Bela Vista exactly on top of the space where Saracura had previously appeared in 1913. Mapped and unmapped in the short span of a decade, the cartographic silencing reflected and anticipated a longer effort to raze this space.

In the early twentieth century Saracura was prominently associated with African descendants. We can discern this spatial identity through an unsigned 1907 article, "Around the World in São Paulo:

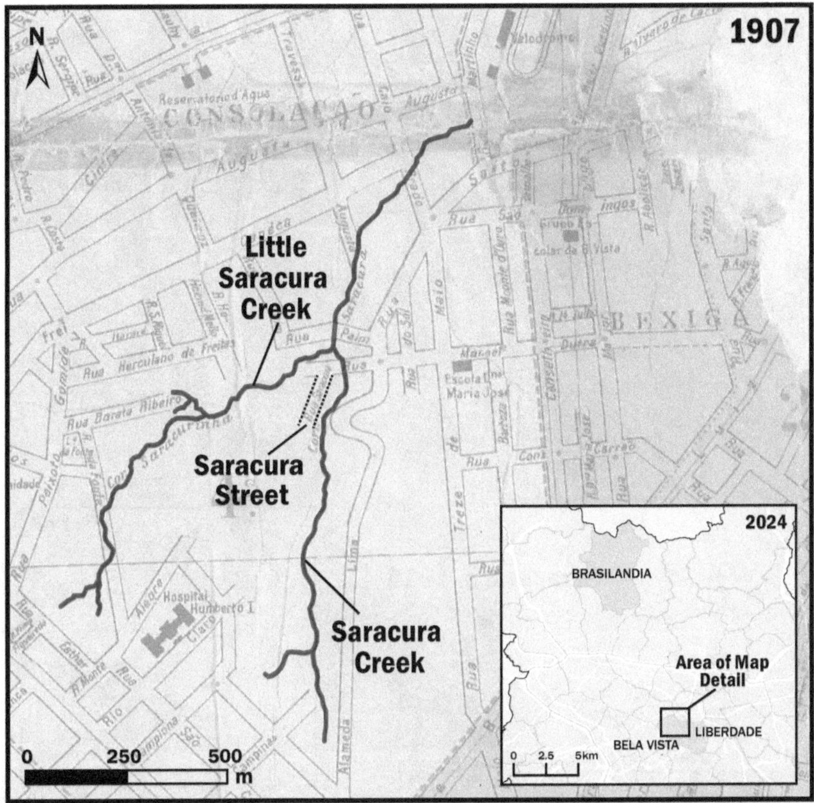

MAP 2.2 · Saracura Creeks and Saracura Street, 1907. Georeferenced basemap is Graccho da Gama, "Planta da cidade de São Paulo," 1907, Arquivo Público do Estado de São Paulo, accessed June 12, 2018, http://www.arquivoestado.sp.gov.br/site/acervo/repositorio_digital/mapa_carto/BR_APESP_IGC_IGG_CAR_I_S_0187_001_001. Other map data sources: GeoSampa; OpenStreetMap (Light Gray Canvas) © OpenStreetMap contributors, Microsoft, Facebook, Google, Esri Community Maps contributors, map layer by Esri. Map by Andrew G. Britt.

Saracura," published in the major São Paulo newspaper *Correio Paulistano*.[23] The brief piece ran under the catchall section "Diverse Facts" and opened with the following: "It is a piece of Africa" full of the "relics of the poor race, impelled by cosmopolitan civilization that invaded the city." Distinct from the maps that depicted a more limited view of Saracura, the prose described the place in three vivid dimensions. The author portrayed a "line of huts on the bank of a stream" with furniture made up of "old boxes and logs of wood" in a valley both "deep and narrow." The article continued in a more sarcastic tone: "Water

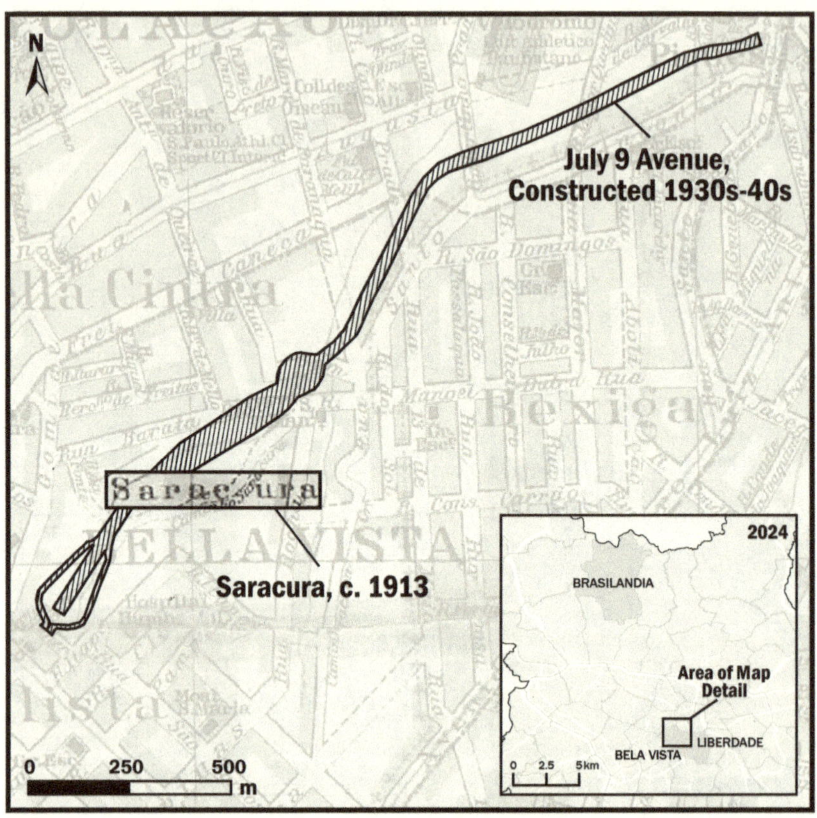

MAP 2.3 · Saracura neighborhood, 1913. Georeferenced basemap is Eng. Civil Alexandre M. Cococi e Fructuoso F.Costa, "Planta da cidade de São Paulo," 1913, Arquivo Público do Estado de São Paulo, accessed June 12, 2018, http://www.arquivoestado.sp.gov.br/site/acervo/repositorio_digital/mapa_carto/BR_APESP_IGC_IGG_CAR_I_S_0296_001_001. Other map data sources: GeoSampa; OpenStreetMap (Light Gray Canvas) © OpenStreetMap contributors, Microsoft, Facebook, Google, Esri Community Maps contributors, map layer by Esri. Map by Andrew G. Britt.

wells turned green mark the places where clay has been transformed into palaces and luxurious residences." The "poor" and "sordid" state of living conditions of Saracura contrasted with the "cosmopolitan civilization" promised by migration of the formerly enslaved into the city after the abolition of slavery in 1888. Homes made of clay, a material symbolizing the time before modern Paulista civilization, made that contrast tactile.

The unidentified author blurred the boundaries between human bodies, animals, and plants in their depiction of Saracura. The piece described "loose goats on the road, seminude Black children making birdcages, geldings with long beards at the feet of the old whitened kinky-haired and thick-lipped from whose mouth hangs a pipe, this gives that dark corner an air of the Congo." The original Portuguese text, like my translation, omits the noun for the only adult human figure in this key passage. Instead, they are reduced to physiognomic features (hair and lips) that mark them as African descendent. The author presents the natural space and its inhabitants as evidence of Saracura's exoticism. More than distinct geographic origins, that foreignness, in this author's representation, amounted to an incompatibility in the present space and time of São Paulo. The author telegraphs this point in the conclusion:

> And there they go slowly dying—sacrificed by the liberty that they did not know how to relish, gathered together by alcohol and agonized by the anguish of the Bright's disease (*Brightismo*) that decimates them, eliminated by the anthropological elaboration of the new Paulista race—those that came on the slave ships, that planted coffee, that fattened the land with sweat and tears, accumulated there, as the leftover scraps of the city, in the dark horrific base of a valley.[24]

While noting the insalubrious and precarious conditions in Saracura, this conclusion places blame for those conditions on the purportedly unfit constitution of the residents themselves. As "the leftover scraps of the city," the author identifies those residents as byproducts of modern urban development: bodies defined by—and conflated as—undesirable space. The "traveler's log" distorts the human and natural landscapes of Saracura as a racialized "piece of Africa" with an "air of the Congo" that, because of its Africanness, stood apart from the materiality, space, and time of a racialized São Paulo modernity.

Fugitives had created settlements in Saracura in the nineteenth century, if not before. Historian Maria Odila Silva Dias writes that in 1831 the São Paulo city council issued a decree that ordered the "closing of a passage between Anhangabaú creek and Bexiga, 'on whose banks thieves and escaped slaves had sheltered.'"[25] Dias asserts that those fleeing captivity long sought refuge on this then periphery of the city, a practice that mirrored similar patterns in cities throughout Brazil: "Since the beginning of slavery, [fugitive slaves] had gone into hiding on the outskirts of the city, in the valleys of Anhangabaú, Bexiga and

Pinheiros."[26] Historian Célia Toledo Lucena offers further evidence of fugitive settlements in the region, writing that the "capoeiras and grasslands surrounding the Tanque Reúno [a key reservoir], in Bexiga, like in other places where the Anhangabaú and Saracura Creek ran, served as places of hiding where rebelling Blacks made *quilombos*. These forests were inviting for hiding places."[27] Saracura existed in relative proximity to nodes of slavery, including local plantations in the contemporary Bela Vista district.[28] In his multivolume study of São Paulo's history and "traditions," historian Ernani Silva Bruno wrote that "in the Bexiga fields themselves, encompassing all of the lands located between Consolação Street and Santo Amaro Street, still in 1870, deer, quail, and fugitive slaves were hunted. Large farms (*chácaras*) circled, on this side, the city." Bruno included an engraving of a *capitão-de-mato*, a fugitive slave hunter, in the Anhangabaú Valley in his book.[29]

As with fugitive communities in the parish of Nossa Senhora do Ó (see chapter 1), few sources survive with the names and stories of those who produced and populated this region. Nonetheless, the official documentation referencing sites of refuge and fugitives indicate that African descendants originally produced the settlement of Saracura as a space of escape. The proximity of Saracura to the urbanized center of the city would draw the attention of urbanists and officials much earlier in the twentieth century than the "Congo" places in the northern reaches of Nossa Senhora do Ó.

Though rare, photographs of Saracura offer an additional perspective on the sociospatial composition of the place in the early twentieth century. An image of Saracura from the Historical Museum of Public Health at the University of São Paulo is not dated (figure 2.2); however, the absence of the July 9 Avenue would place the photo in the 1920s or early 1930s at the latest. While few individuals are discernible in the images, various features of the photo hint at everyday life in Saracura. Clotheslines and laundry weave through the landscape, an indication of the type of work that likely employed local residents. The structures in the images also bear a similarity to the *cortiços* like Navio Parado, discussed in chapter 1. Indeed, some of the residents dislocated from Saracura by the construction of the July 9 Avenue in the 1930s and 1940s may have migrated a short few blocks northeast to live in Navio Parado or other *cortiços* in the Vila Barros complex.

The photos show that housing in Saracura consisted predominately of small, one- or two-story shelters that resembled the structures de-

FIGURE 2.2 · *Cortiço* in Saracura Grande. Undated Image by Geraldo Horacio de Paula Souza. Centro de Memória da Faculdade de Saúde Pública, Universidade de São Paulo.

scribed in the 1907 *Correio Paulistano* article. Anthropologist Claude Lévi-Strauss lived in São Paulo in the mid-1930s and, in his work *Sad Tropics*, published observations about housing in, and the social composition of, a region that resembled Saracura:

> Cow pastures lay at the foot of concrete blocks, a whole area could suddenly spring into being like a mirage, and avenues bordered by palatial houses would stop suddenly on either side of ravines where, between the banana trees, flowed muddy torrents, which served both as sources of water and as sewers for the mud-walled, bamboo-frame shanties housing a black population similar to the one which, in Rio, camped up the hillsides. Goats ran along the slopes. Some exceptional areas of the town managed to combine every feature.[30]

Lévi-Strauss does not specify Saracura in his comments, though his reference to "palatial houses" on avenues (quite possible along Paulista Avenue) juxtaposed with hillside communities in ravines leads me to think he was looking at a landscape similar to figure 2.4 when composing these lines. Writing around the time when planners were beginning the construction on July 9 Avenue, Lévi-Strauss contrasted wealthy residences in areas like Paulista Avenue with the supposedly unurbanized, precarious, and racialized regions like Saracura. As in the 1913 *planta*, Saracura was largely off the map into the 1930s.

Demographic analysis of the ethnoracial composition of Saracura sheds further light on the specific meanings of this neighborhood as a "piece of Africa" in the first decades of the twentieth century. Historian Kim Butler located statistics about births of Afro-Brazilians by São Paulo district in 1925 and 1929. In 1925, she found that 41.4 percent of the children of Afro-Brazilians in the city were born in Bela Vista. The figure increased to 51.6 percent in 1929. The adjacent Liberdade district ranked second in 1925 at 9.2 percent and third in 1929 at 7 percent.[31] In his 1938 study "The Black Element in São Paulo's Population," sociologist Samuel Lowrie analyzed the racial distribution of residents in the city through school enrollment statistics. He published a map with his findings in the journal of the city's Department of Culture, the *Revista do Arquivo Municipal.* Map 2.4 displays Lowrie's map georeferenced onto the city of São Paulo. Comparing Lowrie's map with the position of Saracura on the map from 1913 (map 2.3), we see that between 25 percent and 29.99 percent of schoolchildren in the Saracura region of Bela Vista were either Black or mixed-race (*mulato*).[32] That statistic gave Saracura the highest concentration of African descendants in the city at this time.

Despite a high concentration of African descendants, Saracura and Bela Vista broadly were not ethnoracially homogeneous places. Historian Sheila Schneck offers statistical evidence that supports this point. In her analysis of police records (*boletins de ocorrência*) from 1911–1912, 1914–1915, and 1925, Africans and African descendants appeared in 27.5 percent of the records from Saracura. Portuguese and their descendants accounted for 40 percent. White Brazilians (not ethnically identified as immigrant) counted for 18 percent, while Italians and their descendants made up 14 percent. For the district of Bela Vista broadly, African descendants comprised 17 percent of police records.[33] Such records, of course, do not provide a complete snapshot of the makeup of the neighborhood population. However, the spatial information attached to those records—down to the street level—affords an especially local glimpse of the demographic composition of the region. That view indicates that while African descendants comprised a prominent presence in Saracura specifically and throughout Bela Vista more broadly,

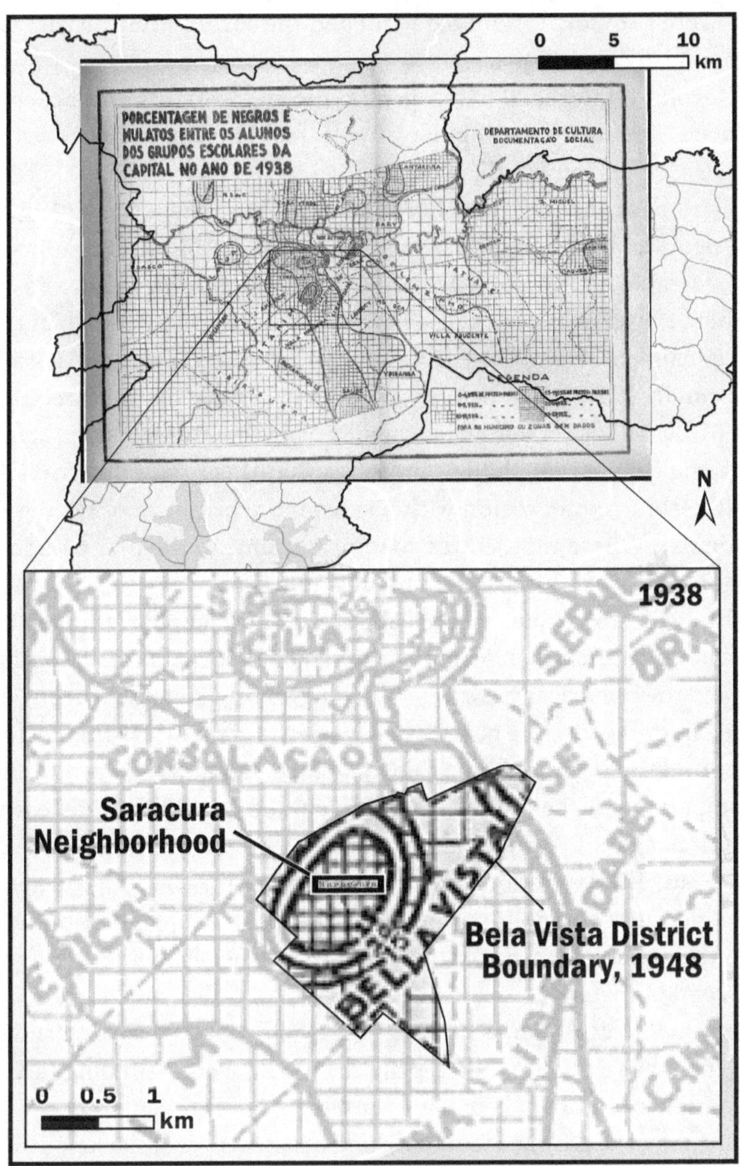

MAP 2.4 · Map showing concentration of non-White population in Saracura in the Bela Vista District, 1938. Georeferenced basemap is Samuel Lowrie, "O elemento Negro na população de São Pauo," *Revista do Arquivo Municipal* 48 (1938), 57. Other map data sources: GeoSampa; OpenStreetMap (Light Gray Canvas) © OpenStreetMap contributors, Microsoft, Facebook, Google, Esri Community Maps contributors, map layer by Esri. Map by Andrew G. Britt.

they were a minority. Both Saracura and the surrounding district were ethnoracially diverse places.

Despite ethnoracial heterogeneity, some residents and observers reduced Saracura to a singular ethnoracial identity as an African or Black space. Italian Brazilian and Bexiga resident Armando Puglisi, for instance, described the neighborhood as follows: There was a place that "the people called Saracura, where many Blacks and Portuguese were concentrated. . . . In Saracura, there were no *mulattoes* (mixed-race people), it was all Blacks, those Blacks who were very dark, all of them descendants of slaves."[34] Nearly a century after the "piece of Africa" article ran in *Correio Paulistano*, Puglisi's emphasis on the foreignness and Blackness of Saracura residents mirrors the earlier 1907 article. At the same time, his statement indicates that this "piece of Africa" had a multiethnic composition with a substantial presence of Portuguese residents.[35] These multiethnic memories point to the first paradox of ethnoracial spaces discussed in the introduction.

The scattered extant records about Saracura help us to understand what political and urban planning elites like Prado and Pretes Maia literally and metaphorically saw when looking south down the Anhangabaú Valley in the 1930s. The contrast between the actually existing material space and the future scheme they imagined can be visualized through a comparison of the photos from Saracura and the elaborate, cosmopolitan design of Avenue July 9 published in Pretes Maia's 1930 Avenues Plan. The aspirational before and after brings into high relief the grand designs of demolition and redevelopment that planners projected onto the region. Silenced for two decades in official city maps, Saracura persisted in material space. Settled as a site of refuge and escape in the nineteenth century, Saracura remained a home for African descendants into the 1920s and 1930s when plans for a new avenue running through the middle of Saracura began to "leave paper."

Through the paving of Saracura and construction of the new avenue, planners aimed to transform the racialized character of this area of Bela Vista. Prestes Maia consistently expressed preoccupations about Bela Vista, which sat between the two southern legs of the "Y system" of avenues central to the Avenues Plan. In his 1930 study he wrote:

> A city's rivers, valleys, railways, etc. create dead-end alleys and *undesirable neighborhoods*, segregated from the normal urban movement: Piques, lower Bexiga, places around the Assembly, hillsides

of Carmo, etc. that differ from the rest of the city. These sectors the ring road will tear open, sanitize, make accessible, and transform into points of passage and commerce. They are, therefore, areas won by the center.[36]

The equation held that the making of avenues—specifically the ring road, in this case—amounted to the sanitation and integration of "segregated," "undesirable neighborhoods." Prestes Maia defined these neighborhoods as socially and geographically marginal spaces, whose "winning" by the "center" sounded decidedly like a military campaign. While during his first mayoral term Prestes Maia would have an institutional position to transform Bela Vista and dislocate Saracura, he was not the only prominent urbanist with such designs. In his introduction to the Avenues Plan, Arthur Saboya had singled out July 9 Avenue with similar rhetoric. With the construction of the avenue, he wrote, "not just the sanitation of the valley and the surrounding zones is assured; also gone is the threat of transforming into new 'favelas' the marginal hillsides of the valley itself."[37]

Much like official city maps after 1913, the mainstream press sometimes depicted Saracura as empty space. A 1939 article about Prestes Maia's ongoing avenues projects explained, for instance, that July 9 Avenue "establishes new connections and valorizes a large nook (*rincão*) that was *abandoned*, although very central inside the city perimeter."[38] The "abandoned" characterization was not accurate, as sources such as Lowrie's study (published the year prior) revealed. Furthermore, records from the city's Department of Expropriations, the municipal sector responsible for demolitions in advance of the construction of avenues, indicates residents lived in the region of Saracura into the late 1930s.[39] Through cartography, mayoral rhetoric, and in the popular press, the representation of Saracura as empty space served to legitimize its material silencing via demolition and the desired displacement of its resident population.

Planners designed a revealing replacement for Saracura. They projected July 9 Avenue to cross the region between the creeks Small Saracura and Big Saracura. At the junction of those creeks, city officials planned and executed a new plaza, named Plaza 14 BIS, in homage to the famous airplane of Brazilian inventor and aviator Alberto Santos Dumont.[40] Redesigned as a public space with a name that indexed Brazilian modernity, the place had previously been a gathering point for

African descendent residents in the region. One of those local residents, Maria Aparecida de Godoy, recalled that "the Blacks would hang around here, where today sits Plaza 14-BIS. The people concentrated here down below, of course everyone would concentrate where there was water and the Saracura Creek passed by below, so the laundresses would wash clothes here for the mansions on Paulista [Avenue]."[41] Godoy's recollection references the first three decades of the twentieth century, before the construction of the new plaza. Her comments reinforce the racialized nature of the local geography and present a gendered perspective, as women gathered at the site with ready access to water to wash clothes for wealthy families on the nearby Paulista Avenue. Historian Maria Odila Silva Dias has shown the connections between women, public fountains, and waterways to be a central feature of São Paulo's geography since the eighteenth century.[42] Historian Richard Morse also drew this connection in his depiction of São Paulo's early nineteenth-century landscape, writing that in the Anhangabaú Valley a traveler "would have seen women slaves crouched over their washing and, coming closer, heard their throaty songs and laughter."[43]

Prestes Maia remained fixated on redevelopment and so-called improvements in Bela Vista from the Avenues Plan through the 1960s. In his 1945 publication *São Paulo Improvements*, he wrote that July 9 Avenue would integrate and valorize "the very depreciated" neighborhood of Bexiga into the city.[44] In the same book he touted the construction of the Jacareí Bridge and associated demolitions as a project "that transformed the appearance of Lower Bexiga."[45] During Prestes Maia's second administration, in 1961, deputy Israel Dias Novaes delivered a defense of the mayor in the state assembly. The speech included the following statement: "The canalization of the Saracura Creek, at the intersection of São Vicente Road, has been contracted, anticipating the urbanization of this central stretch and doing away with the favela there abusively formed."[46] Novaes here offers a candid comment that the "improvement" of the creek's canalization would serve to dislocate an undesirable population. The Saracura favela sat near the former limits of the Saracura neighborhood near the contemporary Praça 14 BIS. The frequency and consistency of these statements reveal both Prestes Maia's continued concern with remaking spaces linked to Saracura within the Bela Vista district and the persistence of residents who contested and frustrated official aspirations.

Saracura was not the only site prominently associated with African descendants in the early twentieth century, of course. Nonetheless, its geographic position—situated between São Paulo's historic business center and emerging elite residential centers in the 1930s—seems to have made it a particularly visible stretch of territory. Nearby elite spaces contrasted sharply the poverty and precarity of life in Saracura, which the observer from the 1907 *Correio Paulistano* piece cast as symbolizing the unfulfilled promises of slavery's abolition. Urbanist-mayors Prado and Prestes Maia designed a project that aimed to transform Saracura from a historic neighborhood associated with Blackness and populated with the city's largest concentration of African descendants into an asphalted roadway, the symbol of modern progress in early twentieth-century São Paulo.

Despite the silencing of Saracura on official maps and the completion of July 9 Avenue, the project to remake the neighborhood by dislocating African descendant populations and associated pasts was incomplete. Some African descendants continued to reside in Bela Vista, and memories of Saracura would, among some, endure. A prominent means for the preservation and reproduction of that spatial identity across generations was samba, especially through Vai-Vai, the *cordão* founded in Bela Vista in 1930. Fernando Penteado, child of one of Vai-Vai's founders and long-time president of the now-samba school, described his origins in the region:

> I was born in Saracura. It was a swamp there. There is a river that passes underneath. . . . All of the water from Paulista Avenue collected there [in the region of Vai-Vai], there it was a swamp and no one wanted to live there. So, the Italians lived on Rocha Street [higher up] and we lived down below. . . . The Blacks lived here all below. And when people talked about Saracura it was pejorative, but we assimilated the nickname. So that now in samba we say: 'It's Vai-Vai from Bexiga, the Pride of Saracura.'[47]

Penteado's comments (published in 2014) highlight the salience of three-dimensional social and racial geographies. Similar to the interpretation of housing in Bexiga discussed in chapter 1, here Penteado maps a topography of neighborhoods within the Bela Vista district that aligned with racialized social stratification. Penteado also describes how residents contested and resignified the negative connotations of Saracura clearly visible in sources such as the 1907 article.[48] While Saracura would be demolished in the 1930s, Vai-Vai would remain in this region through the early twenty-first century, though the school would face infrastructure-related expropriation in the 1960s and have to rebuild once again. Unmapped in São Paulo's official cartography and asphalted for the crown jewel of the Avenues Plan, the story of Saracura highlights how anti-Black violence through dispossession, demolitions, and displacement shaped a key moment of spatial transformation in the 1930s.[49] At the same time, the preservation of this place-name in popular memory and the practice of repossessing and rebuilding after expropriation reflect two core aspects of the spatial praxis of belonging-as-being.

FROM "BEXIGA SQUARE" TO "FLAG PLAZA"; OR, THE FORGOTTEN (IN) GABRIEL MARQUES

An oversized Brazilian flag towers above the plaza where July 9 Avenue and May 23 Avenue converge in the northern limits of the contemporary Bela Vista district (figure 2.3). I have spent afternoons lost in the labyrinthine bus complex that sits in the middle of this plaza, now named the Praça da Bandeira (Flag Plaza), and along the web of pedestrian passages that span across the adjoining avenues. I have spent substantially more time seeking to make sense of 170 years of maps of this space, which reveal extensive geographic and linguistic changes. The Praça da Bandeira was once named the Largo da Memória (Memory Square), the Largo do Riachuelo (Riacheulo Square), the Largo do Piques (Piques Square), and the Largo do Bexiga (Bexiga Square). This century and a half of changes obscure the earlier history of this place. Prior to its consecration as a hallowed plaza uniting two of São Paulo's most significant roadways and, symbolically, the nation itself, parts of this plaza served as a site for the sale and purchase of enslaved people. This past was not passively overlooked but actively unremembered, decades after formal abolition in 1888 and during the 1930s and 1940s, through the spatial project of forgetting.

We have a limited understanding of the geography of the traffic in enslaved persons in the city of São Paulo.[50] We know relatively little, for example, about the locations of sale, the nature of those sites, and, to some extent, the routes that connected markets within São Paulo to the rest of the province of São Paulo. One would expect to find this information in landmark studies of slavery and economy in the city, such as historian Maria Odila Silva Dias's illuminating *Power and Everyday Life: The Lives of Working Women in Nineteenth-Century Brazil.* Dias

FIGURE 2.3 · Praça da Bandeira, looking north along July 9 Avenue, April 2017. Photo by Andrew G. Britt.

charts spaces of sociability and the commercial activities *of* enslaved people, asserting that in the city "slavery was felt as an overwhelming presence"; however, the study offers less information about the geographic dimensions of the commerce *in* captives within the city.[51] Historian Maria Helena P. T. Machado writes that while "the province [of São Paulo] had become, across the nineteenth century and, especially, after 1850, the country's most important purchasing market for slaves, São Paulo had no slave market like the Valongo of Rio de Janeiro, and information about transactions of buying and selling captives in São Paulo's sugar and coffee regions are scarce."[52] Given the importance of São Paulo's sugar and coffee plantations in the expansion of nineteenth-century slavery—what some historians have described as "second slavery"—this is a substantial gap in the historiography.[53]

The transatlantic traffic in enslaved people generated a paper trail that has enabled subsequent generations of historians to reconstruct aspects of the social history of the Middle Passage.[54] The inter-American trade, particularly following the prohibition of the slave trade and, gradually, of slavery throughout the nineteenth century, proves more difficult to chart with such precision.[55] As detailed in chapter 1, the growth of the city of São Paulo was intimately connected to the nineteenth-century expansion of agriculture (especially coffee) in the province, especially in the West Paulista region. The city of São Paulo became a way station for the transport of goods along with enslaved African descendants between the ports of Rio de Janeiro and Santos and the interior of the province. Ian Read has calculated that many of the enslaved people who entered in the port of Rio de Janeiro in the 1870s (he estimates between 5,680 and 6,034 per year) traveled overland into the interior of the province São Paulo, thereby passing through the city of São Paulo.[56] Writing about the internal trade in Rio de Janeiro, Richard Graham explains that planters interested in buying captives "relied on upland middlemen who had contact with fellow merchants in Rio or on mule drivers who delivered coffee in Rio and brought back slaves on consignment for eventual sale."[57]

The sale and purchase of enslaved people do not appear to have taken place at an officially sanctioned site in the city of São Paulo. As Machado notes, the city of São Paulo did not seem to have had a centralized slave market comparable to Rio's Valongo Wharf. At the same time, popular and academic narratives about the traffic and commerce of the enslaved in the city do not depict this activity as randomly dispersed in space. Machado explains how the geography of the local and regionally connected trade was shaped by ready access to drinkable water:

> Important points of encounter in the city, as much for slaves within the city as for the captives that only passed through its streets and alleys, accompanying or even driving troops, were the huts (*ranchos*). . . . The most sought-after hut for those who traveled from Santos were Lavapés and Bexiga, with the latter, located next to the Piques Fountain, at the Memory Square [today Praça da Bandeira], having the best and most abundant waters and therefore becoming the most frequented.[58]

Aroldo de Azevedo describes another factor linking the contemporary Praça da Bandeira with the traffic in the enslaved: "The then Largo do Piques . . . ever since the Bexiga guesthouse (Hospedaria do Bexiga) was put in, became a meeting place for merchants and troops; it was an important 'commercial center of farms, footwear, and leather,' always quite busy."[59] These records suggest that, owing to ready access to good water and a place for lodging, the Largo do Piques (figure 2.4) functioned as an important center of commerce in São Paulo, including in the trafficking of enslaved people.[60]

After a year of fieldwork in São Paulo's archives, I had no suspicion of a connection between the Praça da Bandeira and São Paulo's commerce

FIGURE 2.4 · Paredão do Piques, Militão Augusto de Azevedo, circa 1862. Acervo Instituto Moreira Salles.

in captives. Throughout that year I regularly passed by and sometimes paused at the sole surviving remnant of this space. That place today consists of a waterless public fountain, granite obelisk, and elaborate tilework, all decorated (in 2015–2016, at least) with São Paulo's particular type of graffiti, *pixação*. Searching for this space on a 1954 map of the city (map 2.5), I found its former name—Memory Square (Largo da Memória)—and realized that in the 1950s the site formed part of a larger area that sat at the fulcrum of July 9 Avenue and May 23 Avenue. The 1954 map displayed a much smaller Flag Plaza adjacent to the larger Memory Square. The latter had been nearly completely remade, I subsequently discerned, into Flag Plaza in the course of constructing July 9 Avenue and May 23 Avenue.

For Prestes Maia and other planners working on implementing the Avenues Plan, the juncture of these two avenues held both functional and symbolic significance. The public square sat at the fulcrum of the "inverted Y" system of avenues at the heart of the 1930 Avenues Plan: The two southern legs of the Y were July 9 Avenue and May 23 Avenue; the northern branch, originally named Tiradentes Avenue, now bears the name of the mayor-urbanist himself—Prestes Maia Avenue. The remaking of São Paulo's new and improved transportation network

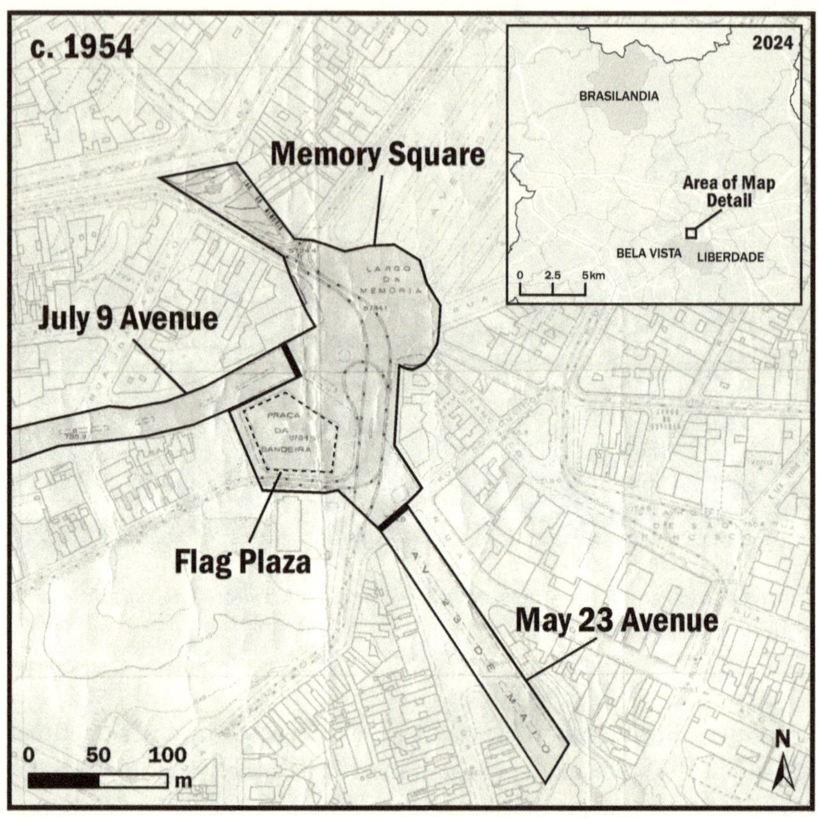

MAP 2.5 · Memory Square and Flag Plaza, circa 1954. Georeferened basemap is "Mapeamento 1954—Vasp Cruzeiro," GeoSampa, accessed June 12, 2018, https://www.geosampa.prefeitura.sp.gov.br. Other map data sources: OpenStreetMap (Light Gray Canvas) © OpenStreetMap contributors, Microsoft, Facebook, Google, Esri Community Maps contributors, map layer by Esri. Map by Andrew G. Britt.

hinged on the successful redevelopment of this central site. Urbanist and historian Raquel Rolnik writes that the region, which she identifies as Piques, had become a "red light district, a zone of black prostitution."[61] Consigning the region to redevelopment, planners projected new roadways and a plaza that would dislocate this population. They justified the project by pointing to environmental challenges and perceived criminal danger. In his 1945 book *São Paulo Improvements*, for instance, Prestes Maia characterized the region as troubled because of storm water drainage problems.[62] Historian Benedito Lima de Toledo wrote subsequently that "it was very dangerous to pass through that region of the valley at night."[63] As with the avenues that it joined, the plaza project encountered delays throughout the 1930s and past Prestes Maia's first terms as mayor. In 1945, Prestes Maia wrote optimistically about a 1942 new decree that would permit (he foresaw) a "more radical" transformation of the place.[64]

While city planners pursued the plaza's material redevelopment in Prestes Maia's first terms as mayor, its name captured the attention of members of São Paulo's city council. In 1949, council member Décio Grisi introduced a measure to rename the place—variously referred to as Largo da Memória or Largo do Piques at this time—as the Praça da Bandeira. He asserted that, in fact, the site was already known popularly as Flag Plaza and that the name merited officialization. His formal petition, signed by fellow city council member and future Brazilian president Jânio Quadros, proclaimed: "If the people make the language—and few, perhaps none, of the moldy grammarians and pedantic purists can stop this—it is also the people that have decisively contributed, in many, many cases to the naming of roads."[65] A newspaper article from the year prior lamenting the "legitimate pandemonium" of pedestrian and automobile traffic at the site referred to the place as the Praça da Bandeira, seemingly confirming Grisi's assertion about popular usage.[66] In a session the following year, the city council approved the name change, thereby making Praça da Bandeira official.[67]

Ironically, no flag seems to have hung in the Praça da Bandeira in the 1940s and 1950s (figure 2.5).[68] Where did the name come from, then? Writer Gabriel Marques, a little-remembered author of African descent in São Paulo, posed this question in a series of articles about São Paulo's history that first ran in the widely circulated newspaper *Folha da Noite* in the mid-to-late 1950s. Marques later compiled and expanded these pieces in his book *Streets and Traditions in São Paulo: A History of Each Street*, published in 1966. In one of its sections, he proposed competing interpretations for the origins of the "flag" moniker at the central plaza.

Perhaps the plaza was named for the flag of the Brazilian Empire, Marques opined. He elaborated on this possibility by reprinting part of the 1869 poem "O navio negreiro" (The slave ship). Abolitionist Castro Alves, known popularly as "the poet of the slaves," wrote the verse:

> Green and gold cloth of my land
> That the Brazilian breeze kisses and sways,
> Banner bathed in sunlight
> The divine promises of Hope![69]

FIGURE 2.5 · Flag Plaza (undated), with no flag visible. Werner Haberkorn, *Vista parcial da Praça da Bandeira. São Paulo/SP*. Museu Paulista (USP) Collection, Wikimedia, accessed June 12, 2018, https://upload.wikimedia.org/wikipedia/commons/a/ac/Werner_Haberkorn_-_Vista_parcial_da_Pra%C3%A7a_da_Bandeira._S%C3%A3o_Paulo-SP.jpg.

Alternatively, Marques wrote, perhaps the plaza referenced the flag of the state of São Paulo, which he depicted through the celebratory verses of São Paulo writer Guilherme de Almeida:

> Flag of my land,
> flag of the thirteen stripes:
> they are thirteen spears of war
> surrounding the soil of the paulistas!

The paired verses present two distinct referents of Brazil's history: the optimism and promise of abolition in the late nineteenth century, and the regionalist identity of São Paulo, which had engulfed the country in war in 1932. Marques concludes that the São Paulo flag must be the true referent, since the square once served as a point of encounter for *bandeirantes* headed on expeditions to the continental interior. Yet this conclusion, delivered quickly and without elaboration, reads as half-hearted. Marques's real interest, it seems, transcended determining the origins of the flag to an inquiry about how—and by what means—the naming of the site obfuscated certain pasts in the then present. Describing the past as "tradition," he writes: "Thus, Progress made it so that the square would get bigger, beautifying it and modernizing it. And it went further, that witch called Progress: It obligated the public officials to change its name, devalorizing tradition. From Largo do Piques it thus became designated Praça—Praça da Bandeira."[70]

As symbols of political and territorial identity, flags can elicit revealing discourses about race, region, and nation. In his comparative study of Brazil, the United States, and South Africa, Anthony W. Marx writes that in all three countries the "issue of how to construct a racial order was central to the historical process of nation-state consolidation, as symbolized by the respective flags."[71] Both of the verses that Marques cites above dissect the formal composition of flags. Their design also caught the interest of Afonso de E. Taunay, the director of the Museum of the State of São Paulo, professor at the University of São Paulo, and prolific author of histories of the city and state, such as *História da cidade de São Paulo*.[72] In 1931, Taunay wrote an article for the mainstream press about Brazilian ceremonial forms, which included the following appraisal of São Paulo's flag:

> A dreadfully ugly symbol, originating in the era of Republican propaganda, they say that Julio Ribeiro invented the flag, the improperly designated "Paulista flag," bleak, unaesthetic, insignificant. Thank God it was never made official, but to our misfortune it is widely adopted. . . . [It is] insignificant today more than ever, because it attributes to the Paulista population a dosage of African blood entirely false since in the lands of São Paulo the percentage of Euro-Americans always was immensely superior to the dosage of Afro, Euro-African, or Afro-American elements.[73]

Taunay's analysis echoes Marx's argument above. Taunay saw in the black stripes of the São Paulo state flag an inaccurate representation of São Paulo's racial composition. His statement reflected his elite, perhaps singular position as one of São Paulo's most prominent historians, however this sentiment was not marginal among influential members of the São Paulo elite in the lead-up to abolition and through the early decades of the twentieth century. The ethos of whitening (*branqueamento*) prescribed the disappearance of African descendants and Blackness through intertwined programs of immigration, republicanism, and industrialization.[74] With the authority to establish official versions of São Paulo's history, Taunay projected a whitened narrative of progress and modernity onto São Paulo's past with this interpretation of the state's most prominent symbol. Marques, who cited Taunay's histories in his work, ends with an alternative conclusion about Flag Plaza: The name change constituted part of the project of "that witch called Progress" in São Paulo. At this point in his writings, Marques's conclusion does not offer an explicit analysis of the racialized significance of the name change or the plaza.

A biographical portrait of Marques's life is neither readily available nor easily reconstructed. We do know, however, that from the 1920s through the publication of *Streets and Traditions* in the 1960s, he authored works of imaginative nonfiction and historically informed fiction that blurred the lines between those genres. His career spanned the breadth of the transformation of São Paulo's city center via avenues, a period during which he narrated the histories of spaces being forgotten in the city, including the pasts buried beneath the Praça da Bandeira. His compelling yet hazy biography is worth examining in detail, as the lack of contemporary memory of the African descendent writer himself parallels the amnesia about the pasts beneath the Praça da Bandeira.

Streets were central to Marques's writing about São Paulo. He opened *Streets and Traditions* with epigraphs from two other authors. The first came from journalist João do Rio, a writer famous for chronicling African diasporic religious practices in Rio de Janeiro: "There is nothing more moving than the beginning of a street." The second reference, from prominent São Paulo figure Guilherme de Almeida, read: "The street lives: the street suffers, the street enjoys / Because of this I believe unwaveringly / That the street has a mysterious soul."[75] Almeida's lines personified streets, ascribing humanlike emotions of suffering and enjoyment to this supposedly inanimate feature of the built environment. Marques seems to have shared the "unwavering" belief: He filled his pages with stories of "mysterious souls" buried beneath—and constitutive with, he asserted—São Paulo's roadways, past and present.

Marques worked at the postal service by day and frequented São Paulo's literary and coffee house scene at night.[76] One of his earliest books was 1922's *The Condemned: Atrocious Tales*, a collection of horror stories set in the city. Prominent São Paulo literary figure Monteiro

Lobato published *The Condemned*, and Lobato biographers suggest that the editor had a particular motivation in doing so. Literary historian Cilza Carla Bignotto writes that Lobato wanted to include a Black author in his "Gallery of the Published," a series of portraits of the authors whom Lobato had published. Biographer Edgard Cavalheiro recalls an anecdote about an unknown Black author who one day entered Lobato's office, asking the editor to review his work for publication. Lobato replied that it was not necessary to read the book and agreed to publication sight (of the book) unseen. Lobato explained his choice: "What I need is a Black in my editorial gallery. From you I just want one thing: a very Black portrait, with no hat on, showing your kinky hair (*gaforinha*)."[77] The cover of *The Condemned* featured a full-page photo of Marques without a hat (figure 2.6). Lobato may have fixated on this racialized visual representation as part of a broader effort to expand the reach of his business to the city's Black readership. Lobato priced Marques's book cheaper than those of other authors, leading Bignotto to surmise "that the editor used the image of the Black author to win over a *specific* readership."[78]

Neither Marques nor Lobato appear to have left written sources about the circumstances described above. One of the sole sources penned by Marques that I located in São Paulo's archives, however, is a birthday letter that he sent to Lobato in 1945. He accompanied a note with a brief story that he wrote about Lobato for broadcast on Rádio Cultura, where Marques was a sometimes host.[79] In his letter Marques wrote playfully, "Well then, Monteiro Lobato, I am around. And don't forget that I continue to be your number-one '*fan*.'"[80] In the radio story Marques described Lobato as "my great and marvelous writer" and "idol of children, and also idol of men young and old!"[81] The story and letter alike imply a relationship of patronage between the two, a plausible dynamic given that Lobato gave Marques one of his earliest, if not indeed his first, publishing breaks.[82]

One of the few (if not only) interviews Marques gave in São Paulo's mainstream press was to the newspaper *A Gazeta* in 1931. The few press articles about Marques (not interviews) rarely made mention of his race; however, the authors of the piece in *A Gazeta* indirectly communicated his skin color by describing him as "from the same land and same race as [João] Cruz e Souza," a famous poet of African descent from Santa Catarina.[83] Most of Marques's responses in the interview were pithy, but he offered a telling, expository reply when the interviewer asked about contemporary social problems. Marques said:

FIGURE 2.6 · Portrait of Gabriel Marques on the cover of *The Condemned*. Gabriel Marques, *Os condemnados: Contos atrozes* (São Paulo: Monteiro Lobato, 1922).

> The capitalist mentality is predominant in the world and from there the stifling environment in which we all live. Wild, cynical, egotistic, inhuman, as it is, it transforms itself into a canker that needs to be and will be fatally eradicated. The poor distribution of capital and silly "favoritism," the profound and painful difference that separates those that have from those that have nothing, those who die from an intoxication of hypercapitalism on the banquet of life to those that perish on sober streets, from cold and hunger.[84]

The lines reveal Marques as a political radical and social critic disdainful of capitalism. While those opinions might have aligned with some of his contemporaries in São Paulo's lettered press and literary scene, they sharply contradicted the project of modernity and progress getting underway through the redevelopment of the city just a year after the publication of Prestes Maia's Avenues Plan.[85] Marques articulated this critique through various metaphors in the response, including the space of the street, a "sober" site where those that have nothing die from "cold and hunger." Note, as well, that the street serves in his response as a space defining social difference.

Marques's early works would advance this social critique through stories about life in urban São Paulo. In 1926 he published *God's Forgotten Ones* (*Os esquecidos de deus*), which received an honorable mention from the Brazilian Academy of Letters. The author of an article about the prize struggled to classify Marques, describing him as "a singular figure among new Brazilian authors," whose "field of observation is, ordinarily, the anonymous life of the humble people, the human wasteland (*o monturo humano*) where great physical and moral suffering ferments." The author characterized his writing style as "bizarre, audacious, insolent, and irregular." The article further revealed that a member of the prize committee had criticized Marques for only writing about "the tragic side of life." Another member disagreed, replying that the "human wasteland" in Marques's work reflected the urban social reality of places like São Paulo, or the "life of hunger, of anguishes, of miseries, of unnamable sufferings and the deaf revolt of humble people in great cities." He concluded: "This misery exists; these sufferings are real; this revolt ferments, and grows in the shadows, and this author [Marques] registers them."[86]

The phrase "God's forgotten ones" appeared in widely circulated newspapers in this era to describe residents facing the precariousness of urban life in São Paulo. A 1928 piece from the short-lived newspaper *Diário Nacional* focused on Canindé, a favela that three decades later would become internationally known through the publication of the writings of one of its Black female residents, Carolina Maria de Jesus.[87] Describing the "marvelous ills" of São Paulo, the author of the 1928 article wrote about a "great number of neighborhoods where the people, with great ownership, call themselves 'God's forgotten ones.'" Roads, once again, functioned to illustrate social conditions: The article included two pictures of unpaved, uneven, and muddied streets in Canindé. The author commented: "It is a legitimate punishment for the passerby to cross these public roadways."[88] It is feasible that Marques himself authored this unsigned article, though no records indicate that he worked for *Diário Nacional* at the time. Another article from

Diário Nacional in 1928 used the same phrase and addressed similar themes.[89] These sources suggest that "the forgotten" signified, among some observers and possibly residents of precarious neighborhoods themselves, the sociospatial contradictions of capitalist progress in the ballooning metropolis.

While his earlier works were mostly fictional stories inspired by real life, in *Streets and Traditions* Marques inverted the equation with imaginative historical narratives. The book includes a section called "Slaves and the Largo do Bexiga," prefaced with a dramatic epigraph introducing the neighborhood of Bexiga as a hub for fugitives and Bexiga Square specifically as the city's slave market. He addresses the reader directly in the subsequent section "Slave Auction": "The reader should know—if they do not already," he begins, "that it was precisely in this Plaza, next to the Memory Obelisk, that, once per week, auctions of slaves occurred." Aiming to rectify the assumed amnesia among readers about the space, he recreates the scene of a slave auction at the square.

In the reimagined scene Marques depicts the social isolation and objectification of African descendent captives. He alternates between descriptions of their bodies and their objectification as "pieces," such as the auctioneer's calls and the tablature where they are listed by price. Social death corresponded to a spiritual forgetting, as well: "And their protector spirits (*orixás*)? What are they doing given that they're not protecting them? . . . In these moments, their *orixás* were traveling far away, very far from there, leaving them forgotten." He establishes a dialogue between figures at the auction in a distinctly African dialect of Portuguese. The exchanges include the following plea from a captive to the young daughter of an interested buyer: "Little miss! I know how to cook! I know how to wash! I know how to iron! I also know how to make *taxada di doce* [sweet treats]! I know how to do *cafuné* [head caresses]! Buy me, little miss!" The repetition of "I know" juxtaposes the intellectual life of the captive with the rampant signs of her objectification, though the list of skills reminds the reader of the productive labor that defined her (market) value. Marques ends the "painful scene" with a baron inspecting and purchasing an enslaved man named Binidito. His sale, along with that of the other captives—including "a future black mother (*mãe preta*) with a far-off glance and robust complexion"—ends the auction.[90]

Marques offers his interpretation after the auction's end. The captives, he writes, "came to live under a new whip. The environment changed, but the suffering not at all." He specifies that environment of suffering: "Sold, they did not have the right to cry. And cry for what? Because they were not going to give their blood and sweat to the enrichment of São Paulo and Brazil? If they didn't know already, they'd learn quickly, as the poet Ciro Costa said well, "'That the fruits of the coffee tree are red globules / Of the blood that flowed from the enslaved black.'"[91] Like Taunay's comments on São Paulo's flag, the poet Costa invoked the blood of enslaved Africans in these two lines. Rather than an "element" to be erased from São Paulo's past and future, however, Costa—and by extension Marques—presents the labor and violence of Africans and their descendants as the source of Brazil's wealth. The lines collapse bodies and commodities in a statement of equivalence: globules of blood are not *like* coffee fruits, they *are* them. They thus emphasize slavery as a racialized system of objectification that served as the foundation of Brazil's wealth.

In *Streets and Traditions* Marques also connected the construction of asphalted urban space in the name of progress to the disappearance of African descendent populations and histories they considered sacred. About the remaking of the Praça da Bandeira in the course of redevelopment for the Avenues Plan, he wrote: "Progress gave a new soul to the place. Progress even changed the name for the purpose, perhaps, of erasing the black past."[92] The sentences recall Almeida's earlier personification of the street as possessing a soul, and they show Marques's understanding of the redevelopment of the site—materially and through its name—as a project of forgetting that silenced the history of African descendants. That project was fundamentally spatial and materialized (as in, made material by city planners) through the substance at the core of the Avenues Plan. As Marques wrote: "It is true that nothing else there records, today, what was, yesterday, that rough piece of Paulistano soil. . . . They buried it beneath the *asphalt*."[93]

In his writings Marques also critiqued the maintenance of racial inequalities after emancipation through commentary on roads:

> Also, when they could, in the slave quarters or on the street, the poor children of Angola, deeply black, like charcoal, would sing their ingenious little verses in a tone of bitter pleading . . .
>
> My miss, my mister,
> I plea for your charity:
> Give me my card of manumission (*carta di forô*),
> I want my liberty!

And After?

After, *came the avenues*, the avenue of Saude (Health), of Lágrimas (Tears) and those that hide thousands of Antônio Tristes, such as described, melancholically, by our inspired poet Paulo Bomfim.[94]

In the first lines—the "before" section—Marques describes enslaved people of African descent pleading in slave quarters or on streets for the liberty. He makes no mention of formal emancipation here, instead shifting from "before" directly to an "after" defined by avenues—the urban spatial form that in São Paulo signaled the height of modernity and progress. These roadways did not bring liberty or equality, Marques indicates. Instead, he suggests that the construction of roadways served to structure racialized social difference and inequality by displacing inconvenient pasts along with undesirable populations in the present.

Marques witnessed the asphalting of São Paulo as an inquisitive researcher residing in the city center. In one of the introductions to *Streets and Traditions*, Marques's peer and author Afonso Schmidt described him as "the pensioner with refined habits, of Tabatinguera Street."[95] This street sits just north of the Liberdade district and east of the city's principal cathedral at Sé.[96] Schmidt asserts that Marques frequented stigmatized places rarely visited by other members of São Paulo's literary elite. About *The Condemned*, for instance, Schmidt wrote:

> In his stories were Bexiga's basements, holes from which, every afternoon, the men went out into the streets, like ants. In the stories were the little bars of Piques, where vagabonds drank until they dropped and the women, when they fought, would pull a razor from their garters and stab at the face of their opponent. In the stories were pigsties without food, where children, deprived of breakfast, drank booze (*aguardente*). In the stories were all the miseries, all the crimes, all the painful things that people find in the last section of the newspaper. [Marques] was a chronicler of subhumanity that did not come to the urban center, but a population that, to find, you must catch the streetcar and get off at the end of the line.[97]

The geography of this quote is telling. In narrating stories about both paved-over pasts and problematic presents, Marques aimed to articulate the quotidian nature—often defined by horror, in his stories—of Bexiga and Piques. These sites did not form part of the "urban center" in the geography Schmidt described. Instead, it seems, his depiction was more reflective of social rather than geographic marginality. While Schmidt implied such lifeways and practices were uncommon, Marques in his various works positioned them at the center of São Paulo's past and present.

Few scholars of São Paulo's urban or literary history reference Marques, suggesting that the author who wrote about forgotten people and the process of forgetting São Paulo's "Black zone" has himself been largely forgotten. He likely died in May or June of 1980.[98] Historian Célio Debes, who was a member of the State of São Paulo Historical Academy, wrote that Marques was a "constant presence" of the academy.[99] Debes writes that "in the memories of his contemporaries, only a cloudy image of him remained; his works, and those were not few, remain totally forgotten among the leading literary figures."[100] The popular forgetting of Marques, a Black author and political radical who excavated forgotten spatial histories in the city, parallels and is intertwined with the silencing of those spaces themselves.

In addition to asphalted avenues, São Paulo officials covered over pasts linked to enslavement at the contemporary Praça da Bandeira by rewriting the local history of slavery. In May 1954, in the same era when Marques first published histories of São Paulo's streets, city council member Paulo Vieira proposed the construction of a memorial at the Praça da Bandeira. He envisioned "a monument commemorating the dates May 23 and July 9, referencing the memory of the young Paulistas Martins, Miragaia, Drausio, and Camargo and the volunteers that fell in the Constitutionalist Revolution."[101] The proposed monument would coincide with the four-hundred-year celebration of São Paulo's founding in 1554, and Vieira could count on broad support for the spirit of the proposal. However, he encountered a significant obstacle: Across town at the new, Oscar Neiemeyer–designed Ibirapuera Park, construction was already underway of a monument commemorating the martyrs of the Constitutionalist Revolution. The council members ultimately decided that the project underway at Ibirapuera took precedence.

Council member Vieira presented a rewritten spatial history of slavery with his rhetoric in support of the monument. In June 1955, the city council reallocated the money that Vieira had originally requested for the monument for the project at Ibirapuera Park. The official resolution for the reallocation explained: "It is right that we erect this monument to our heroes so that future generations can know the sacrifice of the Paulistas at the hour in which they broke the *shackles of slavery* to shout their yearning for liberty."[102] This shackle-breaking referenced the "slavery" imposed on the Paulista population by Getúlio Vargas in the course and wake of his rise to power in 1930. The subject of race followed quickly behind Vieira's exclamation: The monument to 1932 would recognize the movement that the Paulistas led "with their blood in order to dignify the traditions of a race (*raça*)."[103] With such official declarations, slavery, race, and freedom—connected to the Largo do Bexiga but extending beyond—were rewritten in official discourse and through geographic space.

Following the 1960s, historic preservation authorities would promote the official preservation (*tombamento*) of the remaining sliver of space that had served as a market in enslaved people. A group of São Paulo architects in the 1970s petitioned the state of São Paulo's preservation arm, the Council for the Defense of Historical, Archaeological, Artistic, and Tourist Heritage (CONDEPHAAT), for the preservation of the Largo da Memória. The group was led by Carlos Lemos, a prominent architect, urbanist, and historian.[104] Lemos penned multiple letters of support of the preservation with evidence of the historical significance of the square.[105]

The history of slavery at the Largo da Memória appeared in the *tombamento* record, though only as a passing mention. The *tombamento* case file is itself a type of spatial history: a compilation of original evidence and supporting literature organized in linear time and aiming to prove the site's historical significance. Articles from the mainstream press, along with some authored by those lobbying for the *tombamento*, were included in the packet. Pitched at a broad reading public, the articles captured, and would help to shape, popular recollections of the place. For instance, an *O Estado de S. Paulo* piece from January 9, 1972, "Largo da Memória to be Reformed," explained the early history of the site as follows: "There was a well where the animals headed to the livestock market, slaves, and wood (everything had the same value) quenched their thirst or where students, on festive nights, took a dip in the waters."[106] Aside from a handful of similar newspaper articles, the preservation file made no mention of the former use of the place as a site for enslaved commerce or traffic. Throughout the packet and in the official resolution of preservation from April 1975, the architectural characteristics of the Largo received prime attention as symbols of a Paulista prestige set to be "reborn" through restoration.[107] Amnesia about the spatial history of the space variously named Bexiga, Piques,

Memória, Riachuelo, and ultimately Bandeira reflects the effectiveness of the spatial project of forgetting.

Sitting at the Memory Square one afternoon, I recalled reading historian Pierre Nora's work on "sites of memory." Nora argued that sites of memory exist because of the "will to remember," and that they serve "to stop time, to block the work of forgetting, to establish a state of things, to immortalize death, to materialize death."[108] Gazing at the graffitied fountain and the residents enjoying a space of respite in the center of the metropolis, I could not discern any clear "will to remember" at Memory Square. Maybe I, and by extension Nora, were missing something. I then recalled historian James Young's work on Holocaust memorials, *The Texture of Memory*, in which he argued that making a monument does not necessarily serve to maintain memories. Instead, the concretization of the past through austere stone in the present can serve to externalize memories and, in fact, aid the process of forgetting.[109] I surmised that perhaps a different memory project was indeed at play at the contemporary Memory Square: the desire to forget. Despite Marques's efforts to counter that forgetting through alternative histories and imaginative prose, planners actively forgot the spatial history of the Praça da Bandeira through the project of asphalted avenues that spanned from the 1930s to the 1960s.

THE "PICKAXE OF PROGRESS": DEMOLISHING THE REMEDIES

On the morning of June 10, 1883, forty-five enslaved people received manumission certificates in front of the Church of the Remedies (see table 2.1). The leader of the Remedies brotherhood, Antônio Bento, had most likely secured their formal freedom. In the meeting of the brotherhood the week following, Bento requested that "in today's minutes be inscribed the list of those manumitted, so that all of time can attest."[110] The members granted the request, and the names were listed alongside those of their former owners as well as the notary that held their freedom papers. The 1883 event reveals the core elements of the Black liberation project based at the Remedies: the formal abolition of slavery, the public condemnation of enslavers, and the memorialization of those who had succumbed to, survived, or worked to dismantle enslavement and racial violence.

TABLE 2.1 · List of Enslaved People Granted Manumission at the Church of the Remedies, 1883

NO.	NOMES DO LIBERTOS	CARTÓRIO	NOMES DOS EX SENHORES
1	Antonio	Elias	Francisco Antonio Pedroso
2	Antonio	Climaco	Bento Franco de Godoy Lima
3	Antonia	O mesmo	D.ª Maria Jesuina de Camargo
4	Agostinho	O mesmo	Cap. Benjamin José Gonçalves
5	Anacleto	O mesmo	Francisco de Almeida Nobre
6	Armando	O mesmo	Manoel de Queiroz Telles
7	Anna	Fonseca	Dr. Raphael Tobias de Aguiar
8	Benedicto	Climaco	Virgilio Goulart Penteado
9	Benedicta	O mesmo	Joaquim Nobrega de Almeida
10	Balthasar	O mesmo	José Ferreira de Souza
11	Barbara	Fonseca	D.ª Joaq.ª Felicid. da Silva Bueno
12	Barbara	Climaco	Raphael Leite do Canto
13	Brandina	Elias	D.ª Leonôr A. de Lorena Ferreira
14	Canuto	Climaco	Jeronymo José Mendes
15	Camillo	Elias	Dr. Clemente Falcão de Souza
16	Claudina	Climaco	Cap. Benjamin José Gonçalves
17	Candido	O mesmo	Francisco Osorio de Pina Leitão
18	Cecilia	O mesmo	D.ª Maria Ybarra
19	Dorothéa	O mesmo	D.ª Maria Jesuina de Camargo
20	Domingos	Fonseca	Joaquim de Oliveira Lima
21	Eulalia	O mesmo	Dr. Raphael Tobias de Aguiar
22	Emilia	Climaco	Cap. Benjamin José Goncalves
23	Emilia	Fonseca	D.ª Joaq.ª Felicid. da Silva Bueno

TABLE 2.1 · (Cont.)

NO.	NOMES DO LIBERTOS	CARTÓRIO	NOMES DOS EX SENHORES
24	Felisberto	Climaco	Conde de Trer Rios
25	Francisco	Fonseca	D.ª Barbara S. da Silva Caldeira
26	Francisco	Climaco	D.ª Benta Brandina de Moraes
27	Francisca	Fonseca	D.ª Maria Nuncia Gomes
28	Idalina	Elias	Serafim Dias da Cunha
29	João	Climaco	Cap. Benjamin José Gonçalves
30	Joaquim	O mesmo	João C. Mendes Pereira
31	Januario	O mesmo	Dr. Antonio F. de Aguiar e Castro
32	Laurindo	O mesmo	Cap. Benjamin José Gonçalves
33	Laurinda Maria	O mesmo	Henrique Schombourg
34	Luisa	Fonseca	D.ª Joaq.ª Felicid. da Silva Bueno
35	Manoel	Climaco	João Carlos Mendes Pereira
36	Manoel Antonio	Elias	D.ª Leonôr de Mello Sampaio
37	Maria	O mesmo	D.ª Ignacia Candida M. de Oliveira
38	Mariano	Climaco	Firmino A. da Silva Whitaker
39	Paulo	Fonseca	D.ª Joaq.ª F. da Silva Bueno
40	Rita	Climaco	Cap. Benjamin José Gonçalves
41	Rosa	Elias	D.ª Justina M.ª d'Annumpciacão
42	Sabina	Climaco	José Klein
43	Theodoro	O mesmo	D.ª Margarida Junqueira
44	Thomé	O mesmo	Cap. Benjamin José Gonçalves
45	Venancio	O mesmo	O mesmo

Source: "Folha comemorativa da abolição do captiveiro," *A Redempção*, May 13, 1899, 8.

The development of the district surrounding the Church of the Remedies, Liberdade, was inextricably linked to the abolitionist campaign in the 1880s. In the mid-nineteenth century, however, the region's linguistic and material landscapes were organized by markedly different names and practices. In 1850, the place later designated Liberdade consisted of two plazas connected by a street (one block long) running north–south (map 2.6). In 1850, the label printed on the map for the northern plaza in this region was September 7 Square (Pillory) (Largo Sete de Setembro [Pelourinho]). The first part of the name commemorated the date in 1822 when Pedro I, prince of Brazil, declared independence from Portugal. The parenthetical "Pillory" referenced the alternative name for the square, which had served as the epicenter of public punishment in São Paulo. On the same 1850 map, the southern square was labeled Hanging Square (Largo da Forca) and Hanging Hill (Morra da Forca). The punishment and execution of enslaved African descendants and convicted people in São Paulo took place in these spaces. On the adjacent block to the east of the Hanging Square was the Our Lady of the Afflicted (Cap. de N. S. dos Afflictos) chapel and cemetery, dated 1786. This common grave was the first public cemetery in São Paulo and served as the burial grounds for African and African-descendent enslaved people.[111]

The label "Liberdade" appeared on official maps for the first time in this region in 1868 through the renaming of Rua da Liberdade, or Freedom Street, which connected the two squares.[112] As noted previously, multiple principal arteries in colonial São Paulo derived from Indigenous place-names, with Rua da Liberdade formerly known as Jeribatiba. By 1877, the names for the squares that Rua da Liberdade connected had also been changed on maps: "Pillory" had been dropped from "September 7 Square," and "Hanging Square" had been renamed "Freedom Square."[113] Between 1868 and 1877, therefore, the region gained the official place-names that would survive into the twenty-first century. The contemporary boundaries of the Liberdade district are more expansive than this earlier space, which I describe in the following as the *original Liberdade* (see maps 2.6 and 2.7). This territory was the first place in the city of São Paulo where ideals of independence and freedom were inscribed in the linguistic landscape. Those lofty principles were projected onto a region long defined by racialized violence, torture, and death.

Various narratives circulate about the origins of the place-name Liberdade. Some describe it as popularly given in the early nineteenth

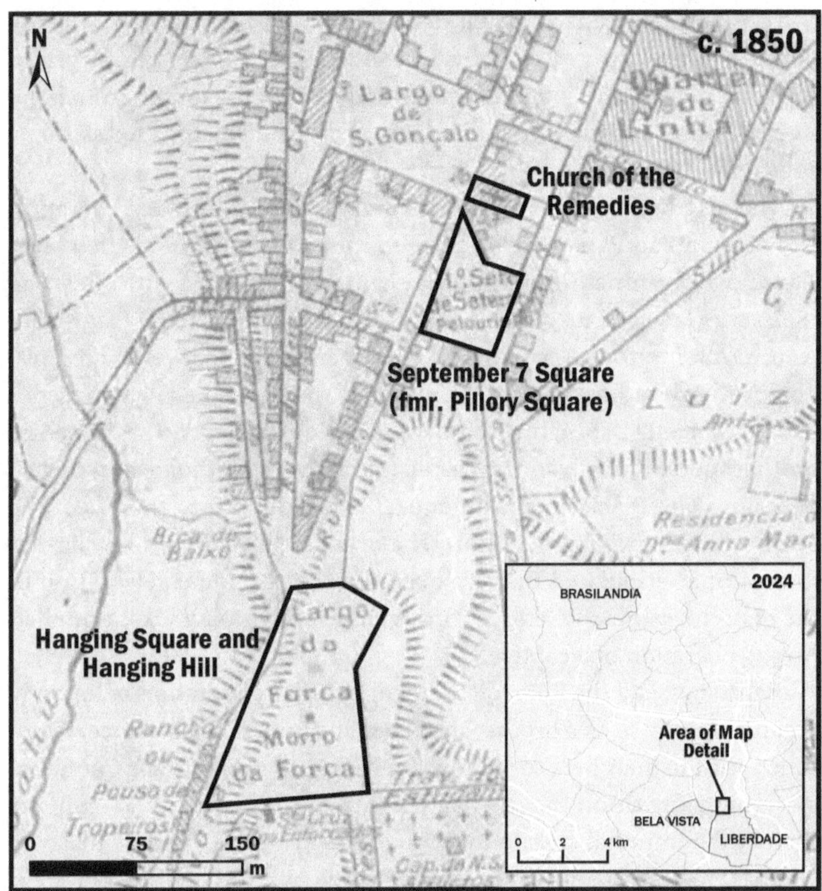

MAP 2.6 · Original Liberdade region in the city of São Paulo, circa 1850. Georeferenced map is Gastão Cesar Bierrembach de Lima, "Planta da cidade de São Paulo 1850," Arquivo Público do Estado de São Paulo. Other map data sources: GeoSampa; OpenStreetMap (Light Gray Canvas) © OpenStreetMap contributors, Microsoft, Facebook, Google, Esri Community Maps contributors, map layer by Esri. Map by Andrew G. Britt.

century, well before it appeared on official city maps. One story holds that the name referenced the freedom that souls gained as individuals condemned to death were executed in the Hanging Square. Another popular narrative points to the thrice-failed hanging of a defiant soldier named Francisco Chagas, or Chaguinhas, who in 1821 nearly escaped death and became a saint of the local Chapel of the Afflicted.[114] Records also indicate that in the middle of the nineteenth century free and enslaved Africans and their descendants in São Paulo were already pursuing antislavery activities in the original Liberdade. A group of freed people, for instance, founded a samba group, named the Zouavos, in the 1850s in the neighborhood that advocated for slavery's abolition.[115]

The original Liberdade became a hub, however, of Black liberation activities in São Paulo during the abolitionist campaign in the 1880s. The most prominent figure of that campaign in São Paulo since the 1860s was lawyer Luís Gama. After Gama's death in 1882, magistrate Antônio Bento took a leading role in organized antislavery activities. The brotherhood based at the Church of the Remedies, which Bento had led since 1880, became a base for abolitionist efforts. The Remedies brotherhood originally incorporated as a formally Catholic lay fraternal order in 1836. Black liberation efforts had figured into the life of the brotherhood since its inception. The organization's founding charter, for example, stipulated that, on occasion of the annual celebration of the church's saint, any leftover financial resources ought to be applied "to the liberation of a captive."[116]

Bento invoked the Remedies's history of Black liberation in his early organizing efforts. In a brotherhood meeting in 1882, for instance, Bento called for the members to "follow the beautiful lead of their founders" by signing a petition that he had composed to the Brazilian emperor against the imperial statute that sanctioned the whipping of enslaved people.[117] Given the proximity of the Remedies church to the pillory in São Paulo, the members of the Remedies brotherhood had likely witnessed firsthand instances of such violence against the enslaved. Not surprisingly, all brotherhood members present at the 1882 meeting signed the petition, an act that marked the intensification of the Remedies's formal involvement in the abolitionist campaign.

In the early 1880s the abolitionist campaign in São Paulo shifted strategies from manumission efforts within the legal system to direct abolition by force.[118] Though likely not the sole architect of this shift, Bento played a principal part putting it into practice. He organized the *caifazes*, a collective composed of freed people, enslaved persons, immigrants, artists, journalists, lawyers, and masons, that was headquartered at the Church of the Remedies. Explaining the group's composition and strategy, historian Emilia Viotti da Costa writes: "The *caifazes* did not content themselves with denouncing the horrors of slavery in the press. The printing press of their journal, *A Redempção*, constituted a

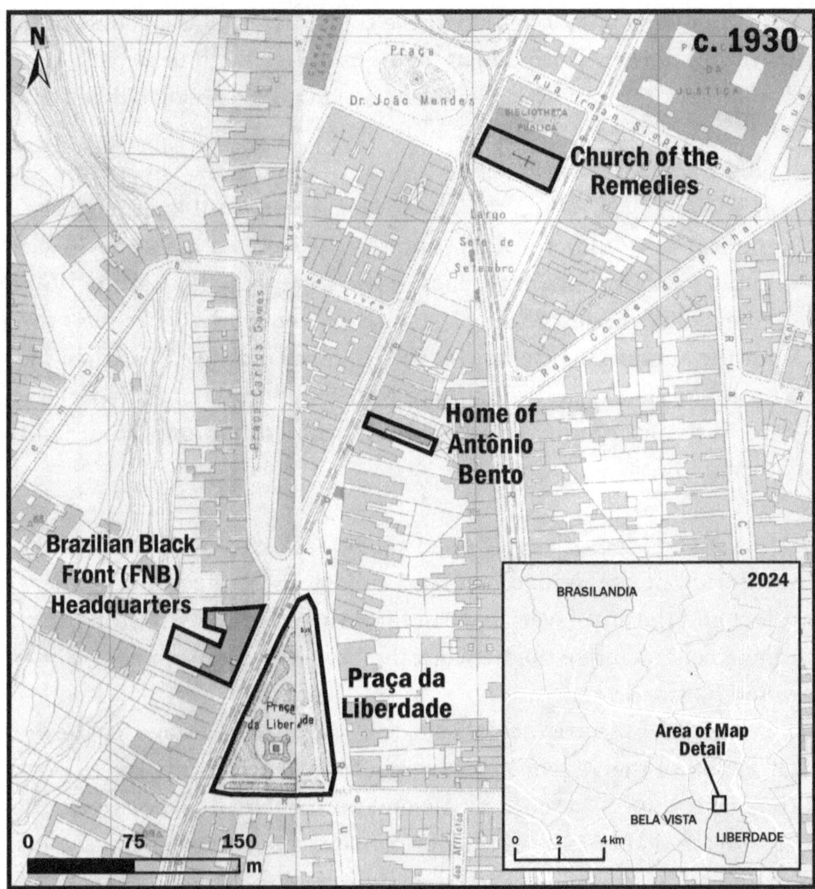

MAP 2.7 · Original Liberdade region, circa 1930, showing the Church of the Remedies, the home of Antônio Bento, the Praça da Liberdade, and the headquarters of the Brazilian Black Front (FNB). Georeferenced map is "Mapeamento 1930—SARA," GeoSampa, accessed June 12, 2018, https://www.geosampa.prefeitura.sp.gov.br. Other map data sources: OpenStreetMap (Light Gray Canvas) © OpenStreetMap contributors, Microsoft, Facebook, Google, Esri Community Maps contributors, map layer by Esri. Map by Andrew G. Britt.

legitimate revolutionary nucleus, where members of the brotherhood of the Nossa Senhora dos Remédios church gathered, a majority being 'working-class Blacks.'"[119] The *caifazes*'s Black liberation project in the 1880s stretched both east and west into the province of São Paulo as members encouraged mass flight from plantations and resettlement in the capital city or in *quilombos*. The *caifazes*'s antislavery campaign also included the forcible freeing of enslaved people within the city of São

Paulo, including at another key space transformed in the course of the realization of the Avenues Plan. In an interview with urbanist Raquel Rolnik, Black movement leader Francisco Lucrécio recalled that

> where today is the Ladeira da Memória, there was an auction site of Black slaves. When the *Irmãos da Alma* [Soul Brothers] knew the slaves would go to auction, they organised a march dressed in purple clothes with torches in their hands. They left the [Remedies] church, descending Riachuelo Street and when it was time for the auction they let loose. The torches became clubs. Then they stole the Blacks and took them to the quilombo of Father Felipe, up in the mountains. He knew the trails in the forest that led to Jabaquara.[120]

The Largo da Memoria, discussed above, sat just a few blocks west of the Church of the Remedies. The similarities between the *caifazes*'s project and the antislavery fight in the United States led historian Kim Butler to characterize the network they constructed as Brazil's Underground Railroad.[121]

In the 1880s the original Liberdade also served as a stage for the dramatization of the violence of slavery. Castro Alves's antislavery poem "The Slave Ship" was set to music and performed at least twice in the 1880s in São Paulo. One of the performances occurred at the São José Theater, a block northwest of the Church of the Remedies.[122] Other performances targeted an audience broader than the theatergoing public. In the 1880s the *caifazes* rescued a recently tortured enslaved person from the interior of the province and transferred him to the city of São Paulo. Bento then placed him at the front of a religious procession led by the members of the Remedies brotherhood. The scene was recorded by Antonio Manuel Bueno de Andrada, a friend of Bento and abolitionist sympathizer:

> Among the saints on the processional floats, suspended on long rods, appeared instruments of torture: shackles, yokes, scourges, etc. In the front, beneath the image of crucified Christ, the miserable captive walked unsteadily and vacillating. . . . The impression on the city was profound. The police did not dare impede the march of the popular mass. . . . Everyone felt profoundly disturbed, except for the wretched, tormented Black man, whose pains had made him mad.[123]

Exhibiting the violence of enslavement through the tortured man, the *caifazes* dramatized the moral campaign against slavery and sought to elicit public support for formal abolition.

In parallel to encouraging mass flight and garnering public support for abolition, abolitionists based at the Remedies church also assembled and organized a material archive that would form the basis of the museum dedicated to the enslaved. In an issue of *O Novo Horizonte*, a newspaper from São Paulo's Black press, journalists remembered the place: "In the vestry of the Church of the Remedies, [Bento] organized a museum with instruments of the martyrdom of slaves, which were presented with the following label: 'All these instruments are authentic and were used.'"[124] Journalist and Brazilian Black Front (FNB) leader José Correia Leite similarly recalled that "the church had a museum of instruments of slave torture."[125] Viotti da Costa wrote that there were "instruments of torture like hooks, irons, chains, found by the members of the brotherhood."[126] In an 1899 commemorative edition of *A Redempção*, one author recounted that "the Remedies brotherhood has precious treasures, the collection of irons taken from the enslaved, which the Paulista Museum would not be able to exhibit."[127] The final comment emphasized the distinctiveness of the Remedies's collection in comparison to one of the city's most eminent patrimonial institutions.

In the years following formal abolition in 1888, the Remedies museum to the enslaved preserved the material realities of racial violence, enslavement, torture, and punishment alongside the material and linguistic elements of the original Liberdade that indexed triumphalist narratives of abolition, including the place-name "Freedom" itself. Creating and preserving this museum represented the significance of remembering and memorialization to the Remedies abolitionists' Black liberation project. The original Liberdade and specifically the Remedies also served as centers of emancipation commemorations beginning in the earliest years after formal abolition. In May 1889, for instance, *O Estado de S. Paulo* recorded the following: "The day before yesterday, in São Paulo the commemorative festivities for the 13th began. Diverse *jongos* of Blacks, in great joy, covered Liberdade Square and Liberdade Street, stopping various times in front of the house of Dr. Antônio Bento. At the side of the house of the beloved abolitionist, they raised an elegant bandstand, where the Remedies band played during the 12th and 13th."[128] These celebrations would continue for decades following and into the 1930s, even in the face of official efforts to suppress them. An article in an 1897 commemorative edition of *A Redempção*, for instance, noted that the local police captain had forced the May 13 celebration to end at ten o'clock. The author critiqued the captain for taking issue with "the dances that the freed people have grown accustomed to performing once per year" while not attending to the "constant robberies that take place in the south of Sé, which even the newspapers have grown tired of reporting because there are so many."[129] José Correia Leite noted that even beyond the May 13 celebrations, the Remedies and the adjacent João Mendes Plaza became "points of concentration for many Black people."[130]

The Remedies and the original Liberdade broadly were also key sites for formal political organizing by Black residents of São Paulo. The FNB headquarters itself sat two blocks south of the Remedies on Liberdade Street at number 196, across from the former Hanging Square.[131] The FNB coordinated May 13 celebrations in the 1930s, which commenced at the Remedies church. The decisions to base the FNB in Liberdade and to begin May 13 commemorations at the Church of the Remedies indicate efforts to link historical and then-contemporary Black liberation struggles through memorialization and political action.

In addition to providing social service programs, the Liberdade-headquartered FNB also advocated against policies and practices of racial discrimination. For instance, FNB organizers in the early 1930s redoubled earlier efforts to overturn the exclusion of Black people from São Paulo's police force, the Civil Guard.[132] Leite addressed this issue in the following, likely fictionalized, scene:

> At the door to a bar, a Black man already of a certain age, half drunk, extends his flattened, calloused hands to a civil guard, an immigrant, with blond hair, eyes like a cat, a majestic prowess like a giant.
>
> —Look at this, the Black man said. This is fifty years behind the plow. *Half a century! Half a century! My youth, my blood, my sweat.* Hoe, shanty, coffee plantation, I left everything in the ground. Afterward, May 13. For years, I would samba on Liberdade Street, in front of the house of Antônio Bento. I drank a lot. May 13. You do not understand any of this. Look at my hands. I am free, young man. Let me drown myself in booze. I am free. It seems incredible. And Blacks can't even be civil guards.[133]

Leite was, as a child, a live-in domestic worker in the home of an Italian family in Bexiga, giving him intimate insight into the dynamics between Black and non-Black immigrant populations in early twentieth-century São Paulo.[134] In his story, the freedman critiques the failed promises of abolition and persisting inequalities through the exchange with the White immigrant, a stand-in for the "free" labor valorized by São Paulo politicians and planters as the country's future beyond abolition. The freedman engages the immigrant as a personification of that historical process and argues for his rights, including by invoking his participation in abolition celebrations at the Remedies in the original Liberdade.[135] The geography in his plea casts that region as a site of memory for the project of formal abolition as well as a mournful, contemporary representation of the continuities of racialized inequalities following the formal end of slavery.

The Church of the Remedies also appeared prominently in author Paulo Cursino de Moura's *Bygone São Paulo* (1932). In a section titled "The Pillory," Moura depicts Pai-João, an archetypal formerly enslaved man in Brazilian folklore, standing in front of the Church of the Remedies.[136] Scanning the church up and down and peering into the adjacent square, he looks for a sign with the square's name, which he is unable to read. He asks a passerby, who tells him that it is the September 7 Square. "Well then, they changed it," he responds. "Here was the Pillory Square." He proceeds to record other changes in the surroundings: "The old Black man did not recognize the local place. . . . Everything had changed."[137]

While invisible in material space, Pai-João recalls the former pillory with acute detail: "A pillar of crude stonework. Solid stones, where two large rings, cemented into the block, hung. Underneath, chains flowing, like snakes, on the flooring, a little taller than the height of the road, forming a type of stage." He also comments on how that spatial history had been buried: "The pillory disappeared. It's good. The memory of the past is erased in the popular soul."[138] A personification of that buried and disappearing past, Pai-João also represented the persistence of memories of racialized violence in the original Liberdade and adjacent to the Remedies church in the 1930s.

Cursino de Moura published this history in 1932, at the beginning of a transformative decade of urban redevelopment in the region surrounding the Remedies. In that first edition the author noted the changes that had already reshaped the original Liberdade, with one significant exception:

> There was sanctuary . . . in other farms of abolitionists, in modest people's homes and in churches. At the Church of the Remedies, at [the Church] of Misericórdia, in the square of that name (demolished in 1888, coinciding with the abolition law, as if to say—"I am no longer needed") and at [the Church] of São Gonçalo. The oldest relic of the times gone by, that the pickaxe of progress has to date still respected—the Church of the Remedies—solemnly attests to the protection of slaves.[139]

Writing in the early 1930s, the refuge of the Church of the Remedies seemed secure from the "pickaxe of progress." The fixture served as the point of reference for Pai-João, representative of a generation for whom the memories of the local space remained acute. Cursino de Moura's allegory served as a type of prose memorial to counter the forgetting that would accompany the razing of the Remedies and other sites meaningful for African descendants in the original Liberdade in the decades following.

In the 1930s, the Church of the Remedies came to occupy a prominent place in first drafts of Brazil's official national patrimony. Mario de Andrade, the famed modernist, was instrumental in creating Brazil's first federal institution focused on historical and artistic patrimony, the Serviço do Patrimônio Histórico e Artístico Nacional (SPHAN). In 1937 Andrade submitted a report to the director of SPHAN concerning "architectural monuments of historical and artistic value" that he argued deserved federal preservation."[140] Andrade recommended eight sites in the city of São Paulo, including the Remedies, which he described in the following:

> It belongs to the Brotherhood of Our Lady of the Remedies and was built on July 17, 1812. The date of the church's establishment is not known at present. The frontispiece on the current facade of the building, which is covered with blue tiles, says 1812. The abolitionists of 1888, led by Luís Gama and others, met in the church. Photos of the facade can already be found in the central headquarters of SPHAN.[141]

Andrade included a description like this for each of the eight sites, providing the rationale for their historical and artistic value. For the Remedies, he highlighted the pivotal links between the church and the abolitionist campaign (historical value) and the tiles on the facade (artistic value), which were atypical in São Paulo. The Church of the Remedies was shortly thereafter featured in the first issue of the national journal of SPHAN, published in 1937.[142] Of the eight sites Andrade recommended for preservation in São Paulo, the Remedies was the only one ultimately demolished.[143]

The preservation of the Remedies, including its potential designation as official national patrimony by SPHAN, would have proved meaningful, most especially in preventing the demolition that would commence the year following Andrade's recommendation. At the same time, such recognition would have followed nearly fifty years of memorialization work already conducted by former abolitionists at the Remedies. While the compilation of a national material memory became an institutionalized, state practice in the late 1930s, former abolitionists had, since the 1880s, pursued their own spatial project of remembering that produced the Remedies church and museum as monuments to the enslaved and freed as well as to the ongoing project of Black liberation, more broadly. That project also helped to support claims of belonging and maintain ties to ancestors in post-abolition São Paulo.

Prestes Maia first outlined the demolition of the Remedies in the Avenues Plan in 1930. An earlier draft of this project, released in 1924 and penned by Prestes Maia and fellow urbanist Ulhôa Cintra, presented a different plan. In that version, the ring road would have been constructed north of the Sé cathedral, a trajectory that would have spared the Remedies church and museum (map 2.8). Four years later, in the much expanded and comprehensive Avenues Plan, Prestes Maia shifted the ring road south of the Sé cathedral (map 2.9), projecting it through the Church of the Remedies, the museum, and likely a burial ground of brotherhood members.[144] This shift accompanied a substantial expansion of the João Mendes Plaza, which would become a crucial stretch of the ring road running along an approximately east–west axis. This revised plan also entailed the linking of João Mendes Plaza with September 7 Square (the former Pillory Square), which would establish a wider road linkage between the Sé and Liberdade districts running south to Liberdade Avenue. This expanded, connected plaza, square, and avenue—which formed a T shape—would serve as a central transportation node for streetcars and the city's growing bus network. Realizing this ambitious plan would require the demolition of a series of structures in these blocks, including the Remedies church and museum and an adjacent building the brotherhood owned. Prestes Maia's appointment as mayor in 1938 gave him the institutional authority with which to execute these key components of the Avenues Plan.

The leadership of the Remedies brotherhood received formal notice of the expropriation and convened a meeting in early March of 1939 to discuss their next move. Their discussion centered on the amount that they understood the municipal government had committed to the expropriation: 3.000 contos (approx. US$177,074).[145] The leader of the meeting and thirty-year head of the brotherhood, Carlos Corrêa de Toledo, found the sum incommensurate with the market value of properties in the area. He cited a prior episode from 1929 when the municipal government had considered expropriation, during which the archbishop of São Paulo had estimated the market value of the church and attached building as *at least* 3.500 contos. Thirteen years later and amid a transformative redevelopment project that would raise local property values, the proposed sum fell well short of expectations.[146]

While the expropriation amount figured centrally into the brotherhood's deliberations at the March meeting, they also kept the history of the church at the forefront of their conversation. Toledo, for instance, directly followed his reading of the expropriation decree with a historical overview of the brotherhood's role in the 1880s antislavery struggle, lauding the "great figures who passed through this place and left indelible marks through their religious and patriotic service."[147] The brotherhood, no doubt, calculated the value of the church based on the local real estate market as much as the place's historical significance to the abolitionist project and the memorialization of the enslaved.

Perhaps surprisingly, the surviving record from the March meeting suggests that the brotherhood did not discuss a move to block the expropriation and demolition. They might have calculated that doing so would prove difficult if not impossible, given the appointment of Prestes Maia to the municipal government and the authoritarian climate of the Estado Novo. The brotherhood's leader, Toledo, instead adopted a moderate negotiation stance that focused on the terms and not the fact of expropriation. He declined "numerous offers" of assistance from lawyers willing to represent the organization before the municipal government out of a desire "to carry out negotiations on totally harmonious grounds." Fresh from the March meeting, Toledo felt "certainty [that] the municipal powers will be the first to recognize

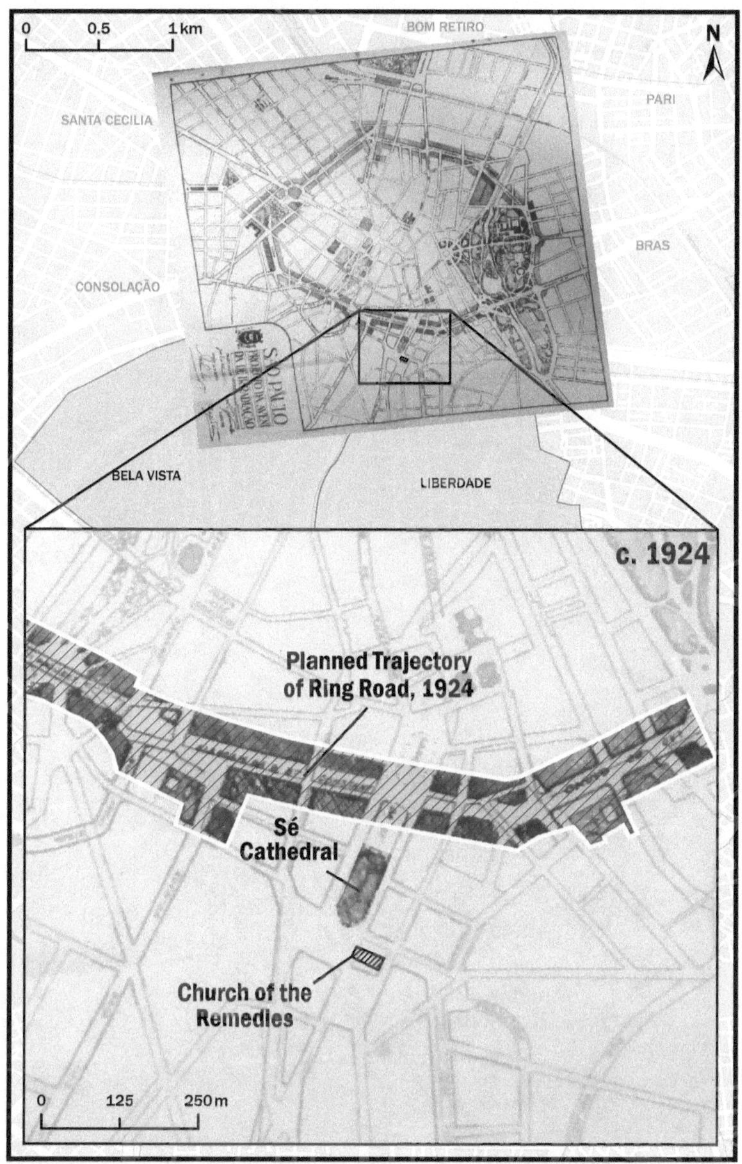

MAP 2.8 · Plan for the ring road drafted by Francisco Prestes Maia and João Florence d'Ulhôa Cintra in 1924. Shaded region north of the Sé Cathedral shows the planned trajectory of the ring road that would have spared the church. Georeferenced map from Francisco Prestes Maia and João Florence d'Ulhôa Cintra, "Um problema actual: Os grandes melhoramentos de São Paulo," *Boletim do Instituto de Engenharia* 6, no. 25 (1924). Other map data sources: GeoSampa; OpenStreetMap (Light Gray Canvas) © OpenStreetMap contributors, Microsoft, Facebook, Google, Esri Community Maps contributors, map layer by Esri. Map by Andrew G. Britt.

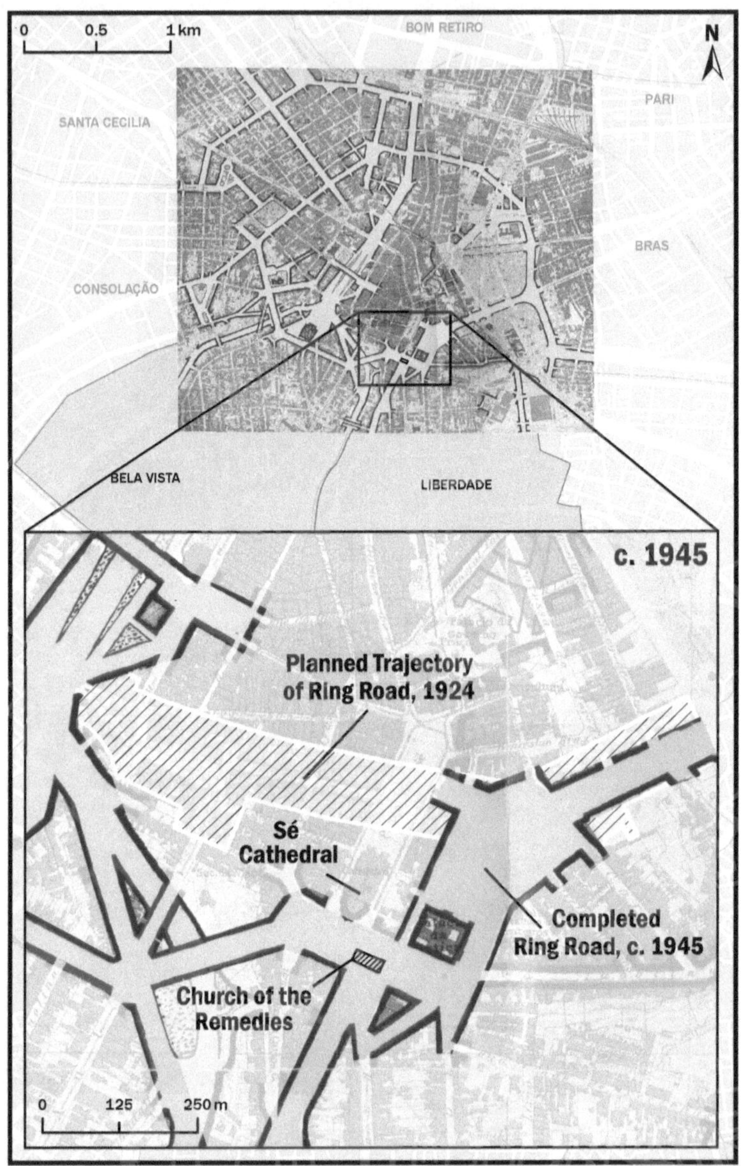

MAP 2.9 · Map of the completed ring road in 1945, showing the alternate trajectory south of the Sé cathedral that necessitated the demolition of the Remedies church. Georeferenced map is from Francisco Prestes Maia, *Os melhoramentos de São Paulo* (São Paulo: Imprensa Oficial do Estado de São Paulo, 1945). Other map data sources: GeoSampa; OpenStreetMap (Light Gray Canvas) © OpenStreetMap contributors, Microsoft, Facebook, Google, Esri Community Maps contributors, map layer by Esri. Map by Andrew G. Britt.

the *high value* of the real estate to be expropriated for the demands of urban progress."[148]

Some observers in São Paulo's mainstream press adopted a similar position, writing appreciatively about the church's historical significance while, at the same time, accepting the demolition as the perhaps lamentable but necessary price of progress. An article from March 1939 pointed to the traffic bottleneck in front of the church as a "serious threat to the future expansion of the metropolis" before concluding: "Now, 218 years later, the traditional Paulistano temple will disappear, in order to attend to the growth of the city's progress."[149] Though noting the church was "one of the few monuments from the colonial epoch," a February 1939 article conceded that "the old temple . . . for necessities imperative to the development of the Paulista capital, is, now, condemned to disappearance."[150] A November 1942 article asserted that the church, "which in that stretch of the city represented old São Paulo," would "open up space, under the pickaxe of urbanism, to the works devised by Mr. Prestes Maia, works that in the short space of almost five years made our central capital among the most beautiful cities of Brazil and America."[151] An article following the demolition concluded that "if, on one hand, we lament the disappearance of 'one more' of the city's historical patrimony, on the other hand we have to agree that the old temple, sitting at the narrowest of bottlenecks that disturbed traffic at the beginning of Liberdade Street, needed to be removed."[152] While such articles gestured toward the church's historical significance, few specified the connections to slavery, abolition, or ongoing projects of Black liberation.

Other observers shared the high appraisal of the value of the church but, instead of accepting demolition as inevitable or necessary, worked to thwart it. These included the prominent cultural figures and city government employees Mario de Andrade and historian Nuto Sant'Anna, who had lobbied for the preservation of the Remedies even before Prestes Maia's appointment as mayor in 1938. After the expropriation decree in 1939, they continued to lobby against demolition. Andrade, for example, discussed the Remedies in correspondence with Luis Saia, an urbanist and ethnographer who would lead SPHAN's São Paulo district office from the late 1930s through the 1970s. Both Andrade and Saia sent letters advocating for the preservation of the Remedies to Rodrigo Melo Franco de Andrade, SPHAN's director. In a letter to Mario de Andrade dated March 7, 1939, Saia wrote:

> About the case of the Church of the Remedies, I also already sent a report to Rodrigo. I don't know if it will stave off the demolition. It's a complicated case, since a lot of work was already put into related expropriations, other construction work has already been carried out, all of this implicating the future demolition of the church. I proposed to Dr. Rodrigo, if the demolition is indeed unavoidable, the budget for a complete model of the church to be made for SPHAN.[153]

Saia's comments seem to draw on backroom conversations with urbanistic and preservation authorities. His observations suggest that already in early March 1939—a week before the Remedies brotherhood had even held their first meeting to determine their response to the expropriation decree—the demolition was inevitable. The brotherhood's leadership itself may have also received this information through back channels, which might help to explain their acquiescence to the fact, if not the terms, of expropriation. Saia's proposal for a scale model of the church, additionally, demonstrates an early effort to imagine alternative modes of preserving the Remedies and the pasts that the brotherhood had memorialized.

The seeming inevitability of demolition did not, however, deter preservationists from continuing to make their pitch, including in São Paulo's mainstream press. Sant'Anna, for instance, wrote a 1942 article in *Folha da Noite* titled "It Was Headquarters of the Enslaved in São Paulo." The piece foregrounded the Remedies's ties to enslavement and abolition and highlighted the proximity of the church to the former Pillory Square. Sant'Anna concluded with a direct appeal to urbanistic authorities: "In the face of all of these facts," he surmised, "the demolition of the traditional Church of the Remedies is lamentable. I believe that, correcting a few urbanistic defects, the temple could be conserved."[154] It is unclear whether those "defects" referred to characteristics of the church or to Prestes Maia's plan for redevelopment at the João Mendes Plaza and September 7 Square. In either case, the historian clearly saw the Remedies church—even in 1942, with the leveling imminent—as both salvageable and worth saving, not incompatible with redevelopment.

Author Afonso Schmidt penned one of the most imaginative pleas for preservation. Schmidt's was one of the only articles from the mainstream press to reference directly the Remedies museum to the enslaved. In his overview of the place's history, Schmidt wrote, "Those who gained their freedom, by flight or by violence, brought their irons, as a pious offering, to the blessed church. The body of the church, little by little, became a museum of torture devices."[155] Schmidt's piece drew on a first-person visit to the church.[156] Neither Mario de Andrade nor Sant'Anna mentioned the museum in newspaper articles or in correspondence relating to SPHAN. Schmidt's unique mention of the museum may have owed to him being one of the few observers to visit the inside of the church and therefore become familiar with the museum's contents. It is also plausible that Andrade and Sant'Anna had visited the church but calculated that highlighting the museum would weaken the case for preservation with urbanistic authorities like Prestes Maia. They may have surmised that officials *might* be sympathetic to a monument to the abolition of slavery—the argument Sant'Anna made in the press—but repelled by a memorial that preserved material instruments and memories of racial violence.

In his appeal for preservation, Schmidt adopted a different approach that kept the material culture of the museum to the enslaved front and center:

> The Church of Our Lady of the Remedies cannot disappear. . . . It should be conserved, even if inside a glass case. . . . It is the Church of Our Lady of Abolition. Almost all countries preserve these antiquities: Governments give them rights as national monuments. Do the same with the Remedies. Raze the block that hides it. Reform it. Encircle it with gates cast with the irons of the enslaved. But do not remove it from there.[157]

Schmidt asserted that the contents of the museum should be dismantled, a suggestion that he, too, may have seen that memorialized material culture and the racial violence it symbolized as incompatible with São Paulo's modernization. At the same time, his proposal that the irons should be melted down and incorporated into a gate surrounding the structure represents the transformation, rather than disappearance, of that material culture and, to an extent, the pasts symbolized therein. Though likely at odds with the wishes of those who had curated and preserved the museum to the enslaved, Schmidt's proposal did steer an imaginative and more reverent, if ultimately unrealized, alternate course.

These impassioned appeals to stop the demolition of the Remedies did not persuade urbanistic authorities, who took control of the structure in September 1942. The Remedies brotherhood ultimately received between 1.2 and 1.4 million cruzeiros (approximately US$61,800–72,100) in the expropriation: substantially less than half of what the leader Toledo understood the city government's valuation of the church to be in the March 1939 meeting.[158] Two sources indicate that judicial authorities settled the final amount of the expropriation, suggesting that what Toledo had hoped would be a harmonious negotiation did not end up as such.[159]

The municipal government may well have reduced their initial expropriation offer by half, a move that the brotherhood, which already found the original proposal of Cr$3 million wanting, would have likely found distressing. It is also possible that a city official communicated the expropriation cost of the entire block, rather than just the Remedies properties, to the brotherhood's representatives. The city government paid Cr$1.1 million for the other privately held building on the block, which together with the Remedies church and attached building would have brought the expropriation total to Cr$2.5 million. Costs associated with other expropriated buildings in the vicinity, or, perhaps, an expropriation cost associated with the municipal library that sat between the Remedies and the other privately held building, could have easily brought the total near Cr$3 million.[160]

Whether either of these scenarios captures what took place, the expropriation ultimately left the Remedies brotherhood with less than half of what they had anticipated and, as noted above, substantially less than the valuation of the church that the archbishop of São Paulo had made in 1929. The brotherhood itself owned these properties, which likely served as a meaningful source of wealth generation and preservation. The reduced expropriation sum, combined with the increase of prices during wartime, were also consequential in hampering progress on the rebuilding of the church in the years following.

The demolition of the Remedies began in late 1942 (figure 2.7), drawing the attention of notable São Paulo residents. Modernist poet Oswald de Andrade, for instance, wrote in his journal of being at the Remedies on the day of demolition.[161] The leveling spanned months, in fact, and was quickly followed by the work to construct a station on the streetcar line at September 7 Square. One source suggests that Prestes Maia moved into his office in the city hall—a few blocks northwest of the demolition site—to be nearby in case any complications arose.[162] The anecdote illustrates the significance that redevelopment in this stretch of the Avenues Plan held for Prestes Maia.

FIGURE 2.7 · Partially demolished Church of the Remedies, 1942. Photo by B. J. Duarte. Acervo Fotográfico do Museu da Cidade de São Paulo.

While the church was razed in 1942 and 1943, not all of the structural elements and objects within the Remedies were ground to dust. São Paulo's archbishop issued a decree in late 1942 with instructions on how to "reduce the . . . temple of the Remedies to profane use, so that it could be demolished." This decree mandated that "all of the objects and sacred implements should be removed by the Brotherhood of the Remedies and stored in a secure place, and recorded in an inventory that will be registered in the minutes of the brotherhood and in this Metropolitan Curia."[163] The contents of the museum to the enslaved may well have been listed in this inventory, however I have not located records to confirm as much in documents from the brotherhood or in the curia. Other sacred material objects from the Remedies, however, were ultimately transferred to the reconstructed church or local museums.

Outside parties took an interest in salvaging some materials from the Remedies. B. J. Duarte, the head of the iconographic section of the municipal Department of Culture, captured the piecemeal dismantling of the Remedies in a series of photos. Duarte's photos from 1944 reveal that doors, stones, and wooden beams from the Remedies had been transferred to a municipal government storage facility. Nuto Sant'Anna lobbied the city government to establish a permanent exhibition to the Remedies composed of these salvaged materials in the Ipiranga

Museum.[164] One of Duarte's photos shows Sant'Anna observing workers at the storage facility reassembling the stone from above the Remedies front door (figure 2.8). The Remedies brotherhood began the effort to reconstruct the church in quick order after demolition. They had acquired land in the nearby Cambuci neighborhood in early 1943 and, by October, had laid the cornerstone for the new church. The increased cost of construction materials during wartime, however, strained the effort to rebuild, as a 1946 article in *O Estado de S. Paulo* explained: "The construction had to withstand the incredible and absurd inflation of the materials most necessary for its progress, such as iron, wood, bricks, etc. Result: the money didn't suffice. The project stopped midway."[165] The church would ultimately be completed; however, the location of the objects from the museum to the enslaved remains unknown into the twenty-first century.

An extraordinary needle in the archival haystack furnishes revealing insight into Prestes Maia's perspective on the demolition of the Remedies. In late 1942 or early 1943 he submitted an extensive report with an update on urban redevelopment projects to the São Paulo state assembly, which was then included in a larger report sent to Vargas. In structure, tone, and detail, the exhaustive document mirrored the Avenues Plan itself. In the early pages of the report, he addressed the construction of the ring road in the proximity of the Remedies church and museum: "The great expansion of the João Mendes Plaza, extended all the way to Tabatinguera Street, required almost three million cruzeiros of expropriation expenditures, including the Church of the Remedies, *of debatable historical and artistic value*, and whose location strangulated the best passage to the neighborhoods of Glória and Liberdade."[166]

Prestes Maia rarely spoke extemporaneously about his projects. He let his voluminous, erudite, and polished technical publications do most of the talking. That pattern makes this six-word value judgment of the Church of the Remedies an unusual and illuminating window into the ideology that animated the decision to demolish the Remedies church and museum and, I suggest, the Avenues Plan more broadly.

Prestes Maia's interpretation of the "debatable" value of the church cannot reasonably be attributed to ignorance about the unequivocal value that the place held for many São Paulo residents, especially, but not exclusively, those of African descent. In the nineteenth century, the church had been deemed of significant enough historical value for inclusion in Militão Augusto de Azevedo's rich collection of photos of São Paulo,

FIGURE 2.8 · Nuto Sant'Anna and workers reassembling a stone from the demolished Church of the Remedies, 1944. Photo by B. J. Duarte. Acervo Fotográfico do Museu da Cidade de São Paulo.

snapped between 1862 and 1887 (figure 2.9). In the more contemporary context of the 1930s (and as already noted), articles about the history of the church had circulated in São Paulo's mainstream press and, in 1937, in SPHAN's magazine (which had a national scope). What's more, Prestes Maia had a well-worn copy of Paulo Cursino de Moura's *São Paulo de outrora* in his personal library—the book with the story of the archetypal Pai-João described above—wherein Prestes Maia's few annotations revealed an interest in the history of African descendants in Brazil, in particular.[167] We would also expect that he was aware of, if not directly involved in debates about, the preservation arguments made by figures like Mario de Andrade. Indeed, the specific vocabulary that Prestes Maia used in his appraisal—"historical and artistic value"—echoed Andrade's language from the 1937 report ("architectural monuments of historical and artistic value") about sites in the city of São Paulo worth federal preservation. His reference to value in that 1942–1943 document also recalls the centrality of that word in the deliberations of the Remedies brotherhood from the March 1939 meeting. These similarities suggest that Prestes Maia's appraisal may have been a direct rebuttal to the arguments that both the preservationists and the brotherhood had put forth about the historical and artistic value of the Remedies. The contrast between the superlative, widely known value that the Remedies held for many in São Paulo and the "debatable" value with which Prestes Maia described it is striking.

The value judgment in the report is also significant because it was rather unnecessary. Prestes Maia could have limited his comments to the latter half of that sentence, which, reasonably, emphasize the transportation bottleneck in front of the Remedies that strained access between the districts of Sé and Liberdade. Or, alternatively, he might have acknowledged that the church indeed held great significance for many in São Paulo while lamenting that, nonetheless, its location necessitated demolition. Many journalists in São Paulo's mainstream press—and, recall, even the leadership of the brotherhood itself in its first meeting after the expropriation decree—adopted this position. Alternatively, still, we might wonder why, among the dozens of structures demolished for the expansion of the João Mendes Plaza, Prestes Maia mentioned the Remedies church at all. Why single out the Remedies and explain the logic of its demolition through this subtle, yet unmistakably dismissive, appraisal?

Prestes Maia's value judgment of the Remedies becomes even more curious in light of his interest in the blue tiles that covered the facade of the church. Mario de Andrade referenced these tiles in his 1937 report as evidence supporting the artistic value of the Remedies. Indeed, though common in other regions in Brazil, such ornamentation was rare in São Paulo. The Church of the Remedies may have been, in fact, the only building in the city with its facade ornamented thusly.[168] One source indicates that Prestes Maia sought to acquire these tiles and requested them from the brotherhood. The brotherhood's members refused. The tiles were initially given to a plant nursery in the park in Ibirapuera and, supposedly, "never heard from again."[169]

Remarkably, 150 of these tiles today hang in the municipal government's library dedicated to architecture and urbanism, which bears the name of Prestes Maia. Prestes Maia coordinated the construction of this library in 1963, and since then it has housed an extensive collection from his own personal archive of books, technical documents, and objects. The label accompanying the tiles indicates that they were restored in 1973, eight years after his death. It is not clear to me how the tiles ended up here, and what role, if any, Prestes Maia might have played in that process. Other tiles from the facade ended up in the São Paulo Museum of Sacred Art and the collection of the Museum of the City.

FIGURE 2.9 · Church of the Remedies, Militão Augusto de Azevedo, circa 1887. Source: Acervo Instituto Moreira Salles.

Whatever the explanation for how the tiles landed in the library named for Prestes Maia, his wish to acquire them starkly contradicts his own appraisal of the supposed "debatable historical and artistic value" of the church and museum.

While we might find Prestes Maia's comments and actions suspicious to the point of duplicitous, does this collection of evidence support the conclusion that anti-Black racism motivated the demolition of the Remedies? Such a conclusion is *not* prominent in the two dominant threads of criticism of the Avenues Plan, which instead concentrate on architectural patrimony and population displacement, respectively. Both lines of criticism present the Avenues Plan as indiscriminate—*not* motivated by or involving racialized social difference—in its destructive and negative impacts.

A 1942 article about the demolition of the Remedies and written by the director of the São Paulo State Archive, Lelis Vieira, for instance, reflects the first thread of Avenues Plan criticism. He wrote: "It is clear that civilization does not respect the city; that progress ignores everything; that comfort is more important than traditions; that so-called aesthetics destroy museums; that urbanism spoils eaves, mutilates moldings, punctures blinds, puts out light fixtures, and achieves the perfection of turning a village into a capital."[170] His criticism lambasted modern architecture and urbanism for its destruction of the city's colonial built environment. A similar sentiment appears in a later article from 1946: For "the expansion of the place and decongestion of traffic, it was necessary to sacrifice nothing less than this historical patrimony of the city, and, with it, the entire block."[171] These criticisms focused on the confrontation between modern architecture and urbanism with earlier urbanistic patterns and building styles, especially religious architecture. We would expect to find comparable criticisms of modern architecture and urbanism in disparate urban contexts. Indeed, the patrimony vein of criticism was not particular to the case of the Remedies or even to the city of São Paulo.

With more attention to the social implications of the Avenues Plan, other observers have critiqued the displacement that demolitions caused. For instance, Anhaia Mello, an architect-urbanist and contemporary of Prestes Maia, criticized Prestes Maia's redevelopment projects in 1945 for leaving an estimated 150,000 people homeless.[172] More recently, scholars such as Nabil Bonduki, Teresa Caldeira, and James Holston have critiqued the displacement caused by the Avenues Plan and the sociospatial inequalities that redevelopment helped to reproduce.[173] While these authors help to elucidate the roots of São Paulo's pronounced contemporary inequalities in the Avenues Plan, the case of the Remedies supports an expanded critical interpretation of this seminal modernization program in São Paulo that foregrounds questions of racial prejudice and racialized inequalities.

The decision to demolish the Remedies went beyond the logic and criteria of transportation planning. Historian Benedito Lima de Toledo gestures toward this conclusion when he writes that Prestes Maia "wanted to demolish the Church of the Remedies—I do not remember his argument why—and arranged the grounds to do so."[174] Toledo here implies that Prestes Maia desired to demolish the church and, subsequently, found an urbanistic basis to support doing so. While this analysis and Prestes Maia's six-word value judgment suggest that he wanted to demolish the church, what other historical context can help us to understand whether, again, this desire was motivated by anti-Black racism, specifically?

A productive parallel example to consider is the proposed demolition of the Church of Our Lady of the Rosary of Black Men, owned by a

Black brotherhood founded in 1711. Between 1903 and 1905, the City of São Paulo had expropriated and demolished the brotherhood's original church, which then relocated to the northeast of the old city center at the Paissandu Square.[175] In the 1930 Avenues Plan, Prestes Maia again set the municipal government's sights on the relocated church, asserting it should be demolished and rebuilt in the Barra Funda neighborhood. In a map of his proposed demolitions from the Avenues Plan, Prestes Maia included the church in an open-ended, catchall category of projects related to "new alignments or modifications." The church sat multiple blocks from the nearest avenue projected for enlargement and, therefore, was an oddly remote choice for demolition.[176]

Prestes Maia, in fact, had no avenue-making plans for the site of the Rosary church at the Paissandu Square. Instead, he intended to erect a monument to Duque de Caxias, a prominent military and political figure of nineteenth-century Brazil.[177] The significance of the Rosary church and Prestes Maia's proposal for replacement suggests that he desired to displace a significant center of Black life in the city and construct, in its stead, a monument that celebrated a White historical figure. The proposed expropriation and demolition also show how Prestes Maia's plan went beyond issues of transportation planning and urban amenities to encompass spatial projects relating to memorialization. Prestes Maia would not succeed in the expropriation of the Rosary church, however, which remains at the Paissandu Square through the present.[178]

Though sparse in the written historical record, some São Paulo residents commented on demolition episodes like those of the Rosary and the Remedies as directly involving anti-Black racism. For example, researcher Virgínia Leone Bicudo recorded the following observation from a Black resident about the proposed demolition of the Rosary church in 1945: "That attitude of prejudice in São Paulo is not exceptional—by the same motive, one thinks about the removal of the church of the Rosary from the Paissandu Square, they say to erect a monument. Discussing the subject with a White Catholic, he told me: 'It is necessary to clean that place, to remove the church from there.'"[179] The quote suggests that the discourses about, and the demolition of, buildings like the Rosary and the Remedies may have served as a concrete means through which Black residents of São Paulo could identify the racial prejudice and inequalities that structured—and continue to structure—Paulistano society yet were frequently denied or veiled.

Analyzing the proposed demolition of the Rosary and the successful demolition of the Remedies in the same frame supports an interpretation of Prestes Maia's project as animated, though perhaps not exclusively motivated, by anti-Black racism. This racism was veiled behind the discourse of urbanistic neutrality and the spatial memory politics embedded in the Avenues Plan, which held places prominently associated with, and often significant to, African descendants as representative of São Paulo's undesirable past. The Remedies brotherhood had memorialized those pasts through the museum to the enslaved. That memorialized material history was at odds, however, with the future-oriented spatial project of whitening, modernity, and progress that Prestes Maia had outlined in the Avenues Plan and that various urban authorities had pursued in São Paulo over generations.[180] Demolition would serve to resolve that contradiction in 1942 and 1943, paving the way for a collective forgetting in dominant memory about the histories of racial violence and Black liberation that the Remedies at once housed, symbolized, and memorialized.[181]

In addition to the Church of the Remedies, urban authorities leveled other sites significant to, and prominently associated with, African descendants in this era in São Paulo and beyond.[182] In the same year that demolition began on the Remedies, for instance, officials in Rio de Janeiro demolished the Praça Onze, a key site in the city's mythical "Little Africa" region, for a new avenue.[183] Such parallels support the argument that the destruction and reproduction of urban space served in the whitening project as well as the maintenance of racialized inequalities in cities throughout Brazil. Prestes Maia's six-word value judgment provides a uniquely incriminating bit of evidence to support this argument for the case of São Paulo, though I would expect that some spatial authorities in other cities shared a similar ideology.

While the case of the Remedies points to broader patterns about the spatial dimensions of the whitening project across urban Brazil, its demolition also helps to illuminate the singularity of the outcomes of that project in the city of São Paulo. The demolition and displacement of São Paulo's "Black zone" in the early twentieth century, combined with state-sponsored projects to produce non-Black ethnic enclaves in its stead in the decades following, would help to concretize the myth of São Paulo as a non-Black city in ways that diverge from Brazil's other major urban centers, including Rio de Janeiro. The demolition of the Praça Onze in Rio de Janeiro, in other words, did not help to set the stage for popular, widely accepted constructions of Rio de Janeiro as a non-Black or White city.[184]

My interpretation of the Avenues Plan as a racialized spatial project of forgetting aligns closely with, and has been deeply influenced by, the work of Gabriel Marques. While throughout this chapter I present original evidence about Saracura, Bexiga Square, and the Remedies church and museum (the latter does not appear in Marques's writings), the arguments I advance here follow and directly support the supposition that he put forth—albeit somewhat delicately—over sixty years ago. I expect that many other African-descendent residents of Liberdade and throughout the city of São Paulo held interpretations similar to Marques's in the mid-twentieth century, even if their voices—like these three key sites in São Paulo's early twentieth-century "Black zone"—were silenced in the decades following.

These narratives and arguments in this chapter point to multiple conclusions about ethnoracial space in Brazil and beyond. While prior scholars have identified space as one of the social domains *least* shaped by racial prejudice, violence, and inequality in Brazil, the episodes presented here indicate that we should not underestimate the force of anti-Blackness, or the significance of ethnoracialized social difference more broadly, in the historical or contemporary production of space. The geography of racialized inequalities in urban Brazil may not align precisely with other ethnoracially diverse, highly stratified contexts in countries like the United States. That misalignment does not, however, automatically correspond to insignificance. Finally, the cementing of anti-Blackness into the infrastructure of the city of São Paulo in the mid-twentieth century suggests that comparably ambitious projects, programs, and practices of repair will be necessary to achieve durable and lasting change in the twenty-first.

THREE

Neighborhoods of Mixture and Massacre

Seventy years after the unofficial settlement of Vila Brasilândia (Brazil-land Village), Google Maps could not correctly identify the location of the neighborhood. Google's digital cartographers placed Vila Brasilândia four kilometers south of its actual location (figure 3.1 and map 3.1). Their mistake was, in part, understandable: Real estate developers originally settled Vila Brasilândia off the map, selling the first parcels in 1947 without official approval from the municipal government and generating decades of spatial confusion. Perhaps accidental, Google's cartographic error was, nonetheless, revealing. Their misplaced neighborhood label covered up a place named Vila do Congo (Congo Village).[1]

Adjacent to Congo Road and Congo Creek, the Congo Village place-name reflected the high population of Africans and their descendants in the surrounding parish, Nossa Senhora do Ó (N. S. do Ô).[2] The present-day superimposition of Vila Brasilândia over Vila do Congo captures a core dynamic in the neighborhood's early history. From 1947 to 1966, city officials and prominent White residents sought to bury sites associated with African descendants in Brasilândia and replace them with a microcosmic "Brazil-land" that both reflected and engendered a nationalistic, and particularly Paulistano, ideal of harmonious ethnoracial mixture.[3]

FIGURE 3.1 · Vila Braslândia, incorrectly positioned, on Google Maps, 2017. This misplaced label is covering up the location of another place named Vila do Congo.

This chapter charts the history of Vila Brasilândia from its foundation in 1947 through 1966, when local residents literally purchased a place for the neighborhood on São Paulo's official map.[4] While the chapter focuses on the foundation of this singular neighborhood, the history of Vila Brasilândia reflected citywide patterns of migration, redevelopment, and the production of ethnoracialized space. The 1930s–1940s execution of city planner-turned-mayor Francisco Prestes Maia's redevelopment project, the Avenues Plan, displaced center-city populations to the city's rural outskirts. There, residents bought cheap lots and constructed neighborhoods such as Vila Brasilândia from scratch. Within two decades, the informally settled Vila Brasilândia neighborhood would

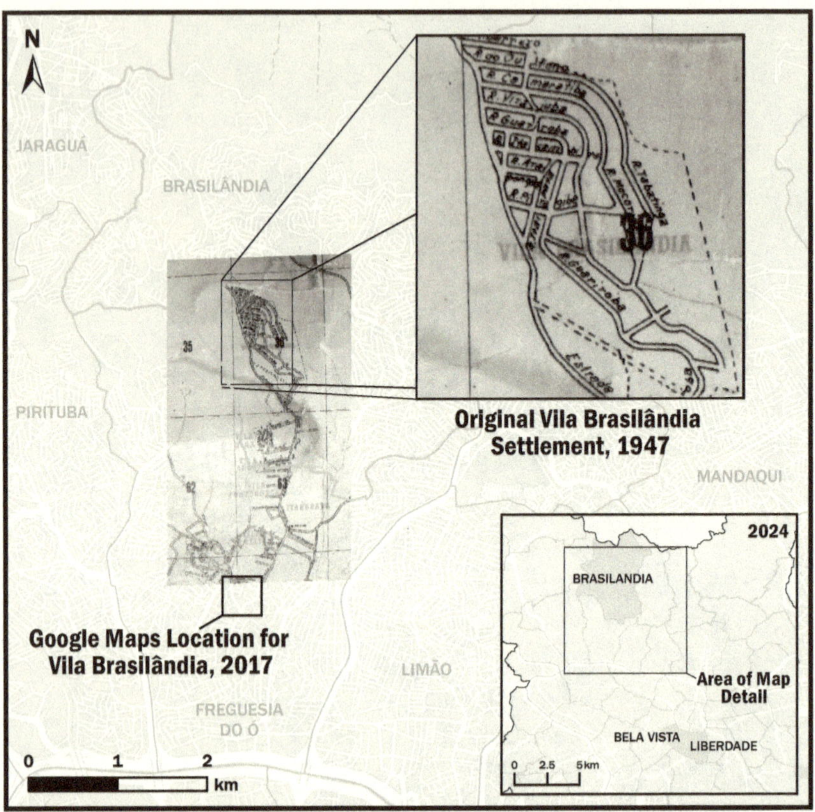

MAP 3.1 · Correct and incorrect locations of the original Vila Brasilândia settlement. Georeferenced basemap is from Osvaldo Nascimento, "Planta da cidade de São Paulo," 1947, Arquivo Histórico Municipal Washington Luis. Other map data sources: GeoSampa; OpenStreetMap (Light Gray Canvas) © OpenStreetMap contributors, Microsoft, Facebook, Google, Esri Community Maps contributors, map layer by Esri. Map by Andrew G. Britt.

become an official subdistrict encompassing approximately thirteen neighborhoods and more than 45,000 residents.

These new neighborhoods were also the products of migration networks that stretched throughout a globally connected Brazil. An array of migrants—ranging from residents of São Paulo's city center and migrants from Brazil's Northeast to Italian and Japanese immigrants and their descendants—settled in and constructed Vila Brasilândia from the 1940s to the 1960s. Amid center-city urban reforms, anti-immigrant prejudice during and following World War II, and interregional migration, some of these newcomers connected over shared experiences of migration and displacement. This population influx and the social cohesion generated among some residents would give credence to the idea of Vila Brasilândia as a microcosm of the nation, constitutive with the ideal of harmonious ethnoracial mixture at the heart of officials' constructions of Brazilianness (*brasilidade*) in this era.

The title of this chapter takes inspiration from Abdias do Nascimento's 1979 collection of essays, *Brazil: Mixture or Massacre? Essays on the Genocide of a Black People*. Penned just a year after the founding of the Unified Black Movement (MNU) and still in the midst of the military dictatorship's strident promotion of the "racial democracy" ideology, Nascimento offered a scathing critique of the centrality of anti-Black violence in Brazil over the long duration and of the "subtle, diffuse, evasive, asymmetrical" character of Brazilian racism.[5] As indicated by the collection's title, Nascimento saw that long duration history as defined by massacre, not mixture. In this chapter, and throughout the book, I aim to show how massacre—defined as anti-Black violence expressed through dispossession, demolition, dislocation, and disinvestment—took place, literally and figuratively, through neighborhood spaces celebrated as sites of mixture. Vila Brasilândia was an exemplary, though not singular, place where these interrelated processes occurred.

THE BEGINNINGS OF BRASILÂNDIA; OR, "UNOFFICIAL SÃO PAULO NEIGHBORHOODS" IS REPETITIVE

The official from the municipal department responsible for maintaining land records of the city of São Paulo delighted in telling me that São Paulo's neighborhoods do not exist. The assertion seemed remarkable: Since my first days in São Paulo, residents had explained the city to me by describing its neighborhoods. What's more, the city government itself has, for over fifty years, bankrolled a series of books about *neighborhood* histories (thirty-three volumes large as of 2006).[6] Was the neighborhood, the spatial category I understood as the organizing principle of the metropolis, in fact a fiction? The places that São Paulo residents refer to as neighborhoods (*bairros*) indeed possess no official definition.[7] Instead, the city of São Paulo is (and has long been) divided officially by the administrative units of subdistrict and district.

Neighborhoods are constructed through an array of practices, from official cartography that position them on maps to residents who describe them in everyday discourses.[8] *Because* they were (and remain) unofficial, popularly produced, and unfixed, neighborhoods in São Paulo serve as especially mutable categories for the construction of meaning.

If São Paulo neighborhoods have no official institutional basis, then where did they originate? Most mid-twentieth-century São Paulo neighborhoods originated in *loteamentos*, (subdivisions) consisting of the division of a tract of rural land into a street grid and parcels for sale. In a 1942 article, Synesio Cunha Barbosa, a leader of the urban affairs organization the Society of the Friends of the City, described *loteamentos* as "the initial rationale of the city."[9] He asserted, furthermore, that this "initial rationale" had not constituted part of traditional urbanizing practices in Brazil:

> Brazilian cities, in general, were formed without any concern for the future. They erected themselves by chance, which has led administrators today to encounter multiple difficulties like supplying them with water, sewage, and so many other indispensable improvements for the development of the lives of their populations. Innumerable cities confirm this assertion. Narrow cities, serpentine, unaesthetic, and precarious, that, only through violent and difficult means, could they be able to adjust themselves to the conditions of progress that they have now reached.[10]

Barbosa advocated for heavily regulated *loteamentos* as the means for productive, future-oriented urban development. Such regulations would help generate planned, ordered, and well-serviced neighborhoods out of those *loteamentos*. Barbosa's optimistic vision relied on the supposedly exceptional character of São Paulo residents: "The Paulista, hard-working and disciplined, proud of his progress and of the greatness of his Brazil, will make of his capital [São Paulo] a modern city, with a perfect *loteamento*, adequate pathways for future movement and rapid communication."[11] These literal and symbolic pathways to the future hinged on the organized development of new neighborhoods from *loteamentos*.

From the 1940s forward, the carrying out of Prestes Maia's Avenues Plan helped to spur the rapid expansion of *loteamentos* on São Paulo's rural outskirts. Extensive demolitions, especially of *cortiços* in the city center, led many residents to seek new housing elsewhere. The freezing of rent prices by Brazilian President Getúlio Vargas's Tenancy Law (1942), real estate speculation, and extensive migration into the city exacerbated the shortage and unaffordability of existing housing stock.[12] Real estate developers capitalized on these circumstances and met the growing demand with *loteamentos* on new frontiers of São Paulo's periphery. The developers of these projects, named *loteadores*, purchased and subdivided tracts of land into parcels, which they often sold at accessible prices. After the sale of individual lots, the *loteador* often passed the responsibility to new lot owners to construct their homes and, sometimes, other features of the built environment. The main vehicle for São Paulo's midcentury urbanization, *loteamentos* regularly defied guidelines set forth by state institutions and were often established without official approval.[13] Architectural historian Nabil Bonduki describes the scale and implications of *loteamento* development in this era: "Between 1940 and 1950, around one hundred thousand families, more than half a million people, began to live in and own their own homes. The great majority of them lived in peripheral *loteamentos*. . . . To confront and dominate the periphery came to be a daily task of hundreds of thousands of workers, who constructed in silence a city much larger than official São Paulo."[14] The "silently constructed" city referenced neighborhoods throughout the region, including in the forested hills north of the geographical center of São Paulo, where the developer of the Vila Brasilândia *loteamento* sold the first parcels in 1947.

The natural geography of the region in and around Vila Brasilândia was not particularly auspicious for urban settlement. Geographer Aroldo de Azevedo visited the northern limits of the Nossa Senhora do Ó parish in the mid-1950s, near the new *loteamento* Vila Brasilândia, and he snapped a picture from Congo Road. Azevedo cast the natural environment as harsh and inhospitable: "In the proximities of Freguesia do Ó, in the direction of Piqueri and Pirituba, granite alone is visible," he wrote. "A true labyrinth of valleys wide and narrow" crisscrossed the region.[15] Although the granite outcrops could provide for profitable commercial activity, Azevedo suggested that humans could best settle elsewhere.[16] His recommendation would not come to pass, as urban settlement elsewhere in the parish, in Vila Brasilândia, had already begun.

Vila Brasilândia was produced literally and symbolically off the map. The municipal sectors responsible for urban planning and infrastructure did not learn about its existence until 1955, eight years after the initial subdivision and construction of homes. In 1955 José Munhoz Bonilha, the *loteador* and owner of Brasilândia Enterprises of Land and Constructions Ltd., requested authorization from São Paulo's Department of Urbanism for a new *loteamento*. Basing their evaluation on a *planta*, or blueprint, of the subdivision and seemingly no field visits, architects and engineers from the Department of Urbanism and the Department of Works reviewed his proposals and responded with a lengthy list of modifications necessary to bring the development up to code. Their requests ranged from the expansion of too-narrow alleyways to the installation of a drainage system. In March 1957, a city engineer reviewing the project declared: "It seems to us that the development, in accordance with the plans presented, does not find itself in condition to be approved by the City."[17] The officials were unaware that Vila Brasilândia was not a proposed *loteamento* but an already-existing material reality, a decade removed from the first sale of lots to newcomers in the neighborhood.

The earliest residents of Vila Brasilândia faced grave local conditions. São Paulo city councilman Homero Silva toured *loteamentos* like Vila Brasilândia in the early 1950s and reported his observations in the city council. Following a tour of the region in May 1953, he described "30,000 souls" that lived in the area as "relegated to the interior and abandoned by the City of São Paulo." The residents were integrated into the city, he said, "by geography, but they are separated from São Paulo in all other respects." Focusing on asphalt, he lamented the condition of the neighborhood's sole commercial artery, Parapuã Street, calling it "a kind of unpaved country road that could be better classified as a narrow path through the woods, a tortuous route on which various buses have already suffered repeated disasters and in which various people were injured and lost their lives." Mortality surfaced again in Silva's conversation with the only doctor of the region, Luciano Rossi, who reported a staggering 80 percent mortality rate among children under age two. Silva implored his colleagues in the city council with the biting plea: "You must go to the periphery, you must see for yourselves the abandonment in which they are living, or better, the abandonment in which they are dying."[18]

The conditions of Vila Brasilândia spurred far-reaching debate in the city council around existential questions such as "What is a city?" In 1953, councilmember Marcos Mélega argued that Vila Brasilândia in fact did not qualify as part of the city: "Materially, we do not consider a place as part of the city where there are not, at the very least, substantial public services, such as water, light, sewage, telephone, and transportation. What is occurring in these neighborhoods can be considered more as people living in encampments than, truly, people living in the city." Mélega's solution was to bulldoze neighborhoods like Vila Brasilândia and for the state to organize the migration and settlement of the residents into the official city as he defined it. Other council members proposed less destructive measures. Among them was William Sálem, who argued that poorly serviced neighborhoods owed not to a lack of resources but to administrative inefficiencies in the expanding metropolis.[19]

Some city council officials explicitly pinned the conditions of Vila Brasilândia on Prestes Maia and the unequal distribution of so-called urban improvements. In the same discussion where Homero Silva recounted his visit to Vila Brasilândia, councilmember Paulo Serei implicated the architect of the Avenues Plan. "The principal person responsible," he exclaimed, "and guilty for this is Mr. Prestes Maia, who took exclusive care of the center of the city, without remembering that São Paulo was also constituted of poor neighborhoods."[20] Prestes Maia had been out of office for nearly a decade in 1953. Serei's comment revealed that the shadow of the urbanist-mayor still loomed large. His admonition also drew a direct link between Prestes Maia's avenues projects in the city center and the precariousness of peripheral neighborhoods like Vila Brasilândia.

Long-term residents of the Brasilândia district also connected the genesis and condition of the neighborhood to the Avenues Plan. Born in Vila Brasilândia in 1954, Célio Pires became a journalist and cofounded the first long-running neighborhood newspaper. Pires had a keen interest in the history of Brasilândia and conducted interviews with residents who had first settled the neighborhood. Pires recorded the link between dislocation from the city center and the foundation of the neighborhood, with Prestes Maia's Avenues Plan a principal push factor for early residents. In 1984 he wrote that the *loteamento* Vila Brasilândia began "in virtue of the expropriations that occurred in the center of the city . . . from the construction of São João, Ipiranga, and Duque de Caxias Avenues. That region was occupied by old mansions (*casarões*) that, subdivided, functioned like *cortiços*, inhabited by an immensity of families that from there were expelled to make way for the avenues."[21]

In this narrative, Pires describes demolitions and displacement caused by avenues projects northwest of the historic city center.

Planners executed some of these projects in the 1920s and early 1930s, well before 1947 when Vila Brasilândia's developers sold the first parcels.[22] As explained in chapter 1, the Avenues Plan spurred multiple dislocations throughout center-city districts like Liberdade and Bela Vista. For instance, residents dislocated by demolitions for the expansion of São João Avenue in the late 1920s were dislocated once again with the demolition of the complex of *cortiços* in Bela Vista named Vila Barros in the 1950s.[23] It is telling, therefore, that in their conversations with Pires, Vila Brasilândia's earliest residents drew a connection between their settlement in the neighborhood and projects from decades earlier linked to Prestes Maia and the Avenues Plan. While broader structural forces figured into this process, Pires himself pulled no punches in his judgment of the responsible parties: Expropriation, demolition, and avenues-making connected to Prestes Maia's projects *expelled* center-city residents to Vila Brasilândia.

Other Brasilândia residents recall similar histories of dislocation and resettlement. The former president of the neighborhood association, the Society of Friends of Brasilândia (Sociedade Amigos da Brasilândia), confirmed that avenues projects in the city center led to migration and pointed specifically to the construction of May 23 Avenue (the roadway that bisects the Bela Vista and Liberdade districts) as a source for dislocation.[24] Given that demolitions for May 23 Avenue continued into the 1960s, his recollection indicates that local migration to Brasilândia may have continued through Prestes Maia's mayoral term in the early 1960s. Another resident remembered that his aunt and uncle lived in Bela Vista before migrating to Vila Brasilândia during this era. Based on his observations growing up in the neighborhood and stories from neighbors, he also affirmed that center-city demolitions and avenues spurred a stream of migrants into Vila Brasilândia. He further implied that this history was common knowledge among long-term residents.[25]

The developer responsible for Vila Brasilândia, José Munhoz Bonilha, himself also linked the neighborhood's origins to center-city avenues projects. São Paulo's prominent newspaper *O Estado de S. Paulo* published a profile of Bonilha in advance of the forty-eighth anniversary of the neighborhood in 1995. The unsigned article included a description of Vila Brasilândia's origins: "The *loteamento* was a success. Professor [Bonilha] remembers that the then-mayor Prestes Maia began to expropriate the central region to widen July 9 Avenue and many people that lived there afterward went to Brasilândia. 'The prices were low.'"[26]

The geography in this description aligns with the high number of expropriations and demolitions along July 9 Avenue in the Anhangabaú Valley. A skeptic might critique some memories of displacement of Vila Brasilândia residents as slanted by the unevenness of urban development and lack of public investment in the region. That critique is harder to levy against Bonilha, who lived across town in the southern region of São Paulo. Despite being a beneficiary of displacement, in other words, Bonilha's recollections mirrored those of Vila Brasilândia residents themselves. His language is softer than the discourse of expulsion in the quote from Célio Pires: Residents, in his estimation, were not expelled from the city center, they simply "went to Brasilândia." The content of the historical narrative, however, is the same. Bonilha's perspective proves valuable, therefore, as further evidence of the links between demolition, avenues projects, and local migration in a geography that tied central districts like Bela Vista to the origins of Vila Brasilândia.

Settlement in peripheries such as Vila Brasilândia was also organized by the leaders of the FNB. In the same era as the Avenues Plan, the FNB launched a resettlement campaign for African descendants to move to, and autoconstruct houses on, São Paulo's periphery. Paulo Barbosa, a member of the FNB, explained the effort: "Many Blacks began to buy lands on the periphery: in São Judas, São Mateus, Barra Funda, Freguesia do Ó, Bairro do Limão, Cantareira. And all of them were poor, they lived hand to mouth. In this way our movement started at the bottom and went up. Priests, various teachers, politicians, and dentists—all Blacks—came from our movement."[27] As the statement indicates, N. S. do Ó (here referred to as Freguesia do Ó), which encompassed Vila Brasilândia after 1947, was a destination for organized resettlement. The leadership of the FNB also temporarily relocated its headquarters to the Casa Verde neighborhood in the Northern Zone, which is adjacent in the east to N. S. do Ó.[28]

Historian George Reid Andrews discusses the results of this project, concluding that "the campaign seems to have met with some success, judging from contemporary observations concerning the movement of black people into those newer sections of the city."[29] In my research I did not locate or encounter specific individuals in Brasilândia or N. S. do Ó who migrated as a part of the FNB project, and I did not identify records about the effort or its results despite the sizable volume of work on the FNB.[30] Social scientist Reinaldo Oliveira sees this process as part of a broader migration: "From 1940, with the implantation of the ideology of single-family homes (autoconstruction), the poor and Black workforce dislocated itself to the São Paulo peripheries, aiming to reduce expenses and make (*compor*) families."[31] Oliveira stresses the agency of migrants in this process, who put into practice "the idea of leaving basements (*porões*) of the city and marching to the periphery."[32]

It is plausible that the FNB organizers developed the project of self-determination through migration and home ownership in part, at least, as a response to Prestes Maia's Avenues Plan. The execution of that redevelopment scheme included the demolition of housing units in neighborhoods with large African-descendent populations as well as the razing of singularly significant sites, such as the Church of the Remedies. That church sat a few blocks away from the headquarters of the FNB. By planning a move in mass to ostensibly unmapped regions on São Paulo's periphery, FNB organizers imagined and sought out spaces of autonomy. Those spaces would serve in the construction of communities along with Black self-determination through an organized program of social and geographic mobility.

Demolitions, the construction of center-city avenues, and organized resettlement were not the only drivers of settlement in Vila Brasilândia. Prestes Maia's Avenues Plan outlined the canalization of the Tietê River, São Paulo's major waterway, which ran serpentinely from east to west and formed the northern margin of the city. The canalization of the waterway—confining it to a linear shape through concrete borders—would permit the construction of adjoining, high-speed avenues. The predictable flow of the waterway would also facilitate urbanization in the surrounding areas, such as N. S. do Ó, and the construction of bridges connecting the region north of the Tietê River to the city center.

Prestes Maia boasted about the completed canalization of the Tietê in his 1945 book *São Paulo Improvements*, in which he included pictures of himself on a ferryboat on the waterway.[33] Engineers completed, and city officials inaugurated, the Freguesia do Ó bridge across the Tietê fifteen years later. This project would establish an asphalted link between the city center and places like N. S. do Ó, paving the way for local migrants and the creation of settlements like Vila Brasilândia.

The horizontal expansion of São Paulo as a result of the Avenues Plan also led to the creation a more extensive and higher-capacity public transportation system. In 1939 Prestes Maia appointed the Commission of Studies of Collective Transportation in the Municipality of São Paulo, which led to the founding of the Municipal Company of Collective Trans-

FIGURE 3.2 · Inauguration of bus line to Brasilândia, 1949. Photo archive of Célio Pires.

portation, or CMTC, in 1947.[34] This new organization reflected a shift from streetcars as the main vehicle for public transportation to a system based on buses.[35] That shift would be facilitated by the development of the asphalted roadway network in the Avenues Plan.[36] The guaranteed daily transfer of low-wage workers from expanding peripheries to the urban center depended on an effective public transportation system.[37] The extension of the first bus line to Vila Brasilândia occurred in 1949 (figure 3.2), though service seems to have been inconsistent throughout the following decade. Bus transportation to Vila Brasilândia remained inadequate through the late 1950s, when the neighborhood came to the center of a public controversy about municipal transportation. Officials sought to privatize bus lines to distant, peripheral areas like Vila Brasilândia, arguing that their operation was too costly. Critical articles in the press noted that riders along the privatized lines would be susceptible to "changing buses mid-way and [therefore] paying double fares."[38]

In 1958 members of the city council asserted that an "irregular concession" had been granted for the privatized Vila Brasilândia line. Some accused Mayor Adhemar de Barros of having business ties to the company that received the contract.[39] Eight days after the initial story broke, the superintendent of the CMTC, Durvalina Vieira, admitted to irregularities with the following explanation:

> That line [to Brasilândia], despite having been made available for competition, never had a party interested in operating it. With complaints increasing, in the form of legitimate petitions from residents, and there being difficulties for the Company to dispatch more vehicles with that itinerary, it was resolved to give away the contract, in an insecure and transitory manner, until the announcement of a new competition, to a group of people with interests connected to the neighborhood. There is no permanent contract. Just the provision of services, without a secure contract, that will be legalized with the firm that wins the competition for the contract.[40]

Vieira here revealed an aversion to the operation of the line to Vila Brasilândia. Residents had petitioned authorities for reliable service, and the City's fix was to make official the temporary bus transport facilitated by "a group of people with interests connected to the neighborhood." If the accusations against Adhemar de Barros were correct, those interests involved the mayor himself. The controversy over the bus line suggested a prejudice against the neighborhood ("that line . . . never had a party interested in operating it") as well as a willingness among city officials to let Vila Brasilândia's residents fend for (seemingly precarious) transportation themselves.

Despite speeches about Vila Brasilândia in the city council as early as 1953 and the bus controversy in 1958, officials from the Departments of Urbanism and Works seem to have not known about the actual condition of the *loteamento* until after the developer requested its authorization in 1955. As those officials pushed for rectification to what they thought was a proposed development in the late 1950s, they forced the hand of the *loteador* Bonilha. He confessed that, in fact, he had sold most of the lots, and new residents already occupied them. The "planned" development already existed. With Vila Brasilândia residents living on properties that they owned within the *loteamento*, modifications to correct what one city architect described as "grave irregularities" could not be made. Contrary to the shady permissiveness of city officials regarding the irregular bus line, these records suggest an underresourced Department of Urbanism unable to keep tabs on the practices of private developers on São Paulo's swelling periphery.[41]

The conflict between the City and Bonilha escalated rapidly, with both sides reinforcing their positions rather than acquiescing to compromise. Municipal engineer Antonio Fiorito concluded in 1958: "From the motives that were exposed it seems to us, we repeat, the fact the developer sold aquatic lots does not justify the nonobservance of the minimum that is required in relation to drainage and rainwater. Consequently the developer should fully observe our requests."[42] Shortly thereafter, Department of Works Director Marcello de Godoy resolved that "the acceptance of the present development will provoke severe damages to the City, for the exclusive benefit of the developer himself."[43]

Bonilha aimed to turn the tables. He argued that because he sold the lots in 1947, before a new series of urban regulations were passed in 1953–1954, the City could not hold him responsible for the stricter, more recent standards. His argument ignored, of course, the fact that he sold the lots originally without official approval and that he had subsequently misrepresented the status of the development when requesting permission for its construction in 1955. Bonilha, predictably, did not fare well in the eyes of those officials. In 1959, official José Fernandes Berlula wrote that it was clear that "the entirety of the lots has already been sold by the developer, desirous of immediate profits and, also, of dividing his responsibility with approximately 1,400 buyers who, in their faith and respectful humbleness, were certain they were conducting business in accordance with all legal requirements." Berlula derided Bonilha's subsequent legal maneuvering as "clever and Machiavellian."[44]

City officials condemned the clandestine construction of irregular *loteamentos* along with the developers responsible for them. City councilman Farabulini chided *loteadores* like Bonilha as "urban *latifundiários*" who sell lots that they know will "never receive the necessary public improvements."[45] *Latifundiários* were the landowning heads of feudal, large-scale farms, or *latifundios*.[46] The application of this term to real estate developers in the urban context asserted a continuity between *loteamentos* and prior spatial forms characterized by stark inequality and power asymmetries. That continuity likely had an acute historical resonance in Vila Brasilândia, echoing the local history of slavery in the nineteenth century and the sixteenth-century founding of the parish through the large landholdings and enslavement of Indigenous people by Manoel Preto (discussed in chapter 1). The dispute between the City and Bonilha was ultimately transferred to judicial authorities, ending when a São Paulo judge decided that the developer would pay for his actions. In 1965, ten years after Bonilha's request for official approval of the *loteamento*, and nearly twenty after the actual material construction of Vila

Brasilândia, he received a fine of 5,000 cruzeiros.[47] The fine was likely trivial for Bonilha: 5,000 cruzeiros made up 7.58 percent of the monthly *minimum wage* for a worker in São Paulo in 1965.[48] The penalty did not alter or rectify the "grave irregularities" of the urban development itself.

Vila Brasilândia was the earliest of approximately fifty *loteamentos* created in the contemporary district of Brasilândia through the 1980s. São Paulo's historical archives, such as one of the city's principal historical repositories, the Arquivo Histórico Municipal, contain almost no records of these *loteamentos*. I located and gained access to sources about them in still-active municipal institutions charged with regulating urban redevelopment and real estate. These institutions have produced a paper trail in the course of attempting to rectify what they describe as the "urbanistic irregularities" of *loteamentos* settled off the map. These documents, therefore, retain a practical utility less common for the sources in places like the Arquivo Histórico Municipal. Indeed, I was unable to access to some of the *loteamento* records in 2016 because planners, architects, and engineers from the City were actively utilizing them in an effort to address neighborhood conditions in a process termed *regularization*. Map 3.2 displays *loteamentos* within the district of Brasilândia that were registered with the City from the 1950s through the 1980s.[49] In the center is the outline of the original *loteamento* Vila Brasilândia, which is not included in this layer. Its exclusion reflects the circumstances of its founding and long irregular urbanistic status, the consequences of which local residents and municipal authorities have been contending with ever since.

AUTOCONSTRUCTION, BEYOND BRICKS AND TILES: FROM "CONGO" TO "BRAZIL-LAND"

I had no idea what *tijolos* were, and my ignorance seemed to faze Célio. The journalist and long-time Brasilândia resident pantomimed bricklaying and proceeded to explain the original location of the kiln that cooked Vila Brasilândia's foundational bricks (*tijolos*). That was my first visit to the neighborhood but not the last mention of bricks in Vila Brasilândia and elsewhere. A former resident of the Bela Vista district, for instance, would later tell me about how pioneering Brazilian critical theorist and educator Paulo Freire privileged bricks in his adult literacy initiatives. Freire used the word and physical object to spur his mostly poor students, many of whom worked in construction, to question

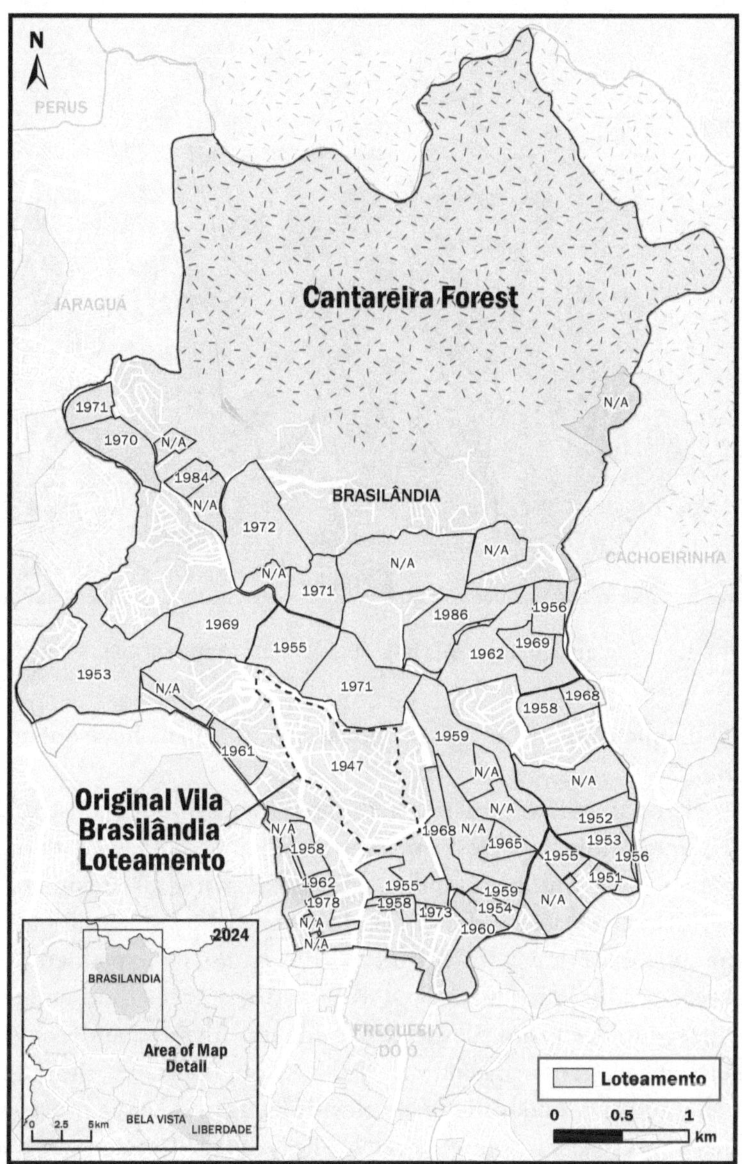

MAP 3.2 · Visualization of *loteamentos* registered with the City of São Paulo in the contemporary district of Brasilândia and (when available) year of charter. Data sources: Arruamentos (ARR) layer, Prefeitura Municipal de São Paulo; GeoSampa; Open Basemap Light Gray Canvas Base—Sources: Esri, TomTom, Garmin, GeoTechnologies, Inc.; METI/NASA; USGS; © OpenStreetMap contributors; Microsoft; Esri Community Maps contributors. Map by Andrew G. Britt.

FIGURE 3.3 · Undated photo of Vila Brasilândia. Photo archive of Célio Pires.

social inequalities, as in: "I make houses. Why don't I have one made of bricks?"[50]

Bricks occupied a central role in the literal and symbolic construction of Vila Brasilândia. In a clever marketing scheme, the developer of the *loteamento*, José Munhoz Bonilha, offered the materials to construct a house, including bricks and roof tiles, to anyone who purchased a parcel. In the 1995 interview with *O Estado de S. Paulo*, he explained: "The brickyard produced the bricks and we gave two or three thousand units and three hundred roof tiles to the residents." The demand exceeded even the developer's expectations: "People would purchase the land on Saturday and by Monday they were already living in at least a provisional house: 'It was so fast no one believed it,'" he recalled.[51] An undated photo (figure 3.3) exhibits what this neighborhood in the making looked like.

As with similar *loteamentos* on São Paulo's periphery, residents produced Vila Brasilândia through the process of autoconstruction (*autoconstrução*). The *auto* prefix denotes that residents themselves constructed homes gradually over time and in lieu of the real estate developer, licensed builder, or state institutions. Autoconstructing residents built São Paulo's expanding periphery from the 1940s through the 1980s; however, the significance of that practice transcended the obvious material utility of bricks and roof tiles.[52] The autoconstruction of Vila Brasilândia as a material place and a neighborhood identity invites an additional reading of *auto* as synonymous with *the self.* While producing the *loteamento*'s built environment by themselves, Vila Brasilândia residents also engaged in the production of themselves. In this process, new and long-term residents alike confronted the region's spatial history of slavery and reconstructed ethnoracialized spatial identities in negotiations over the local built and linguistic landscapes.

Slaveholding, sugarcane agriculture, and large concentrations of enslaved and fugitive African descendants characterized the parish of N. S. do Ó in the nineteenth century. N. S. do Ó served as a waystation for transportation between the city center and the interior of São Paulo until the late 1860s, when the construction of a rail line between Santos and Jundiaí isolated the parish. With negligible population growth and scanty urban development, N. S. do Ó would change little from the end of the nineteenth century through the 1940s, when developers began to produce *loteamentos* like Vila Brasilândia.[53] The developers and autoconstructing residents who produced those new *loteamentos* encountered a built and linguistic landscape that referenced the region's African descendent populations. That landscape included places like Congo Road, Congo Creek, and Congo Village. In the course of the region's urbanization, some residents sought to erase these spaces and replace them with a microcosmic Brazil-land that reflected the ideal of harmonious ethnoracial mixture and proximity. Place-names and roadways served as two principal sites for the production and contestation of this autoconstructed space and identity.

In 1956 a group of residents of Cruz das Almas sent a petition to the city council to replace three local place-names.[54] Situated to the southwest of the Vila Brasilândia *loteamento*, Cruz das Almas bordered Congo Road on its western side. Presented in the city council by council member Agenor Lino de Mattos, the petition called for "the change of the name of the neighborhood to 'Vila Monteiro Lobato,'" and of Congo Road to "Estilac Leal Avenue."[55] The proposal envisioned a renovation of the local linguistic landscape to celebrate the two notable individuals: the author Lobato (discussed in chapter 2 and chapter 4) and Leal, a Brazilian general and minister of war under Brazilian president Getúlio Vargas from 1951 to 1954.[56] These were major features of the local environment: Cruz das Almas was the name by which the local region was identified on official maps, and Congo Road served as a principal roadway connecting the center of the parish of N. S. do Ó in the south with Cruz das Almas and the interior of the state of São Paulo to the north. The request also, significantly, entailed a redefinition of the category of the "Congo" roadway: from *estrada*, a word for road associated with rural areas, to *avenue*, the symbol and way of modern progress that planners had, in the two decades prior, used to reshape the city of São Paulo.

What motivated the residents of Cruz das Almas to petition for the name changes? In a 2006 interview conducted by reporters from a local newspaper, the *Jornal Cantareira*, long-term Cruz das Almas resident Adelina Gomes da Costa Leal provided insight into the popular significance of these names. Born in Portugal in 1944, Leal arrived in Brazil in 1948. She recalls the history of Cruz das Almas as such:

> It is said that in the time of slavery, here close by there were slave quarters. It is said as well that many Blacks died near here, and in memory of the souls of the slaves it became known as Cruz das Almas (Crossing of the Souls). Cruz das Almas Street, today Manoel José de Almeida Street, was the path of Blacks from the slave quarters to Itaberaba.[57]

Map 3.3 displays the geography that Leal outlines. She was twelve years old, and had lived eight years in Brazil, when local residents petitioned for a new name for Cruz das Almas.

Another resident, LS, was born in Vila Itaberaba, a *loteamento* south of Vila Brasilândia and east of Cruz das Almas, in 1928. LS spent his career as a bus driver with routes throughout São Paulo. After marrying, he began autoconstructing a home near the former Cruz das Almas Street, where he has remained ever since. The route of enslaved persons to Itaberaba described by Leal likely passed very close to his home. What's more, his relatives possessed substantial land holdings in this area through the mid-twentieth century, including Brasílio Simões, the man commonly credited with owning the tract that was sold to Bonilha and later subdivided as Vila Brasilândia.[58]

Google Maps positions LS's home within the Cruz das Almas neighborhood. If you repeat this place-name to him, however, he will quickly correct you. His home sits in Vila Timoteo, he explained to me, the namesake of his ancestor Timoteo, whose portrait hangs in the living room of the original part of the house. Historian Máximo Barros asserts that Timoteo was one of the earliest producers of the local brand

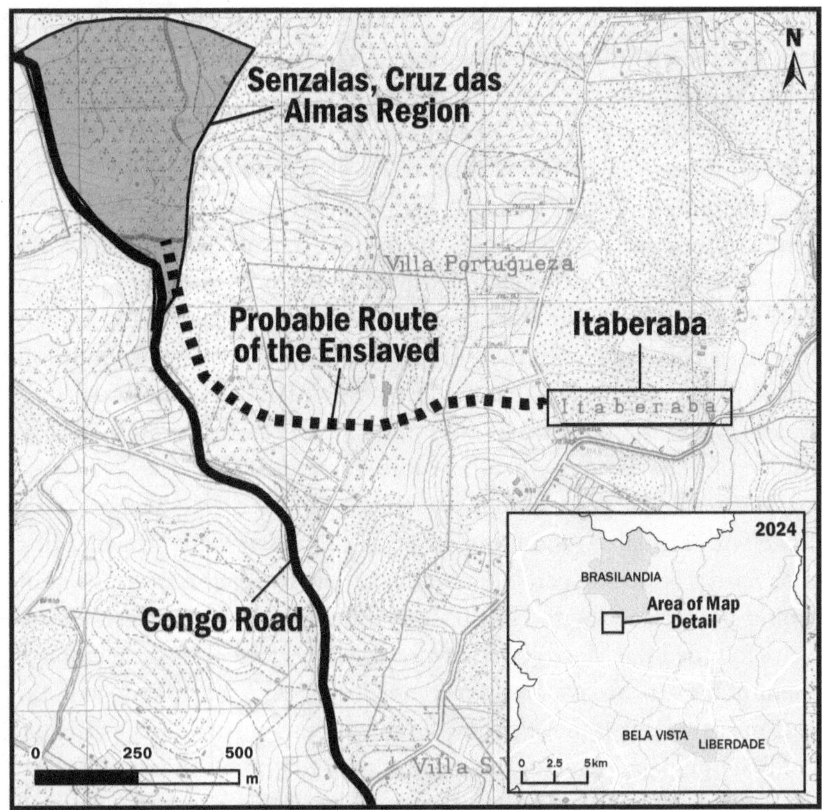

MAP 3.3 · Geography of Cruz das Almas as described by Leal and interviewee LS. Georeferenced map is "Mapeamento 1930—SARA," GeoSampa, accessed June 12, 2018, https://www.geosampa.prefeitura.sp.gov.br. Other map data sources: GeoSampa; OpenStreetMap (Light Gray Canvas) © OpenStreetMap contributors, Microsoft, Facebook, Google, Esri Community Maps contributors, map layer by Esri. Map by Andrew G. Britt.

of cachaça, the Caninha do Ó.[59] LS's insistence on the preservation of the place-name of his ancestor reflects a familial pride. That pride is especially acute because most of the inheritors of these landholdings sold to *loteamento* developers in the middle of the twentieth century. His emphasis on "Vila Timoteo" also echoes the petition from Cruz das Almas residents sixty years earlier. LS aims to maintain the identity of the space in popularly imagined, if not official, geographies with a name that recalls his ancestor, not local African descendants.

São Paulo's city council did not approve the 1956 request to rename Cruz das Almas, which retains this name to the present. However, in the immediate years following municipal officials accepted other, similar appeals, including the renaming of Congo Road. The stone quarry Morro Grande sat between Congo Road and Vila Brasilândia. Morro Grande was a main source of employment and commercial activity in the region, and its managers seem to have played a fundamental role in the renaming of Congo Road. In 1957 representatives of Morro Grande sent a request to the municipal government to pave Congo Road.[60] Asphalt would ease the transfer of stones from the rock quarry to a processing site a few kilometers south, they argued. Adelina Gomes, who like other residents often measures historical periods by the conditions of roadways, remembers that the "only street that had gravel was Congo Road . . . where oxcarts passed pulling stones from the stone quarry Morro Grande to be crushed near Itaberaba Avenue."[61]

The municipal government consented to replace the gravel on Congo Road with asphalt in 1960, the same year that São Paulo Mayor Adhemar Barros issued a decree to rename Congo Road. The previous name would be replaced with "Elísio Teixeira Leite Avenue—Meritorious." Leite founded the Morro Grande quarry, at this time under the management of his son-in-law, Thomaz Melo Cruz.[62] As a mayoral decree, this action seems not to have produced debate in a forum such as the city council or a paper trail of documentation. Other than the request from the Cruz das Almas residents a few years previous, therefore, I have not located other official evidence expanding on the mayor's motivation for issuing the decree.

The simultaneous asphalting and renaming of Congo Road as an avenue do not seem coincidental. LS recalls that a representative from Morro Grande helped to lead the initiative to rename Congo Road. LS suggests that the unidentified representative's desire reflected a broad sentiment within the region that the name was "not appropriate."[63] The mayor and other government officials may have acceded to the renaming because the asphalting had been delayed. The action likely also, however, reflected a consensus among Morro Grande's leadership and officials that "Congo" was indeed inappropriate. The paving and renaming of Congo Road paralleled the asphalting of city-center sites prominently associated with African descendants in the course of executing Prestes Maia's Avenues Plan.

Some observers describe the stones carted down Congo Road from the Morro Grande quarry as exceptional. Similar to the autoconstructing residents producing a microcosmic "Brazil-land" surrounding Morro

Grande, the quarry's products served in the literal and symbolic construction of São Paulo's and Brazil's future. Roadways, not surprisingly, figured centrally into those constructions. Geographer Aroldo de Azevedo described granite extraction in the northern limits of N. S. do Ó:

> Another economic activity of the Cantareira region consists in the exploration of its diverse granite outcrops, which is carried out by the Municipality of São Paulo, by the State of São Paulo Department of Roads and Roadways, and also by private companies, that from these quarries they extract paving stones for the paving of Paulistana streets and material destined for the paving of roads and civil construction projects. Many of the stones can be found in very visible locations; but there are others that hide themselves in the forest or behind breaks in the terrain.[64]

Morro Grande supplied the raw stone material for the asphalting of Via Anhanguera, a path used as early as the seventeenth century for *bandeirante* expeditions to the interior and reinaugurated in the 1940s as one of the first modern, asphalted highways in the country.[65] Advertisements for Morro Grande echoed the rhetoric and imagery of the *bandeirantes*, the colonial settlers who hunted mineral wealth and enslaved people in the interior of the Brazilian colony and served to expand its territorial reach.[66] A 1948 advertisement from Morro Grande and focused on Via Anhanguera read: "Eloquent demonstration of Paulista dynamism, Via Anhanguera opens new horizons for our economy, by connecting our productive centers, for which it offers a wide path" for the "driving force of our progress."[67]

The Morro Grande advertisement for Via Anhanguera resembled the discourse of Fábio da Silva Prado about July 9 Avenue (discussed in chapter 2) and further emphasizes the high stakes that political and urban planning elites in São Paulo attached to roadways. While Morro Grande's marketing pitched the business as the force paving the path for the locomotive of São Paulo to drive the country into the future, the unpaved Congo Road represented the past. Linked to African descendants, slavery, and Black self-determination, the past seemed to have been considered undesirable by the quarry's leadership and the city officials who approved the name change. They may have deemed Congo Road particularly inappropriate because the raw material transported along it would comprise the building blocks of São Paulo's material and symbolic future.

While Morro Grande commercialized the mineral extraction for large-scale projects in the twentieth century, other records suggest that stones from N. S. do Ó had long served in local construction. In her study of colonial São Paulo, historian Maria Odila da Silva Dias makes the following passing, but significant, reference: "Women would bring stones in their carts for building works in town, or firewood for the inhabitants to use: those who came from Freguesia do Ó travelled along the borders of Santa Ifigênia and, from there, came across the Acu and Constituição bridges, driving their carts towards Largo de São Bento at the heart of the old commercial centre of São Paulo."[68] The observation suggests that residents in, and raw material from, N. S. do Ó had long participated in building the city of São Paulo.

Roads feature centrally in contemporary recollections of residents when describing Vila Brasilândia's history. Resident MB, for example, describes traveling across them between the neighborhood and more central regions of the city. Women would gather in early mornings at a spring in the center of Vila Brasilândia to launder clothes. Following the early-morning labor, they would walk across steep hills to Parapuã Street and then to the nearest bus stop in Vila Itaberaba. The bus would transport the women to more central areas of the city, where most worked as domestic laborers. Roads, in her memories, are rarely paved, with the material substance of clay (*barro*) occupying a central role in people's daily lives. She emphasized the strategies used to traverse muddy roads and arrive clean at work. Most commonly, they used galoshes (overshoes) and switched to clean shoes once they arrived on asphalt.[69]

An undated photo (figure 3.4) from the collection of the journalist Célio Pires shows a group of residents walking down the unasphalted Parapuã Street. The composition of the picture, faceless individuals together traveling down the dirt road, appears mundane at first. The fact that someone deemed the scene worthy of a photographic image, however, suggests they understood this as a meaningful event. Perhaps the photographer was motivated to record residents along the route to or from parts of the city where they had lived previously, before urban redevelopment in the name of asphalted avenues led them to unpaved places like Vila Brasilândia.

The asphalting and renaming of Congo Road as Elísio Teixeira Leite Avenue signaled a continuity in the story of asphalted avenues silencing spaces associated with African descendants in São Paulo. While

FIGURE 3.4 · "Stretch of Parapuã Street." Photo archive of Célio Pires.

one chapter in this avenue's history occurred in Vila Brasilândia, Prestes Maia's original project continued to unfold in the city center. The urbanist-mayor won an additional term in 1961 with the campaign pledge to complete the avenues first outlined decades before, especially the successively delayed May 23 Avenue separating the districts of Bela Vista and Liberdade. Those projects would continue to reshape the material environments and spatial identities of the Liberdade and Bexiga neighborhoods decades after the razing of Saracura, Bexiga Square, and the Church of the Remedies (discussed in chapter 2). Meanwhile, in the northern zone of the city, the silencing of Congo Road and the development of the Vila Brasilândia *loteamento* would also contribute to efforts to remake ethnoracial space.

DISPOSSESSION AND THE ETHNORACIAL GEOGRAPHY OF N. S. DO Ó AND BRASILÂNDIA

Efforts to transform place-names associated with African descendants in Brasilândia took place in what some locals remember as a racially divided region in the decades before and following the *loteamento* of Vila Brasilândia. Recalling this racialized sociospatial division, one local resident described the contemporary area of the Brasilândia district in the north as a locus of Black settlement. He said that Whites were concentrated in areas to the south, closer to the center of the parish, and were unwelcome in the northern region.[70] In an article about the parish's history, journalist and historian Sandra Santos describes a similar geography with a particular focus on religious practices: "Like in other churches in São Paulo, in the central church of the parish there was no place for the religiosity of Black people, whose geographic space, since very early, was delimited: The periphery of the parish is Black; the center of the parish is White."[71] An 1855 land record notes the existence of a place popularly named Mandinga in Morro Grande, which is today the northern region of Brasilândia.[72] This name is prominently associated with African descendent spiritual practices.[73] We will find further support for this geography in the final section of this chapter, which traces the creation of São Paulo's first officially registered *terreiro de Candomblé* in Brasilândia in the late 1950s.

While few records survive to shed light on this geography of racial segregation, land records provide some insight into the potential concentration of African descendants in the northern reaches of N. S. do Ó. The following announcement ran in *O Estado de S. Paulo* in 1879: "Emancipations: Refer to the *Tribuna* [another newspaper] that Dona Joaquina Alves de Siqueira died leaving free seventeen slaves she possessed, bequeathing to them a large farm (*sítio*) in Freguesia do Ó and a house in the city."[74] Siqueira's 1874 will provides more details about the inheritance, including the names of some of the individuals who gained their freedom and property upon her death:

> And by not having any older relatives, nor descendants, for the lady to freely dispose of her goods, I leave them to my freedman (*liberto*) Francisco Alves, who I institute as the universal heir. I confirm the liberty I granted to Ignacio, Benedicta, and as such to Benedita, their daughter, João Pedro, Anna, Antonio, and Balbina, whose freed papers you will find registered in the records of the first and second notary. . . . These freed people are to serve me while alive and I will send each one [illegible] from their work and they will say six masses for my soul.[75]

These freedpeople may have been part of a settlement of African descendants in the northern reaches of N. S. do Ó. The name Francisco

Alves Siqueira appears on an eligible voter list from the region in 1906, suggesting that the executor of her estate remained in N. S. do Ó.[76] The name Siqueira also appeared in *loteamento* projects in areas adjacent to Vila Brasilândia in decades following, including Vila Siqueira Penteado to the southeast.[77] The appearance of Siqueira in other *loteamentos* makes it plausible that the original *sítio* was located in one of those areas. Francisco Alves de Siqueira's *sítio* might have spurred the settlement of other African-descendent freedpeople after those original seventeen in the late nineteenth and early twentieth centuries, creating an enduring settlement among African descendants.

We find an additional, though still sketchy, clue about the region's racialized social geography in the original deed of sale for the Vila Brasilândia *loteamento*. There was a surprising degree of ambiguity in the record of sale, which read:

> This tract, which they together own and in the following proportions—of the following signees: Dona Esperança Alves de Oliveira had one-fourth of said farm in the will of Dona Francisca Maria de Jesús, processed by the 4th Notary of Orphans of the capital, ratified on October 13, 1919, and transcribed under number 13,785 in Record of the 2nd Circumscription (Circunscrição) of this region; Ernesto Alves de Oliveira and his wife had a sixth in the same will, according to transcription number 10,279 of the same Record of the 2nd Circumscription; and each one of the remaining grantors had a dozen grandparents on said farm, in the inventory of dona Julia Alves de Oliveira Simões.[78]

The sale occurred in an official context recorded by a notary, yet the precise ownership of *more than half* of the farm was unaccounted for. Esperança Alves de Oliveira possessed a fourth and Ernesto Alves de Oliveira and his wife owned a sixth, totaling 41.67 percent. The record describes the other approximately 60 percent of the *sítio* as having been occupied (or still being occupied) by the vague quantity of "dozens" of grandparents presumably related to those selling the *sítio* to the *loteador* Bonilha. The record describes those grandparents as listed in the will of Julia Alves de Oliveira Simões, and an obituary for a person by that name ran in a newspaper article in 1929.[79] Who were these dozens of grandparents? Were they still alive? If so, why had they not been present at—or at least mentioned by name—in the selling of what was, ostensibly, their property? If not alive, why were their wills not cited as proof that those listed as selling that sixty percent of the property were the lawful inheritors of it?

The lack of clarity about the ownership of the original nucleus of Vila Brasilândia raises important questions about land transfer across time and the details of the original sale. Given what records suggest about the large presence of African descendants in N. S. do Ó, especially in the north of the parish, the urbanization of this region through the *loteamento* of Vila Brasilândia may have constituted the dispossession of lands held by African descendants.[80] The connection between an unclear bill of sale and possible dispossession was not unique to Vila Brasilândia. In her study of Indigenous struggles for land access and dispossession throughout the city of São Paulo, including in the district adjacent to Brasilândia, geographer Camila Salles de Fária encountered similar ambiguities in the archival record. Through a meticulous dissection of land records in the Jaraguá region, which is today home to one of the city's officially recognized Indigenous territories, Salles documents numerous examples of public notaries having certified land sales in the 1920s without proper documentation and on what those notaries successively described as the good faith that came from having a personal relationship with the seller or sellers.[81]

Salles's research increases my suspicion that the original *loteamento* of Vila Brasilândia may have involved dispossession. The extant sources do not provide sufficient evidence to settle these suppositions, however. The name, or names, of the *sítio* itself are not identified in the original deed of sale, and to date I have not located the land ownership records from the late nineteenth or early twentieth centuries that corresponded to this space. Those records would likely provide information that could be cross-referenced with other sources to compile a more complete picture of occupation and property ownership in the region before the 1947 sale.

The development of Vila Brasilândia would reshape the region's ethnoracialized geography in ways that mirrored prominent nationalist discourses about harmonious ethnoracial mixture. LS credited the *loteamento* with improving the racial segregation that had divided the parish of N. S. do Ó. The establishment of the new urban settlement, he asserted, reduced divisions and established greater physical and social proximity.[82] This process of integration was also aided by the diversification of the resident population through vast local and regional migration.[83] In addition to the erasure of certain sociospatial relations and histories, therefore, the urban development of Vila Brasilândia had a futurist orientation that involved a racialized reimagining of the composition of the nation through local neighborhood space.

The name of the new *loteamento* reflected this futurist orientation. At least two stories offer explanations for the origin of the name "Brasilândia." One indicates that the name was almost an afterthought. The credited owner of the original tract, Brasílio Simões, arrived at the notary to register the then-nameless area before selling it to the developer Bonilha. The notary indicated that Simões would have to choose a name. He decided to give his own, thereby creating the "land of Brasílio," with Brasilândia. Supporting this version of the history, the neighborhood newspaper *O Jornal da Brasilândia* indicates that Simões "was the inspiration for the *loteamento*."[84] The second story holds that the name came from Bonilha himself. The 1995 article in *O Estado de S. Paulo* backs this version: "The patriotism of Bonilha was decisive in deciding the name of the village. 'I always liked anything related to the name Brazil,' he affirmed. 'I named the company Brasilândia Enterprises of Land and Construction and, later, the place Brasilândia itself,' he recounts. 'It stuck.'"[85] The fact that the development company also bore the name, and that the source comes directly from him, leads me to see Bonilha's story as the more accurate version. Whichever of the origin stories is correct (if either), local residents likely interpreted "Brazilland Village" as a space deeply interwoven with nationalist constructions of identity.

The practice of constructing the nation through urban space extended far beyond Vila Brasilândia in this era. On the federal level in the 1950s, urban planners, architects, and politicians designed nationalist development schemes around modern urban forms. Brazilian president Juscelino Kubitschek (1956–1960) committed to "50 years of development in five," with the crown jewel of his program the city of Brasília, to be the nation's new capital.[86] Designed by internationally renowned architect Oscar Niemeyer and urban planner Lúcio Costa, Brasília celebrated the ascendant country and paved a concrete path for its continued progress. The construction of Brasília drew migrant laborers from around the country, including some residents from Vila Brasilândia.[87] As those residents built the nation symbolically through the new national capital, they also autoconstructed Brazil and Brazilianness on the local scale of the neighborhood. In silencing spaces associated with African descendants, especially the places named Congo in N. S. do Ó, some of the early producers of "Brazil-land Village" endeavored to create an urban space that both reflected and engendered ideals of ethnoracial harmony, proximity, and mixture. Crucially, however, those ideals of mixture privileged non-Blackness and, thus, the massacre of African descendants.

SPACES OF MIXTURE THROUGHOUT SÃO PAULO: THE "BRASILANDENSE RACE" AND JAPANESE-BRAZILIAN BANDEIRANTES

Vila Brasilândia appeared in São Paulo's mainstream press for one of the first times in the year following the clandestine sale of its first lots. Headlined "With 10,000 Residents and 3,000 Buildings, Vila Brasilândia Continues Without Transportation," the 1948 *Jornal das Notícias* article described the place as a quintessential São Paulo neighborhood, defined by rapid growth and ethnoracial mixture:

> São Paulo is a metropolis that grows dizzyingly. Neighborhoods that emerged yesterday today are true cities, with their necessities, their suffering, and their problems. As during the war, whose effects we feel even now, the city does not stop growing. Skyscrapers continue rising here and there, the population grows considerably, *individuals of all races and all creeds*, they come here to try their luck, with that very human and understandable desire to find a better life. New neighborhoods appear miraculously, attesting to the capacity for progress and achievement among our people.[88]

The influx of populations of "all races and creeds" into Vila Brasilândia aided efforts to remake the geography of the northern region of N. S. do Ó in an image of harmonious ethnoracial mixture. That effort was not confined to Vila Brasilândia, however.

Officials and individuals connected to state institutions in São Paulo throughout the 1940s and 1950s, especially in the context of World War II, expressed preoccupations about the ethnoracial distribution of immigrant and non-White populations in space. Displacement spearheaded by state officials, combined with networks of more willing migration, helped to create neighborhoods of ethnoracial mixture. In the face of the official premium on mixture, some residents responded by producing alternative, unofficial spaces that facilitated the maintenance of distinctive cultural identities and practices. This section charts the production and negotiation of such spaces of mixture with a focus on Vila Brasilândia, São Paulo's first "Japanese neighborhood" (Conde de Sarzedas), and public monuments designed to symbolize harmonious ethnoracial relations.

From the 1940s to the 1960s, migrants from the center of the city of São Paulo, the interior of the state of São Paulo, Minas Gerais, and the North and Northeast regions of Brazil all constructed Vila Brasilândia. Italian, Japanese, and Portuguese immigrants and their descendants lived alongside longtime White and non-White residents whose roots stretched deeper into N. S. do Ó's past, including a high concentration of Africans and their descendants.[89] The influx of migrants propelled what the 1948 *Jornal das Notícias* article described as a "frightening" rate of population growth in Vila Brasilândia.[90] Urbanist Jorge Wilhelm calculated N. S. do Ó (inclusive of Vila Brasilândia) among the top five fastest-growing districts in São Paulo in the 1950s in terms of population.[91] Sparse records mean that estimates about numbers and the composition of the population in the 1940s vary drastically. For instance, while the article above estimates 10,000 residents in 1948, councilmember Homero Silva suggested 30,000 in 1953, and some city urbanists indicated 1,400 in 1959. This inconsistency may have reflected the imprecision of the limits of Vila Brasilândia: Observers like Silva may have calculated 30,000 based on a geography that encompassed the entirety of the northern section of the N. S. do Ó parish (i.e., multiple *loteamentos*), while city urbanists might have restricted their estimates to the borders of the Vila Brasilândia *loteamento* itself.

The image of Vila Brasilândia as a space of ethnoracial mixture appears prominently in early editions of *O Jornal da Brasilândia*, the first long-running neighborhood newspaper. This publication printed some of the first written accounts of local history through interviews with older residents in the 1970s and 1980s. Similar to the recollections of LS already discussed, the newspaper's articles celebrated the foundation of the Vila Brasilândia *loteamento* as a triumph of multiculturalism owing especially to the influx of immigrants. An article in one of the earliest editions, headlined "The Founders of the *Brasilandense* Race," privileged Italian, Japanese, Spanish, and Portuguese immigrants as the pioneers of the neighborhood.[92] The piece represented the place as quintessentially Brazilian because of its multiethnic immigrant and immigrant-descendent populations. That celebratory discourse also connected the foundation of the neighborhood to the creation of a new race: the "*Brasilandense* race." In doing so, the article collapsed biological, ethnoracial, and spatial referents of belonging into a new, ethnoracialized neighborhood identity construct. African-descendent residents, long prominent in the region, were rendered invisible in that representation.

Another, more recent celebratory narrative about the neighborhood's foundation, compiled in a 2006 documentary, privileges Italian and Japanese immigrants and their descendants in the neighborhood's foundation. Produced with financial support from the City of São Paulo, the documentary is titled "The Brasilândia District and its Histories." The first two interviewees are Dante Coiro, born in Santo Arsênio, Italy, and Lídia Yamasaki, whose father's family immigrated to Brazil from Japan. The documentary weaves their stories, which stretch across the globe, into Vila Brasilândia's origin story. Coiro recalls a double displacement in his recollection of transatlantic and local migration. His family fled Italy during World War II and settled in a *cortiço* in the center of São Paulo, which he characterizes as peopled largely by Italians. The demolition of that *cortiço* in the context of the Avenues Plan required the family to move again, this time to Vila Brasilândia. Depicting the founders of Vila Brasilândia as unified by shared experiences of dislocation and hardship, Coiro explained that the neighborhood was founded "by the humblest people: Northeasterners, people from the interior, foreigners."[93]

As in the article about the "*Brasilandense* race," however, the 2006 documentary about Vila Brasilândia's history privileges the presence of immigrants and their descendants. The region's historic and contemporary African-descendent populations remain unrecognized until a prominent local samba musician, Luiz do Pandeiro, appears with the film's score. In another allusion to the salience of roadways in Brazilian social life, the principal line of his song runs, "The roads were just *poeira* [dirt] . . . our cinema made just from *madeira* [wood]." The visibility of African descendants increases as the documentary continues, especially through interviews with actor and musician known as Black Gero, whose family lived in Bela Vista before moving to Brasilândia.[94]

While praising the immigrants who helped to found Brasilândia, the documentary also highlights the prejudices that Japanese-Brazilians faced during and in the decade following World War II. Brazil's entry into the war on the side of the Allies, combined with the emergence of militant secret societies (among the most well-known being Shindo Renmei), fueled both official and popular anti-Japanese sentiment in this period.[95] During the fascist-inspired Estado Novo regime (1937–1945), Brazilian president Getúlio Vargas initiated a Brazilianization campaign that would affect Japanese immigrants and their descendants. The "homogenization program," historian Jeffrey Lesser writes, "sought to preserve Brazilian identity from the encroachment of ethnicity by eliminating distinctive elements of immigrant culture."[96] Especially after 1942, officials in São Paulo sought to disperse concentrations of Japanese-Brazilian populations. Officials targeted the space that journalists and some residents had deemed the city of São Paulo's first "Japanese" neighborhood, Conde de Sarzedas (named after the street along which it sat), which was located just north of the contemporary Liberdade district.

Most Japanese immigrants in the early twentieth century worked in agriculture on rural colonies (*colônias*) in the interior of São Paulo and the adjacent state to the south, Paraná.[97] From 1912 forward, some Japanese immigrants and their descendants began to establish an urban "colony" in the city of São Paulo along Conde de Sarzedas Street. In popular discourse, this place was both a street and a neighborhood, though the name derived most obviously from the roadway along which it stretched.[98] Conde de Sarzedas attracted immigrants and rural-to-urban migrants because of its proximity to employment opportunities in the city center and the availability of cheap housing.[99] Demographic records indicate that from the 1910s to the 1930s, Conde de Sarzedas Street concentrated the largest population of Japanese families and businesses owned by them in the city.[100] The region's built environment was not decorated or designed to emphasize Japaneseness, however. Author and artist Tomoo Handa explains that "perhaps some imagined that Conde was a commercial street with a strong Japanese color." However, aside from Japanese language characters outside of commercial sites, he explained, "in its external aspect it was like any other São Paulo suburb, with nothing particularly special."[101]

Some observers nonetheless described Conde de Sarzedas as a distinctly Japanese space. A 1936 article from one of São Paulo's most prominent newspapers, *Correio de S. Paulo*, referred to Conde de Sarzedas as São Paulo's "Japanese neighborhood" (*bairro nipponico*).[102] The authors of a 1935 article, "The Symphony of the Metropole," from the same paper delighted in the irony that some Conde de Sarzedas residents born in Brazil nonetheless identified as Japanese. They recounted a telling exchange with a boy along a street parallel to Conde de Sarzedas:

> Are you Japanese?
> I am, yes sir.
> Where were you born?
> Over there. And the boy points to Tabatinguéra Street.[103]

The same article endeavored to explain why Japanese immigrants and their descendants concentrated in a singular space: "They gather in neighborhoods, where they seek to establish the customs of their country. This is human. Any Brazilian would feel at home in a Brazilian neighborhood installed in the middle of a foreign nation." While the author identified phenotypical characteristics of the local population as distinguishing the neighborhood from others, they pointed to the most salient manifestation of the ethnoracialized space as part of the built environment. "Here and there," the author explained, "the crude characters of their complicated language, mark the principle of the Japanese neighborhood."[104] As with other examples, such as Congo Road, the popularly determined, local linguistic landscape served to produced ethnoracialized social difference in space.

Fueled by wartime anxieties, the government-led Brazilianization campaign aimed to impose ethnoracial mixture on the neighborhood scale in places like Conde de Sarzedas. Among restrictions on the use of certain foreign languages (Japanese, Italian, and German), the seizure of assets, and prohibition on schooling, a specific tactical operation sought to displace immigrant families from Conde de Sarzedas Street.[105] Twice in 1942 the Estado Novo police force, the Department of Social Order, forcibly removed Japanese immigrants and their descendants from this region. Historian Sachio Negawa recounts an interview with local resident Mr. Me, who described one of the forced evacuations:

> I believe it was 1942 when an evacuation order was given by the Security Bureau to leave the Conde within 24 hours. My older brother and I went to the police and asserted that we were Brazilians who had even done military service. However, the policeman stated that, "All you people with Japanese faces are Japanese." In the end, we had to close down our business and move out.[106]

Fleeing families would spread into other regions around the city, such as Acclimação, Vila Mariana, and Saúde, leaving Conde de Sarzedas uninhabited in the years following.[107]

Anti-Japanese discrimination in São Paulo also prompted the settlement of Japanese immigrants and descendants in Vila Brasilândia. Lídia Yamasaki (featured in the 2006 documentary previously discussed) was born in Vila Brasilândia in 1947, the same year the developer sold the first lots. Yamasaki's father and paternal grandparents emigrated from Japan and first lived in Sorocaba in the agricultural interior of the state of São Paulo. The family then moved to Pedra Grande, a region north of the contemporary Brasilândia district. Anti-Japanese prejudice prompted the family's next move in the mid-1940s, as Yamasaki explains: "My father was on the farm of a Brazilian who expelled the Japanese, who said the Japanese could not live here. So my father came to live here in Brasilândia."[108] Yamasaki's memory echoes narratives of displacement among other local populations, including Italian immigrants and their descendants and African descendants, when describing the origins of the neighborhood. Those common experiences of migration and displacement, despite distinct circumstances and different geographies, likely created bonds among the varied newcomers to Vila Brasilândia.

The Vargas-led homogenization campaign tried to dissolve Japaneseness by destroying distinctive cultural practices but succeeded primarily in pushing them underground.[109] In the commercial heart of Vila Brasilândia on Parapuã Street, for instance, locals established a Japanese-language and Judo school. The founders gave the school a "typical" Portuguese name to conceal it from authorities. One migrant born in Japan moved to Brasilândia in the 1950s from the interior of São Paulo and opened a watchmaking shop a few blocks north of the school on Parapuã Street. A future president of the local commercial association, he autoconstructed his shop along with an adjoining house, today a sprawling, two-story complex with an elaborate garden. His son traveled a few blocks down Parapuã Street to attend the Japanese-language school through his adolescence. Despite an improved climate that permitted instruction in Japanese, in this era the school retained its Portuguese name, a testament to its clandestine founding during the war.[110]

While displacement and underground practices characterized the wartime years for Japanese-Brazilians throughout São Paulo, the decade following would see public efforts aiming to promote Japanese-Brazilian reconciliation, including through the production of space. In 1952 Japan and Brazil restored diplomatic relations.[111] Parallel to increasing commercial and political relations were spatial projects that aimed to make the rekindled friendship publicly visible and tactile. The 1954 celebrations of the city of São Paulo's four-hundred-year anniversary offered a privileged opportunity for demonstrating reconciliation. The anniversary prompted the construction of the monumental Ibirapuera Park in the south of the city, and celebration organizers included a Japanese pavilion in the space. An external group, the Collaborative Commission of the Japanese Colony for the Fourth Centenary of São Paulo, proposed the idea to the organizers, petitioning "to be permitted the construction, by our risk and payment, of a *genuinely* Japanese pavilion."[112]

Surrounded by a "garden also characteristically Japanese," the pavilion was designed as a "reproduction of the Summer Palace of the Japanese emperor constructed in Kyoto in 1590."[113] Constructed in Japan, the pavilion was shipped to and assembled in São Paulo. There it would serve as a "demonstration of architectonic originality" of the Japanese and serve as an exhibition space for exclusively "Japanese art . . . painting, sculptures, engravings, and other objects produced by Oriental artistic artisanry (folklore)." The Commission organized buses for tourists and festivalgoers staying in São Paulo's center and decorated the route with "typical" Japanese lanterns.[114] Very distinct from the predominately concrete, modernist structures elsewhere at the Ibirapuera Park celebration, the architects of the Japanese pavilion project aimed to showcase ethnically distinct authenticity imported straight from the old country. The public, officially sanctioned, and "typically" Japanese pavilion would also signal a step toward reconciliation. Situating the pavilion within the monumental Ibirapuera Park signified both the maintenance of Japaneseness and a close association of that ethnic identity to regional Paulista and national Brazilian identities. The production of the Japanese pavilion as ethnoracial space was one of the first coordinated efforts of its kind in São Paulo and a crucial precursor to the neighborhood-wide "Orientalization" project that would begin to remake Liberdade in the 1960s (the subject of chapter 5).

In addition to the Japanese pavilion, the Collaborative Commission of the Japanese Colony organized a bilingual publication, the *Album of the 4th Centenary of the Foundation of São Paulo*. A message from Brazilian president Getúlio Vargas in the album linked São Paulo's prosperity to the contributions of Japanese immigrants and their descendants. Vargas's comments betrayed a continued preoccupation with ethnic difference and nationalist integration: "The sentiment of cordial hospitality," he stated, "will serve, without question, as incentive for the continued productive efforts of the Japanese colony and its complete identification with the people and customs of our country."[115] Jânio Quadros, then mayor of São Paulo, penned a more grounded message, praising Japanese-Brazilian skill at growing tomatoes, cotton, and potatoes, in addition to their work in the "rationalization and technical advancement of farming itself."[116] This measured praise was less ambiguous in one of the album's full-page images (figure 3.5). The image depicts a *bandeirante* towering over São Paulo's cityscape and saluting the unified flags of the state of São Paulo, Brazil, and Japan. In addition to signaling the iconic *bandeirante*'s approval of reconciliation, the image absorbs Japanese immigrants and their descendants into that same historical myth, casting them as quintessential Paulistas along with nonimmigrant, White Paulistanos.

Behind the celebratory rhetoric and optics of reunification, the album communicated a subtler message about ethnoracial difference and space. The "album" of the title alluded to a vast collection of photographs that fell into two categories. The first consisted of before-and-after images of the city of São Paulo that compared iconic sites from the late nineteenth century (well before Japanese immigration to Brazil began in 1908) with images of the same sites in the 1940s and 1950s. Skirting the overwhelmingly rural history of Japanese-Brazilians in the country, the images aimed to rewrite Japanese-Brazilians into the narrative of modern urban progress in the city of São Paulo. The second, more numerous collection entailed hundreds of photos of Japanese-Brazilian families pictured in front of sites of commerce or agricultural production. In addition to the names of the families, the album listed the addresses of their businesses or homes. While concentrated mostly in the state of São Paulo, the range of locations communicate diffuseness. The collection and composition of the photographs stress the productive value of Japanese-Brazilians while simultaneously, it would seem, aiming to alleviate any concerns about the threat of ethnoracial concentration in space.

The authors of the 1952 album might have created it in response to ethnoracial mapping of populations of Japanese descent conducted over the preceding decade. Unlike their peers elsewhere in the Americas, who in this period employed maps to ensure ethnoracial separation, government-affiliated researchers in São Paulo employed maps with the stated goal of measuring, and thereby guaranteeing, neighborhoods of

FIGURE 3.5 · *Bandeirante* saluting the flags of São Paulo, Brazil, and Japan. *Album do IV Centenário da Fundação de São Paulo*, 1954, Library of the Museum of Japanese Immigration.

mixture. In his 1940 study "Ethnic Cysts" ("Enquistamentos étnicos") in the municipal government–sponsored *Revista do Arquivo Municipal*, researcher Oscar Egidio de Araujo wrote about the ethnic distribution of Japanese, Syrians, and Jews in the city. Araujo wrote: "It is in São Paulo where best can be analyzed the many-sided foreign influence over the untamed spirit of savagery, the romanticism of the Blacks and the courage of the Portuguese."[117] He emphasized the exoticism of the "Japanese neighborhood," Conde de Sarzedas: "In periods of intense daytime movement . . . many are the physiognomies of Oriental traits that we see headed for this part of the city. We could even think that we are in some symbolic piece of Japan."[118] Araujo measured the distribution of Japanese populations in the city, calculating an especially notable concentration in one block (presumably along Conde de Sarzedas Street): "In one block alone, with 1.08 hectares, more than 35 percent of the Japanese lived."[119]

Araujo used elaborate methods to map the distribution of Japanese populations in space. He explained his approach: The map was created "by the process of isometric curves devised by engineer Bruno Rudolfer, which consists of the application of the principle of leveled curves in ecological representations."[120] I have not found source materials that outline this methodology in a more accessible manner. Araujo published a map of the Liberdade district, titled "Ecological Distribution of Japanese by Block and Isometric Curves."[121] He explained the importance of research on concentrations of immigrant populations in São Paulo as a matter of measuring assimilation, writing that "some ethnic groups present an accentuated tendency to form concentrations, while others spread themselves out. . . . But, we also arrive at these inevitable questions: Which of these two immigrant groups is more advantageous and what is the grade of assimilation of each? Precise answers to these questions represent, for Brazil, an incalculable importance."[122] Araujo's study was one among multiple conducted in this era that mapped the ethnoracial social composition of in São Paulo. Two editions of the *Revista do Arquivo Municipal* in 1938 also included maps of the ethnoracial distribution of São Paulo's populations.[123]

A map titled "The Region of Conde de Sarzedas Street, the Oasis of Japanese Immigrants, 1910–1940" (figure 3.6) was displayed in a historical exhibit in the Museum of Japanese Immigration in Liberdade.[124] Tomoo Handa created this map and published it in the 1970s.[125] Contrary to the maps produced by researchers like Araujo, Handa's map aimed to preserve ethnoracial difference in the face of an official emphasis on mixture and assimilation. The map depicts commercial and social sites, including stores, restaurants, hotels, a tennis court, and a school. Handa labelled the topography of the region, especially the steepness of Conde de Sarzedas Street, and the location of basements that residents rented, areas where sidewalks sat lower than the street, and places especially humid because of flooding issues. These details emphasized the hardships of housing and highlighted the productive local commercial activity. The map does not, on its surface, depict the neighborhood as ethnoracial space different from surrounding neighborhoods.

The very structure of the map, however, harkens to distinctive Japanese cartographic traditions. Handa's map echoes the style and form, for instance, of the Shōhō castle plans, a series of maps commissioned in Japan from 1644 to 1648 (figure 3.7). Officials from Japan's then political authority, the Tokugawa Shogunate, ordered castle towns throughout Japan "to compile and to submit plans showing the locations of their capitals."[126] The Conde de Sarzedas castle, located near the geographic center of Handa's map and still standing along that street, perhaps reminded the author of this distinct cartographic form.

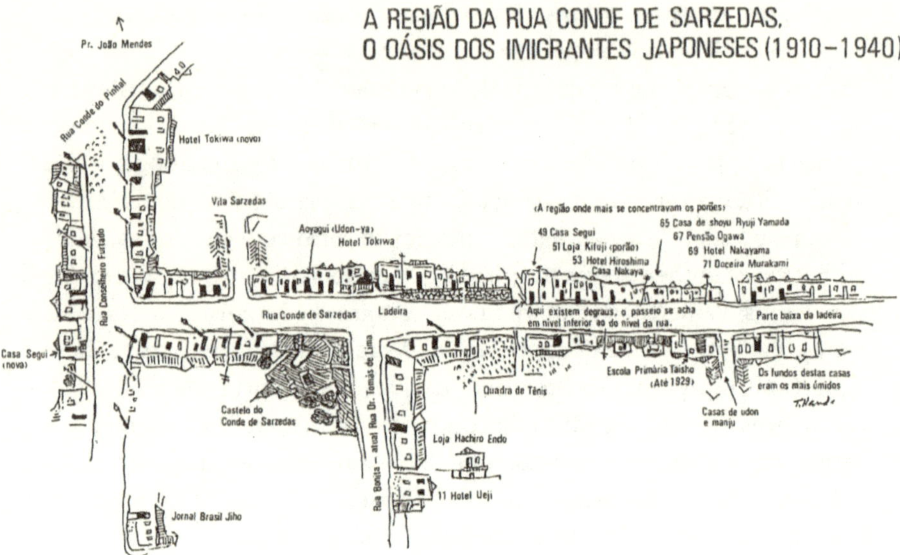

FIGURE 3.6 · "The Region of Conde de Sarzedas Street, the Oasis of Japanese Immigrants (1910–1940)." Tomoo Handa, *O imigrante japonês: História de sua vida no Brasil* (São Paulo: T. A. Queiroz, Centro de Estudos Nipo-Brasileiros, 1987).

The orientation of the map also followed Japanese cartographic customs that differed from Euclidian representations of space in Western cartographic and visual traditions. As historian Kaxutaka Unno explains: "Users would then sit or kneel around them and rotate the maps as necessary, and so multiple points of view were preferred over a single one."[127] By concealing overt references to Japanese identity, the map of Conde de Sarzedas communicated the full potential for integration of Japanese immigrants and their descendants. Yet Handa embedded in the map cartographic traditions preserved from the old country. In doing so, he preserved ethnoracial difference in a way that likely resonated with Japanese immigrants and immigrant descendants.

While Japanese-Brazilians in the 1940s and 1950s negotiated prejudice and assimilation through spaces of mixture, some local African-descendent populations in the same era also contested official projects that privileged ethnoracial mixture and harmony. The organizers of the 1954 celebration supported the construction of a monument to the archetypal Mãe Preta (Black Mother), the idea for which dated to the 1920s. At that time, a majority of the lettered Black elite in São Paulo

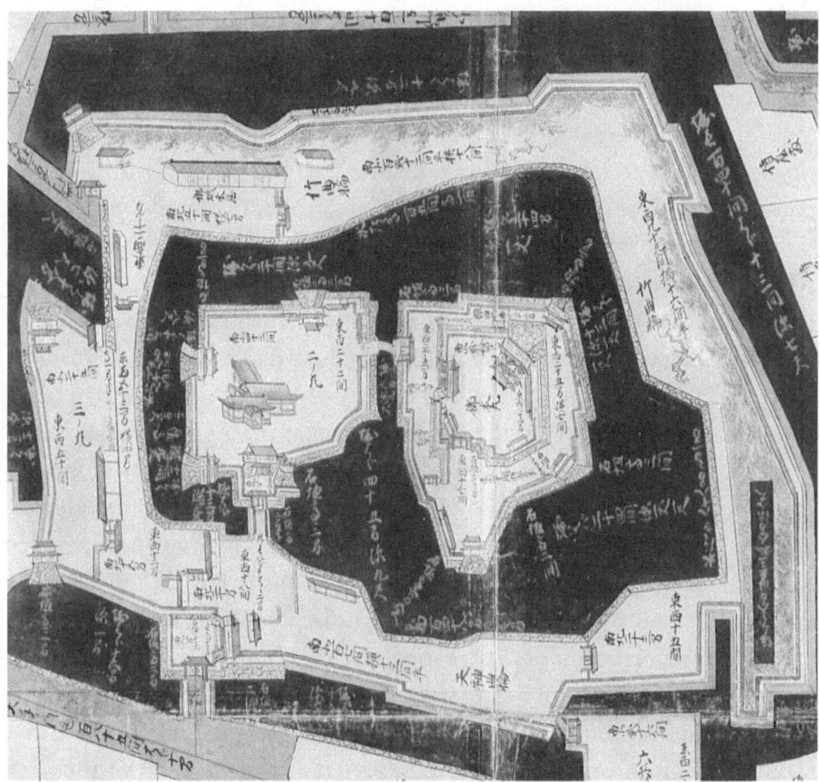

FIGURE 3.7 · Mino-no-kuni Ogakijo ezu, Shōhō castle plans, 1644. National Archives of Japan Digital Archive, accessed June 12, 2018, https://www.digital.archives.go.jp/DAS/pickup/view/detail/detailArchivesEn/0305000000_4/0000000439/00.

supported the monument project as a means "to proclaim the unequivocal centrality of blackness in Brazilian society."[128] Three decades later, the officials coleading the new effort described its significance quite differently. For example, an article from the mainstream paper *Folha da Manhã*, "The Black Mother and the City Councilman," offered the following statement of support for the project:

> This is the great miracle of our generous land that dissolves all into one unity of understanding and love. And those who arrived later also participate in the present of our new land and work toward the creation of its future. But the greater beauty is . . . when the children of immigrants themselves begin to participate in our past, distant from the land in which they were born.[129]

The author interpreted the Black Mother as a representation of ethnoracial mixture and harmony, with all differences "dissolved" into a singular "unity." The *true* "beauty" emerges, however, when immigrants (i.e., "those who arrived later") embody the nationalist ideal of integration and come to identify fully with the nation's past and future. The comment achieves impressive rhetorical acrobatics by celebrating immigrant, ethnoracial integration through the figure of the enslaved, African-descendent mother.

The statue was inaugurated in 1955 at the Largo do Paissandú (figure 3.8), adjacent to the Igreja Nossa Senhora do Rosário dos Homens Pretos (Church of Our Lady of the Rosary of Black Men) that had been saved from demolition during the execution of the Avenues Plan in the prior decade (see chapter 2). The narrative represented by the monument proved controversial: an enslaved woman breastfeeding, a practice that slaveholders commonly required Black women perform for their children. The monument did not draw broad acclaim from São Paulo's lettered Black elite.[130] FNB organizer José Correia Leite, for example, criticized its design, especially the figure's exaggerated features.[131] Historian Micol Seigel writes: "Celebrating the Black Mother's self-sacrificing dedication to the well-being of her master and his family, [the monument] supporters buried any discussion of the present under an unctuous nostalgia."[132] The statue reflected the limited scope of acceptable memorials to slavery or African descendants and brought into high relief the contradictions in the rhetoric of harmonious ethnoracial mixture. Historian Paulina Alberto writes that the silence in reaction to the statue from Black journalists in the period reflected "an increasing disenchantment on the part of black thinkers with the direction that the discourse of racial democracy seemed to take in the mid-1950s."[133]

TERREIRO SANTA BÁRBARA: CONTINUITIES AMID CHANGE FOR AFRICAN DESCENDANTS IN SÃO PAULO

Pulquéria Albuquerque had resolved to stay quiet. She had planned for her lawyer to do most of the talking in the 2016 meeting with the city officials planning a new avenue project. The proposed extension of Avenue João Paulo I, which began at the Tietê River and ran north five

FIGURE 3.8 · Mãe Preta Statue, May 2017. Photo by Andrew G. Britt.

kilometers into Brasilândia, would require the municipal expropriation and demolition of Pulquéria's home. In the two years prior, that residence and the surroundings had been recognized by federal and state historic preservation entities as the first officially registered Candomblé *terreiro* (spiritual house) in the city of São Paulo. Pulquéria's spiritual mother, Manudê, had established the *terreiro* over fifty years before, and Pulquéria had worked to gain official recognition of Terreiro Santa Bárbara from historic preservation authorities since Manudê's death in 2004. With city officials seeking to demolish the site for the extended transportation corridor, Pulquéria decided to speak up for the histories rooted in the space that she and Manudê constructed over decades.[134]

Despite efforts to produce a microcosmic Brazil-land and to erase spaces associated with African descendant from the late 1940s through the early 1960s, newcomers to Vila Brasilândia also produced new spaces significant to African descendants. The migration streams that brought thousands of newcomers to Vila Brasilândia in this period included Julia Lima da Silva, born in Bahia sometime in the late nineteenth century.[135] Lima came to São Paulo by way of the Northeastern state of Sergipe. In 1965, Lima—also named Mãe Manudê (sometimes

Manodê or Manaundê)—registered the Candomblé *terreiro* she had founded in Vila Brasilândia in the mid-1950s with the local notary. This act made Terreiro de Candomblé Santa Bárbara the first official *terreiro* in São Paulo, perhaps the first south of Rio de Janeiro.[136]

Manudê long maintained distance from journalists and researchers. Only a handful of written sources remain about the history of Terreiro Santa Bárbara or her biography. One of the sole sources comes from an interview she gave to anthropologist Reginaldo Prandi in the mid-1980s. Recounting her trajectory to São Paulo, Manudê explained:

> I arrived here in São Paulo and when I opened my Candomblé, I registered my house at the notary as a house of Candomblé. Directly from Sergipe to São Paulo. My spouse had a house in São Paulo and another in Sergipe. Because I had in-laws in São Paulo and when I visited, I gave a party there at the site and they made a *barracão* [place where ceremonies are held], with true Candomblé. But before this I spent time with my mother [*mãe-de-santo*] in Sergipe, where she was sick. I went, talked with my mom and there she taught me, and everything that she taught me I did in my house. I opened the house and my *mãe-de-santo* came to inaugurate it and all of this I did there in Sergipe. It was when this girl here [Oiadeci or Pulquéria?] left from here in São Paulo to search for me and went to Salvador, but she did not find me in Salvador, I was in Sergipe. Then she went from here to Salvador by plane and from Salvador to Sergipe by bus. Her family brought me. She is always with me and *fez a obrigação* of twenty-five years here in the *barracão*. After I arrived here, I did, I also brought her sister [Oiadeci?]. These my two daughters are within the old rhythm really, everything in the old rhythm really. I went making *iaô*, much *iaô* [creating many spiritual children, or *filhos-do-santo*]. I continued here. . . . I came to São Paulo because the family of this girl that I raised there brought me, so that I would work with her. And when I arrived here there was no Candomblé, the first that registered Candomblé was Manudê, in 1965. There was no one that had Candomblé here. For this reason the first Candomblé in São Paulo was Manudê. Here before there was only Umbanda.[137]

The testimony provides a number of illuminating historical details, such as her migration path and social relationships. Manudê also affirms that when she arrived in São Paulo she did not encounter other Candomblé *terreiros*. Two other sources provide further information into the compelling life of Manudê and the founding of Santa Bárbara: oral histories with Pulquéria Albuquerque, Manudê's daughter and the current saintly mother of Santa Bárbara, and a magazine profile, "The First Candomblés of São Paulo—Manaundê, Pioneer of the Northern Zone of São Paulo."[138]

While we know that Manudê arrived in São Paulo from Sergipe, the date of her arrival could have been as early as the 1940s and as late as the early 1960s. It seems that shortly after her arrival she secured employment as a domestic worker in the home of Jânio Quadros, who during these years served as mayor of São Paulo, governor of São Paulo, and then (briefly) president of Brazil. Manudê's first residence was a rental house (potentially procured with Quadros's assistance) in Vila Itaberaba, a *loteamento*-turned-neighborhood just south of Vila Brasilândia.[139] Through the 1950s Itaberaba was relatively sparsely populated, affording Manudê space "to live and play with hands (*tocar com palmas*), clandestine sessions to the *orixás*."[140] The distinction of playing with hands instead of the usual drums (along with the sessions being clandestine, of course), suggests Manudê's aimed to avoid discrimination against Candomblé in São Paulo at this time.

While living in Vila Itaberaba, Manudê began working in the house of the family of the developer of Vila Brasilândia, José Munhoz Bonilha. While in this role one of the Bonilha daughters became ill and the doctor who normally attended to the family could not resolve her sickness. Manudê intervened with a treatment that proved successful. As a recognition of gratitude, Bonilha gave Manudê a plot on Ruiva Street. In the years following—likely after 1958 but before the notarial registration in 1965—Manudê established the terreiro, registered officially in 1965 as Santa Bárbara.[141] Manudê's use of the saint's name may have reflected an interest in appropriating Catholic symbols into her practice, however it was also a strategic move to head off harassment from authorities.

Despite substantial development nearby, the north side of Ruiva Street where Manudê opened the *terreiro* remained nearly empty through the late 1950s (map 3.4). A zigzagging creek, Rock Creek (Córrego das Pedras), ran parallel to Ruiva on this northern side of the low-lying street. The certainty of flooding in the area might have explained the lack of settlement and availability of the land. In fact, Ruiva Street appeared in the City's investigation into living conditions in Vila

Brasilândia in the late 1950s. In 1957 engineers requested copies of the receipts for lots sold on Ruiva.[142] There was no indication in the engineers' documents of why, out of dozens of streets within Vila Brasilândia, Ruiva would be one of only two streets for which they solicited more detailed information from the developer. Given the topography and Munhoz's willingness to part with the land, however, the area may have been precarious from an urban development perspective. City engineers may also have been trying to confirm that Munhoz had given title to those who purchased the lots.

However precarious in the eyes of urban planners and engineers, the stretch of land on Ruiva Street served as an opportunity for Manudê to establish a space of her own. Manudê planted roots on Ruiva Street, taking advantage of the natural and spiritual resources provided by the surrounding Atlantic Forest and planting trees at the entrance to the site. She autoconstructed the place, beginning with an "improvised shed covered with canvas."[143] Pulquéria explains that over the years Manudê carried out expansions and reforms, such as the installation of bricks, by herself. Pulquéria further explains that Manudê produced the *terreiro* with her *orixás*, making decisions about design and autoconstruction in dialogue with spirits.[144]

The production of space is an important part of Candomblé practice. The Portuguese word *terreiro*, "maker of land," itself indicates this aspect of the religion. Crucial to Manudê's project was the making of a covered, interior space with an earthen floor where Candomblé ceremonies would be held, known as the *barracão*. Anthropologist Daniele Ferreira Evangelista describes "the Candomblé *terreiro* as a specific kind of architectural complex—with a building pattern more or less characteristic—where the forces and divine energies act in a way to create and perpetuate the connections with human beings."[145] That interior space was surrounded by a compound of homes where dozens of Manudê's spiritual children lived, many of them having followed her migration path from the Northeast to São Paulo from the 1950s on.

Mãe Manudê faced popular and official anti-Candomblé sentiment. Pulquéria recalls regular police harassment and multiple incidences where Manudê was arrested.[146] Silvio recorded that "it was a daily routine, constantly the police would come by and the persecution took control of her [Manudê's] life, various times it got to the point where they invaded the *terreiro* and even broke saintly objects (*assentamentos de santo*)."[147] Manudê confronted resistance from some neighbors, as well,

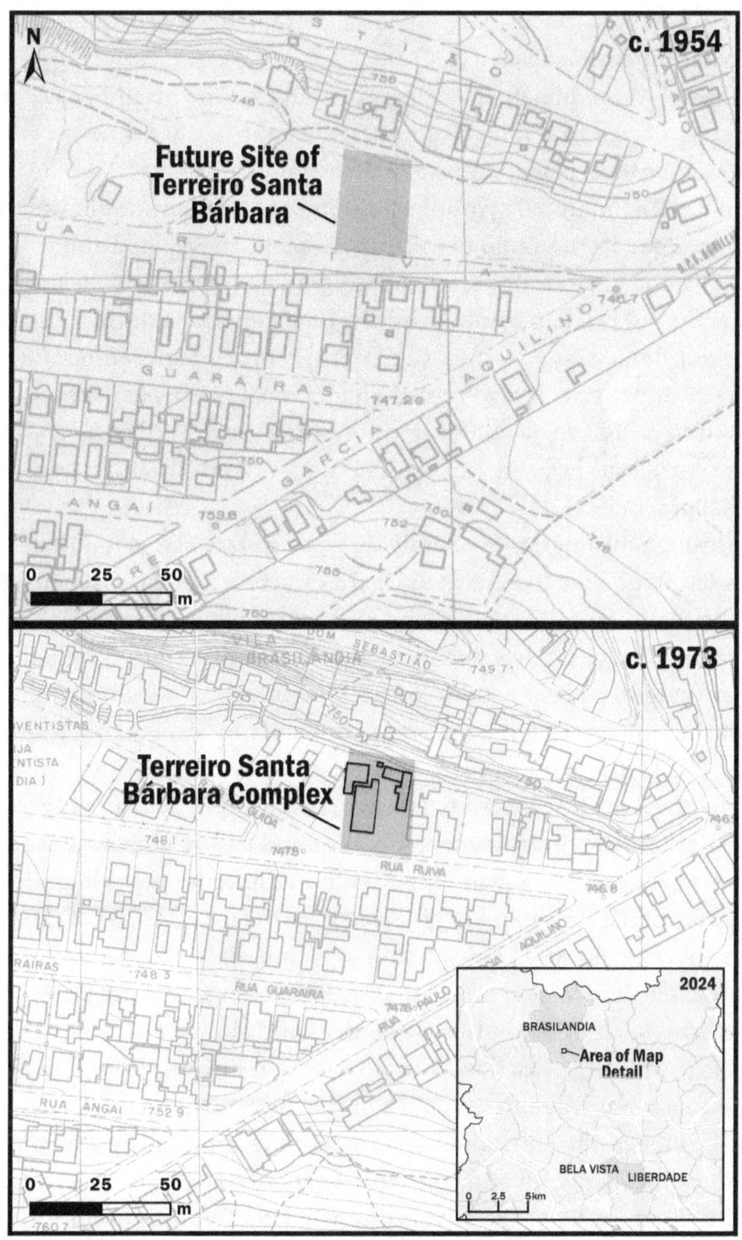

MAP 3.4 · Terreiro Santa Bárbara site, circa 1954 and 1973. The 1954 georeferenced basemap is "Mapeamento 1954—Vasp Cruzeiro," GeoSampa, accessed June 12, 2018, https://www.geosampa.prefeitura.sp.gov.br. The 1973 georeferenced basemap is "São Paulo—GEGRAN," 1973, Acervo Técnico Gegran/EMPLASA. Other map data sources: GeoSampa; OpenStreetMap (Light Gray Canvas) © OpenStreetMap contributors, Microsoft, Facebook, Google, Esri Community Maps contributors, map layer by Esri. Map by Andrew G. Britt.

who, "upset with the installation of a Candomblé *terreiro* in the region," collected a petition against it.[148]

One of Manudê's chief strategies to address the prejudice entailed hanging a large Brazilian flag under the roof in the *barracão* where ceremonies took place, a strategy that Manude used to allay the fears of police. The national symbol would indicate, Manudê believed, that the space and its inhabitants were unthreatening. Situated amid—both spatially and temporally—an emerging microcosmic Brazil-land, the placement of the flag symbolized the contradictions in the discourse of racial democracy in mid-twentieth-century São Paulo. While a strategy of defense, it also represented a local rewriting of the meanings of *brasilidade*, with the symbol of the nation subsumed within a structure that housed African descendent and Brazilian spiritual-spatial practices.

Through the migration of individual priestesses like Manudê and the foundation of sites like Santa Bárbara in urban metropolises like São Paulo, Candomblé practices changed. Anthropologist Reginaldo Prandi describes how cities drove that change. Prandi describes the Candomblé of "Bahia and other states as Black populations' religion," different from the "universalized heiress" of Umbanda in São Paulo. He elaborates: Cities like São Paulo are where "ethnicity is lost, where the gods are involved in the plot of social relations of capitalism already to the fullest, where the time that controls work and leisure already is the time of the salaried regime, where the buildings and the asphalt eliminate the space of the forest and of the beaten earth (*chão batido*) of the gods in the old Bahian way."[149] Asphalt here symbolizes broader forces and change, but it also serves as an active force engendering it: a threat to African descendent cultural practices and ethnoracial identity. The interring of Congo Road with asphalt, which occurred roughly in the same years that Manudê established the *terreiro*, indeed reflected the significance of the substance as a material that buried spaces prominently associated with and sometimes sacred to African descendants.

The production of the *terreiro* signaled continuities despite efforts in Vila Brasilândia and beyond to raze spaces associated with African descendants. Corresponding to high populations of African-born, the parish of Nossa Senhora do Ó was long a locus for African and African-descendent spiritual practices. In her study of African descendants and Italians in São Paulo, anthropologist Teresinha Bernardo finds that Freguesia do Ó was one of the city's privileged spiritual spaces for Black women, in particular: "There were festivals also in remote places like Freguesia do Ó, or even Pinheiros, where the 'drums sang loudly,' in the words of one old Black woman."[150] The distance likely facilitated an autonomy unavailable in more central regions: Black women "did not want to be in the same space, because they did not want to leave their mark; these happenings were the target of persecutions, of discriminations: 'a Black thing,' '*macumba*,' it was 'badness' that emerged from the drumming (*atabaques*), according to the official reading."[151] Bernardo explains that the women who conducted these spiritual practices "lived in places with few residents, the majority Blacks, like Casa Verde or Freguesia do Ó."[152] The remoteness of N. S. do Ó, and then Brasilândia, from the city center provided a measure of autonomy for these spiritual practices.

It may be a coincidence that Manudê established her *terreiro* in Vila Brasilândia, situated within a region that had long been a privileged site for African-descendent spiritual practices. However, the histories in this chapter and chapter 1 point to the more likely conclusion that N. S. do Ó had a special significance as a site of Black self-determination and autonomy. In this reading, Vila Brasilândia provided to Manudê an appealing place where, even if she were regularly harassed, she could practice Candomblé and create a *terreiro* with some measure of autonomy. Manudê could, in other words, productively pursue a spatial praxis that connected the creation of a place of belonging to the ontological condition of survival. Her decision in 1965 to officially register the *terreiro* reflects the relative security that living in Brasilândia, I surmise, uniquely afforded her and some other African descendent residents of the region.

Efforts in this era to produce Brasilândia as a microcosmic "Brazil-land" would conclude with a cartographic victory: What began as an irregular settlement gained a place on official maps of São Paulo. In February 1964 an administrative-territorial reform led to the creation of the city's fortieth subdistrict, Brasilândia (without the "Vila").[153] Two years later, in 1966, a group of local and "particularly active residents" succeeded in getting Brasilândia on the official state map by paying a fee to the Geographical Institute of the State of São Paulo.[154] The process of securing this position—of becoming part of the formal city in terms of cartographic representation—coincided with some notable efforts to erase local spatial histories associated with African descendants and to construct a dominant identity of the neighborhood as a non-Black, multicultural microcosm of the nation.

Such neighborhoods of mixture would provide support for representations of Brazil as lacking the racialized social divisions that plagued other societies in the mid-twentieth century. A 1952 article focused on Japanese immigration from *Jornal Folha Carioca* summarized the official premium on spatial integration in this period:

> Racial discrimination is anachronistic, at least official discrimination. We recognize that there are certain ethnic groups that isolate themselves strategically, always causing hassles of unfortunate consequences. But to officialize racism, this is revolting and inadmissible for a future world that has the present as its beginning. Much less in Brazil, which an eminent sociologist has classified as the sole racial democracy that exists in the whole world.[155]

The author positioned integration and assimilation as fundamental to the futurist project of Brazil and antithetical to "anachronistic" racial prejudice. In postwar São Paulo, multicultural neighborhoods were privileged, local, and everyday manifestations of this futurist project. Neighborhoods of mixture served as the building blocks for a city and a country defined by mixture.

This representation was echoed in Aroldo de Azevedo's 1958 book *A cidade de São Paulo: Estudos de geografia urbana*, where he offered a map of the city of São Paulo's ethnoracialized geography. He wrote,

> From the ethnic point of view, the marks are very visible: Syrian-Lebanese and Armenians concentrated at March 25 Street and surrounding; Japanese, in the blocks around Conde de Sarzedas Street; Jews from west-central Europe, in Bom Retiro; Italians in Brás, Mooca, and Bela Vista; Blacks, in Barra Funda, Casa Verde, and also in Bela Vista; foreigners of varied provenance disseminated in many "Garden City neighborhoods," and all of them coexisting, in the most complete harmony, with those that pride themselves in descending from old colonial stock or from other corners of the State of São Paulo and other regions of the country.[156]

While depicting the city of São Paulo as a place of mixture, Azevedo described, on the same page, the city's growth as "an incessant fever of constructions . . . of popular *loteamentos* executed in a disordered manner, symbolizing the staggering growth of the city, which, in the last few years, has come to construct, on average, one house every twenty minutes!"[157] In these adjacent paragraphs, he connected the city's "disordered," fertile urbanization with its ethnoracialized and supposedly "harmonious" landscape of mixture. Representations like these did not only reflect constructions of *brasilidade*; they also participated in the everyday project of sociospatial nation-building by locating the ideal of harmonious ethnoracial mixture in the urban landscape of the nation's most populous city.

Discourses about mixture at the scale of the neighborhood shaped, and were shaped by, broader currents. Perhaps most famously, in the decade following the end of World War II, supposedly harmonious ethnoracial relations in Brazil caught the attention of officials at the United Nations Educational, Scientific and Cultural Organization (UNESCO), who commissioned a series of studies about how Brazil had supposedly avoided the racial antagonisms and segregation that structured former slave societies elsewhere. Initially concentrated on the state of Bahia alone, the project ultimately expanded to include research teams in Rio de Janeiro, São Paulo, and Pernambuco. Sociologist Marcos Chor Maio explains that the project organizers expanded the geographic scope beyond Bahia because it seemed "important to investigate race relations in São Paulo, a state experiencing rapid industrialization and urbanization and showing clear signs of racial tension."[158] Researchers would, not surprisingly, document racial prejudice and inequality in São Paulo, including through analyses provided by current and former residents of Bela Vista.[159] The urban redevelopment project that remade the city center through demolitions and dislocation in decades prior had likely exacerbated racial tensions in São Paulo.

This chapter examines how discourses about urban space intersected with ideals of harmonious ethnoracial mixture and the realities of anti-Black massacre in 1940s–1960s São Paulo. Those realities would be more widely recognized in the decades that followed, especially through the work of Black movement organizers. At the same time, the ideological power of landscapes of harmonious ethnoracial mixture would also endure and, in Liberdade and Bexiga, be channeled into concrete, neighborhood-scale projects of ethnoracialization.

In highlighting this dynamic between mixture and massacre at the scale of the neighborhood, this chapter suggests that representations of urban spaces that emphasize their postracial, non-Black, or White characteristics in cities like São Paulo may reflect historical projects and practices of anti-Blackness, rather than actually existing socio-spatial realities.

FOUR

Belonging-as-Being

Brasilândia as "Little Africa"

Surrounding a circular table draped with the state flag of São Paulo, the samba composers and Brasilândia residents end each Tuesday night gathering by singing in unison the anthem of the group Samba do Congo. The lyrics resonate throughout the Casa da Cultura da Brasilânida, a community center in the contemporary district of Brasilândia. Many of the musicians share new compositions, ranging from a song about roots samba on São Paulo's coffee plantations to a piece about migrating from the Northeast. The composers distribute the lyrics for new songs on quartered sheets of paper for us to follow and participate in shaping melodies and lyrics. No one needs a copy of the lyrics for the concluding anthem, which we begin somewhat rotely, until the familiar lyrics and driving instruments lift the room's energies:

Paulistano blood
Born in the *terreiro*
Samba do Congo, fruit of Brazil[1]

While founded in 2011, the past permeates Samba do Congo's music and mission. Composers seem to take as much pride in the songs they write as the stories and histories with which they preface them.

The story that binds them together is the former Congo Road, one of Brasilândia's principal roadways that was, I argue in chapter 1, likely a significant site for fugitives in the nineteenth century in the surrounding parish of Freguesia do Ó. São Paulo's mayor approved the renaming and asphalting of Congo Road as Elísio Teixeira Leite Avenue in 1960. That roadway, which the founders of the samba collective recalled from their childhood, served as the inspiration for the founding of Samba do Congo. In their lyrics, stories, and gatherings, the group's members exhume commonly forgotten and silenced histories that extend from the history of Congo Road to encompass pasts and presents significant for African descendants in Brasilândia and beyond.

A research contact in Brasilândia told me about Samba do Congo in 2014. My introduction to the group came shortly thereafter at an event titled "Afro-Bantu Paulista" that featured the *velha guarda* (old guard) of samba composers in Brasilândia and centered on a discussion of the Bantu, or Central African, roots of samba and African-descendent culture in São Paulo. That event paralleled other twenty-first-century initiatives aiming to investigate and valorize the Bantu cultural origins of African descendants in São Paulo.[2] "Afro-Bantu Paulista" and eighteen months of subsequent Samba do Congo gatherings served as key sites in my effort to understand the historical construction and contemporary meanings of Brasilândia as a "Little Africa." This chapter draws heavily on informal conversations, formal interviews, and the music of Samba do Congo played at the Casa da Cultura da Brasilândia and elsewhere in the city of São Paulo.

The discourse of a "Little Africa" or "Black territory" recurs in urban contexts throughout Brazil and beyond. Academics have played prominent roles in chronicling, and also helping to produce, these spatial identities. Perhaps the most notable Brazilian spaces in this type of geographic imaginary are the "Little Africa" region of Rio de Janeiro and the historic center of the city of Salvador in Bahia.[3] "Black territories" have also been identified in regions less commonly associated with African descendants, such as the cities of São Paulo and Porto Alegre, located in Brazil's southernmost state, Rio Grande do Sul.[4] I first encountered a reference to Brasilândia as a "Little Africa" in an article about Black territories by urbanist Raquel Rolnik. Rolnik termed the neighborhood São Paulo's "Little Africa" and noted the especially high population of Black residents.[5] Sociologist Edward Telles made a significant if similarly brief mention of Brasilândia:

Greater racial segregation, no matter what the cause, often means the existence of dynamic ethnic neighborhoods, where ethnic affinities create a greater valuation of shared residential space, promoting cultural life and helping to empower ethnic groups toward greater participation by uniting common interests and controlling political spaces. The case of black (*negro*) districts like Liberdade in Salvador—where Afro-Brazilian music and culture are produced—Brasilândia in São Paulo, and Madureira in Rio de Janeiro are prime examples.[6]

Despite Rolnik's and Telles's comments about Brasilândia's significance on a national scale, very little information is available in either English or Portuguese about how Brasilândia became such a significant space. Nor are there available sources that elaborate on what it means, precisely, for Brasilândia to be a "Little Africa." This deficit of understanding contrasts with the voluminous literature about the other sites Telles mentions in Salvador and Rio de Janeiro. This chapter is an effort to address these inquiries and chart the production of Brasilândia as a space particularly significant to, and prominently associated with, African descendants.

Demographic figures provide some context for the ethnoracialization of Brasilândia as a "Little Africa." In the 1980 census, 24.6 percent of the population of São Paulo identified as non-White (*pardo* or *preto*). In Brasilândia, in the same year, 42.4 percent of residents identified as non-White. This proportion placed Brasilândia second only to the eastern district of Guianazes, which logged 42.6 percent of its population as non-White, among all of São Paulo's fifty-six districts.[7] Brasilândia, therefore, had one of the highest percentages of non-White residents in the city. The neighborhood's population remained quite ethnoracially diverse, however, with non-Black residents representing a majority. What did it mean, then, for Brasilândia to be considered a "Little Africa," and how was this identity constructed?

While the demographic composition of a neighborhood plays a role in the construction of an identity associated with it, the history of Brasilândia and similar spaces reveals the more complicated processes involved in ethnoracialization. As noted in chapter 3, from 1947 through the mid-1960s, an influx of ethnoracially and regionally diverse migrants settled in and constructed (Vila) Brasilândia. Some locals in this period imagined the neighborhood as a microcosmic "Brazil-land," representative of the harmonious ethnoracial mixture at the heart of mid-twentieth-century constructions of Brazilianness (*brasilidade*).[8]

In the mid-1960s, however, the dominant identity associated with Brasilândia began to shift. Spatial projects originating from within and outside of the region would transform popular perceptions of the place from a multicultural microcosm into a marginal region marked as Black and African-descendent.

In this chapter I chart three histories involved in the production of Brasilândia as a "Little Africa" in the 1960s and 1970s, especially: a shift in dominant approaches to urban planning, the founding of a championship samba school, and the application of a racist nickname to the region through a novel "reality radio" program. These narratives concentrate in the period from the mid-1960s through the mid-1970s and reveal both significant instances of anti-Blackness along with the creation of Brasilândia as a privileged site through the spatial praxis of belonging-as-being among some African descendants.

FROM MULTICULTURAL MICROCOSM TO MARKED MARGIN IN AN ERA OF "INTEGRATION"

In August 1975, Brasilândia arrived on thousands of newsstands and mailboxes across Brazil. The magazine *Veja*, which supplied national and global news to Brazil's expanding professional and intellectual class, published two articles with references to Brasilândia in their special August issue, titled "How to Measure Urban Poverty."[9] The first issue of the weekly in 1968 had a massive circulation of 695,000 and a readership of potentially four times that.[10] While those figures had contracted in the mid-1970s (before ballooning again in the decades following), *Veja's* impact on the dominant classes remained consistent.[11] One of the 1975 articles that mentioned Brasilândia, "Living Without Water," profiled the family of Edeuzita Souza Silva. She was described as a "resident of the *catastrophic* neighborhood Vila Brasilândia, whose living children have gastrointestinal infections—as did two of three that already died." The apocalyptic description continued: "Along with millions of other poor São Paulo residents, the family of Edeuzita consumes water from a private well . . . literally contaminated from physical, chemical, and bacteriological points of view."[12] Paired with the Silva family story were images snapped by the *Veja* photographer: six wincing children, huddled around their mother and the insalubrious well (figure 4.1). Through the wrenching image and sensationalist prose, the piece

FIGURE 4.1 · Edeuzita's family in Brasilândia. A caption reads, "Edeuzita, her children, her well: Waiting for piped water." "Vivendo sem água," *Veja*, August 6, 1975, 51. Image available at https://acervo.veja.abril.com.br/#/edition/34191?page=51§ion=1 (last accessed June 11, 2018).

presented the space of Brasilândia and its residents as symbolic of urban social and environmental pathology in the 1960s and 1970s. Circulated throughout Brazil, this representation and the grave social realities it reflected marked Brasilândia as an emblematic periphery in this era, dangerous both to its inhabitants and to residents of the city of São Paulo.

National as well as local changes in approaches to urban planning contributed to the identification of Brasilândia as such in this period. The installation of a technocratic military dictatorship in 1964 contributed to the consolidation of new approaches to official city planning on multiple scales in Brazil.[13] In São Paulo, that approach concentrated on efforts to curb four decades of unchecked horizontal expansion. The municipal and state governments had helped to facilitate that growth with a hands-off approach to urbanization, a sentiment epitomized by São Paulo governor Adhemar de Barros's 1947 statement: "You can construct your houses without official plans; the City will close its eyes."[14] The construction of neighborhood subdivisions (*loteamentos*), often without state approval and without concern for building or city planning regulations, helped to expand the city's footprint fourfold between 1950 and 1970.[15] As São Paulo's limits continued to balloon, national and local planning officials developed a new planning doctrine that prescribed a more comprehensive approach to city planning and the incorporation of the scattered *loteamentos* that residents and real estate developers had sometimes settled clandestinely. Those planners termed this approach *integrated development* or *integrated planning*.[16]

While planners developed projects of integrated development for cities throughout Brazil, the ethos had special purchase for the nation's most populous city and its financial and industrial hub. Decades of unregulated growth and informal, illegal settlements had produced precarious conditions and a disconnected city. Urbanist and historian Céline Sachs-Jeantet describes "the immense São Paulo periphery" in this era as an "archipelago of *loteamentos* in different stages of consolidation."[17] Integrated development promised improved conditions in peripheral places through expanded utility networks, public housing programs, and more functional transportation systems. Planners, however, found the ideal of integration much easier to study and elaborate in discourse than to realize in practice. Increasing awareness of precarious conditions, documented and disseminated by urbanists and journalists on an unprecedented scale in this era, brought the realities of *dis*integration to a broad audience. That awareness would make Brasilândia recognizable in São Paulo and beyond.

The first step toward the integration of Brasilândia into the city of São Paulo occurred in 1964, when a municipal government reorganization made the unofficial neighborhood of Vila Brasilândia the city of São Paulo's fortieth subdistrict. The institutional realignment paralleled fast-paced population growth in the region: from just under 20,000 residents in 1950, Brasilândia reached nearly 50,000 residents by 1960 and nearly 115,000 by 1970.[18] The elevation of status to subdistrict marked a step toward incorporation into the formal city of São Paulo, though the multiple promises of integration—improved transportation, housing, and parity in public services—remained unrealized in practice. Continued pressures from in-migration, along with the failures of integrated development, made life precarious for many Brasilândia residents throughout the 1960s and 1970s.

In São Paulo, the project of integrated development promised a shift from what was long the predominant emphasis in city planning: growth and development through transportation infrastructure. Transportation planning had dominated planning on paper and in practice in São Paulo since the 1930 publication of Francisco Prestes Maia's Avenues Plan. As discussed in chapter 1, the Avenues Plan outlined the structure of the city-to-be-created from the 1930s through the 1960s. Prestes Maia sought to execute the Avenues Plan in practice through his three terms as São Paulo's mayor from 1938 to 1945 and from 1961 to 1965.[19] The completion of his 1961–1965 term signaled the beginning of the end of this era, as urbanists and politicians in the decade following began to develop alternative approaches to planning, including integrated development.

The first significant step in that shift occurred in 1968. In that year the City of São Paulo released the Basic Urbanistic Plan (Plano Urbanístico Básico), or PUB. The PUB presented an outline for a proposal of integrated development for the metropolitan region of São Paulo. The authorship of the PUB included "an international consortium of business consultants" and represented, in the analysis of anthropologist Teresa Caldeira, "the basis for the first general urban plan of the city."[20] The study broached an array of issues, ranging from social development and public administration to questions of land use and zoning. While prevalent, transportation planning reminiscent of the Avenues Plan formed just one part of a larger, more comprehensive whole. The PUB's authors aimed "not just to orient the construction of avenues and viaducts, but to serve the sectors of education, culture, and health, parks and gardens."[21]

The study also revealed the multiple meanings of integration as a spatial and cultural project. The PUB singled out, for instance, migrant populations in São Paulo as being "subjected to constant and painstaking effort in the search for economic and social improvement. The challenges of access to the labor market and the inadequacy of services and social programs restrict opportunities for greater mobility and social integration."[22] The comprehensive approach to city planning in the PUB outlined a shift from the almost exclusive emphasis on transportation planning from the 1930s to the early 1960s. Furthermore, it provided a roadmap for the geographic and social integration of spaces and populations throughout the metropolis.

Officials did not support the transformation of the PUB from a study into a plan. Instead, the São Paulo city council approved a narrower proposal, the Directing Plan for Integrated Development (Plano Diretor de Desenvolvimento Integrado, or PDDI), three years later in 1971. The PDDI was the first comprehensive plan adopted by city officials since Prestes Maia's avenues proposal forty years earlier. The PDDI maintained the principle of curtailing São Paulo's unwieldy horizontal expansion but otherwise little resembled the PUB. Lacking the more comprehensive approach to planning, the PDDI signaled, for urbanist historian Sara Feldman, "the negation of the concept of a master plan."[23]

Despite efforts to develop a more comprehensive planning practice, prominent city officials continued in the 1960s to privilege the São Paulo mainstay of transportation planning. The shadow of Prestes Maia loomed large. Urbanist and Prestes Maia biographer Benedito Lima de Toledo writes that the urbanist-mayor's 1961–1965 term focused on "putting the municipal government in order." Prestes Maia set the stage, however, for the more project-centered mayoral administration of his successor, trained engineer José Vicente Faria Lima (in office 1965-1969). Toledo explains that "when Faria Lima was elected, he found it possible to execute all of the projects that Maia had elaborated in his second term . . . the dinner was already served up for him. When he was elected, he used the famous expression: 'I don't want planning (*planejamento*), I want doing (*fazejamento*).'"[24] Like Prestes Maia, Faria Lima privileged projects like the widening and elongating of avenues in an effort to update the transportation system. He also aimed to grow circulation capacity from 160,000 vehicles in 1960 to 3.6 million by 1990.[25] Similar to the Avenues Plan, Faria Lima's vision of urban development sought to bring together spaces in the metropolis through a new and improved transportation infrastructure.

An urbanization project involving Brasilândia during Faria Lima's administration reflected this vision. The 1968 plan outlined the construction of a massive, sixty-meter-wide avenue running north–south along Brasilândia's eastern edge. The city council approved the proposal despite complaints from three council members, who asserted that the studies for the project were half-baked and that another avenue of comparable size, running in the same direction just six hundred meters to the west, had already been approved.[26] Instead of elaborating programs to address dismal public services, an ambitious, potentially redundant roadway project received public funding.

Brasilândia residents themselves entered the debate over urban integration through roadways. In 1967 a commission of residents from Brasilândia took a request to Faria Lima for the paving a road in the region of Vila Santa Terezinha. This *loteamento* sat north of the original Vila Brasilândia *loteamento* and was identified as a locus of Black settlement in an interview with one resident.[27] The new road would connect Terezinha to areas in the west of Brasilândia along the former Congo Road. Deep, parallel valleys running north–south in Brasilândia made such east–west connections uncommon. Faria Lima balked at the residents' request, however, asserting that the project "would be a piece of junk, because the roads are only slightly wider than eight meters and we cannot throw away money on this." Faria Lima complained further that the Brasilândia commission had approached him with "inadequate solutions" multiple times.[28] Faria Lima's support for the possibly redundant 1968 north–south avenue proposal contrasted sharply with his disdain for this grassroots request one year later.

While municipal administrators continued to privilege planning through transportation infrastructure, housing became an urgent concern. An economic boom in the late 1960s and early 1970s fueled continued migration into the city of São Paulo.[29] Migrants confronted a severe housing shortage. A 1967 special edition of the newspaper *Folha de S. Paulo*, titled "Poor Great City," noted that 72,000 houses needed to be built per year in the metropolitan region by 1970 to meet the deficit.[30] Federal and local government authorities created new institutions in this era, such as the National Housing Bank (BNH) and Metropolitan Company of São Paulo Housing (COHAB), in an effort to meet housing needs.[31] The units generated through these public housing and mortgage assistance programs, however, fell short of demand.[32]

The ubiquity of irregular housing developments further challenged municipal and federal urban reform efforts. Since the 1930s the city of São Paulo's Department of Urbanism had identified many *loteamentos* as irregular, including the original settlement of Vila Brasilândia. This diagnosis meant that the developments did not conform to municipal regulations in terms of infrastructure, the minimum size of parcels, and the allocation of spaces for public use as roads, parks, and schools. The *loteamentos* that private developers and residents produced often bore little resemblance to those outlined in municipal code. A common practice for families in Brasilândia and elsewhere, for instance, was to purchase a single lot and subdivide the parcel into minilots.[33] These practices helped families to generate capital and create rungs for social mobility, even if they disobeyed the required minimum size of a lot established by municipal legislation. Over four decades, urban policymakers successively reduced the minimum size of lots in the hopes of bringing municipal codes in line with actually existing, informal spatial practices.[34]

After decades of half measures, urban policymakers shifted their approach in the 1960s and 1970s. They increasingly enforced code regulations or, alternatively, relaxed requirements so that irregular developments became regular overnight. Municipal laws passed in 1967 and 1972 required developers to prove the successful completion of basic infrastructure such as roads, sewage, and water networks before a project was approved by the City. Crucially, they provided mechanisms to penalize developers if they failed to meet code. The 1972 law proved more effective in enforcing regulations, representing the "first profound change in the intervention of public authorities" in the era of permissive urban development.[35]

The enforcement of new, stricter regulations resulted in the freezing of legal urban developments, as effective enforcement inadvertently cut off the supply of cheap housing and moved the production of *loteamentos* fully underground. Between 1972 and 1979, São Paulo's Department of Urbanism only approved seven new *loteamentos*. This corresponded to a boom in the production of clandestine and, most often, irregular *loteamentos*. In sharp contrast to the seven authorized developments, informal planners and developers coproduced an estimated 3,567 irregular *loteamentos* in the 1970s. Those places covered nearly 35 percent of the city's territory by the end of the decade.[36] By finally succeeding in curbing the state's permissiveness in the face of irregular *loteamentos*, state officials inadvertently spurred an even more precarious pattern of urban development and spatial disintegration.

Irregular and clandestine *loteamentos* were the norm rather than the exception in the urbanization of Brasilândia. The region's first *loteamento*, Vila Brasilândia, was developed without approval from the Department of Urbanism in 1947 and has remained irregular into the twenty-first century.[37] In the late 1960s and 1970s, new *loteamentos* increasingly pushed into the dense Atlantic Forest in the northern region of the district.[38] The remote environment likely appealed to developers keen on producing irregular settlements away from the increasingly watchful eyes of authorities.

The settlement of Jardim Damasceno, a *loteamento* whose boundaries stretch deep into the Atlantic Forest, exhibits this pattern. One of the first settlers in the area, QV, purchased his lot in 1971 and realized the year following that the developer had only given him a bill of sale for the purchase of his parcel, not title to the land itself. QV worked building São Paulo's first metro line, and he constructed his home in the *loteamento* along with many neighbors' residences. He sought title for his property in the city government, an act that unwittingly informed the City of the existence and condition of the clandestine development. Municipal urbanists then initiated an effort to regularize and legalize the development.[39] Filling the vacuum in housing previously met by permissive urban expansion, clandestine *loteamentos*/neighborhoods like Jardim Damasceno stretched the limits of Brasilânida into ever more remote, forested regions throughout the 1970s.

The restriction on *loteamentos* also prompted a sharp increase in favelas in São Paulo, with Brasilândia a principal area of their concentration. While favelas surged in Rio de Janeiro at the beginning of the twentieth century, they appeared for the first time in the city of São Paulo in the 1940s and as a result of the housing crisis discussed in chapter 1. One of the most noteworthy favelas in Brazil, São Paulo's Canindé, became internationally famous as a result of the 1960 publication of the diaries of one of its residents, Carolina Maria de Jesus.[40] Prestes Maia coordinated the removal of Canindé and resettlement of residents in the first year of his 1960s term in office, describing it as a "stain" on the city.[41] While prevalent since the 1940s and internationally known in the 1960s, São Paulo's favelas did not comprise an especially prominent feature of São Paulo's landscape. Architect and urbanist Nabil Bonduki affirms that their growth "remained restricted until the 1970s, as much a result of the discrimination and repression that their inhabitants suffered as the enormous offering of peripheral lots [i.e., *loteamentos*]."[42]

The number of residents living in favelas and the number of favelas themselves surged in São Paulo in the 1970s. The occupation of land and construction of favelas helped to meet housing demands, especially given the restrictions on *loteamentos*. From 41,000 residents in 1971 (0.75 percent of the city's total population), the number of São Paulo residents living in favelas grew to 117,237 (1.60 percent) in 1975 and 866,500 (8.63 percent) by 1985.[43] One article described São Paulo as "the city that became a favela."[44] A 1967 article in *Folha de S. Paulo* commented on the then-incipient phenomenon with a dubious if revealing opening: "The favela is not only the place where samba is danced. It is also a place where comfort is an unknown word. Hygiene, electric light, piped water, sanitation systems do not exist. The shacks stack up in any way possible and do not receive the light of the sun or vegetation."[45]

Favelas emerged in the 1950s in Brasilândia; however, a spike in the 1960s and 1970s resulted in the subdistrict having one of the largest numbers of favelas in all of São Paulo. Map 4.1 displays the settlement of favelas in the contemporary district of Brasilândia from the 1950s through 1995. In 1973, the district surrounding the subdistrict of Brasilândia, Freguesia do Ó, accounted for the highest number of favelas in the city at 110 (or 20 percent of São Paulo's total). The next highest was the Santo Amaro district at 82.[46] From three in the 1950s, favelas in Brasilândia grew to 23 in the 1960s and reached 61 by the end of the 1970s.[47] One study cast the region as a place of last resort: "The Northern Zone does not afford favorable topographic conditions for the construction of adequate housing, suffering an intense process of land devaluation. As a result many areas were occupied by low-income populations . . . [who] stretched into empty areas, forming favelas, despite these areas' considerable, life-threatening risks."[48] Brasilândia's remoteness provided a measure of autonomy for those seeking land and for *loteamento* developers keen to capitalize on the vast housing demand.

The development of *loteamentos* and favelas in Brasilândia often took place simultaneously. Map 4.2 offers a close-up view of Jardim Elisa Maria, a *loteamento* in the northeast of the district. Jardim Elisa Maria was granted approval for construction from municipal authorities in 1962. In that same year, residents settled the first favelas, Gato Preto I and Gato Preto II. Overlaying the approved *loteamento* blueprint and a layer of favelas displays a precise alignment between the spaces designated for public use and these favelas. The eight additional favelas settled in Jardim Elisa Maria in years following would continue this pattern, which was common throughout Brasilândia. Mapping how residents informally settled public and vacant lands within officially approved *loteamentos* illustrates the close connections between informal and formal development.

Brasilândia residents faced severely limited infrastructure and services in this era. An estimate from 1970 indicated that of the 20,769 buildings in Brasilândia, only 2,262 (or 10.9 percent) had piped water and just 82 (.004 percent) had access to the municipal sewage network. Those numbers compared unfavorably even to the adjacent Nossa Senhora do Ó subdistrict, where 10,768 (47 percent) of the buildings had running water and 2,991 (13 percent) had access to the sewage network.[49] The figures for both Brasilândia and Nossa Senhora do Ó were

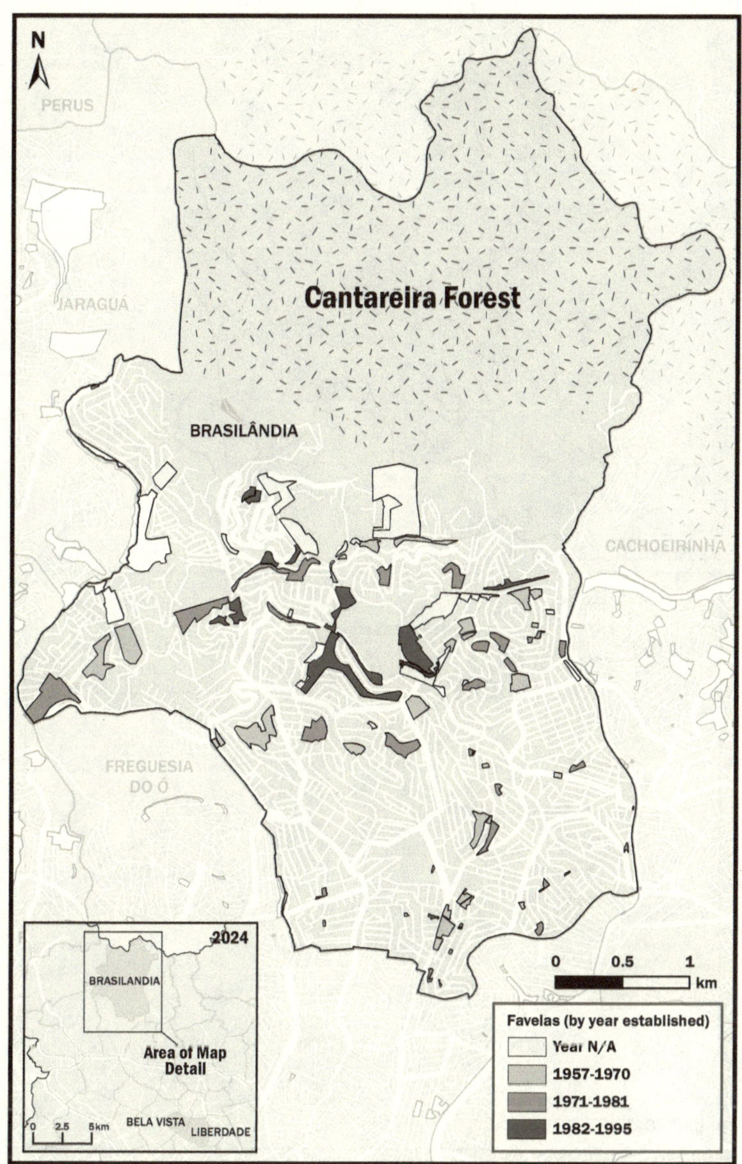

MAP 4.1 · Favelas in Brasilândia by year of settlement (if available). Data sources: Secretaria da Habitação e Desenvolvimento Urbano; GeoSampa; Open Basemap Light Gray Canvas Base—Sources: Esri, TomTom, Garmin, GeoTechnologies, Inc.; METI/NASA; USGS; © OpenStreetMap contributors; Microsoft; Esri Community Maps contributors. Map by Andrew G. Britt.

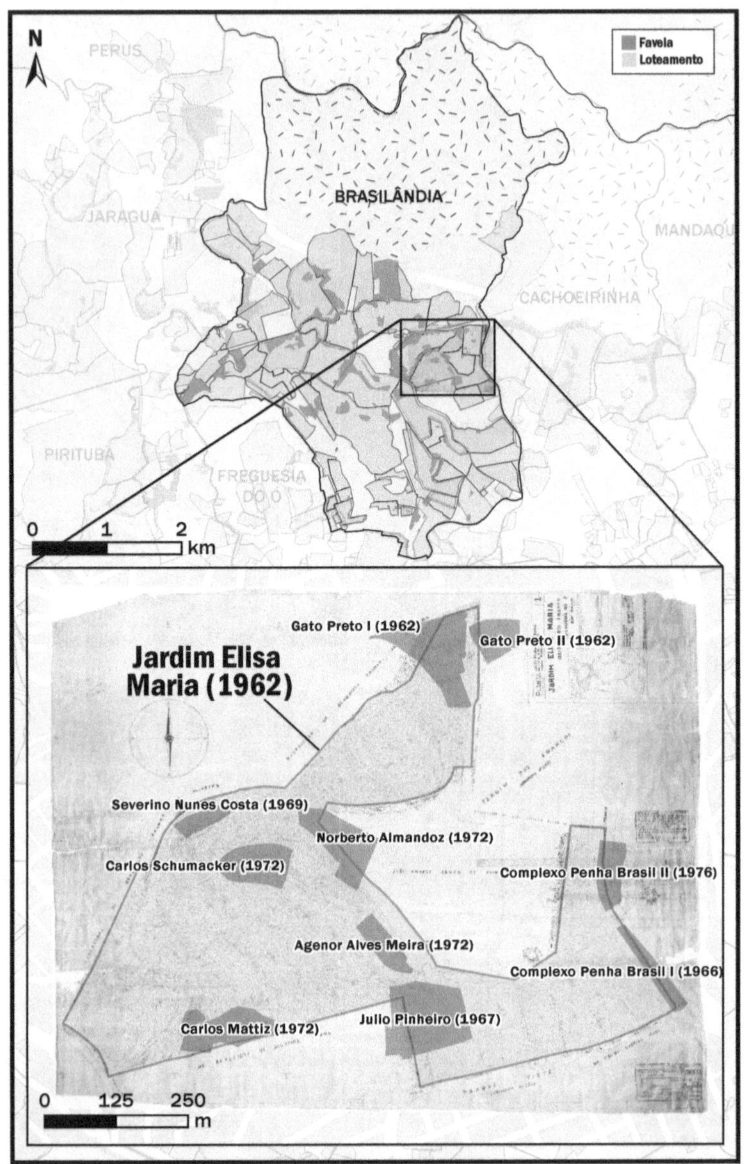

MAP 4.2 · Jardim Elisa Maria *loteamento* and favelas, showing their settlement in public spaces. Georeferenced map is the original *loteamento* plan for Jardim Elisa Maria. Data sources: Coordenação de Gestão de Documentos Públicos, Prefeitura de São Paulo; Secretaria da Habitação e Desenvolvimento Urbano; GeoSampa; OpenStreetMap (Light Gray Canvas) © OpenStreetMap contributors, Microsoft, Facebook, Google, Esri Community Maps contributors, map layer by Esri. Map by Andrew G. Britt.

relatively far off from averages for the city as a whole: In 1973, 56 percent of houses citywide had running water, while 35 percent were connected to the sewage network.[50] While services and infrastructure were limited or absent in neighborhoods throughout the city, the conditions in Brasilândia were exceptional.

Some Brasilândia residents responded to these conditions by creating, in 1978, the Center for the Defense of Favela Residents (*Centro de Defesa do Favelado*). Founded in the Icaraí favela in the original Vila Brasilândia *loteamento*, the organization advocated for the rights of favela residents and taught strategies of nonviolent resistance, especially to contest threats of demolition and displacement from officials. They also coordinated the collective construction of brick houses and sewer systems, helping to create more secure housing and urban infrastructure in the absence of private developers or public authorities.[51]

At the end of the 1970s, likely in part in response to resident organizing, officials would begin to attempt to rectify poor infrastructure and precarious conditions throughout São Paulo in a comprehensive regularization effort. Brasilândia was, not surprisingly, a prime region of focus.[52] The regularization of Jardim Elisa Maria (discussed previously) took place between 1981 and 1983. By 1976, ten favelas had been settled in this *loteamento*, a substantial portion of the total in Brasilândia (estimated at sixty-one in the late 1970s) and perhaps the highest concentration of any *loteamento* in the region. Records suggest that officials had little awareness of conditions in the *loteamento* following its approval in 1962. In 1981 they conducted the City's first official site visit. The architect sent to investigate, Lucia Noemia Simoni, learned that a significant portion of the proposed development had not, in fact, been constructed and that residents had not been given title for their property. Simoni also documented the settlement of favelas, which encompassed housing complexes and one elementary school, in public squares within the *loteamento*. She captured the precarious landscape of Jardim Elisa Maria in dozens of photos, evidence to support her conclusion that the irregular development should be rectified at the developer's expense. Regularization of most of the *loteamento* would take place in short order, with one significant exception.

Residents settled the Carlos Mattiz favela in the southwest of Jardim Elisa Maria in 1972. Part of this favela stretched into, and was described as blocking, Street 11, a road that the developer should have constructed in the 1960s but did not. The regularization of the *loteamento* in the early 1980s depended on the completion of this road. Officials from different municipal sectors debated the correct course of action. Some recommended the removal of the favela, arguing that *loteamento* residents who had purchased lots along the other side of Street 11 had the right to use this thoroughfare and could later sue the City if they were not granted access. Another official, from the São Paulo State Company of Sanitation (SABESP), argued against the removal, referencing a 1978 decree that favelas should be removed only in the service of the broad public interest or in cases where conditions were life-threatening.

The debate continued into 1982 and 1983. One official suggested a compromise: only the homes blocking Street 11, not the whole favela, should be removed. Another, in support of removal, described the residents of Carlos Mattiz as *maloqueiros*, a derogatory term for favela residents. The back-and-forth culminated in February 1983, when a separate official visited Carlos Mattiz and concluded, sympathetically: "We don't have the conditions for [removal], since there are people living in these shacks, and they don't have anywhere to go." The debate ended six months later, when yet another official visited and determined that, while not as wide as first planned, Street 11 was wide enough for cars to pass. The favela residents were allowed to remain, and the *loteamento* was considered regularized.[53] The regularization of Jardim Elisa Maria reveals internal municipal debates about how to address urban precarity and the reality that, for some residents, official efforts to improve conditions had the potential to worsen them (through displacement, in this case).

Indeed, favela residents in Brasilândia in this era faced threats of displacement both amid and in parallel to regularization efforts. One particularly dramatic episode (unrelated to regularization) took place in 1981, when officials from SABESP sought to demolish the Salvaterra favela, located along the former Congo Road. Officials initially relocated Salvaterra residents to an undesirable location near Jaraguá. The residents returned to Salvaterra, rightly expecting a confrontation with SABESP officials and police. With support from the Center for the Defense of Favela Residents, residents deployed a strategy of nonviolent resistance in an hours-long standoff. They secured their relocation to a new development elsewhere and the right to remain in Salvaterra until resettlement. The episode provides another example of Brasilândia residents facing repeated displacement and highlights strategies they used to contest official hostility and the specter of further dislocation.[54]

From its founding in 1947 through the middle of the 1960s, Brasilândia had existed largely outside the formal city of São Paulo. In that era, an array of ethnoracially diverse residents and real estate developers constructed an identify for the neighborhood as a microcosmic, multiethnic "land of Brazil." The ethos of integrated development in the late 1960s and early 1970s presented a new geography for the city premised on the incorporation of informal, remote places like Brasilândia. That approach, of course, glossed over the connections that had long tied the neighborhood and its residents to more central areas of São Paulo. Nonetheless, integrated development promised to formalize these connections: planners would incorporate Brasilândia and its residents into the official city, affording to both the space and its residents the benefits therein. In practice, however, residents continued to face precarious conditions throughout the 1970s, and Brasilândia became increasingly known as an emblematic, exceptional urban margin.

Widely circulated representations of Brasilândia, including the *Veja* article noted previously, also likely helped to shift popular perceptions of the neighborhood from a multiethnic microcosm to a marginal and racialized periphery. Photographer André Cservenka snapped striking images in Brasilândia for the magazine *Movimento*, an antidictatorship publication founded in 1975.[55] His photographs gave a face to the urban crisis and to the quotidian realities of Brasilândia as an emblematic racialized periphery. Figure 4.2 displays one of Cservenka's images: a landscape of wooden shacks built on top of one another on a Brasilândia hillside. A young resident, almost indiscernible, peers casually and, seemingly, cautiously toward Cservenka's lens. The exposure obscures the young man, whose body is darkened by the shadows of the doorway and made nearly indistinguishable from the surrounding built environment. The composition, nonetheless, positions him at the center of the image, representing him as the concealed human reality at the core of the place.

Another photograph by Cservenka (figure 4.3) depicts the interior of a residence in Brasilândia. An elderly Black woman in the background, feet resting on a dirt floor, stares directly at the camera over the shoulder of a child, perhaps her grandson, in the foreground. The composition of the image suggests continuities across time: the woman, representative of the past, occupies the space of the present along with the young

FIGURE 4.2 · *Favela*, by André Cservenka, 1979. Collection from the magazine *Movimento*. Arquivo Público do Estado de São Paulo.

boy, symbolic of the future. The boy's distracted and curious expression contrasts with the woman's more ambivalent, knowing stare. That stare seems to articulate the continuities of everyday life in Brasilândia and the sociospatial inequalities in São Paulo across generations.

Circulated in major publications, such images depicted Brasilândia's marginality in both geographic space and time. The subheading of a 1979 article in *O Estado de S. Paulo* about local conditions in the region—"Images from the Beginning of the Century"—made the point about time even more explicitly.[56] These images also educated readers and viewers about the racialized social composition of Brasilândia. City planners rarely discussed race explicitly in relation to Brasilândia or other regions. However, the photographs of shadowed, non-White Brazilians with—and confused as—a landscape of urban precarity and disintegration within the city likely helped to make Brasilândia recognizable in this era as a non-White periphery. These representations, in turn, probably laid the groundwork for more explicit processes of ethnoracialization. In the following two sections I examine those processes: first, through the founding of a samba school, and second, through the popularization of a racist nickname for Brasilândia on São Paulo's radio waves.

FIGURE 4.3 · Untitled photograph of interior in Brasilândia in 1979, by André Cservenka. Collection from the magazine *Movimento*. Arquivo Público do Estado de São Paulo.

FIGURE 4.4 · Former site of Rosas de Ouro samba school, facing north toward the original Vila Brasilândia settlement, May 2017. Photo by Andrew G. Britt.

SAMBA, ASPHALT, AND ROSAS DE OURO

In the middle of a vacant, overgrown lot in the commercial heart of Brasilândia, there were few obvious signs that I was standing *someplace else*. São Paulo samba composer and musician Geraldo Filme wrote "I'll Samba Someplace Else" ("Vou sambar n'outro lugar"), eulogizing one of the city's most significant centers of samba in the early twentieth century, the Largo da Banana (Banana Square). Located in São Paulo's Barra Funda neighborhood, this site was demolished for the construction of an overpass in the late 1950s. Urban redevelopment projects had spurred dislocation and local migration throughout the city of São Paulo from the 1930s forward, and by the 1960s a critical mass of samba composers and musicians had settled in Brasilândia.[57] In the midst and wake of these dislocations, African descendants transformed Brasilândia into *someplace else*. One of the most significant local spaces in that transformation took place in the now overgrown lot (figure 4.4), where, in 1971, local residents established the headquarters of the samba school Rosas de Ouro (Roses of gold). In the following decades, Rosas de Ouro would win eight titles at carnival, becoming one of the city's most celebrated samba schools.[58] This site and the samba school headquartered here—along with a handful of others throughout São Paulo—became the heirs to the Largo da Banana.[59]

From the inception of this samba collective, the members produced songs whose central themes addressed topics such as spatial belonging, anti-Black violence, and multiracial democracy. This space and the performances that Rosas de Ouro led—both within Brasilândia and on avenues in the geographical center of São Paulo—helped to define the neighborhood in the early 1970s as a privileged locus of Black self-determination: a "Little Africa." That definition served to contest the increasingly racist and broadly negative stereotypes associated with Brasilândia and its residents. The violence represented by, and that took place (literally and figuratively) through, those stereotypes would only get worse in the years following, as the next section shows. Rosas de Ouro, nonetheless, would serve as a key site for the spatial praxis of belonging-as-being from the 1970s through the 1980s.

The official establishment of Rosas de Ouro occurred in 1971 when an interracial group of individuals secured the previously mentioned lot in the heart of the neighborhood along Parapuã Street. Eduardo Basílio, a White businessman from Brasilândia, helped to acquire the space and assumed the presidency of the school, which he would occupy until 2003.[60] Rosas de Ouro stayed at this site in Brasilândia until the early 1980s, when it moved to the more developed part of the adjacent neighborhood of Freguesia do Ó in the south. The move, which disappointed many Brasilândia residents, entailed splitting with some of the original, Brasilândia-based musicians who had founded and frequented the school in its earliest years.[61]

Some residents recall a longer history of Rosas de Ouro and date its origins before the 1971 purchase of the lot on Parapuã Street. WB and MB, members of Rosas de Ouro in this era, place its origins in an area of the original Brasilândia settlement called the Catimbó, which had a large concentration of Black residents. Musicians would play music and store their instruments in the Catimbó. Such spaces were hard to come by in this period, owing to both limitations of space and official hostility to samba.[62] Multiple residents of Brasilândia remember that police were particularly hostile to samba gatherings in the late 1960s.[63] An early 1970s article titled "Samba According to São Paulo" in the magazine *Realidade* described some of these challenges. An image in the article depicted a crowded corner of a living room with instruments strewn about. Its caption read, "Without practice areas and without headquarters, the São Paulo leaders transform their homes into rehearsal studios and instrument depositories."[64]

The Catimbó does not exist on official maps of Brasilândia. Like the Largo da Banana and other popularly named spaces throughout São Paulo, the area existed principally in popular geographic imaginaries. Born in the interior of the state of São Paulo in 1923, Geralda Luiz Galdino settled in Freguesia do Ó in the 1930s and later participated in Rosas de Ouro for many years. She remembers the Catimbó as "a village of houses where Blacks lived, at the corner with the deep pit."[65] At the center of the Catimbó was a fork in the road that led uphill. With windows stretching along the same horizontal line of these houses, some residents remember this collection of structures resembling, and known locally as, the "slave ship" (*navio negreiro*).[66] The shape of the roads that bordered the Catimbó created a sharp oval somewhat reminiscent of the outline of a vessel. Recall that *navio negreiro* was also the name for the *cortiço* on May 13 Street in the Bela Vista district, the neighborhood of origin for some residents who settled in Brasilândia. The area's name also referenced African-descendent culture: Catimbó was an African Brazilian and Amerindian spiritual practice common in Brazil's Northeast.[67]

The denomination of a housing complex with a large Black population as a *navio negreiro* may have implied that the African descendants who lived in that complex did not belong, either within Brazil broadly or the city of São Paulo, specifically. At the same time, the positive usage of this name among multiple Black residents I interviewed suggested that some—perhaps many—residents of African descent saw such places as sites of refuge and belonging. Such sites were especially pivotal in the mid- to late 1960s, as Brazil's military government promoted postracialist ideologies of mixture and integration on an unprecedented scale.[68] With a large concentration of African descendants and a hub for cultural practices like samba, the Catimbó would have been likely perceived by officials as a threat to those dominant ideologies. The residents of Catimbó, nonetheless, produced in this corner of Brasilândia a place that would provide a measure of protection from the real threat of anti-Black violence and the discursive denial of the existence of anti-Blackness or Blackness itself. At the same time, the Catimbó also served as a site for the creation of an active samba collective. That collective would be formalized as Rosas de Ouro through the interracial alliance and land acquisition in 1971. The school's origins are intimately tied to the spatial praxis of belonging-as-being that the residents of the Catimbó pursued in the years prior.

PSO grew up in Brasilândia and composed some of Rosas de Ouro's earliest sambas. His father settled in Brasilândia in the 1950s, purchased a lot, and constructed his home along with his wife. Those original bricks, oversized in comparison to the kind commonly used today, are exposed along the entryway to his home. "Black people built this community," PSO remembers.[69] His conception of "built" was not metaphorical. In addition to concentrating many African descendants, Brasilândia urbanized through the spatial practices of residents themselves. These practices included the autoconstruction of residences, a widespread method of home building (discussed in chapter 3) wherein families construct residential complexes gradually over time and without degreed architects or engineers.

Locals in Brasilândia also produced the neighborhood on more collective scales that transcended individual homes. While grand avenues occupied the minds of São Paulo's official planners, residents in Brasilândia who were engaged in constructing the built environment also concerned themselves with roads and pavement. Almost invariably and without provocation during interviews, residents in Brasilândia would broach histories of paving. Like PSO, residents commonly articulated precise timelines for when and how a road was paved and who participated in the labor or negotiations with urban services authorities to make that paving happen.[70] These recollections follow a trajectory, emphasizing the transformation from the time when "everything was forest" (*era tudo mata*) to the arrival of stone, concrete, or asphalt roadways. PSO recalls an instance of locals taking road construction into their own hands. When he was a child, his father organized other residents of Plínio Rocha Pinto Street, where their house was located, to carry out a paving project. They contracted to purchase stones from the nearby rock quarry and paved the road themselves.[71] These actions reveal the determination of residents in neighborhoods like Brasilândia to address the everyday consequences of scant investment in infrastructure from urbanistic authorities and real estate developers.

At the same time, the prominence of paving, and particularly asphalt, in conversations with Brasilândia carries additional, intriguing symbolism. Asphalt is not just a mundane, if essential, material in Brazil. A common view of Rio de Janeiro divides the city between *morro* (hill) and *asfalto* (asphalt). These terms distinguish, in the geographic imaginary, the formal city, defined by asphalt, from the informal city, defined by unpaved favelas on hillsides. This distinction is also commonly understood as aligned with other aspects of sociospatial difference: between the rich city and poor city, and the White city and non-White city.[72] This distinction reveals how seemingly mundane features of the built environment, such as asphalt, can acquire an ethnoracialized significance. The racialized hill-asphalt binary is more commonly associated with Rio de Janeiro than São Paulo, perhaps because of the latter's distinct patterns of urban development across a larger expanse of territory and a more recent history of favela settlement. Brasilândia, however, proves an exception to this rule, as stories about hills and pavement arise frequently in interviews with some of Brasilândia's earliest residents, as well as in the lyrics of Rosas de Ouro.

Hills featured prominently in the first samba *enredo*—the song composed for and performed by a samba school during Carnival competitions—that Rosas de Ouro produced for carnival in São Paulo in 1971. PSO recalls the song "History of Vila Brasilândia," which contrasted (while also connecting) the hilly topography of Brasilândia with the geographic center of the city:

> Sing the high hills
> A monumental panorama
> From which you can see
> All of our city.[73]

In a city where broad, horizontal landscapes are hard to glimpse, Brasilândia's high elevation had provided uninterrupted views of the verticalizing center (the tallest in Latin America at the time) of São Paulo since the inception of the *loteamento* in the 1940s.[74] Despite the twelve kilometers between Brasilândia and the center, the view from the steep hills generated a perception of proximity with the city's geographic core. The daily experience of traversing unpaved roads from Brasilândia to the city center and back put a premium on pavement. The persistence of roads (even primary arteries) without asphalt into the 1960s—the era of integrated development—signified Brasilândia's lack of integration and, therefore, its marginal status. The absence of pavement thereby defined a spatial hierarchy dividing the city along lines of rich/poor and White/non-White, with Brasilândia falling on the marginal periphery. Singing about "*our* city," Rosas de Ouro members countered that geography and made a claim to belonging within both the material and symbolic space of São Paulo.

The city of São Paulo's tourism arm officialized carnival celebrations in 1968, meaning that the municipal government took over the organization and regulation of the festivities and parades. Ethnomusicologist Shuhei Hosokawa asserts that this officialization "transformed carnivals into less dangerous, less marginal, more industrialized and concomitantly more inclusive events. The commercial development of samba schools also facilitated easier access to the world of carnival for the middle and upper classes and the non-Black population."[75] The City likely recognized the business potential in samba and aimed to capitalize on the transformation of the supposedly "marginal" and "dangerous" cultural practice into an accessible feature of São Paulo's cultural life. From 1968 to 1977, the carnival parade marched down São João Avenue, one of center-city São Paulo's principal arteries. Some Brasilândia residents surely knew the area well, having lived nearby in decades prior.

In 1973 Rosas de Ouro's *enredo* engaged themes of anti-Black violence, multiracial democracy, and Black self-determination. The *enredo* was titled "Ethnic Formation" ("A formação étnica"), and the lyrics ran:

> Indians, Whites, and Blacks
> Began the evolution
> And their names and deeds
> Our history will tell
>
> Diogo Álvares Correia Caramuru
> Gave his heart
> To the young Indian Paraguaçu
>
> From this blood mixture emerged
> The strong Brazilian folk
>
> The Blacks how they would suffer
> In the slave quarters
> Seeking refuge
> In the *quilombo* of Palmares

At the sound of the whip you could hear
The loud shout
Of the overseer proclaiming

Catch hold of the Black
This Black
Wants to flee to the *quilombo* of Palmares
With the King Zumbi[76]

The song nearly reads as two discrete compositions. The first three stanzas present a dominant myth of Brazil's founding as taking place through the racial mixture of "Indians, Whites, and Blacks." That narrative is elaborated by reference to the affective relationship between an Indigenous woman and Diogo Álvares Correia (known by the name Caramuru in the Indigenous language Tupi), a Portuguese colonist and icon of cultural in-betweenness.[77] The tone of the song shifts markedly after the third stanza, with the remaining lines foregrounding anti-Black violence, enslavement, and Black self-determination.

"Ethnic Formation" reproduces a conventional narrative of Brazil as a postracial, racially harmonious society in the first three stanzas. The authors may have done so to appease the ears of officials of the military regime, who had doubled down on that national myth since seizing power in 1964. Alternatively, those first three lines may have served as the setup: They present the orthodox narrative of Brazil's "ethnic formation" before proceeding to radically contrast it in the remaining lines. That contrast positions anti-Black violence and control, as well as the threatening (to the overseer) desire for Black self-determination, as an equal, if not even more constitutive, element in the "ethnic formation" of Brazil. Sung on the center-city avenues linked to urban redevelopment in the then-recent past, these concluding lyrics may have also been intended as a critique of the role of anti-Blackness in the spatial development of the city, including the displacement and disinvestment that had shaped Brasilândia.

Two years later, Rosas de Ouro's samba-*enredo* adopted a different tone but focused on a recurring theme: streets. Titled "Rosas de Ouro on the Street," the *enredo* was inspired by "The Street," a poem by Guilherme de Almeida, the prominent literary and cultural figure discussed in chapter 2.[78] The exuberant, playful *enredo* chronicles, "in a true tempest of joy," vivid images from a quiet, carefree day in a São Paulo *praça* into a revelrous night on a São Paulo street. Zeca da Casa Verde, a composer well known throughout São Paulo, was credited for this samba-*enredo*, and Rosas de Ouro took an impressive second place in its first year competing in the top tier of samba schools.[79] The centrality of streets in this *enredo* again emphasizes the significance of this urban form.

Rosas de Ouro would remain at its original site in Brasilândia for nearly a decade before the school's president, Eduardo Basílio, coordinated its move to the adjacent district of Freguesia do Ó in the late 1970s. In the local newspaper *Jornal da Brasilândia*, Basílio explained that its purpose was to acquire more space and to avoid complaints about sound from nearby residents in the densely populated center of Brasilândia.[80] The move proved controversial for some residents in Brasilândia, who saw Black membership in the school steadily diminish after the relocation to Freguesia do Ó.[81]

For carnival in 2006, Rosas de Ouro marched with the song "The African Diaspora: A Crime Against the Human Race." The design for the parade included a float in the shape of a slave ship, described by a journalist in *O Estado de S. Paulo* as "a living sculpture. The form will be totally made of Blacks, including both the shell and the holding areas." The article quoted the then-president of Rosas de Ouro as saying, "We are all African descendants." The author also asserted that "the school of Freguesia do Ó has not forgotten its roots in Vila Brasilândia, and will give due homage to Blacks." Some residents recalled that, given the school's diminished Black membership, the organizers of the 2006 parade had to seek out African descendants in Brasilândia to form the social composition of the slave ship.[82]

In the 1960s and 1970s, residents of Brasilândia faced increasingly negative characterizations of the neighborhood. In the earliest days of Rosas de Ouro, and likely before in the Catimbó, some Brasilândia residents responded with critical and lyrical spatial histories that recast the neighborhood as a "Little Africa": the continuation in a long line of sites of refuge, self-determination, and belonging for African descendants. Such efforts intersected with broader expressive currents in São Paulo. For instance, in 1971 São Paulo's Center for Black Culture and Art (CECAN) staged a theatrical production titled *And Now . . . We Speak.* Written by academics and activists Eduardo de Oliveira e Oliveira and Thereza Santos, the play covered centuries of history of Africans and African descendants in the diaspora, broaching topics ranging from slavery in the African subcontinent to police brutality in São Paulo. In her history of CECAN, Joana Maria Ferreira da Silva writes that "the theatrical group was heterogenous: They ranged from Black students from the [elite private university] Mackenzie to individuals with almost no schooling. The group was composed of a middle-class segment and of poor members, residents of Vila Brasilândia."[83] Historian George Reid Andrews writes that CECAN was founded in Bexiga, a fact that would make the participation of Brasilândia residents in this play all the more significant.[84] The reference to social class also points to the quite plausible conclusion that Brasilândia was, in the early 1970s, exceptional in the city of São Paulo as a hub of both African-descendent and poor, nonelite populations.

Historian Kim Butler, in her study of post-abolition life in São Paulo and Salvador, argued that "it will be important to conduct further research on the less visible strategies of those who retreated into universes of their own creation as yet another expression of self-determination in the post-abolition era."[85] Brasilândia's history exemplifies, in my eyes, what Butler termed "universes of their own creation," especially though not exclusively among African descendants outside of São Paulo's Black middle class or elite. The creation of the neighborhood falls between the two seminal periods of flourishing Black social and political organization, marked by the dissolution of the FNB in 1937 and the founding of the MNU in 1978. Brasilândia's history thus helps to illuminate consequential processes of racialized displacement and disinvestment in this period as well as the forging of spaces of survival, Black self-determination, and belonging on São Paulo's geographic and social margins.

BROADCASTING BRASILÂNDIA: CRIMINALITY, REALITY RADIO, AND RACIST STIGMA

In 2017 the newspaper *Folha de S. Paulo* published an article headlined "Map of Death." Based on a study conducted by newspaper staff, the piece mapped the spatial distribution of murders in the city of São Paulo in 2015. The subheading, "The Map of Death in São Paulo Goes from Switzerland to Mexico; Locations of Crimes Recur," referenced the gulf between the comparatively low murder rates in certain São Paulo neighborhoods (likened to those in Switzerland) and the much higher rates in others (likened to those in Mexico). "Locations of crimes recur" asserted a continuity in the geography of violence in São Paulo, and the authors presented the district of Brasilândia as a longtime locus of "recurring" crime.[86] They stated, for example, that Brasilândia had the sixth-highest rate of murders in the city. Seven murders occurred on Elísio Teixeira Leite Avenue (the former Congo Road) in 2015, the second-highest of any roadway in the city.[87]

The *Folha de S. Paulo* article presents a narrow definition of violence in Brasilândia and throughout the city of São Paulo as exceptional moments of bodily harm. That definition excludes more quotidian forms of structural violence, such as poverty and gravely substandard urban infrastructure.[88] In doing so, the article participates in what anthropologist Teresa Caldeira has termed the "talk of crime," a discourse about perceived violence and crime that she shows exacerbated sociospatial segregation and inequality in São Paulo in the 1980s and 1990s, especially.[89] Brasilândia has long occupied a significant role in discourses about violence and crime in the city. However, in the 1960s and 1970s, the stigmatization of the neighborhood as a center of danger took on a more evidently racialized character. In this section I trace the racist construction of Brasilândia as a dangerous place, including through the novel reality radio programs of a popular broadcaster named Gil Gomes. Beginning in the late 1960s, Gomes broadcast sensationalized stories of violent crime in São Paulo and, in the years that followed, would help to popularize a racist epithet, "Monkeyland" (Macacolândia), to describe Brasilândia.

As noted previously, I first learned about the neighborhood of Brasilândia through references to it as São Paulo's "Little Africa." In the course of fieldwork, however, São Paulo residents who did not live in Brasilândia rarely brought up the "Little Africa" neighborhood identity without my prompting. Instead, my casual mention of the neighborhood most often elicited comments about the place as a locus of danger and violent crime. One such interaction took place when registering with Brazil's Federal Police (a process all foreigners must complete early after arriving). Casual conversations with the functionaries at the multiple stages in this process are common. The affable person charged with reviewing my documentation had previously lived in a district to the east of Brasilândia. Realizing the connection, I mentioned to her that my research focused on Brasilândia. She responded with a cautious sigh and explained that my appearance, especially my White skin color, would create problems for me in the neighborhood. I did not push her to expand the logic of her comment, which I nonetheless interpreted as an allusion to the supposedly high index of violent crime and Black population in Brasilândia. While anecdotal, such interactions reveal contemporary perceptions of the neighborhood as defined by a criminalized and racialized stigma.

I have deleted this section twice and twice clicked *undo* out of concern that the following narratives will reproduce a simplified and racist stigma of Brasilândia. My aim is, to state the obvious, much to the contrary. By documenting the construction of the stigma, I aim to complicate and, ultimately, counter it. The following is not a comprehensive analysis of actually existing patterns of violent crime over time. Instead, the section centers on the history of the stigma of Brasilândia as a dangerous place, one chapter in how the stigma took on a racialized form, and some of the strategies that residents have employed and still employ to navigate or contest it. This enduring stigma, a racist rendition of the "Little Africa" neighborhood identity, serves to pathologize the neighborhood and its residents. The stigma also helps to obfuscate broader conceptions of violence—and especially anti-Black violence—as manifesting in widespread poverty and substandard urban infrastructure, both acute realities (as detailed in the first section above) of most residents' daily lives in Brasilândia in the 1960s and 1970s, before, and since.

Despite the sensationalized discourse of the "talk of crime," it is important to note initially that some Brasilândia residents describe the fear and reality of violence as a significant feature in the everyday lives.[90] While such recollections indicate the prevalence of violence in Brasilândia, it does not follow that the neighborhood's residents were exceptionally violent. As explained in the first section of this chapter, Brasilândia was singular in São Paulo for having a severe lack of public services and for exceptional rates of urban poverty. These issues were causes, symptoms, and indeed forms of violence. Some locals drew the link between the lack of adequate urban infrastructure, for example, and conventional definitions of violent crime. Neighborhood organizations, known as Societies of Friends of the Neighborhood (Sociedade dos Amigos do Bairro) sprouted up throughout São Paulo from the late 1950s through the 1980s.[91] The Society of Friends of Brasilândia lobbied the municipal government for resources for the neighborhood, such as electricity and public illumination, with the explicit aim of improving safety.

A 1972 article in *O Estado de S. Paulo* drew the connection between infrastructure and public safety, noting that "the installation of streetlights on roads and in plazas and the extension of police patrolling to more distant, less frequented places are the primary demands from Societies of Neighborhood Friends on the São Paulo periphery."[92] The article singled out Vila Brasilândia for inadequate policing: "The existing police precincts, as well as military detachments, don't have the means to cover the full area. While some neighborhood roads have lots of movement that help to keep delinquents away, the Vila also has the so-called Catimbó, situated in a tumultuous region difficult to patrol."[93] Similar to the 2017 *Folha de S. Paulo* study, the author of this article flattened the more complicated social reality of violence as relating to structural poverty and poor urban infrastructure. That simplified representation presented the Catimbó and Brasilândia as nodes of crime, peopled by stigmatized and marginalized "delinquents." The explanations for violent crime in Brasilândia in the 1960s and 1970s rarely conformed to such simplistic characterizations.

State authorities, including some officially responsible for public safety, sometimes contributed to violent crime in Brasilândia. In addition to increased police scrutiny and surveillance of neighborhood residents, dramatic confrontations between residents and state security officials occurred in the neighborhood during Brazil's military dictatorship. In 1968, for instance, Brasilândia became a shooting ground for a group of rogue police detectives known as the Esquadrão da Morte (Death squad). José Francisco dos Santos Filho, known as Cabo Verde, lived in Brasilândia and newspaper reports suggested that he controlled the local commerce in marijuana. In late December 1968, two members of the Esquadrão da Morte tracked Cabo Verde in the Catimbó. They subsequently captured and drove him to a city in the São Paulo interior, where they murdered him.[94] In the years following, members of the Esquadrão da Morte faced trial for the murder along with allegations of being involved in the illicit trade themselves. They were accused of murdering competing traffickers or, in the case of Cabo Verde, traffickers who would no longer supply pay-offs.[95]

The military dictatorship also prompted violent resistance in Brasilândia. In November 1971, five participants from the antidictatorship organization the Popular Liberation Movement (Movimento de Libertação Popular), or MOLIPO, set a bus on fire at a plaza in Brasilândia. A member of the military police named Nelson Martinez Ponce happened upon the scene and attempted to intervene. The MOLIPO militants supposedly killed the officer, and the press in São Paulo ran stories about the five "terrorists" accused of the murder. The caption of an image of Ponce's funeral in *Veja* magazine described him as "the latest victim of the violence."[96] An article in *O Estado de S. Paulo* from three months later identified the militant Hiroaki Torigoi as one of the five participants in the bus bombing and murder.[97] MOLIPO adopted urban guerilla warfare tactics made famous by Brazilian Carlos Marighella, who influenced militant movements across the globe.[98]

The bus incident aligned broadly with those tactics; however, their decision to set fire to a bus and in Brasilândia may have had a broader significance. I have not located sources that indicate why MOLIPO militants chose Brasilândia or if the neighborhood served as a site for organized antidictatorship networks. The fact that a street in the Jardim Elisa Maria region of Brasilândia today commemorates Marighella suggests a plausible link.[99] The 1971 incident, nevertheless, likely provided further evidence to support the stigma of the neighborhood as a locus of dangerous crime.

A novel series of sensationalized radio programs exaggerated popular perceptions and realities of violent crime throughout São Paulo in the 1960s and 1970s. These programs drew on a much longer tradition of popular media focused on crime in Brazil and beyond.[100] Broadcaster Gil Gomes was one of the most prominent purveyors of the genre on São Paulo's radio waves. He got his start in 1968, when a man attempted (unsuccessfully) to kidnap an administrative assistant in the office building where he worked as a sports reporter. Gomes grabbed his microphone and covered the unfolding drama in real time. The experience provoked "a new and dazzling emotion," Gomes remembers. "When everything finished I sensed that this could be my new path. A live police program. We would transform police news into facts that would be narrated."[101] In the years following he would make a name for himself as a "truth-bearing" journalist and amateur detective, narrating violent crime along with "various types of everyday drama in a large city . . . stories of abandonment, of homosexuals, of prostitutes, of transvestites, or cases whose themes were supernatural forces, like the one about a 'spirit that fought with a drunk in a *terreiro de macumba*.'"[102]

Journalist José Wilson penned a scathing critique of Gomes's program and others like it in *Lua Nova*, a publication founded in 1984 by the São Paulo–based Center for Studies of Contemporary Culture (Centro de Estudos de Cultura Contemporânea) as a forum for articles on contemporary issues.[103] Broadcasters like Gomes described, Wilson wrote, "in a sensational and frightening form the most terrible crimes of daily life, making clear that these could happen to anyone." Though other cities broadcast comparable programs, São Paulo distinguished itself with "specialized narrators" who became celebrity millionaires on par with television and soccer stars. "Mornings on São Paulo radio," Wilson wrote, "are bathed with blood, terror, and hate."[104] Gomes's shows opened with the tagline "the greatest reporter of Brazilian radio" before proceeding to the "fantastic cases" of the day.[105]

Gomes's show made an impact. He shared a daily audience of two million listeners with the other major broadcaster in the genre, Afanásio Jazadji.[106] Wilson writes how fabricated parts of Gomes's stories were sometimes adopted by authorities as the official version of events.[107] Beyond official or popular perceptions of crime, the programs served to stoke anxieties and, in fact, had the potential to increase crime rates. Gomes incentivized, Wilson asserted, "the population to participate in assassination operations against criminals who operate in the neighborhood or, at the very least, to remain silent in the face of the groups that formed to hunt bandits."[108] A 1979 article celebrating fifty-two years of radio in Brazil noted that "Gil Gomes, by drawing attention to violence in the greater region, ends up being a harbinger of spectacular crimes."[109]

With stories about often petty crimes in marginalized areas in poor regions on the outskirts of the city, the programs aided in the criminalization of geographically marginal regions in São Paulo like Brasilândia. Broadcasters like Gomes assumed roles as spokespeople for popular justice, and the listening audience often lived in the very areas where the "fantastic" cases took place. Poor residents formed long lines at radio stations to solicit judgments from broadcasters such as Gomes, while others sent letters requesting "solutions for cases that the police were not able to solve."[110] One resident described Gomes as "my only hope for justice. The police, you know how they are, they don't do anything."[111] Gomes would ultimately be recognized by police authorities as a popular arbiter of justice: "Gomes has already received various trophies from the police, for his prominence and his contribution in the fight against crime in Brazil. One of them was a trophy with his name, given by the First Battalion of the Metropolitan Military Police."[112]

Oral histories with Brasilândia residents suggest that Gomes helped to popularize (if not coin) a nickname for the neighborhood as "Macacolândia," or "Monkeyland." I first encountered the term in the dissertation of Reinaldo José de Oliveira, who conducted interviews in Brasilândia and cited a resident who described broadcasters using the phrase on the radio.[113] In my own research, I first encountered Gomes's name when a longtime Brasilândia resident attributed use of the term to the broadcaster's shows in the early 1970s. Resident LN also cited the racist epithet, presenting it as evidence of discrimination against Brasilândia residents, though without naming Gomes.[114] Another resident, CP, remembers first hearing a related association when he commuted to the neighborhood of Braz, known as a hub of Italian immigrants and their descendants in São Paulo, for work in the early 1970s. After CP told a new coworker that he lived in Brasilândia, a colleague responded: "Aren't there just a bunch of monkeys there?"[115] Another resident suggests that Gomes exaggerated the significance of Brasilândia in the distribution of crime in the city of São Paulo. He explains that Gomes would attribute any crime that happened in the Northern Zone, the expansive region of the city of São Paulo above the Tietê River, to Brasilândia.[116] To date, I have not located recordings or transcripts of Gomes's broadcasts to track the precise usage of this term, including specific years.

Decades before the ascription of "Macacolândia" to Brasilândia, prominent and best-selling São Paulo author Monteiro Lobato published a collection of children's fables with one short entry, "Two Voyagers in Macacolândia."[117] Released in 1922, *Fables* (*Fábulas*) was celebrated by an article in *O Estado de S. Paulo* for being "enormously distributed throughout the whole country" and adopted in São Paulo for classroom curricula.[118] The fable opens with two travelers lost in the *sertão*, an arid and impoverished region of Brazil's Northeast commonly represented in political and literary discourses as an uncivilized region populated by mixed-race Brazilians and standing in the way of national order and progress. Lobato's two travelers—one a "diplomat," the other an "irritated, bitter friend of truth"—stumble accidentally upon the kingdom named "Macocolândia." They are seized by "fierce guards" who take them to meet the king, named Simão III.

Lobato represents "Macacolândia" as a farcical kingdom ruled by an unthinkable monkey king. With "that monkey curiosity," Lobato writes, the sovereign Simão examines each of the travelers and then asks them to appraise his kingdom. Responding first, the diplomat offers lavish praise: "I have never seen a people more handsome, a court more brilliant, nor a king of more noble appearance than Your Majesty." Responding second, the "friend of truth" dithers through his evaluation: "What do I think? It's good! I think it is!" Simão cuts him off, demanding candor. "It's nothing," he tells the king, "Monkey here, monkey there, monkey on the throne, monkey on the flagstaff." Furious, the king sentences "the miserable slanderer" to a week in a burning caldron. "Friends of truth," Lobato concludes, must "cover their backs with armor."

Lobato does not situate "The Two Voyagers in Macacolândia" in a specific historical era; however, certain details within the story seem to reference large *quilombos*, perhaps especially the famous Palmares kingdom. Founded in the early seventeenth century, Palmares was the largest such collective in Brazilian history and lasted for nearly ninety years before being overtaken.[119] By placing "Macacolândia" in the Northeast region, where Palmares rose and fell, Lobato perhaps makes a subtle allusion to the *quilombo*. The fact that Simão is the third generation on the throne also parallels Palmares, where the name of the leading figure Zumbi repeated over generations. Lastly, the final place to fall in the war to destroy Palmares—and, by some accounts, the capital of the kingdom itself—was deemed the "Royal Court of Monkeys" (*Cerca Real dos Macacos*).[120] Lobato may have avoided the name Palmares in order to hew to the fable genre, which derives its moral force in part from anthropomorphized, ahistorical unreality. Palmares figured prominently in the surge of Black associative life in São Paulo in the 1920s, including the 1926 founding of the Palmares Civic Center.[121] Seen in that historical context, the fable may also suggest apprehensions about Black political leadership.

Lobato's works remained prominent in the decades following, and even today the official children's library in the city of São Paulo bears the author's name.[122] A 1972 article from *O Estado de S. Paulo* noted Lobato's firm place in "the pantheon of national letters," especially through continuing high sales of children's books.[123] Stories such as "The Two Voyagers in Macacolândia" provided didactic material for young Brazilians about racialized social hierarchies as manifest both in geographic space and human bodies. Historian Carl Degler writes about the significance of Lobato's racialized discourse in relation to Lobato's 1934 book *Voyage to the Sky* (*Viagem ao Ceu*). Degler describes the prominent character Aunt Nastacia within that book as "nothing less than that of the Negro mammy as she used to appear in the United States in the form of Aunt Jemima. The sketches . . . show her with a fat, shapeless body, thick lips, large eyes, large flat feet, and a kerchief on her head. As a personality she is loving, hard-working, superstitious, fearful, subservient, and ignorant." Degler explains that such racial caricatures proved consequential for generations of children: "From such books children, principally middle- and upper-class whites, learned how to perceive blacks."[124] The story about "Macacolândia" may have, similarly, helped to naturalize racialized hierarchies in the guise of aphoristic universals for generations of young Brazilians.

Gomes grew up in São Paulo when Lobato's children's literature was a staple of the public curriculum. No records indicate, however, that his use of "Macacolândia" derived directly from Lobato's *Fables*. The prominent history of slavery and records of *quilombos* in the region of Brasilândia, formerly the Freguesia do Ó parish, bore some resonances to Palmares. The composers of Rosas de Ouro had invoked the history of Palmares directly in their theme for carnival in 1973, drawing an implicit connection between Brasilândia as a "Little Africa" and the Palmares kingdom. Even if these parallels did not register directly with Gomes, in the ears of some of his listeners the use of the spatialized monkey metaphor would have drawn on generations of racist "common sense" in Brazil and throughout in the Americas.[125]

The racist nickname depicted Brasilândia as the modern manifestation of a dangerous, farcical "Macacolândia" populated and ruled by Black Brazilians. Updated to 1970s concerns about violent crime, the term cast the neighborhood as a primitive Black periphery, antithetical to order and progress and dangerous, perhaps all the more so because it served as a locus for Black self-determination. Gomes's broadcasts likely both reflected and contributed to anxieties about Blackness on the city's geographic and social margins.

"Macacolândia" was not the only racist nickname applied to Brasilândia or its residents. CF recalled another nickname popularly associated with the company that ran the Brasilândia bus line through the early 1970s, Transportes Urbanos Sociedade Anônima Limitada (TUSA), and that was also broadcast over the radio. The nickname, based on the acronym, was "Transporte de Urubú Sem Asa" (a literal translation is "Transportation for vultures without wings"). I did not know the meaning of *urubú* as vultures in my initial conversation with CF, who subsequently explained that it had a meaning similar to the racist monkey epithet.[126] I later found Degler's explanation of common usage of *urubú*: "Black children are instructed quite directly on the low value of their color. At an early age little black boys are called *urubu* (a black vulture) or *anu* (a small black bird)."[127] Not unique to contemporary São Paulo, such racist nicknames likely served to reinforce inequalities that are both sociospatial and racial.[128]

With the broadcasting of racist nicknames on São Paulo's airwaves, non-White and White Brasilândia residents alike confronted the stigma associated with the neighborhood throughout the city. In his dissertation on segregation in São Paulo, Oliveira recorded the following commentary from a resident about this experience:

> When I was young, Brasilândia carried a heavy weight of prejudice. To live in Brasilândia was to be considered a thug (*bandido*). . . . Brasilândia was synonymous with everything that didn't work out . . . everything that happened in Brasilândia would appear in the press: Crime in Vila Brasilândia, they killed so and so! And businesses didn't hire people that lived in Brasilândia.[129]

Locals developed strategies to counter this stigma. For instance, residents sometimes claim residence in another neighborhood or district when talking with a potential employer.[130] Oliveira's interviewee explains: "People, when they went to look for work, would omit this [the name Brasilândia]. . . . People would say they lived in Freguesia do Ó, that they lived wherever, but like this, you didn't say you lived in the subdistrict of Brasilândia, no one ever said it."[131] This sentiment endures: A documentary film produced in the neighborhood included a group interview with adolescent residents. They all admitted to using names other than Brasilândia when talking with nonlocals to describe where they lived and to avoid the stigma.[132] A taxi driver explained a similar sentiment to me with a creative twist: "When it's for a job, I say I'm from Freguesia do Ó. When it's the taxman, I'll say Brasilândia." These strategies reveal residents keenly aware of, and adept at navigating, the racist social stigma attached to Brasilândia.

Not everyone I met, including long-term Black residents deeply invested in the history of the region, had heard of the nickname of Brasilândia as "Macacolândia." Most, however, likely confronted the consequences of the broadcasting of that racist epithet. Gomes's program, along with other media that exaggerated violent crime in the region, contributed to making Brasilândia a racialized point of reference throughout São Paulo. The racist nickname would further set Brasilândia apart from similar places throughout the city's geographic periphery, where poverty, a grave lack of public infrastructure, and precarious living conditions were types of everyday, structural violence that many locals knew well. The stigmatization of Brasilândia served to gloss over those more complicated manifestations of violence and mark the residents and the space of the neighborhood itself as a dangerous, non-White margin.

By the 1980s, Brasilândia had one of the largest concentrations of African descendants in the city of São Paulo. Produced through the spatial praxis of belonging-as-being, the neighborhood had acquired a special significance among African descendants in the city.

That significance was encapsulated in 1982 by Genival Candido da Silva, a Brasilândia resident running for City Council in that year's elections. In an article printed in the neighborhood newspaper, Silva wrote:

> It is often said, with a certain amount of pride, that in our country there is no racism. The people of Brasilândia have something to say about this. There was a time when the neighborhood, whose population is predominantly Black, was known as "macacolândia." There was a time when the police, in a clear discriminatory attitude, would burst into the houses and shacks of our people looking for "marginals," arresting indiscriminately, and "cleaning up" the streets of the neighborhood. The residents then decided to fight back. By always moving together, organizing associations, recreating their culture, and returning to their roots, they achieved several improvements. Streets were asphalted, schools were constructed. But transportation continues to be terrible, and insecurity is still high. What we really gained was a consciousness of our Blackness (*negritude*), of the racism that surrounds us, and of the need to win, to demand from those in power, dignity in our lives.[133]

Referencing the racist epithet, criminalization, police harassment, and disinvestment, Silva critiqued the anti-Blackness that had shaped Brasilândia over the preceding decades. That history, he asserted, equipped residents with powerful evidence to contradict boastful representations of Brazil as a postracial society. At the same time, Silva stressed how residents had worked collectively to make Brasilândia a place of belonging for African descendants and a base from which to struggle for fundamental human dignity, including the very right to exist. Written thirty-five years after the sale of the first lots in Vila Brasilândia, Silva's comments echoed core features of the spatial praxis of belonging-as-being.

The privileged role that Brasilândia held, along with another manifestation of key aspects of the spatial praxis of belonging-as-being, surfaced in the 1985 renaming of a public square in the neighborhood for

Luiza Mahin. Mahin is commonly remembered for her involvement in uprisings of enslaved and free Africans in Salvador, Bahia, in the 1830s, perhaps the most dramatic period of antislavery rebellions in Brazilian history.[134] In the years following the thwarted revolts of the 1830s, Mahin fled Salvador to an unknown fate. Her son, Luís Gama (discussed in chapter 2), meanwhile, was enslaved and transported south to the city of São Paulo. There, he obtained legal freedom and a law degree, which he used to spearhead antislavery campaigns in São Paulo's courts through his death in the early 1880s.

The Black Women's Collective of São Paulo spearheaded an initiative to rename a public square in Brasilândia, which sat just a few blocks away from the former Congo Road, for Mahin. They advertised the event with a poster that featured Mahin's visage (figure 4.5). At the inauguration in March of 1985, the prominent African-descendent poet Cuti delivered a few verses of celebration and reflection:

> Luiza Mahin is in the square
> for the dignity of the race.
> What is the secret
> of the language of spaces
> and statues?
> Between the being who passes
> unaware
> and the immovable stone or plaque
> the message whistles
> against the silence of the farse.
> Who has a past
> So secret
> To be chosen for the names of streets and plazas?

Echoing other African-descendent residents of São Paulo such as Gabriel Marques, Cuti here argued for the significance of place-names in countering the "silence of the farse," a reference to the common practice of rendering African descendants invisible in São Paulo's past, present, and future. The creation of Luiza Mahin Plaza contested that anti-Black silencing, which had indirectly spurred the creation of Brasilândia (through displacement) and directly led to the renaming of Congo Road. The decision to place Luiza Mahin Plaza in Brasilândia reflected the significance of this neighborhood as a hub for survival, Black self-determination, and belonging among the residents of Brasilândia and African descendants throughout São Paulo.

The naming of Praça Luiza Mahin coincided with the consolidation of the neighborhood as a "Little Africa." This construction of the neighborhood's spatial identity signaled a shift from the previous decades and earliest years of the *loteamento*, when migrants of diverse ethnoracial and geographic backgrounds represented this neighborhood-level "Brazil-land" as a harmonious, multiethnic microcosm of the nation. From within the neighborhood in the period following, some locals sought to construct Brasilândia as a locus of both ethnoracial diversity *and* Black self-determination. From without, dominant characterizations of the neighborhood rarely accommodated such complexity. In an era when urbanists privileged an ethos of integration as the solution to a burgeoning urban crisis, figures like Gomes and others helped to create a durable image of Brasilândia as a racialized Other and dangerous margin within the city of São Paulo.

The construction of Brasilândia as a "Little Africa" existed, nonetheless, alongside the continued and substantial ethnoracial diversity of the local population. Locals experienced that diversity every day in the commercial core of Brasilândia along Parapuã Street. That street bisected Rosas de Ouro Street, along which sat the headquarters of the samba school. A block southwest was the Yamamato Judo Association, the Japanese language and Judo school discussed in chapter 3 that was founded clandestinely in the early 1950s. On the same block was J. Vagliengo Plaza, named in 1966 by a city council decree for the Italian-born head engineer of the railway between Santos and Jundiaí.[135] Concentrated within the span of two blocks in the commercial heart of the neighborhood, these place-names reflected the African-Japanese-Italian-descendent demographic and spatial reality of Brasilândia and similar spaces throughout the city of São Paulo. That reality coexisted alongside racialized inequalities, violence, and prejudice within Brasilândia and the city of São Paulo more broadly.

The erasure of center-city spaces associated with African descendants set the stage for the production of Brasilândia as a "Little Africa," and Brasilândia appears in hindsight as one of the destinations that Geraldo Filme anticipated in his resolution, "I'll Samba Someplace Else." While some urbanists and journalists defined the neighborhood as a pathological periphery, residents in Brasilândia appropriated that

FIGURE 4.5 · Poster celebrating the inauguration of Praça Luíza Mahin. Geledes Collection, AEL – Arquivo Edgard Leuenroth, UNICAMP.

spatial designation and resignified the meanings of the margin. Their construction of Brasilândia as "Little Africa" echoes bell hooks's definition of the margin as a "site of radical possibility, a space of resistance." In *Feminist Theory: From Margin to Center*, hooks wrote:

> To be in the margin is to be part of the whole but outside the main body. As black Americans living in a small Kentucky town, the railroad tracks were a daily reminder of our marginality. *Across those tracks were paved streets*, stores we could not enter, restaurants we could not eat in, and people we could not look directly in the face. Across those tracks was a world we could work in as maids, as janitors, as prostitutes, as long as it was in a service capacity. We could enter that world but we could not live there. We had always to return to the margin, to cross the tracks to shacks and abandoned houses on the edge of town. . . . Living as we did—on the edge—we developed a particular way of seeing reality. We looked both from the outside in and from the inside out. We focused our attention on the center as well as on the margin. We understood both. This mode of seeing reminded us of the existence of a whole universe, a main body made up of both margin and center. Our survival depended on an ongoing public awareness of the separation between margin and center and an ongoing private acknowledgement that we were a necessary, vital part of that whole.[136]

Despite the thousands of miles and myriad other differences that separate rural Kentucky and São Paulo, hooks's reflection mirrors the language and content many residents of Brasilândia use when describing the neighborhood's history and the sociospatial dynamics of São Paulo broadly.[137] hooks's characterization of segregation and racial division as determined by, and defined as, paved streets would have been immediately recognizable to many Brasilândia residents along with notable figures like Geraldo Filme and Gabriel Marques. These parallels point to the racialized significance of material features of the built environment and their work in structuring and reinforcing racialized social inequalities in varied contexts throughout the Americas.

FIVE

Producing Ethnoracial Infrastructures

Making "Japanese" Liberdade and "Italian" Bexiga

On his first tour of South America in October of 1997, United States President Bill Clinton spoke to business leaders in the city of São Paulo.[1] Clinton complimented the commercial elite at the gathering, describing São Paulo as the "economic heart of the continent" and the "city of the future." He also flexed his knowledge of local culture, which he articulated through a description of the city's neighborhoods: "The neighborhoods of São Paulo are a window on the world. The colors of Italy enliven Bixiga. The flavors of Japan infuse Liberdade. The spirit of the Middle East fills Bom Retiro. The rhythms of Africa pervade every quarter. People from everywhere call this place home."[2] Clinton presented São Paulo's ethnoracialized neighborhoods as representative of the city's seemingly distinctive brand of ethnoracial mixture and supposedly harmonious interethnic relations. The Brazilian attendees may have nodded with agreement and satisfaction at Clinton's depiction of São Paulo as a multicultural metropolis. Some of them, however, may have also recalled the more complicated pasts involved in constructing this local landscape of mixture.

Indeed, one significant space from that past sat remarkably close by. The gathering took place at the Memorial to Latin America in the Barra Funda neighborhood, just a few blocks from the former Largo da

Banana.[3] City officials buried that sacred space beneath an asphalted avenue and concrete overpass in 1958. For those who remembered the Largo da Banana or similar places throughout São Paulo, that demolished site attested to the planning and dislocations involved in producing the landscape of harmonious ethnoracialized neighborhoods that Clinton celebrated.

For many readers, the ethnoracialized neighborhoods Clinton described likely sound familiar. So-called ethnic enclaves are common, prominent features of populous, multiethnic cities in the Americas and beyond. The conventional popular and academic wisdom about ethnic enclaves holds that they emerge through settlement patterns among immigrants and their descendants.[4] According to this line of thinking, Liberdade is "Japanese" because Japanese immigrants settled there, established businesses and other institutions, and, over generations, maintained a significant-if-not-dominant presence relative to other ethnoracial groups. Liberdade is "Japanese," in other words, because Japanese immigrants and their descendants have lived there.

Settlement patterns and population proportions certainly figure into the construction of ethnic enclaves. I have yet to encounter an example of a "Little Italy," for instance, that did not have at least some discernible history of settlement by Italian immigrants and their descendants. Nonetheless, ethnic enclaves are neither the inevitable nor the organic result of settlement patterns among immigrants and their descendants. What's more, the reasonable, intuitive supposition that the specific identity of an ethnic enclave reflects the demographic composition of the local resident population does not always align with the sociospatial realities of such places, in São Paulo and beyond.

Japanese and Italian immigrants and their descendants, for instance, have long formed one among multiple ethnoracial groups in Liberdade and Bexiga. In fact, Liberdade became "Japanese" through the "Bairro Oriental" project at a time when migrants from Brazil's Northeast, along with immigrants from China, Korea, and Vietnam, made up sizable minorities of the resident population. Similarly, migrants from Brazil's Northeast constituted a substantial portion of Bexiga's population in the 1960s and 1970s. These demographic realities point toward the limitations of the ethnic enclaves model and invite us to reexamine the specific processes through which ethnoracialized neighborhoods are constructed, including who participates in their construction and, crucially, what populations and other identities those spatialized identities are constructed against. Liberdade and Bexiga offer apt and compelling settings within which to carry out this reexamination. As I will show, the dominant ethnoracialized identities of these neighborhoods were produced in relation and, at times, direct opposition to contemporary in-migrant populations (Northeasterners, especially) as well as the former African-descendent residents who had made these two neighborhoods core places in São Paulo's early to mid-twentieth-century "Black zone."

As discussed in chapters 1 and 2, from the late 1920s through the mid-1960s, urban redevelopment centered on the construction of avenues began to reshape Liberdade and Bexiga, at the time two of the most significant centers of African-descendent settlement in São Paulo. Expropriation and demolitions dislocated many long-term African-descendent residents, paving the way—literally and figuratively—for the transformation of Liberdade and Bexiga into *former* cores of what Geraldo Filme described as São Paulo's "Black zone." The previous chapter charted the remaking of that zone on São Paulo's geographic periphery in Brasilândia, which came to be known as a "Little Africa." This chapter returns the frame fully to the city center, where, from the mid-1960s through the mid-1980s, an array of planners produced two of São Paulo's most iconic and seemingly natural ethnic enclaves: "Japanese" Liberdade and "Italian" Bexiga.[5]

Ambitious redevelopment schemes and unwieldy, unchecked urbanization had generated an urban crisis in the metropolitan region of São Paulo from the late 1960s through the mid-1970s.[6] Official city planners in São Paulo identified the districts of Liberdade and Bela Vista as key sites of urban decay, all the while pursuing disruptive transportation projects that continued to exacerbate local conditions. In this context, self-appointed neighborhood representatives in Liberdade and Bexiga partnered with official city planners to pursue projects of neighborhood revitalization fueled by the logic that historic centers of Japanese and Italian settlement deserved better. Tourism-oriented economic development drove the campaign to make Liberdade "Japanese," while the project to make "Italian" Bexiga centered on state-sponsored historic preservation.

These combined ethnoracialization and urban revitalization efforts ushered in extensive material changes in the local built environment. Those changes included the installation of an ethnically themed infrastructure—what I term an *ethnoracial infrastructure*—of valuable, durable urban services rare in most São Paulo neighborhoods at the time. This infrastructure included public illumination, sidewalks, parks, bridges, signage, and more. The substantial public and private investment in this infrastructure both reflected and reinforced the social prestige of Japanese and Italian ethnoracial identities in the city of São Paulo. At the same time, the infrastructure further contributed to the burial of spaces significant to African descendants in Liberdade and Bexiga, the continued dislocation of African-descendent residents from these regions, and the deepening of racialized urban inequalities in the city on the whole.[7] This infrastructure, therefore, helped to concretize ethnoracialized social difference in ways that deepened ethnoracial inequalities in São Paulo while, simultaneously, establishing a tangible, material basis of support for representations of São Paulo as a non-Black, ethnically immigrant multicultural metropolis.

As noted in previous chapters, there is a crucial distinction between the categories of district and neighborhood in São Paulo. The narratives in this chapter take place within the spaces officially classified as the districts of Bela Vista and Liberdade. Those districts have existed formally—with officially demarcated boundaries—since the first decade of the twentieth century. The neighborhoods of Liberdade and Bexiga are distinct from, but located largely within, these formal districts. As with all São Paulo neighborhoods, these neighborhoods have no formal or official boundaries. They are fluid constructs defined or redefined through everyday spatial practices and discourses. They are also the products of larger-scale redevelopment projects that center on, and are framed by, specific neighborhoods. The making of "Japanese" Liberdade and "Italian" Bexiga are examples of such larger-scale projects. Both projects aimed to redefine these informal, unofficial neighborhoods through the production of ethnoracial space. Readers will note that throughout the chapter I use quotations when describing the ethnoracialized identities of these neighborhoods (as in, "Italian" Bexiga and "Japanese" Liberdade or "Bairro Oriental") so as to emphasize their constructed nature.

THE DEMOGRAPHICS OF ETHNORACIAL NEIGHBORHOODS

Census data measuring race and ethnicity are problematic, in Brazil and beyond, and such data must be used cautiously and in dialogue with other sources of quantitative and qualitative information. Census information can, nonetheless, provide useful insights about the ethnoracial composition of certain spaces, especially in the context of formal projects centered on the ethnoracialization of those spaces. As noted earlier in the book, quantitative data—especially but not exclusively from Brazil's census—about the ethnoracial composition of districts in São Paulo is quite challenging to access and generate.

These methodological challenges owe to the small scale of the district level and the methods by which race has been measured in official censuses. In Brazil, race is not measured on the universal questionnaire, which all citizens fill out, but on the complementary questionnaire, which derives from a sampling of a segment of the population. Access to the source data—not just the summary conclusions from that data—from the complementary questionnaire is necessary to calculate demographic data on race at the district level. For censuses before 1960, the source data from the complementary questionnaires has been lost. For the 1960 census, the source data is available, however census authorities sampled only 5 percent of the population for the complementary questionnaire. That small sample size prevents us from computing ethnoracial identification at the district level with a necessary degree of statistical confidence. In 1970, authorities expanded the scope of the complementary questionnaire, applying it to 25 percent of the population. However, the military dictatorship in 1970 omitted race from the census under the logic that racial categories could not accurately capture the ethnoracial diversity of Brazil's population.[8]

Race was reinstated in the 1980 census, and the complementary questionnaire from that year sampled 25 percent of the population. The source data from the complementary questionnaire is still available, and researchers from the University of São Paulo's Centro de Estudos das Metrópoles (CEM) have conducted the harmonization of the 1980 census data, a key step in demographic research. The 1980 census provides the earliest dataset, therefore, with information both usable and directly relevant to this study. Ideally, we would have data available from prior censuses to capture a longitudinal view of how the ethnoracial composition of these neighborhoods has changed over time. The limitations outlined above, however, prevent us from gaining such a view. While data from one census year does not capture change over time, the 1980 census does provide an illuminating snapshot of Liberdade and Bela Vista toward the end of the projects that transformed them into iconic ethnic enclaves. I will introduce core features of this snapshot, the calculation of which was led by sociologist André Marega Pinhel and geographer Rodrigo Fernandes Silva, and then refer back to this demographic context throughout the chapter as I narrate the ethnoracialization projects in both neighborhoods.

In our calculations we aggregated the four original racial categories listed on the 1980 census into just two: *White* and *non-White*. The original four categories were *preta* (Black), *parda* (Brown), *branca* (White), and *amarela* (Yellow). The Brown category—*parda*—included those who identified as Indigenous. Census officials added a separate category for Indigenous in the 1991 census. In our calculations, the *non-White* category includes respondents from the *preta* and *parda* categories. The MNU advocated for the aggregated category *negro* in the 1980s to contest the practice of whitening among Brazilians of African descent on the census.[9] Our usage of *non-White* aligns with their argument, though we opt for *non-White* instead of *negro* given that *parda* included people who identified as Indigenous. The aggregated *non-White* category also reflects conclusions from studies of racialized inequality in Brazil, which have found that the socioeconomic conditions of people who identify as *preta* and *parda* are similar enough—and, crucially, distinct enough from *branca*—to merit aggregation.[10]

The aggregated category *White* includes respondents from the *branca* and *amarela* census categories. CEM researchers included *amarela* in the *White* aggregate category in the process of data harmonization. Their motives for this aggregation are not entirely clear, though they most likely did so to increase the statistical confidence of their calculation. Their decision also reflects influential Brazilian racial ideologies that position Japanese immigrants and their descendants as non-Black and, in some cases, White.[11] The aggregation of *branca* and *amarela* means that data from the 1980 census does not offer a clear estimate of residents who identified as *amarela*—and thus most likely as Japanese immigrant descendants—in Liberdade (or Bela Vista, for that matter). The census does include other variables that provide suggestive clues, however. For instance, the religion category reveals that in 1980 Liberdade had the highest concentration of residents of any São Paulo district who practiced an "Oriental religion" (the census's term). Those practitioners constituted just 4.6 percent of the total resident population in Liberdade, however. This measurement positions Liberdade as significant for Japanese spiritual practices relative to São

Paulo on the whole, though the small number of practitioners again reveals the lack of homogeneity—in this case, religious/spiritual—of the district.

Mapping ethnoracial distribution in São Paulo in 1980 according to census data largely confirms the transformations that took place in these districts before 1980 and as outlined in the previous chapters. In 1980, 24.6 percent of São Paulo residents identified as non-White, while 18.4 percent of residents in Liberdade and 13.8 percent of Bela Vista residents identified as non-White. These figures placed Liberdade at thirty-first and Bela Vista at forty-first among the city's fifty-six districts for the percentage of its population that was non-White. These numbers quantify how thoroughly these neighborhoods had transformed over the middle of the twentieth century: After having two of the highest concentrations of African descendants in the 1930s, by 1980 they ranked in the lower half among all districts for the portion of residents who identified as non-White.

These demographic features of Liberdade and Bela Vista also align with the broader racialized geography of the city in 1980, as more central districts displayed a higher proportion of White residents compared to those on the geographic margins of the city. As noted in chapter 4, Brasilândia had the second-highest proportion of non-White residents in the city in the 1980 census, reflective of the concentration of non-Whites in the geographic periphery and especially the city's Northern Zone. High proportions of non-White residents also concentrated in the Eastern Zone and Southern Zone, as shown in maps 5.1 and 5.2. These maps illustrate the effects of the decades of racialized displacement that had transformed these districts and São Paulo more broadly across the middle of the twentieth century.

While Bela Vista and Liberdade had higher proportions of White residents than the city of São Paulo broadly in 1980, they were not ethnoracially homogenous. For instance, the 1980 census showed sizable immigrant populations among the residents of the two districts: 9.4 percent of Liberdade residents and 8.9 percent of Bela Vista residents were born outside of Brazil. By contrast, only 0.8 percent of Brasilândia residents were immigrants according to the 1980 census. The largest immigrant groups in Liberdade were Japanese (40.8 percent), Korean (10.3 percent), and Chinese (6.9 percent). In Bela Vista, the largest immigrant groups were from Portugal (17.4 percent), Italy (15.4 percent),

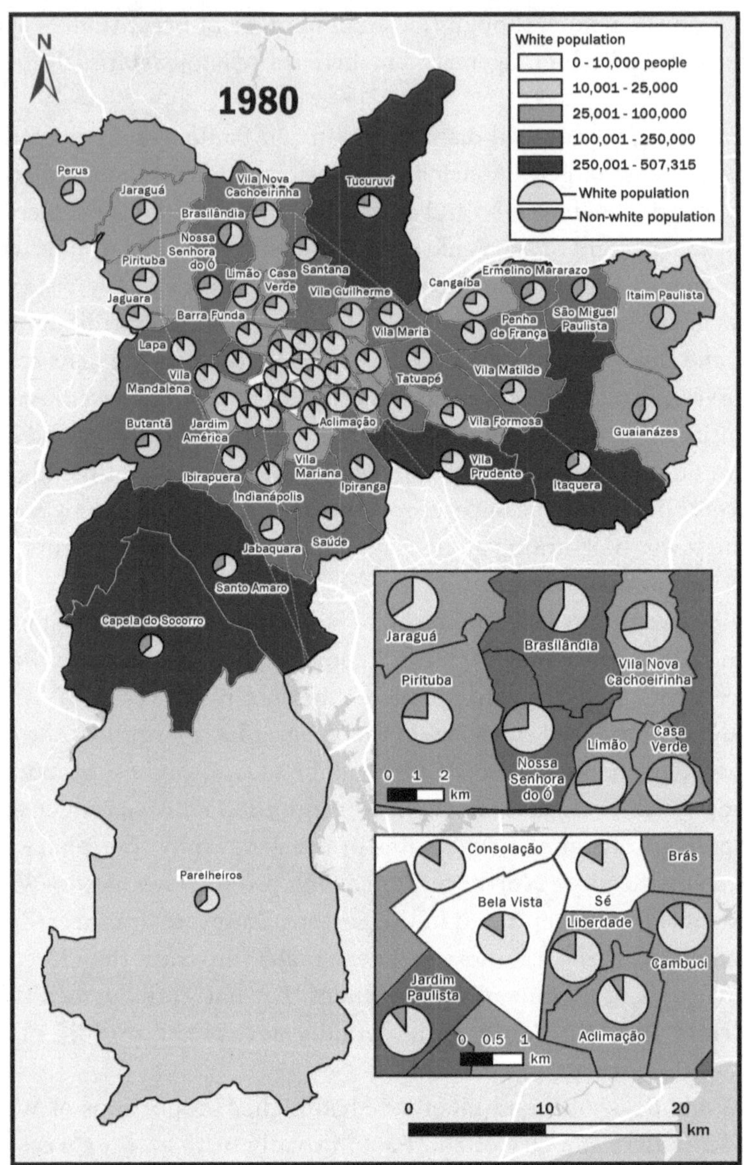

MAP 5.1 · Distribution of White São Paulo population by district, 1980. Data sources: Censo/IBGE; OpenStreetMap (Light Gray Canvas) © OpenStreetMap contributors, Microsoft, Facebook, Google, Esri Community Maps contributors, Map layer by Esri. Map by Rodrigo Fernandes Silva, André Marega Pinhel, and Andrew G. Britt.

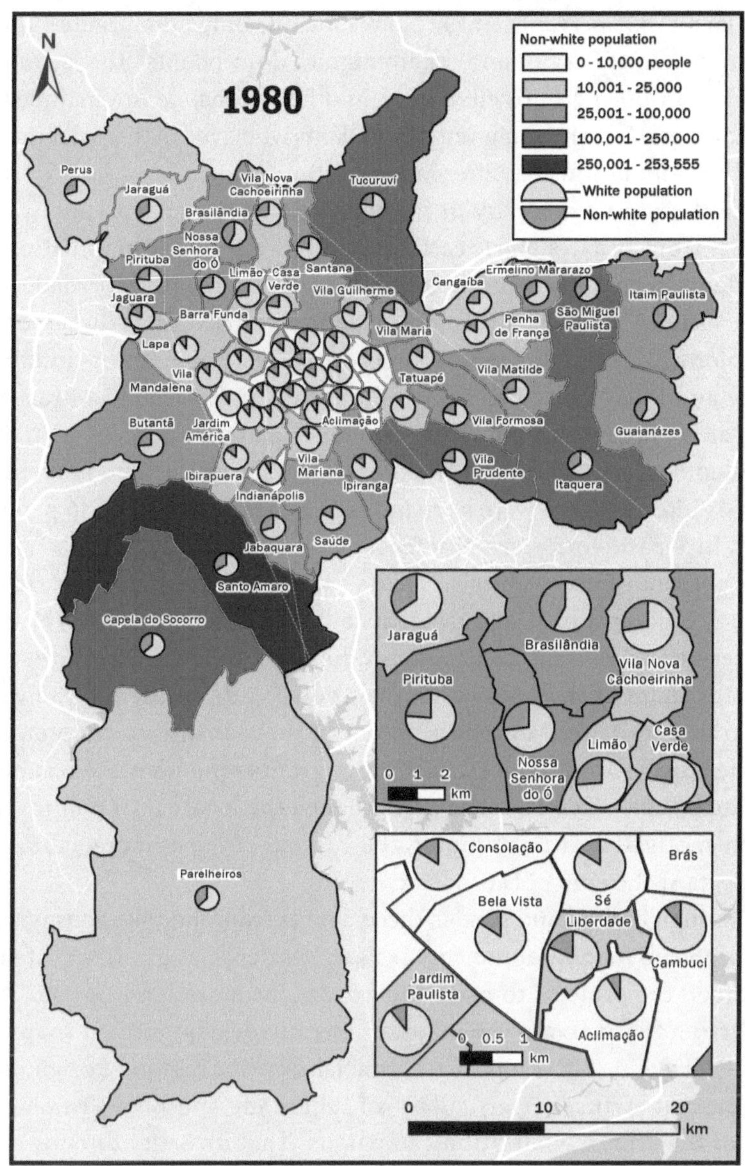

MAP 5.2 · Distribution of non-White São Paulo population by district, 1980. Data sources: Censo/IBGE; OpenStreetMap (Light Gray Canvas) © OpenStreetMap contributors, Microsoft, Facebook, Google, Esri Community Maps contributors, map layer by Esri. Map by Rodrigo Fernandes Silva, André Marega Pinhel, and Andrew G. Britt.

and Japan (15.2 percent). These figures include only immigrants—those born outside of Brazil—and not immigrant descendants. The Japanese- and Italian-born groups cited here, in other words, do not include the Japanese and Italian immigrant descendants who lived in these districts.[12]

The populations of Liberdade and Bela Vista also displayed significant regional diversity in the 1980 census. Not surprisingly, migrants from Brazil's Northeast constituted the largest population of residents born outside of the state of São Paulo in both Liberdade and Bela Vista. A similar pattern occurred in Brasilândia, as discussed in chapter 4. The racial composition of Northeastern migrants in Liberdade and Bela Vista differed from Brasilândia, however. In Brasilândia, 26.9 percent of non-White residents and 21.9 percent of White residents were born in the Northeast. In Liberdade, 43.9 percent of non-White residents were born in the Northeast, while just 16 percent of White residents were Northeasterners. Similarly, in Bela Vista, 36.1 percent of non-White residents came from the Northeast, while only 13.6 percent of White residents did. In Liberdade, in fact, Northeasterners who identified as non-White (43.9 percent) comprised a greater share of the population than non-White residents who were born in São Paulo (36.9 percent). As I discuss in this chapter, the higher proportion of Northeastern migrants who identified as non-White in Liberdade and Bela Vista shaped the local racial politics and likely motivated, at least in part, the authors of the ethnoracialization projects at the core of this narrative.

Though limited and partial, these figures from the 1980 census shed light on the demographic context and ethnoracial politics that surrounded the projects to make Liberdade "Japanese" and Bexiga "Italian" from the 1960s to the 1980s. They provide a quantified snapshot of the diversity—in terms of ethnoracial identity, region of origin, and immigrant status, in particular—of Liberdade and Bela Vista in the era of the ethnoracialization campaigns. That diversity directly contradicted the essentialized identities being projected on and produced through the transformed infrastructure of these two neighborhoods. That contradiction reinforces the conclusion that the ethnic enclaves hypothesis—that Bexiga is Italian because Italian immigrants and their descendants live there—does not sufficiently capture the dynamics that factor into the making of ethnoracial space. How and why, then, did Liberdade and Bexiga become "Japanese" and "Italian," respectively? The following sections offer answers to this inquiry.

FIGURE 5.1 · Torii in Liberdade, June 2017. Photo by Andrew G. Britt.

DEMOLITIONS AND THE BUSINESS OF ETHNORACIAL SPACE

At first, the president of the Liberdade Shopkeeper's Association, Tsuyoshi Mizumoto, rejected the proposition. Torii were hallowed gateways placed at entrances to Shinto temples in Japan, and the streets of Liberdade were not sacred. At least, not yet. Other Liberdade business owners helped convince Mizumoto to adapt the sacred symbol for the extensive project to make Liberdade São Paulo's "Bairro Oriental."[13] The project sought to capitalize on popular fascination with exoticized Oriental culture through the remaking of Liberdade into an ethnoracialized neighborhood fit for tourism and commerce. The red torii stood tall over the neighborhood along Galvão Bueno Street at the inauguration of the "Bairro Oriental" in 1974 (figure 5.1). The construction of the gateway consecrated the neighborhood as the "Bairro Oriental"; however, the reproduction of Liberdade began years earlier with a more destructive practice: expropriations and demolitions relating to avenues projects.

This and the following section chart the planning and production of the "Bairro Oriental." Extending from the late 1960s through late 1970s, the campaign involved the extensive reproduction of the local built environment with material forms designed to index Japaneseness.

The effort drew an array of participants into collaboration, from Japanese-Brazilian business elite and ordinary neighborhood residents to authorities from the municipal and state governments of São Paulo. The project provided the district of Liberdade with an improved urban infrastructure, including public illumination, sidewalks, parks, and bridges, all valuable urban amenities scarce in most São Paulo neighborhoods in the era. These changes did not transform Liberdade into a middle- or upper-class neighborhood in the years following.[14] Nonetheless, the project's completion represented official support for, and the concretization of, a Japanese ethnoracial identity in the geographic center of São Paulo. While valorizing Japaneseness, the inauguration of the "Bairro Oriental" further dislocated African descendants from Liberdade and helped to obscure significant local spatial histories relating to slavery, abolition, racial violence, and Black self-determination.

Ethnoracialized neighborhoods often change over time in ways that belie clear beginnings or endings; however, one of São Paulo's original "Japanese" neighborhoods came to a decisive conclusion in 1942. As discussed in chapter 3, in June 1942 state officials dealt a destructive blow to the Conde de Sarzedas neighborhood, located north of the contemporary Liberdade district along Conde de Sarzedas Street.[15] The declaration of war against Japan and Germany prompted a nativist Brazilianization campaign that demanded the at least superficial assimilation of Japanese-Brazilians.[16] Assimilation meant the suppression of minority cultural practices such as language as well as the desegregation of Japanese-Brazilians within the space of the city of São Paulo. State authorities forced the dislocation of residents from Conde de Sarzedas in 1942, sparking the dispersion of families into other districts throughout the city.[17] Few sources remain about the precise timeline or geography of this migration. Some of the residents dislocated from Conde de Sarzedas, however, did not remain gone for long. Historian Sachio Negawa explains that many families returned to the area in the second half of the 1940s and throughout the 1950s. Some of these returnees, he writes, "avoided the Conde District and resettled in different parts of the Liberdade District along Galvão Bueno Street and São Joaquim Street."[18] The reconstitution of a "Japanese" neighborhood, beginning in the 1950s and extending through the mid-1970s, aligned with this new geography of settlement south of Conde de Sarzedas Street.

Economic development drove postwar reconciliation between the Japanese and Brazilian governments as well as neighborhood-level changes in Liberdade. In 1953, a prewar immigrant and successful grain dealer named Yoshikazu Tanaka founded a 1,500-seat movie theater, Cine Niterói, on Galvão Bueno Street.[19] Anthropologist Alexandre Kishimoto describes Cine Niterói as "the first cinema dedicated exclusively to showing Japanese films in Brazil."[20] The earliest years of the theater coincided with a golden era of Japanese cinema, and Cine Niterói showed films by such famed Japanese directors as Akira Kurosawa. Kishimoto and Negawa describe the Cine Niterói as the initial spark, and long-time hub, for Japanese-Brazilian commercial activity in postwar Liberdade. That activity included an especially vibrant film scene, spread over five different cinemas by the end of the 1950s, and the establishment of neighborhood commercial organizations.[21] Cine Niterói's founder Tanaka became the first president of the Liberdade Shopkeeper's Association in 1965. In 1974 that institution was reorganized as the Cultural and Assistance Association of Liberdade with Mizumoto at the helm.[22] The leaders of those organizations would spearhead the "Bairro Oriental" effort in years following.

Official and academic histories present the founding of Cine Niterói in 1953 as the beginning of the reconstitution of a "Japanese" neighborhood in Liberdade. Negawa, for instance, asserts that "what caused the area to become the new Japantown that replaced the Conde District was definitely the opening of the Cine Niterói."[23] Kishimoto classifies the 1953 inauguration as the "retaking of the Japanese neighborhood."[24] "Retaking" encompassed both the reconstitution of Liberdade's identity *and* the expansion of local commercial activities: "Cine Niterói transformed the residential area into a shopping district."[25] A 1982 article similarly explained that the "Bairro Oriental" project began at Cine Niterói.[26] This narrative about Liberdade's transformation has cemented in official discourse, as evidenced by a 2017 decree from São Paulo's city council about Liberdade: "Galvão Bueno Street came to be the center of the Japanese Neighborhood, growing around Cine Niterói, having received a part of the businesses expelled from Conde de Sarzedas Street. It was there that the Japanese could find a little corner of Japan and satisfy their nostalgia for the homeland."[27]

Liberdade's Cine Niterói was not the only center for Japanese-Brazilian cultural and commercial life in São Paulo. Similar spaces elsewhere in São Paulo included, for instance, Vila Brasilândia, the destination for

FIGURE 5.2 · Cine Brasilândia (undated). Photo archive of Célio Pires.

some residents dislocated from Liberdade during urban redevelopment projects in decades prior. In the same year of Cine Niterói's founding, a Japanese-Brazilian Association based in the district of Freguesia do Ó founded a movie theater in Vila Brasilândia. Kishimoto writes that the Association had existed since 1933 (nearly fifteen years before the founding of Vila Brasilândia).[28] Figure 5.2 shows the wooden cinema in Vila Brasilândia, which multiple current residents of the district mentioned in interviews.[29] While Japanese-Brazilians founded cinemas in both Liberdade and Vila Brasilândia in 1953, in decades following the former neighborhood would become known as the "Bairro Oriental" and the latter a "Little Africa." This divergence invites us to consider further the other factors—beyond the founding of Cine Niterói—that contributed to the construction of Liberdade as the "Bairro Oriental."

City planning projects relating to transportation infrastructure set the stage for the making of Liberdade as the "Bairro Oriental." City planner and two-time mayor Francisco Prestes Maia ran successfully for a third term in 1960 with the promise to complete key components of his 1930 Avenues Plan once and for all. In his 1960s term Prestes Maia expanded the scope of his project to include the construction of the first stretch of São Paulo's metro system.[30] Cleverly, he pitched the avenues and metro projects as a package deal, with the first line of the metro running parallel to the May 23 Avenue along Liberdade's western edge.[31] Demolitions and excavation for the metro line began in the early 1960s and continued into the mid-1970s.[32] State officials pursued a third ambitious transportation scheme in this area in the same period. Starting in 1968 residents in Liberdade and Bela Vista had to contend with the construction of the Radial Leste-Oeste Avenue. Spearheaded by the military dictatorship, this avenue extended east–west through the Liberdade and Bela Vista districts and connected to the elevated highway that would become known popularly as the Minhocão, or "Big Worm."[33]

This array of transportation projects in the 1960s and 1970s took a substantial toll on the landscape and commercial activity in the district. Representatives from the city's Department of Urbanism, Public Works, and City Services admitted that the projects had caused violent, potentially irreversible changes: "The scars left in the urban landscape by the opening of the grand avenues and the implantation of the Metro may never be restored without more planning."[34] A Liberdade restaurant owner told a journalist from *O Estado de S. Paulo* in 1974 that "we have suffered much in these last three years from the metro construction."[35] The same article calculated that demolitions and construction had caused up to a 60 percent decrease in sales among neighborhood businesses.[36] A later publication from 1987 explained that the Radial Leste-Oeste Avenue "mutilated a considerable stretch of the urban fabric, demolishing a great number of buildings. . . . It created an unpassable division in the total extent of the neighborhood."[37] Demolitions for the Radial Leste-Oeste Avenue included the iconic cornerstone of the postwar "Bairro Oriental": the Cine Niterói. The cinema would relocate, however, just a few blocks away and continue to screen films into the 1980s.[38] See map 1.1 for a visualization of the demolitions in Liberdade and Bela Vista linked to the Radial Leste-Oeste.

Rather than razing the nascent "Bairro Oriental," the 1960s demolitions in Liberdade in fact helped to lay the foundation for a much more expansive ethnoracialization project. In the late 1960s and early 1970s, city officials began to address the negative effects of these transportation projects in Liberdade. In 1973 they promised to "recompose the landscape" along the eastern side of May 23 Avenue.[39] Their proposal envisioned, in fact, a wholesale remaking of the neighborhood through what they termed its "reurbanization." The official municipal document approving the plan explained that "there will be constructed commercial buildings, institutional buildings, buildings for offices, public buildings, hotels, parking for vehicles, community resources, and public areas."[40] São Paulo Mayor Miguel Colasuonno (1973–1975) endorsed the reurbanization project in 1973, explaining that the "impact triggered by the metro on the development of adjacent areas will be considerable."[41] The official documentation from the 1973 plan made no explicit mention of Japanese-Brazilians or of Liberdade as a "Japanese" or "Oriental" space. However, the plan's open-ended, expansive scope provided substantial latitude for a broad interpretation of "reurbanization" as the transformation of the identity of the neighborhood itself.

MAKING THE "BAIRRO ORIENTAL"

The idea for the "Bairro Oriental" appears to have originated with *O Estado de S. Paulo* journalist Randolfo Marques Lobato. A 1993 article from *Diário Nippak*, one of Liberdade's Japanese-language newspapers, chronicled the genesis of the project with the headline "The History of Liberdade: A 'Gaijin' [foreigner or non–Japanese-Brazilian] Created the Bairro Oriental." In 1969 Lobato attended a meeting of the recently appointed municipal secretary of tourism, Amadeo Papa. "In thirty seconds," the piece explains, Lobato conceived of the "Bairro Oriental" project and suggested it to the new secretary as a way to "'mark' his time in the administration." Lobato argued that this public investment in the neighborhood would both create a draw for tourists and improve safety conditions. Paulo Maluf, São Paulo's then-mayor, supposedly "shook" (*vibrou*) with excitement at the idea.[42] Maluf and Papa named Lobato head of the project to make Liberdade "Japanese." Lobato was not Japanese-Brazilian and had admittedly few close associations who were. Through a connection with the Japanese consulate, he connected with Liberdade business leader Tsuyoshi Mizumoto. Mizumoto, who is commemorated in contemporary São Paulo with a statue in the Praça da Liberdade, assembled more than one hundred of Liberdade's business owners for a meeting about the proposal.[43]

The Commission for the Implantation of the "Bairro Oriental," composed of Lobato and business owners in Liberdade, steered the project. They coordinated the reproduction of the local built environment through the construction of tangible and recognizably "Japanese" forms. In addition to the torii mentioned above, the changes carried out in the project included red light posts with three white lanterns designed to resemble cherry blossoms (*suzuran-tô*); Japanese pine trees; a "typical" Japanese garden; an original, Japanese-themed sidewalk design; bridges crossing the Radial Leste-Oeste Avenue; and a remodeling of the exteriors of businesses to include "strong colors" and Japanese-language signs.[44] Initiated in 1969, the project remained unfinished until the mid-1970s. Like all places described as neighborhoods in São Paulo, the neighborhood of Liberdade did not have a set legal definition. The project, however, established ethnically identifiable markers in the built environment that defined the limits of the ethnoracialized Liberdade neighborhood.

Central to the reproduction of Liberdade as the "Bairro Oriental," roadways suffused official discourse about the project. City councilman Mario Osassa, for instance, explained that the project intended "to make it so that the *streets* [of Liberdade] present those typically Oriental characteristics and therefore cause attraction." Key material changes involved in the "Bairro Oriental" project centered around roadways: the torii, sidewalks, the decorative light posts, and bridges crossing the Radial Leste-Oeste Avenue. The sidewalks were the subject of a November 1969 decree about the "so-called 'Oriental zone'" by Mayor Paulo Maluf. The decree outlined the locations for the installation of new or refurbished sidewalks, with the stipulation that they were "to be executed in the Portuguese type of mosaic, with a design characteristically oriental."[45] The design ultimately installed along the refurbished sidewalks displayed *mitsudomoe*, a symbol associated with Japanese samurai.

The sidewalks are, somewhat curiously, the singular element of the project that I found discussed in official documentation in an array of historical archives and municipal government institutions in São Paulo. The lack of extant, official documentation may owe to the records having been lost or, alternatively, to the processes by which the project was executed. The collaborative nature of the initiative, involving urban authorities as well as local residents in the construction and transformation of various features of the built environment, suggests that execution of the project may have been atypical enough not to be precisely logged in official documentation. Without surviving official records, however, and no light shed from interviewees, the absence of these records remains a mystery.

The authors of the project frequently described the new Liberdade as the "Bairro Oriental" instead of the "Bairro Japonês." In doing so, the name transcended a narrower reference to Japanese immigrants and their descendants to include other residents of East and Southeast Asian descent.[46] Lobato recalled, in fact, that the initial idea was "not to create a Chinatown, per se, but a neighborhood for the Japanese, Korean, and Chinese communities."[47] As noted in the demographic overview, Liberdade residents born outside of Japan in Southeast and East Asia made up sizable minorities of the neighborhood's population.[48] While Japanese immigrants constituted the primary migratory group from East Asia from 1908 through World War II, postwar migratory streams included Chinese, Korean, and Vietnamese immigrants.

Liberdade's ethnoracial diversity compelled journalists from São Paulo's mainstream press. A 1982 piece entitled "Liberdade: A World of Sounds and Colors" sensationalized the subject with rhetorical questions such as "Where else in the world do Japanese, Chinese, Koreans, and even Vietnamese coexist peacefully? . . . [Liberdade] is a piece of the Orient." The same article asserted that many of the immigrants in Liberdade did not have legal immigration status in the country and that some of the newcomers developed creative strategies to navigate their undocumented status. One anonymous resident described a "common practice" among locals: "Friends loan each other identification documents and, since to Brazilians all Orientals look alike, there is not the least danger in being discovered."[49] Despite adopting the more inclusive, umbrella category "Oriental," the architects of the project chose material symbols—like the torii, cherry blossom lanterns, and samurai-inspired sidewalks—principally associated with Japan.

The labor of constructing the "Bairro Oriental" in material space involved ordinary local residents along with municipal officials. A *Diário Nippak* article noted that "it was decided that the City would take care of the infrastructure works and the community would take care of painting the facades and placing signs on shops in the oriental style, with translation to the Portuguese."[50] A 1974 article recorded the extensive popular participation in the project, with residents involved in "the process of eliminating all Western traits and the concomitant valorization of everything Oriental."[51] Japanese-Brazilian architect Tomio Kimura participated in the effort, drafting a plan to remake the Liberdade Plaza and metro station with a Japanese theme: "There will be a pagoda, stones, a mirror of water, a fountain, plants, and vegetation of Japanese origin."[52] Despite support from both the mayor and engineers from the metro for Kimura's plan, the full-scale reproduction of the plaza and station did not occur. These examples indicate, nonetheless, the extent of official and popular participation in the production of the ethnoracialization initiative.

The "Bairro Oriental" project drew inspiration from earlier constructions of ethnoracialized space in São Paulo. Postwar reconciliation efforts between the Brazilian and Japanese governments included the production of a "Japanese" space in Ibirapuera Park, as discussed in chapter 3. The showpiece of that space, named the "Japanese Pavilion," was a wooden structure fabricated in Japan and modeled after a sixteenth-century imperial palace in Kyoto. The pavilion was inaugurated as part of the celebration of the city of São Paulo's four-hundred-year anniversary in 1954. In 1969 Japanese-Brazilian city councilman Mario Osassa praised São Paulo's head tourism officer Papa, whom he described as "preoccupied with characterizing the São Paulo neighborhoods considered typical, like Liberdade, and Bom Retiro . . . to accentuate the characteristic customs they present."[53] At the same time, Osassa urged Papa to remember that the municipal government already possessed a "historical patrimony donated exactly by the Japanese collective." Osassa noted that the Ibirapuera pavilion was "almost completely abandoned" and requested that officials restore "that relic, that corner of Japan within the city of São Paulo" for "all tourists and Paulistanos to see." The secretary of tourism did not heed Osassa's request but instead went all in on the "Bairro Oriental" initiative in Liberdade.

What might be considered mundane features of the urban built environment—street illumination, sidewalks, and public parks—were amenities scarce in most São Paulo neighborhoods. The city government's investment in the "Bairro Oriental" project transformed Liberdade's streetscape in ways that positively impacted the built environment and the ordinary lives of locals.[54] The extensive public illumination system received particular attention in the press. Photographs of a handful of the 450 newly installed streetlamps exhibit the drastic change they created (figure 5.3). Journalists identified public illumination as a key feature of the "Bairro Oriental." A 1974 article about the neighborhood's inauguration in *Diário de S. Paulo* explained, "When the three keys that light the new lanterns on Galvão Bueno Street and adjacent streets were activated, last night . . . Liberdade came to have a new name: 'Bairro Oriental.'"[55]

FIGURE 5.3 · Lampposts and *torii* in Liberdade, 1970s. Acervo da Fundação de Energia e Saneamento.

In *Veja*, Brazil's most widely circulated national magazine, the lighting and electricity company Peterco ran an advertisement with stunning images of the neighborhood at night and the tagline "the first Brazilian company that makes light in Japanese."[56] Public illumination and electricity represented urban modernity, a sentiment that *Veja* journalists emphasized in the article about the inauguration of the "Bairro Oriental." A photograph of the torii included a text overlay with the words "modern life." The significance attached to public illumination in Liberdade also owed to the scarcity of this resource in most neighborhoods throughout the city of São Paulo at the time. One source from 1968 indicated that 76 percent of streets in São Paulo lacked public illumination.[57] A business owner involved in the Liberdade project noted that, not surprisingly, the substantial public investment in the "Bairro Oriental" generated complaints from residents of other neighborhoods.[58] The public illumination element of Liberdade's ethnoracialized infrastructure shows how the ethnoracialization project helped to further deepen inequalities between São Paulo's neighborhoods.

Not all Japanese-Brazilians or residents of Liberdade approved of the project and the production of commercialized ethnoracial space. Sociologist Hiroshi Saito expressed ambivalence about the campaign in a 1973 article in *Veja*. He lamented the lack of "research about the neighborhood population, their customs and their needs," and he predicted that the result of the project "will be the capitalization of an entire culture for the sake of commercial profit."[59] An article from the following year in *O Estado de S. Paulo* recorded discontent among both "young second-generation Japanese-Brazilians " (*os jovens nisseis*) and "the Japanese of the old guard" (*os japoneses da velha guarda*). The author concluded that "the transformation of Liberdade into a typically Oriental neighborhood is received with an almost total indifference."[60]

In 1980 a group of scholars of Japanese-Brazilian culture and history gathered for a symposium at the University of São Paulo and debated the significance of the "Bairro Oriental." The ethnoracialization of the neighborhood was not a formal, predetermined topic of the symposium but was broached during the debate section following a panel titled "Adaption and Social Participation." Historian Masao Daigo presented a positive view of the project, arguing:

> Despite the neighborhood being around for a long time, it was considered quite "foreign" (*estranha*). The signs in Japanese were as discrete as possible. However, since 1970, obtaining the authorization of the municipal government and the name of "Bairro Oriental," a new life began. After that they began to think that the signs with Japanese characters should be as visible as possible. Activities that were more or less hidden, such as the *bom-odori* (a Japanese dance and the Artisanal Fair), started to be presented extensively in public and contributed to giving the bairro oriental characteristics of one of São Paulo's principal commercial zones.[61]

These comments seem particularly conditioned by the experiences of Japanese-Brazilians during and in the immediate aftermath of World War II, when Japanese cultural expressions, such as language, were driven underground by Brazilian authorities. In chapter 3 I discussed this period in depth, including how the creation of a precursor to the "Bairro Oriental"—the Japanese Pavilion in Ibirapuera Park, opened in 1954—marked a significant step toward the symbolic reconciliation of Japan and Brazil and, relatedly, renewed acceptance of Japanese and Japanese-Brazilian cultural expression. Daigo cast the "Bairro Oriental" project as the celebratory culmination of this process, arguing that it "represented a phase in the process of integration" among Japanese immigrants and their descendants into Brazilian national culture.[62]

Other Japanese-Brazilian observers took issue with Daigo's resolutely positive view of the "Bairro Oriental" project. Judicial official Kazuo Watanabe disagreed strongly with Daigo's conclusion and levied a broader critique against the creation of ethnoracialized space in Brazil. Such spaces only made sense, he argued, in a country where racial discrimination is enforced through urban spatial segregation, "such as in the United States."[63] The implicit premise in Watanabe's comparison—that Brazil lacked racial discrimination in urban space—is, of course, suspect. Nonetheless, his wider critical stance on the production of ethnoracialized space in Brazil captures the more complicated processes involved in creating ethnic enclaves. That stance also set up Watanabe's critique of the "Bairro Oriental." Absent official segregation as its prime motive, São Paulo's "Bairro Oriental" was created, he argued, because of "businessowners' interests, support from politicians (not only Japanese immigrant descendants, but also from an entire community) that resulted in profits for the businessowners and, for the public authorities, greater tax revenues."[64] Watanabe's critique of the business of ethnoracial space echoed the same made by the sociologist Saito in *Veja* in 1973.

Watanabe concluded his comments at the USP symposium by presenting an alternative view about the ideal path for the integration of Japanese descendants into Brazilian society. "Japanese culture will only survive," he explained, "if it mixes with Brazilian culture and, from this mixture, generates a culture typically Brazilian, as happened with African culture in relation to Brazilian culture. New cultural values will be created through this form of participation." With this theory of cultural change, Watanabe saw the creation of a distinctly Japanese—not Japanese-Brazilian—infrastructure in the "Bairro Oriental" as representing "a step backwards in the history of Japanese immigration in terms of integration."[65]

Hiroshi Saito also weighed in on the subject at the USP symposium, perhaps attempting to steer somewhat of a diplomatic middle course between Daigo and Watanabe. Seven years removed from his critical comments on the project in *Veja*, Saito offered a distinct interpretation of the specific functions and broad significance of the "Bairro Oriental." "As for the existence of the Oriental and/or Japanese neighborhood," he explained, "and the possibility that commercial and political interests motivated its construction, I believe that its existence is based in a symbiotic organization, a symbiotic conviviality, in an ecological sense, to provide access to portions of the population that have interests and specific needs."[66] Saito elaborated his point in more concrete terms, explaining that Liberdade offered "specialized stores, Japanese and Chinese restaurants, and other specialized institutions and establishments to meet customer demands for specific needs. This is why there are neighborhoods made up predominantly of *sírio-libaneses*, of Jews, and of other ethnicities, including the Italian neighborhood, which is already disappearing: they exist to exercise certain functions that these ethnic groups need or that they can offer."[67] Saito's comments on the project display a shift from a critical stance on the commercialization of Japanese-Brazilian identity toward a more utilitarian argument about the functions such spaces serve.

Saito concluded his comments by linking ethnoracialized neighborhoods in São Paulo broadly, and Liberdade more specifically, to the national ideal of racial democracy. Comparing Brazil to the United States, Saito explained that while the latter had established a strong political democracy, "democracy in the racial sense" did not exist. Brazil, on the other hand, still struggled to establish total political democracy (a resonant statement given that Brazil's military dictatorship remained in power). "Racial democracy," however, "is already complete." Saito's linking of neighborhoods in São Paulo to racial democracy reveals how, in the eyes of some observers, the ethnoracialization of these spaces served to bolster the discourse of Brazil as a postracial society.

The indifference expressed about the "Bairro Oriental" project may not have surprised or troubled the authors of the initiative. Explaining the motivation behind the project, the president of the shopkeeper's association, Mizumoto, said that "we are working so that Liberdade truly distinguishes itself as a typically oriental neighborhood." Local business owners did not simply hope to increase sales, he continued, "but also to motivate the population of São Paulo to know the culture and customs we represent, in a truly touristic sense."[68] Mizumoto's comments indicate the organizing committee's intentions to boost tourist traffic and commercial development by predominately, even if not exclusively, targeting a public that was not of Japanese descent.

While the "Bairro Oriental" project displeased or proved disinteresting to some locals, its execution helped to make the neighborhood a representative space of Japanese-Brazilian identity, culture, and history. The effort helped to pave the way for other, related state-sponsored initiatives. In 1978, for example, the City of São Paulo assisted financially in the construction of the Historical Museum of Japanese Immigration in Brazil along São Joaquim Street in Liberdade.[69] Japan's Prince Akihito and Princess Michiko and the president of Brazil's military government, Ernesto Geisel, attended the inauguration of the museum, which coincided with the seventieth anniversary of the arrival of the first ship of Japanese immigrants to Brazil. Though based in the neighborhood, the museum would have a broad geographic reach, housing archival material relating to Japanese immigrants and their descendants from around the nation.[70]

The "Bairro Oriental" initiative prompted some locals in Liberdade to make comparisons with similar ethnoracialized neighborhoods beyond Brazil. The head of Cine Niterói, Tanaka, described the differences of Liberdade from San Francisco's Chinatown. While "known internationally," he explained, the San Francisco neighborhood "is very different from our 'Bairro Oriental.' For starters, it is typically Chinese, not Japanese. Second, it is very old and not cared for like the one we are making. When completely finished . . . I can guarantee ours will be one of the greatest tourist and commercial attractions in the world."[71] A 2009 neighborhood guide that commemorated forty years of the "Bairro Oriental" struck a similar tone. The editor of the guide, Luis Handa, explained: "Liberdade is the face of São Paulo . . . it was constructed in the mold of Chinatown and Little Tokyo, but it is very Brazilian, it has sushi men from Bahia and Brazilian churches frequented by Orientals."[72] Such comments emphasized mixture as a core value of Brazilian national identity while also implying how successfully Japanese immigrants and their descendants had performed this nationalist ideal.

At the same time, Handa's observation also emphasized the compelling fact that Liberdade's resident population included substantial ethnoracial and national diversity. As noted in my discussion about demographics earlier in the chapter, the uniformity of the "Oriental" or "Japanese" built environment masked the demographic fact and lived realities of ethnoracial diversity and cross-cultural exchange in Liberdade before and after the completion of the "Orientalization" project. A 1982 article from *Folha de S. Paulo* explained, for instance, that the Chapel of the Afflicted, a significant site for African descendants in São Paulo, "receives daily visits from Orientals who pay for prayers and light candles."[73] Later, in the carnival of 1998, Bela Vista's famous Vai-Vai samba school celebrated the ninetieth anniversary of Japanese immigration to Brazil with the theme "Banzai Vai-Vai!"[74]

The demographic and cultural diversity of Liberdade was not unique to São Paulo. For instance, Liberdade's mid-twentieth-century history paralleled a Los Angeles neighborhood in the same period. In 1942, US officials forcibly displaced Japanese Americans from the place popularly known as "Little Tokyo" in Los Angeles. Shortly after, during World War II, African Americans settled in the neighborhood, which subsequently became known as "Bronzeville." Japanese Americans returned to the area following the war, and in the 1940s and 1950s the area became known as "Little Bronze Tokyo," according to historian Hillary Jenks. A 1946 article in *Ebony* magazine described the neighborhood as a cross-racial union, though it notably stopped short of emphasizing cross-racial mixture: "Bronzeville and Little Tokyo have been betrothed. Out of a marriage of convenience has come a genuine attachment and affection between the two peoples."[75] Beginning in the 1960s, Japanese American and state officials collaborated to remake "Little Tokyo." Over three decades, Jenks explains, "the enclave was physically remade and packaged for Japanese tourists and Pacific Rim consumption."[76] The product of that project, Los Angeles's "Little Tokyo," bore a similar timeless, organic appearance of a typical ethnic enclave. The trajectory of this Los Angeles neighborhood bears striking similarities to Liberdade. Those parallels show how state-sponsored projects supporting the spatialization of singular ethnoracial identities in ethnoracially diverse neighborhoods have characterized the production and lived realities of other "ethnic enclaves" across space and time.

The inauguration of the "Bairro Oriental" marked a significant step in rewriting Liberdade's significance as a core neighborhood in São Paulo's "Black zone." That rewriting owed to both the explicit campaign of ethnoracialization and the demolitions caused by transportation planning projects in decades prior. The expansive demolitions involved in the construction of the Radial Leste-Oeste Avenue may have, like avenues projects in the preceding decades, dislocated African-descendent populations from the district of Liberdade. Dislocation relating to that project took place in the adjacent district of Bela Vista (as the following section shows), however few sources remain to shed light on that history in Liberdade.

African descendent residents of Liberdade did comment on transportation infrastructure projects in this era.[77] The samba school Lavapés, founded in 1937 in Liberdade by Deolinda Madre (known popularly as Madrinha Eunice), marched in the carnival of 1969 with an *enredo* titled "Old São Paulo and Modern São Paulo." The song contrasted the "modest and beautiful" São Paulo of old with the modern city. That modernity was represented by what, in the sung version, sound like plaintive lines: "The new avenues are there, the new viaducts are there, O, O, O, here comes the metro."[78] The Lavapés musicians who also resided in Liberdade had witnessed the coming of modern São Paulo up close in the 1960s, and the transportation schemes that heralded it shortly preceded the "Bairro Oriental" project. Following nearly four decades of demolitions, that project fully reconstructed the built environment of the place that had once been the headquarters of abolitionism in São Paulo and a hub of twentieth-century Black political organizing.[79]

Neither demolitions nor the "Bairro Oriental" project fully erased the historical and contemporary significance that African descendants attached to Liberdade, however. The samba school founded by Geraldo Filme, Paulistano da Glória, continued to gather and play along Glória Street with "Japanese" lanterns hanging along the street in front of its windows. The eighteenth-century Chapel of the Afflicted, protected from demolition by the state's historic preservation board, has remained standing in the Alley of the Afflicted into the twenty-first century (figure 5.4).[80] In 2018, in fact, archeologists discovered nine bodies of formerly enslaved people from the Cemetery of the Afflicted.[81] In January 2020, São Paulo's city government approved a project to create a memorial at this site, "aimed at the preservation of the archeological archive and memory of the Black men and women who lived in the Liberdade neighborhood, in the center of São Paulo, during the period of slavery."[82] While noting the pre-abolition history of African descendants in Liberdade, that sentence notably omitted the significant twentieth-century presence of African descendants in this space. In 2022, the founder of Lavapés mentioned above, Madrinha Eunice, was honored with a statue in the Liberdade Plaza. This statue constitutes part of a broader initiative, led by São Paulo's Department of Historical Patrimony, honoring five Black São Paulo residents with statues throughout the city (including

FIGURE 5.4 · Chapel of the Afflicted, Liberdade, 2017. Photo by Andrew G. Britt.

Geraldo Filme). The cemetery and statue projects align with increasing official recognition of African-descendent Paulistanos and sites that intersect with histories of racial violence, enslavement, abolition, and Black self-determination in Liberdade, specifically, and throughout São Paulo, more broadly.[83]

In Liberdade, these memorialization projects run parallel, however, to continued efforts to assert the exclusively Japanese identity of the neighborhood. In 2018, for instance, the São Paulo state government renamed the local metro station from "Liberdade" to "Liberdade—Japão." The change—which centered on all-important transportation infrastructure and was broadcast on metro maps far beyond Liberdade—emphasized the links between Liberdade and Japan while, simultaneously, serving to further veil the history of Liberdade's African-descendent populations. In 2020, São Paulo state deputy José Américo introduced legislation to rename the metro station again, to "Japão—Liberdade—África." As of early 2024, the proposal has not passed. These competing trends amount to an unprecedented public contestation over the ethnoracialized infrastructure inaugurated in the "Bairro Oriental" initiative in the mid-1970s. Whether that contestation will significantly reshape the visible or dominant imagined landscape of Liberdade in the years ahead remains to be seen.

POSTAPOCALYPTIC URBAN AND ETHNORACIAL RENEWAL

The short film opens with a close zoom from an aerial view of seven children jumping around a sandy pit. One of the kids face-plants and the camera pans out, revealing a rugged landscape of skyscrapers adjacent to excavations and two-story homes that seem centuries old. A solemn voice intercedes: "Caetaninho went out one afternoon like always to play soccer and was hit by a car. That is progress." A critique of progress in the form of modern roadways suffuses this ten-minute 1971 film titled *Bexiga: Year Zero*.[84] The short depicts Bexiga as a site of postapocalyptic urban deterioration, where demolitions, real estate speculation, and new highways obliterated what the narrator characterizes as the "most Paulistano of neighborhoods," built by and for Italian immigrants. The film climaxes with a shot of land cleared for new avenues stretching through the center of the neighborhood. The somber voice-over returns: "Bexiga, a heap of doors and windows stacked between the caverns (*bolsas*) of grand avenues and viaducts. Bexiga did not change, it simply disappeared." The film's mostly funereal piano music then gives way to an up-tempo, Tarantella jingle. Seven older, presumably Italian women—the supposed last vestiges of "Italian" Bexiga—walk across the avenue that replaced their homes and turned the clock on *their* neighborhood back to "year zero" (figure 5.5).

Bexiga: Year Zero reads as an exaggerated representation of rupture. However, the following sections reveal how an array of individuals—from state urban planners and preservation officials to local journalists and self-appointed neighborhood representatives—diagnosed changes of apocalyptic proportions transforming Bexiga. Beginning in the late 1960s and continuing through the mid-1980s, those individuals negotiated the material and social consequences of urban redevelopment through the lens of Italianness. Some pointed to Bexiga's supposed "Italian" identity as a legitimation for much-needed urban improvements. At the same time, they created a project to realize those improvements through an "Italian" built environment. Their proposed project centered on architectural preservation and aged structures in the neighborhood, and it conflated urban renewal with a celebration of Italianness through ethnoracialized space. Their effort helped to construct an incomplete, yet enduring, "Italian" identity for

FIGURE 5.5 · Still from *Bexiga: Ano Zero*, 1971. Governo do Estado de São Paulo; Secretaria de cultura, esportes e turismo; Conselho estadual de cultura; and Comissão estadual de cinema. Regina Jehá, dir., *Bexiga: Ano Zero*, Lauper Filmes, 1971, Filmoteca da Emplasa, posted November 26, 2014, by Emplasa, YouTube, https://www.youtube.com/watch?v=Ee5xRCsbsSE.

Bexiga that stood in opposition to both historical and contemporary alternatives.

As in the adjacent district of Liberdade to the east, roadways projects took a substantial toll on Bela Vista in the 1960s and 1970s. The City expropriated and demolished scores of structures for the completion of the May 23 Avenue along with the Radial Leste-Oeste Avenue and the Minhocão. While earlier avenues projects involved extensive expropriations and demolitions, they stretched through low-lying valleys whose inhospitable environmental conditions had limited settlement typical of center-city São Paulo. The Radial Leste-Oeste Avenue, by contrast, extended through an area of dense settlement and involved comparatively more expropriations and demolitions. Historian Antônio Rodrigues Porto estimates the construction of the Radial Leste-Oeste alone involved the demolition of "more than one thousand houses, shacks and livelihoods, in an extension of one kilometer long by fifty meters wide."[85]

City planners maintained an optimistic tone in public comments about the long-term prospects for the affected districts. In 1971 the director of the Department of Urbanism, Werther Krauss, downplayed the impact of these roadways projects as a transitory, unexceptional feature of urban development in São Paulo and other cities. He explained: "The urban phenomenon transformed the area into a zone of urban deterioration, which is a global problem of large metropolises. . . . But when the area arrives at the lowest rate of deterioration, the recovery begins and the neighborhood escapes the decomposition." Krauss concluded that the natural cycle of the market would help to rectify conditions in Bela Vista, along with three plazas that the Department of Urbanism planned to build locally: "More or less ten years from now, these areas will be recuperated."[86] Like other generations of planners before and after him, Krauss's prediction would prove wildly optimistic.[87]

The construction of the Radial Leste-Oeste Avenue and Minhocão dislocated local residents from Bexiga. Geographer Francisco Capuano Scarlato, who wrote extensively about the neighborhood in this era, explained: "Countless expropriations disfigured the neighborhood's landscape and expelled a significant part of the long-term residents. Between the end of the 1960s and beginning of the 1970s, a large part of the neighborhood became a 'job site.' The view of the neighborhood on the ground-level was of mutilated houses and streets."[88] The dislocation of residents occurred through the expropriation of parcels but also as a result of broader market forces. A 1971 article in *O Estado de S. Paulo* addressed the thorny relationship between expropriation, public works projects, and real estate speculation. Expropriations raised the value of adjacent, nonexpropriated plots, incentivizing those property owners to sell, charge higher rents, or stay and deal with higher taxes. This relationship had preoccupied urbanists in São Paulo since the early twentieth century, and Bexiga proved to be another example where market forces shaped how redevelopment plans were put into practice.[89] The 1971 article cited one property owner on the subject: "I am going to sell this lot soon because it is easier in the beginning, the valorization of this plot is going to give me a big headache, and also I don't have the means to demolish the house and build a better one or an apartment building."[90] The valorization of land in Bela Vista paralleled the verticalization of some parts of the district, as developers constructed high-rise apartment buildings for middle- and upper-class residents.[91] Such development would remain decidedly uneven through the following decades.

Some popular and academic histories of Bexiga in the 1970s gave the impression that Italians were the only ones dislocated from the neighborhood. A 1973 article cited then seventy-year-old resident Luiza Tulsi: "Today everything is ending. There are few Italians still here. Many died from grief, with the expropriations. Others got together and went to live in these new neighborhoods."[92] Her words implied a constitutive, essential relationship between Italian residents and neighborhood structures. The same piece featured an image of a tight cobblestone street with the caption "The Bexiga of old constructions, of narrow streets. . . . Everything is coming to an end to give way to the new reality of viaducts and avenues."[93] Scarlato identified the descendants of Italian immigrants as the primary category of "long-term residents" displaced by the roadway projects. He wrote: "The population of Italo-Paulistas that was always dominant, began to diminish each day more."[94] These individuals described demolitions and displacement as an existential threat to the Italian identity of Bexiga and its residents of Italian descent.

These popular and academic discourses made no mention of the effects of roadways projects and real estate speculation on the contemporary African descendants who lived in the district of Bela Vista. Ferando Penteado, former president of the Vai-Vai samba school and a native of Saracura, explained in a 2012 interview: "Today the neighborhood has few Black families. The construction for the Minhocão created the first great devastation of Bexiga. It passes through the very center of Bexiga. Because of it a bunch of families had to leave."[95] Social scientist Reinaldo Oliveira interviewed Milton, a former resident of Bela Vista, who was dislocated by real estate speculation and roadways projects in the neighborhood. Oliveira writes: "Many *cortiços* and old homes in Bexiga were demolished for the construction of high-rise apartments for the middle and upper class. . . . Milton and the poor and Black population that lived in Bexiga in this era had no other choice" than "involuntary segregation" in the center or moving to the city's geographic margins.[96]

As in decades prior, expropriation and demolitions from the roadway projects spurred another wave of dislocation to both new and old peripheries on the edges of São Paulo. Nascimento and Oliveira identified the district of Casa Verde in the Northern Zone and the housing complex Cidade Tiradentes in the Eastern Zone as primary destinations for dislocated Black populations from Bela Vista in this era.[97] That dislocation reshaped the ethnoracialized geography of the city's neighborhoods, whitening center-city districts like Bela Vista and producing new centers of Black settlement on the geographic periphery. Nascimento cites one resident from Casa Verde, Maria Aparecida de Godoy, who explained: "I arrived in Casa Verde, where I saw this large Black population, and I said: 'What is this?' I was used to never seeing Black people anywhere I went. There [in Casa Verde] it was different, Blacks are on every corner, and I said: 'Now I know where the folks from Bela Vista ran to.'"[98] Casa Verde borders Freguesia do Ó to the east, and it was not a new destination for dislocated Black Paulistanos. Organizers from the FNB had relocated the headquarters of the organization to Casa Verde and coordinated a program of planned resettlement in the middle of the twentieth century.[99]

Articles in the popular press made no mention of the contemporary dislocation of African descendants from Bela Vista, however, rendering that population as a bygone element of the neighborhood's nineteenth-century past. For example, a 1971 piece from *O Estado de S. Paulo*, entitled "Bexiga: All That Remains Is Nostalgia," described the neighborhood in 1902 as an "agglomeration of houses and shacks, constructed by Blacks and Italians." The same article noted that Bexiga became famous in the nineteenth century "as a place of refuge where runaway slaves were hunted." The piece prominently mentioned Saracura, the name of a creek and a neighborhood settlement for freed people paved for the construction of the July 9 Avenue (see chapter 2).[100] A separate piece from 1973 described Black Paulistanos as "the first residents of the neighborhood."[101]

While crediting the foundation of Bexiga to African-descendent freed people and noting silenced places like Saracura, these articles ignored the actually existing African descendants who still lived in Bexiga. They did not broach the histories of how some of those individuals, along with the spaces where they lived, disappeared. They did not draw a parallel to the avenues projects of decades past that had already dislocated residents from Bexiga, including to peripheries like Brasilândia. Instead, the authors described a natural and linear progression of the neighborhood's social composition: Founded by African descendants, the settlement of Italian immigrants had supposedly transformed the neighborhood into an essentially Italian place that was, in the 1970s, under threat of disappearance.

MAKING "ITALIAN" BEXIGA

Beginning in the 1970s a handful of locals in Bela Vista developed grassroots initiatives to preserve neighborhood history associated with Italian immigrants and their descendants. In 1978 resident Armando Puglisi founded the Museum of Bexiga in his childhood home along Ingleses Street. Puglisi was the youngest of four sons of an Italian immigrant and tailor. He was born in Bexiga but had what one article described as a "very strong accent" from his father's homeland.[102] Puglisi's neighborhood museum consisted of an array of memorabilia, from the unsurprising, such as photographs from the early twentieth century, to the unconventional: index cards with the nicknames of the "first" residents of the neighborhood (all Italians), boxing gloves, and an English sewing machine brought to São Paulo by Italian immigrants in the nineteenth century.[103] Though the museum sits closed as of 2017, a plaque on the museum's exterior still displays "Museu do Bexiga" and the year of its founding. An adjacent sign proudly exhibits the segment of Bill Clinton's 1997 speech about São Paulo's ethnoracialized neighborhoods.

Historic preservation initiatives expanded in the district of Bela Vista in the early 1980s. Officials from the state of São Paulo historic preservation agency, CONDEPHAAT, and local residents developed a new initiative in a meeting at the Museu do Bexiga in 1982. Dubbed "Street of the Past," their project aimed to recreate "old Bexiga" in a one-block stretch of May 13 Street, a road named after the date of the formal abolition of slavery in Brazil. The restoration sought to rectify the apocalyptic urban decay depicted in *Bexiga: Year Zero* and turn the clock back to the perceived glory days of the neighborhood in the 1920s and 1930s. An article about the project from *Jornal da Tarde* explained that "the visual panorama of the 1920s will be recreated, the era when the majority of the homes in this part of the street began to be constructed."[104] Though not framed as a project to create "Italian" space with ethnic identity markers, the effort centered on the buildings that Italian immigrants had constructed.[105]

"Street of the Past" received official support from the secretary of culture of the state of São Paulo, Bexiga native João Carlos Martins. Martins explained that he hoped the initiative would "transform the street into even more of a tourist attraction that it already is."[106] Officials did not supply resources to refurbish those structures' interiors, which one journalist described as, "in general, deteriorated." Structures that did not represent the Italian identity of the neighborhood were prevalent, but their connection to non-Italian populations went unmentioned. The plan included, for instance, the restoration of the exterior of what one article termed "the most imposing mansion on this block of May 13 Street—the so-called 'Navio Negreiro,' today the headquarters of a *cortiço*."[107] The author made no further mention of the past or then present of the *cortiço*, which was a historic hub of settlement among Black residents of Bela Vista and may well have remained as such in the early 1980s.

The museum and May 13 Street preservation projects set the foundation for a neighborhood-wide project that combined historic preservation, urban revitalization, and the production of a recognizably "Italian" built environment. I first met the man responsible for this initiative, Walter Taverna, at the annual neighborhood festival Cake of Bexiga. Founded with the (ultimately successful) goal of baking the world's biggest cake, the festival featured Taverna reverently as the "informal mayor" of Bexiga. Taverna owned a restaurant along May 13 Street and in 1980 established the Society for the Defense of the Traditions and Progress of Bela Vista (SODEPRO). I interviewed Taverna at the headquarters of the newly named Cultural Center for the Memory of Bexiga along May 13 Street.[108] The headquarters doubles as a museum to Taverna's nearly four decades of promoting the Italian, and more specifically Calabrian (from the southern Italian region of Calabria), history and culture of Bexiga. Taverna extended other neighborhood historic preservation efforts, which did not have an openly ethnoracialized character, into an explicit project to make Bexiga "Italian." Taverna had (or made) friends in high places, and in the early 1980s his project received buy-in from top municipal officials in the city of São Paulo.

Taverna's project called for the construction of material signifiers of Italianness and the installation or refurbishing of decaying features of the built environment. He outlined his project in letters to tourism, urban planning, and historic preservation officials. Taverna deemed it "crucial" for city tourism authorities to install three signs in the neighborhood to read "Welcome to the Italian touristic center of Bela Vista / Sponsorship: SODEPRO—City of São Paulo—Paulistur."[109] His other proposals included the restoration of the urban tree canopy; the creation of pedestrian walkways with tiles that showed the map of Italy; Italian-themed public illumination; the repaving of roads and sidewalks; marketing to promote the neighborhood; increased policing; tourist attractions, such as a streetcar tour of the neighborhood; the official *tombamento* of a subregion of an area he described as "more than integral to the formation of old Bexiga"; and improved signage, especially stoplights and signs for one-way streets. Taverna envisioned an ambitious, multifaceted remaking of the neighborhood that would define Bexiga as unmistakably Italian. He outlined a geography for the "area to be demarcated as the Italian touristic center of Bela Vista." This geography would define the ethnoracialized neighborhood—a fluid construct without official definition or limits—in official discourse and material space.[110]

In the requests he submitted to the municipal government, Taverna asserted that the making of "Italian" Bexiga would return the neighborhood to its glory days. He defined those days with a particular focus on streets and sidewalks. In a letter to São Paulo's mayor, Taverna explained: "The construction of these pedestrian sidewalks will bring back, at least in a part of Old Bixiga, the tranquilities of our old streets, where our ancestors could get together in front of their homes."[111] A piece from *Jornal da Tarde*, "Let's Go to Bexiga. The Past Is There," echoed this sentiment by remembering the neighborhood's sidewalks as "a natural continuation of living rooms, where people pulled out chairs and spent hours in conversation with neighbors." Scarlato identified this practice as emblematic of the Italian identity of the neighborhood: "It was in this space that we can invoke the symbolic image of that Italianism of the neighborhood—the '*oriundi*' [an Italian-born immigrant] and his chair on the sidewalk."[112] The construction of new avenues threatened what was described as a distinct Italian neighborhood culture built around the street. If successful, Taverna's project would help to stem the tide of change.

The project to make Bexiga "Italian" bore strong similarities to the "Bairro Oriental" effort in the adjacent district of Liberdade. In at least one case, the nearby project served as a direct inspiration for Taverna. In his original proposal as submitted to municipal urbanism and tourism authorities, he requested that Paulistur, the state organization responsible for tourism, develop an original type of "Italian" lamppost in the same way the "typically Japanese" lampposts were "developed for the Liberdade neighborhood."[113] The development of tourism was, as in Liberdade, an explicit goal of the project, and Taverna communicated directly with the head of the tourism agency Paulistur. Whereas the Liberdade Shopkeeper's Association blended tourism with commercial development, however, Taverna insisted that the project to produce "Italian" Bexiga was not driven by any motivation for profit.[114]

Also similar to the project in Liberdade, high-ranking city officials participated in the campaign in Bexiga. In 1974, officials in the city council had raised the idea of creating a special zoning provision to control land use and development in the districts of Bela Vista and Luz, the latter located on the northern side of the historic city center. The suggested provision seemed particularly suited for Bela Vista's aged architecture, as it called for "specific projects of reurbanization, for the preservation of buildings of historic and cultural value."[115] In 1980 and 1981, planners from the Municipal Urban Development Company of São Paulo (EMURB), a department responsible for city planning projects, began drafting plans for an initiative that aimed to improve local conditions and "preserve" the Italian character of the neighborhood. The director of city planning for the state of São Paulo, Paulo Julio Valentino Bruna, also took part in the project to make Bexiga "Italian." He attended at least one neighborhood meeting about the campaign, and in a 1982 letter to another official about the initiative explained, "We developed the project in question . . . as a process of urban renovation and revitalization."[116]

The Bexiga project had a distinct focus on the neighborhood's built environment. Common discourses about the identity of Bexiga presented the neighborhood's Italianness as synonymous with its buildings and the individuals often credited with constructing them: the *capomastri*, or Italian master craftsmen. The film *Bexiga: Ano Zero* celebrated the *capomastri*, crediting them with the construction of the neighborhood and noting that they worked "without using blueprints." Similarly, in the *Jornal da Bela Vista*, Italo Bangnoli wrote: "With the passage of years, many of the Italian customs and traditions were lost to time and the principal mark left by this population was its architecture, which could be observed in the details of antique homes. However, these details are also getting lost. . . . The Italian presence in Bexiga will enter into history only as a memory."[117] Scarlato repeated this narrative in an academic context a few years later: "In Bexiga, the Italian 'capomastri' built the neighborhood, leaving their cultural influence on its landscape."[118] This discourse endures to the recent past, as well. In 2011 the governor of the state of São Paulo, Geraldo Alckmin, commemorated the migration of the more than 1.6 million Italians to Brazil in the nineteenth and twentieth centuries by declaring the "Year of Italy" in São Paulo.[119] His proclamation centered on Italian contributions to the city's built environment, including the "great number of revered buildings . . . constructed or designed by Italians." He continued: "But it was not only the great Italian architects and engineers who marked their passage through São Paulo. Workers, master craftsman, the 'capo-maestri,' as they were called, changed the face of the city, substituting constructions of mud and wattle and daub, for modern buildings that reproduced European patterns."[120]

The celebration of Italianness through and, crucially, *as* São Paulo's built environment excluded non-Italian populations. In her neighborhood history of Bela Vista, Nádia Marzola argued that of the many manifestations of Italian culture in São Paulo—from language to music and food—the spatial reigned supreme. "It was in relation to the art of building, and therefore, the very physiognomy of the city that we find . . . the most important contribution of the *peninsulares* [immigrants from the Italian peninsula] who settled in the city of São Paulo."[121] The silencing of non-Italians in these spatial histories is sometimes striking, as in the case of Marzola's interpretation. On the next page, following the paragraphs about the "great influence" of Italians on the architecture of the city of São Paulo, she included a picture of the Navio Negreiro *cortiço* on May 13 Street. Marzola made no mention of the historic and contemporary significance of this *cortiço* for African descendants in the neighborhood.[122]

The representation of Italianness as constitutive with the built environment differentiated the remaking of Bexiga from the project in Liberdade. Changes to the built environment figured centrally into the "Bairro Oriental" project, of course, as the extensive material constructions throughout the streets of Liberdade in the 1960s and 1970s indicated. However, that project's organizers did not describe their effort as the preservation of a Japaneseness already manifest in the built space. They sought instead to concretize a Japanese identity through *additions* to the built environment. By contrast, Taverna, Puglisi, and other self-appointed neighborhood preservation authorities in Bela Vista conflated the neighborhood's built environment and Italianness and asserted that neither could be saved without the conservation of both.

FIGURE 5.6 · Planned streetscape for "Italian" Bexiga. "Bela Vista: Plano de reurbanização," EMURB, Architect Vera Lucia de A. S. Kitazato, October 1984. SP-Urbanismo archive.

São Paulo city officials adopted the grassroots plan for "Italian" Bexiga in the 1980s. EMURB published a 1984 study that outlined the wholesale remaking of the neighborhood. The introduction to the study explained: "With the goal of strengthening the character of the Bela Vista neighborhood as the Tourist 'Center' of the Italian Colony, EMURB has drafted a reurbanization plan." The authors of the plan conducted "meetings with representative people from the neighborhood," who offered proposals relevant to tourist development and the conditions of the built space. The project called for sidewalks with the map of Italy, the painting of streetlights with the colors of the Italian flag, and the hanging of flags on a gateway that represented different regions of Italy.[123] Mock-ups of the latter (figure 5.6) bore a clear resemblance to the torii erected in Liberdade. The study also repeated the claim about the exceptionalism of the local built environment: "Here, different from other neighborhoods of immigrant colonies, like Liberdade, for example, the typology of the old constructions still standing define and characterize the area."[124] The 1984 study did not express tacit support for a project predominately centered on the installation of new urban services. Instead, the study represented an explicit endorsement for what its architects imagined as the simultaneous revitalization of the neighborhood and its transformation into an unmistakably "Italian" place.

A "NORTHEAST" IN "ITALIAN" AND "JAPANESE" SÃO PAULO

As with the making of the "Bairro Oriental," there was a central demographic paradox to the making of "Italian" Bexiga. The neighborhood received official state recognition as "Italian" at a moment when the local population of Italian descent had declined significantly. Marzola chronicled these demographic changes in the late 1970s: "But today, the population [of Bela Vista] is not predominantly Italian; the neighborhood has changed very much, the Italians moved out and only memories survive of 'old Bexiga.'"[125] A few years later, in 1983, the municipal secretary of culture conducted a study on "environmental heritage" throughout São Paulo, with Bela Vista and Liberdade the first neighborhoods under examination. The study registered significant aspects of the neighborhood's built and natural environment, as expected, yet it also affirmed a finding that "has already been expressed by neighborhood leaders . . . the large presence of Northeasterners."[126]

The settlement of migrants from Brazil's Northeast in these neighborhoods generated tensions between newcomers and longer-term residents. The 1983 municipal secretary of culture study explained that "the old population of the neighborhood, not only those of Italian origin, but also the Blacks that participated in the formation of the neighborhood, do not look fondly on the Northeastern migrants in the neighborhood." As already noted, Northeastern migrants who identified as non-White outnumbered those who identified as White by a margin of nearly three to one. Racialized, anti-Northeasterner sentiment surfaced in interviews with local residents. Scarlato writes that the "traditional population" of the neighborhood considered the influx of Northeasterners and their occupation of abandoned structures as "one of the most important causes of the loss of the cultural identity of the neighborhood." Those residents developed a "strong xenophobia . . . carrying themselves as a retrograde minority beneath an unfurled flag of Italo-Paulistanism."[127]

Such sentiments also surfaced in the built space of the neighborhood. A 1983 article from the local newspaper, *Jornal da Bela Vista*, for instance, pictured a graffitied wall with a swastika and the scribbled phrase "Get Out Dirty Bahians." Bahians referred to residents from the Northeastern state of Bahia; however, the term was likely used as a more general reference to migrants from the Northeast.[128] The neighborhood newspaper author explained the "repulsion" evident in the graffiti as reflecting either racial prejudice or the supposed lack of participation of migratory populations in neighborhood activities and institutions.[129]

Debates about the true or desirable identity of Bela Vista took place through discussions that centered on the neighborhood's built environment. Observers who had previously conflated Italianness with the built environment of Bela Vista also "materialized" Northeasterners, confusing them with *cortiços*. In the *Jornal da Bela Vista*, Italo Bangnoli wrote: "Across the years Bexiga took on a new appearance, leaving the European profile introduced by Italian immigrants behind."[130] He continued: "Time also brought new residents to Bixiga, and in the tenements of Rui Barbosa Street, you don't anymore find Mr. Giuseppe, Geovani, Pepino, Mrs. Concheta, Marieta and Assunta."[131] These archetypal Italian residents had been replaced, the quote implied, by migrants from the Northeast.

Bexiga: Year Zero also linked the settlement of migrants from Brazil's Northeast to *cortiços* in the district of Bela Vista. The film depicted the dislocation of "traditional families" from the neighborhood, opening the door for newcomers who "will continue following the path of demolitions." In other words, these residents continued seeking available housing in expropriated structures that municipal authorities had not yet demolished. The narrator of the film termed these families "marginals" and featured footage of them within the crumbling interiors of expropriated homes. The video portrayed the mostly dark-skinned individuals as both symptoms and causes of Bexiga's deterioration.[132]

Scarlato similarly drew a connection between the settlement of Northeastern migrants in Bela Vista and the expansion of precarious housing, especially *cortiços*, throughout the neighborhood. Quoting a study conducted by the municipal secretary of planning (SEMPLA) in 1989, Scarlato noted that Bela Vista and Liberdade had the highest density of *cortiços* in the city of São Paulo at 155 per square kilometer.[133] Both *Bexiga: Ano Zero* and Scarlato described the deterioration of the neighborhood's "Italian" identity through changes to the built environment. Those changes transformed the supposed masterpieces of the *capomastri* into *cortiços* occupied by poor Northeastern migrants. Scarlato wrote: "The neighborhood gradually lost its romantic air as a residential place, where the presence of the 'capomastri,' and close relationships between neighbors, people that in the majority lived nearly two generations in the same *cortiços*, gave way to a neighborhood that transformed into the symbol of one of the cruelest forms of housing exploitation—the *cortiço*."[134] The sources I located indeed provide evidence for extensive demolitions and material disruptions from the execution of public works projects like the May 23 Avenue, metro, and Minhocão/Radial Leste-Oeste. I did not locate sources on the expansion of *cortiços* in the neighborhood to confirm the discourse that suggests as much. The supposed expansion of *cortiços* locally and associated degradation of the neighborhood may well have been exaggerated by the negative perceptions of newcomers from the Northeast.[135]

What is ironic about the blaming of Northeastern migrants for the expansion of *cortiços* is that prior residents of Bexiga, especially Italians, had constructed or lived in *cortiços* since the nineteenth century.[136] *Cortiços* figured centrally in the built landscape of Bela Vista since the earliest days of the neighborhood's formal existence. Such structures included iconic *cortiços* like those of the Vila Barros complex, demolished in the context of Prestes Maia's Avenues Plan in the 1940s. The identification of Northeastern migrants as responsible for the proliferation of *cortiços* glosses over this history and falsely implies that these newcomers introduced a novelty into Bela Vista's landscape.[137] Historical sources suggest instead that the predominant groups who lived in those *cortiços* changed: "From the 1950s forward the principal social alteration that occurred in the neighborhood was the type of resident of *cortiços*—the Italian immigrant and Black gave way to the national migrant who generally came from the North and Northeast of the country."[138]

The project to make "Italian" Bexiga, replete with the romanticization of the *capomastri* and construction of a visible and tangible "Italian" built environment, occurred in direct opposition to the local settlement of Northeasterners. A 1982 article in *Veja*, titled "Bexiga Puts Up a Fight," observed that the "projects designed by immigrants and their descendants could sour the racial cauldron of Bexiga." The article quoted a nineteen-year-old Bahian who lived in a *cortiço* on May 13 Street. "Society wants to throw us under the bridge," he began. "And I ask: Who works in the neighborhood's restaurants?" With his rhetoric heating up, the young man articulated his anger at the prejudice against Northeasterners: "You can write this: If the Italians expel us, I will set fire to all of Bexiga's restaurants and bakeries."[139] The same article quoted Walter Taverna—the chief protagonist of the Italianization project—as saying that "marginals are invading Bexiga."[140]

Some migrants would contest those sentiments through discourses about São Paulo's built environment. Listen, for example, to the song "Every Building Constructed in São Paulo Has the Salt of the Sweat of the Northeasterner."[141] Sung in the traditional *repentista* form from the Northeast, the song was composed by Sebastião Marinho, a native of the state of Paraíba, and Andorinha (also known as José Saturnino dos Santos), from Pernambuco. Marinho and Andorinha both migrated to the city of São Paulo in the mid-1970s, and in 1988 they founded an organization dedicated to Northeastern culture on the edges of the Liberdade district on Teixeira Leite Street.[142] A section near the introduction of their undated song runs:

> Every building constructed in São Paulo
> Has the salt of the sweat of the Northeasterner
>
> Northeasterners construct beautiful homes
> They don't earn much working on constructions
> They make pretty houses and mansions
> Only they have no right to live in them
>
> They live in the shacks of favelas
> Where the voice of hope echoes an anthem

Later in the song, the authors comment on racialized regional difference through a reference to the different colors of land in Brazil's Northeast and the state of São Paulo:

> To leave the land that has your color
> Lazing in the emerald sun
> To exchange for a reddish-purple color[143]
> The setting all dull and polluted

The lyrics aim to counter the antimigrant sentiment and racist stigmatization that many Northeasterners faced as "marginals" in neighborhoods such as Bexiga.[144] Marinho and Andorinha counter that prejudice and make a claim to belonging by highlighting the daily hardships and social inequalities of migrant life. That discourse has likely recurred among migratory populations across time and region. In the refrain of the song, however, they make a more specific and distinctive claim of belonging based on the productive labor of Northeasterners in constructing the city's built environment. Like the neighborhood residents, officials, and journalists of Bexiga who idealized the *capomastri,* Marinho and Andorinha asserted their claim of belonging by highlighting their participation in the construction of the city of São Paulo.

The "Italian" Bexiga project excluded contemporary Northeastern migrants in Bela Vista along with African descendants. Journalists rarely asked either group for their opinions on the effort. The author of the 1982 *Veja* article, however, attempted to capture popular sentiment among African descendants in conversations with members of the Vai-Vai samba school: "The rosy Italian appearances that decorate bakeries, cantinas, and pizzerias of Bexiga—or Bixiga, for the traditionalists—provoke resigned smiles from the members of Vai-Vai."[145]

I located just two articles in the popular press criticizing the making of "Italian" Bexiga for excluding African descendants. Historian Ernani Silva Bruno authored both articles. Bruno cited figures for the high presence of African descendants in Bela Vista at midcentury and noted that "the subject seems not irrelevant, at a moment when São Paulo's neighborhoods, through the productive enterprise of their own residents, seek to identify their roots and preserve their cultural values."[146] He addressed the organizers of the Bexiga initiative more directly elsewhere: "Nothing prevents, obviously, the organizers . . . to seek to preserve the marks that residents of Italian origin left on the appearances of the neighborhood. . . . But a question remains in our spirit: Can the traces left by residents of Black descent be excluded from the Memory of Bexiga?"[147]

In 2002 the Department of Historic Preservation for the City of São Paulo declared the historic preservation, or *tombamento,* of a sizable portion of what they described as the "neighborhood of Bela Vista, in the district of Bela Vista."[148] The action meant that modifications to any of the 906 buildings included in the historic area would have to be approved by municipal preservation authorities. Without any reference to the culture of the neighborhood, the official preservation document described Bela Vista as exceptional because it still preserved many older buildings, not because of its Italianness. The choice to describe both the neighborhood and the district as "Bela Vista" seems to be a subtle rejection of "Italian" Bexiga or an evasion of the spatialized identity altogether. Scarlato argues that from the 1950s through 1970s, Bela Vista was the name commonly ascribed to the region. The use of Bexiga from the 1970s forward, he asserts, coincided with the "rediscovery of the neighborhood" as an area of "Italian traditionalism."[149] Though absent in the official declaration, Walter Taverna preserved the Italian association in the press in his comments on the declaration. An article about the *tombamento* quoted him as saying: "A neighborhood that has neither a memory nor a history does not have value and this place is precious. Here, various Italian immigrants made their lives."[150]

The contemporary *tombamento* of Bexiga shows how popular and official discourse about neighborhood identities shift over time. Architectural historians Clara Correia d'Alambert and Paulo Cesar Gaioto Fernandes offer the following appraisal of the 2002 action: "The preservation of Bela Vista, as related in the [2002] tombamento record, involved not only architectural and urbanistic aspects, but also others of a socioeconomic, even anthropological nature, such that the urban space of the neighborhood reflects, in a broad sense, the *unquestionable cultural and ethnic miscegenation* that took place there."[151] The assertion of neighborhood-level "cultural and ethnic miscegenation" in Bela Vista accurately reflects the contemporary and historical ethnoracial diversity of resident populations. That demographic mixture is, it should be emphasized, not exceptional: All São Paulo neighborhoods exhibit an unmistakable degree of ethnoracial heterogeneity. However, the premium on mixture in the twenty-first-century discourses about the preservation of Bela Vista reveals a notable shift away from official sponsorship of the ethnoracialization of space. As with similar discourses of ethnoracial mixture in Brazil, however, that discourse dissolves actually existing historic and contemporary social difference. In doing so, it glosses over the enduring inequalities and prejudices between various ethnoracial and regional groups, including Northeasterners, who call Bexiga home.

While recent official historic preservation and planning documents omit references to "Italian" Bexiga, the traces of decades of Italianization efforts can still be seen in the contemporary built environment. The posts of streetlights throughout the neighborhood are painted with the red, white, and green of the Italian flag, including the post in front of the Saracura mural discussed in chapter 2 (figure 2.1). The visage of prominent samba composer and musician Adoniran Barbosa, whose parents came from Italy and who chronicled São Paulo's Italian culture in song, features in the light signs for local pedestrian crosswalks (figure 5.7). Locals also coordinated the construction of a bust of Barbosa

FIGURE 5.7 · A pedestrian crossing light with the face of sambista Adoniran Barbosa in Bela Vista, 2014. Photo by Alexandre Tokitaka.

in 1983, and a street bears his name in the north of the district.[152] These features attest to the discernible, yet incomplete, campaign to create "Italian" Bexiga.

It can be tempting to view ethnoracialized neighborhoods like Liberdade and Bexiga as exceptional, singular places. Indeed, the array of planners who produced the neighborhoods described them as unique, and the customized collection of material markers they designed for their infrastructure bolstered those claims. The similarities between the two ethnoracialization projects in Liberdade and Bexiga, however, challenge such exceptionalist assumptions. By 1978 both neighborhoods had a museum dedicated to the ethnoracial group most identified with the neighborhood. By the mid-1980s, the state had bankrolled projects of simultaneous ethnoracialization and urban revitalization that transformed their built environments, providing a valuable and bespoke infrastructure of urban amenities that residents of most other São Paulo neighborhoods could only dream of. In the course of demolitions and new constructions, both projects transformed two historic centers for African descendants in the city of São Paulo into neighborhoods associated with non-Black immigrants and their descendants. By charting the parallels that made these two projects more similar than different, this chapter counters the representations of ethnic enclaves like the "Bairro Oriental" or "Italian" Bexiga as singular, in São Paulo and beyond.

This chapter also shows that while social identities are unstable, continuously in flux, and negotiable, the production of ethnoracial space in Liberdade and Bexiga reveals how social difference can become fixed in—and fixed as—material space. Ethnoracial space thus reminds us of the material significance of *construction* in our understanding of identity as a social construct. The ethnoracialized infrastructure in Liberdade and Bexiga served to concretize ethnoracial identity and ethnoracialized inequalities in consequential ways.[153] The transformation of these neighborhoods deepened inequalities while, paradoxically, creating a hypervisible, durable, and seemingly natural ethnoracialized landscape that supported representations of São Paulo as both a non-Black, ethnically immigrant city and a multicultural metropolis. Only in the third decade of the twenty-first century, approximately fifty years after the completion of the ethnoracialization projects, are some successful challenges being waged against the exclusion and silencing generated and sustained by these projects.

The construction of ethnoracial space in Liberdade and Bexiga also provides illuminating historical context for contemporary planning practices and development schemes in populous, multiethnic cities, particularly those with historic links to slavery, worldwide. These histories are partly instructive, in other words, because comparable projects of ethnoracialization continue to capture the imaginations of state officials. For instance, former São Paulo mayor João Doria (2017–2018), who headed the city's tourism division during the campaign to produce "Italian" Bexiga, has pursued a similar initiative just a few kilometers from Liberdade and Bela Vista. In 2017 Doria outlined his aspirations for a tourism/revitalization project in São Paulo's Bom Retiro neighborhood, a population hub of Korean immigrants and their descendants, on a trip to South Korea. Partnering with multinational corporations based in Korea such as Samsung and Hyundai, Doria proposed to reproduce Bom Retiro as a "Little Seoul" (Little Séul).[154]

The making of "Italian" Bexiga and "Japanese" Liberdade should give officials like Doria pause, or at least serve to moderate the often ambitious reach planned for such projects. The parallel projects of urban revitalization and ethnoracialization in Bexiga and Liberdade fell well short of city planners' expectations. Their shortcomings demonstrate that so-called place-making initiatives, which sometimes (inadvertently or deliberately) double as ethnoracialization projects, are questionable instruments for economic development as well as spatial changes that improve living conditions for local residents in long-lasting and equitable ways.[155] Public or private investments in those projects, even when they are couched in language of ethnoracial inclusivity, can serve to exacerbate, rather than ameliorate, social exclusion along with ethnoracialized inequalities.

EPILOGUE

Early 1970s: "Asphalt Has Today Covered Our Ground"

Each Tuesday night, before they sing original compositions, the members of Samba do Congo warm up by playing roots samba, or *samba de raíz,* from members of São Paulo's old guard. One favorite is Geraldo Filme's "Tradition (Go to Bexiga and See)," composed in the early 1970s.[1] Though Filme founded and directed the Paulistana da Glória samba school in Liberdade, in the 1970s he became a regular at Bexiga's Vai-Vai. The main two verses of "Tradition" are:

> Samba no longer raises any dirt
> Asphalt has today covered our ground
> The memory I have of Saracura
> The nostalgia I have for our *cordão*[2]
>
> Bexiga today is only skyscrapers
> And you don't see the moonlight anymore
> But Vai-Vai is steady in its place
> It's tradition, and the samba continues.

Samba do Congo members sing "Tradition" amid the continuing transformative impacts of the arrival of the metro's new Orange Line, the future station for which sits just a few blocks from the place where they gather weekly. The playing of Filme's "Tradition" seems connected to this moment, yet the song's narrative also invokes earlier episodes from São Paulo's spatial history. Filme composed "Tradition" in the context of the ethnoracialization projects discussed in chapter 5. The 1970s–1980s campaign to make Bexiga "Italian" was spearheaded by an organization with "tradition" in its very name: The Society for the Defense of the *Traditions* and Progress of Bela Vista. With a samba school headquartered in Liberdade and composing music for Vai-Vai in Bexiga, Filme's lyrics counter the representation of Italian "Bexiga," in particular, with an alternative history centered on Saracura, asphalt, and Vai-Vai.

Filme's take on tradition, however, extended even before and beyond 1970s–1980s Bexiga. The silencing of places like Saracura, he suggests, was a customary and recurring practice—a *traditional* one—in the city of São Paulo throughout the twentieth century. Through the execution of the Avenues Plan, asphalted roadways remade Bexiga as well as Liberdade, two of the most significant neighborhoods for African descendants in the city of São Paulo since the nineteenth century. Progress entailed the razing of structures throughout the neighborhoods and the paving of significant, sometimes sacred places for African descendants. Pavement had a special resonance given the African descendent cultural practices in Brazil that attach a spiritual significance to unimpeded contact between bare feet and beaten earth (*chão batida*).[3] Asphalted avenues disrupted that spatial relationship. They were the material trappings of progress, reflective and generative of a racialized urban modernity.

While Filme concludes "Tradition" with the resolute assertation that Vai-Vai remains "steady in its place," the sociospatial reality of the samba school has been nowhere near that secure. "Tradition" itself was composed just a few years after the leaders of Vai-Vai had to relocate their headquarters from a rental property on Rua 14 de Julho elsewhere in Bela Vista. That headquarters was expropriated in the late 1960s for the construction of the Elevado Presidente Costa e Silva, or Minhocão (known officially, today, as Elevado Presidente João Goulart), also discussed in chapter 5. While Filme's "asphalt today covers our ground" likely invoked earlier episodes like the paving of Saracura and the Largo da Banana, the line likely also referenced the then-recent, material burial of Vai-Vai's headquarters beneath pavement. In the wake of the late 1960s expropriation and demolition, Vai-Vai's leadership acquired a new property a few blocks southwest of Rua 14 de Julho, at the corner of Rua São Vicente and Rua Doutor Lourenço Granato. Vai-Vai would remain "steady in [this] place" for more than a half-century following.

The last, resolute line of "Tradition" sounds different in the third decade of this century. After nearly a decade of murmurs about the possibility, in September 2021 the leadership of Vai-Vai reached an agreement for the expropriation and relocation of their headquarters once again. The impetus? The construction of the metro station in Bela Vista that will serve as the penultimate stop on the southern end of the new Orange Line. The Spanish company in charge of the infrastructure project will fund the construction of a new headquarters for Vai-Vai further south in Bela Vista, along Rua Almirante Marques de Leão. While Vai-Vai's leadership acquiesced to these terms, in the press they also articulated a clear lament for the loss of the headquarters, including by invoking Filme's songs "Tradition" and "I'll Samba Someplace Else."[4]

In February 2023, a group called Mobiliza Saracura Vai-Vai submitted a judicial petition to preserve a section of the site under demolition and construction for the Orange Line as an archeological zone. The excavations following the demolition of Vai-Vai have led to evidence of settlement from Saracura in the early twentieth century, and the activists expect further work could unearth remains from the *quilombo* in the nineteenth century if not before. Gisele Brito, the coordinator of the Right to Antiracist Cities at the Instituto de Referência Negra Peregum, argued that, as a significant site of Black resistance and permanence in the city, Vai-Vai's headquarters should not have been expropriated in the first place. "We are not against the metro, although its construction did not require the removal of Vai-Vai," she said. Brito then linked this episode to the recurring, traditional pattern of spatialized anti-Black violence recounted throughout this book: "This is a strategy of whitening the territory."[5]

Nearly a century after the publication and execution of the Avenues Plan, the construction of the Orange Line has once again connected Bela Vista and Brasilândia through processes of dispossession, demolition, and displacement. The striking parallels between the Avenues Plan and the Orange Line suggest that the reproduction of racialized inequalities through infrastructure projects, including in these privileged neighborhoods for African descendent residents of São Paulo, endures. And yet, some countervailing trends have, in the very recent past, begun to emerge. These competing currents highlight the endurance of the paradoxes of ethnoracial space in São Paulo into the present.

APRIL 2022: "A NEW SETTLEMENT"

The new statue features a life-sized, bronze cast of Geraldo Filme. His eyes fix on the horizon, with one hand halfway out of his pants pocket—"ready to pull out a recently-composed samba," as the municipal government press release put it—and the other hand holding a microphone.[6] The City inaugurated this statue in April of 2022 in the Barra Funda neighborhood at the Praça David Raw, a sliver-size public space today occupying what was once the much more expansive Largo da Banana. The demolition of that public square in 1958 for the construction of the Pacaembu overpass inspired Filme's composition "I'll Samba Someplace Else." That song encapsulated both the anti-Black violence and persistent Black self-determination that shaped mid-twentieth-century São Paulo's spatial development.

The daylong ceremonies celebrating the new statue included an official inauguration, capoeira circle, ceremonial cleaning, series of concerts, and more. Samba collectives from around the city of São Paulo and beyond came to mark the occasion. Multiple groups raised their banners (*estandartes*) during the inauguration ceremony. At one point, immediately behind the statue, framing Filme's head, hung the orange and white *estandarte* of Brasilândia's Samba do Congo (figure E.1). One of the group's founders, Fernando Ripol, described the ceremony as the inauguration of an *assentamento* (settlement), a consecrated object or place that serves as the physical and spatial representation of an *orixá* (divine spirit) in Candomblé. Samba do Congo's presence attested to the outcomes of the spatial praxis of belonging-as-being, which had secured a *someplace else* in the form of Brasilândia, broadly, and the creation of the Samba do Congo collective, more narrowly.

The inauguration of the statue to Filme constituted part of a wave of similar projects in the last few years. In 2016, a monument to Zumbi dos Palmares was erected at Praça Antonio Prado, the original site of the Igreja Nossa Senhora do Rosário dos Homens Pretos. In 2020, the municipal secretary of culture inaugurated a memorial to Joaquim Pinto de Oliveira, known prominently as Tebas (1721–1811), adjacent to the Praça da Sé. An enslaved architect and craftsman, Tebas participated in

FIGURE E.1 · Samba do Congo *estandarte* at the inauguration of the statue of Geraldo Filme, 2023. Prefeitura da Cidade de São Paulo.

the design and construction of multiple iconic structures from colonial São Paulo and purchased his freedom from the proceeds of this labor.[7] Geraldo Filme memorialized Tebas in the 1974 composition "The Slave (Sé Plaza)" ("O Escravo [Praça da Sé]"), which served as Paulistana da Gloria's entry into carnival in the same year.[8]

Two years after the construction of the Tebas statue, the municipal government inaugurated five statues to African descendants in São Paulo, including the bronze cast of Filme along with a statue in the Praça da Liberdade of Deolinda Madre (or Madrinha Eunice), the founder of the city's first official samba school, Lavapés (discussed in chapter 1). The other monuments honored writer Carolina Maria de Jesus, musician Itamar Assumpção, and Olympic athlete Adhemar Ferreira da Silva. Some observers described this municipal initiative as a response to the demands of activists who, amid a global swell of antiracist organizing in 2020 and 2021, set fire to a massive statue dedicated to the *bandeirante* and enslaver Borba Gato.[9] The designer of the Borba Gato statue also designed the Mãe Preta statue (discussed in chapter 3), the target of much critique from some Black residents of São Paulo upon its inauguration in the mid-1950s.

Contemporary Black movement activists have spearheaded related memorialization projects in Liberdade in the last few years. As noted in chapter 2, São Paulo's first public cemetery for enslaved African descendants, the Cemetery of the Afflicted, sat in Liberdade behind the Chapel of the Afflicted, which remains standing through the present. The cemetery, however, had long been interred beneath a complex of asphalted highways and concrete buildings. In 2018, the demolition of a building next to the Chapel of the Afflicted prompted an excavation, and archeologists discovered nine bodies of the formerly enslaved and other artifacts from the Cemetery of the Afflicted.[10] In the years following, responding to calls from neighborhood residents and local activists and organizers, São Paulo's city government approved a project to create a memorial at the site along with the restoration of the chapel. In September 2025, those calls persuaded the city government to approve and coordinate the removal of the cherry-blossom lanterns in the alley that leads to the Chapel of the Afflicted, the Beco dos Aflitos.[11]

These projects reflect an emerging pattern in São Paulo of official support for the memorialization of sites significant to African descendants. Such initiatives, as recounted throughout this book, have long figured centrally into the spatial praxis of African descendants in São Paulo. However, the officially sanctioned statues of African descendants throughout the city and the memorial project in Liberdade represent a commitment from municipal authorities to an official memorialization that seems to diverge from the anti-Blackness that has long shaped official and public attitudes in São Paulo. Remembering, forgetting, and place have figured centrally in discourses about these projects. For instance, Geraldo Filme's niece, Leonilda de Fátima, described the significance of the statue of her uncle like so: "We are reliving a history that, until now, we thought might not have *anywhere* to exist, that perhaps he would be forgotten, but today he is being honored."[12]

Similarly, the description on the monument to Tebas includes the following: "A Black man who achieved his freedom at fifty-seven years old and remade São Paulo's eighteenth-century architecture. His principal achievement was to free himself from chains and take flight into eternity. The collective nature of his legend freed him from being forgotten." These new memorialization projects have the potential to contribute to the disruption of the "traditional" pattern of anti-Blackness that has rendered African descendants invisible in certain spaces in the city, especially, though not exclusively, in the neighborhoods that constituted São Paulo's early-twentieth-century Black zone.

MAY 13, 20XX: THE MARCH AGAINST "FALSE ABOLITION"

There are no guarantees that this wave of memorialization will continue or, necessarily, have the effects its advocates might hope for. The proliferation of memorials in and to São Paulo's former "Black zone," while not insignificant, also does not, of course, signify a deep commitment to address anti-Black violence and racialized inequalities in São Paulo or beyond. Indeed, the piecemeal reassembly of memorialized fragments of São Paulo's "Black zone" runs the risk of reproducing the core paradox of ethnoracial space: bolstering discourses of postracial inclusivity that conceal the enduring reality of deeply rooted racialized inequalities and anti-Black violence.

Many African descendants have long cultivated caution over the promise of positive and durable social change. For example, José Pompílio da Hora, a leader in the Black movement organization Union of Men of Color, appraised the significance of political change in 1946, one year following the end of the authoritarian Estado Novo regime and redemocratization of the nation. Pompílio asserted: "Democracy for Blacks has been the right to clean roads, to build buildings where they are not allowed to live."[13] The built environment, for Pompílio, here symbolized the *absence* of actual change for African descendants despite the supposed triumph of redemocratization. The possibilities for actual multiracial democracy remain uncertain today as in that era.

A similar sentiment is expressed annually on May 13, the date of slavery's formal abolition in 1888, by the group Ilú Obá de Min. Both of the founders of this all-female group, Beth Beli and Girlei Luiza Miranda, grew up in Brasilândia.[14] The membership is multiethnic, and the music and performances are deeply indebted to African-descendent spiritual practices like Candomblé. On the date of formal abolition, the members of Ilú Obá de Min lead a march from a local site known as the "grand staircase of Bexiga" on May 13 Street in Bela Vista. This staircase sits adjacent to the Navio Negreiro *cortiço*, one of the surviving testaments to the Africans and African descendants in Bela Vista, which I discuss in chapter 1. Organizers begin the event with speeches at the staircase, where they offer critiques of May 13 as a date of "false abolition" that masks enduring racialized inequalities and privileges the agency and generosity of Princess Isabel in advancing Black freedom.[15] Following the speeches, the group proceeds down the staircase and May 13 Street, passing Italian cantinas and Italian-flag-themed lampposts on their way into the heart of the neighborhood, toward Avenida Nove de Julho and the former headquarters of Vai-Vai.[16]

Such demonstrations contest enduring and, for many, alluring triumphant narratives of abolition, including those cemented into São Paulo's spatial and linguistic landscape at places like May 13 Street in Bela Vista. In neighboring Liberdade, recent changes to local place names have revealed the endurance of the practice of Black erasure and the contrary currents that might limit the reach and significance of "Black zone" memorialization projects (as noted in chapter 5). In 2018, for instance, the São Paulo state government renamed the local metro station from "Liberdade" to "Liberdade—Japão." This change emphasized the connections between the neighborhood of Liberdade and Japan while, simultaneously, serving to obscure the history of Liberdade as part of São Paulo's "Black zone." More recently, in December 2022, the municipal government announced plans to create a twelve-million-square-meter esplanade in Liberdade that would link the neighborhood's three bridges across the Radial Leste-Oeste (figure E.2). Dubbed the "Oriental Esplanade," the project would create a commercial center, exposition plaza, and center of innovation and culture, all in a style directly inspired by Japanese architecture.[17] These contemporary examples reveal that, while the state-sponsored transformation of Liberdade into a "Japanese" neighborhood in the 1960s and 1970s concluded with its inauguration in 1978, elements of that project—and the ideological roots from which it drew sustenance—remain alive through the present. The paradoxes of ethnoracial space, in other words, remain unresolved in the heart of Brazil's multicultural metropolis.

FIGURE E.2 · Rendering of planned "Oriental Esplanade," 2023. Prefeitura da Cidade de São Paulo.

MAY 2018: "THIS IS OUR PLACE. . . . PEOPLE COME FROM EVERYWHERE"

From its founding in 2011 through early 2018, Samba do Congo played at the Casa da Cultura da Brasilândia, a public community center. In May 2018 the group acquired its own headquarters in the Morro Grande region. The headquarters sits between the future Brasilândia metro station and the former Congo Road (now Elísio Teixeira Leite Avenue), a symbol and space of continuity amid uncertain urban change. The ethnoracially diverse members of Samba do Congo will, for the foreseeable future, continue to assemble in this space in a circle beneath the group's orange and white *estandarte* and around a table draped with the flag of the state of São Paulo. They will continue to compose and play songs about their individual and collective histories and the spaces that tie them to each other and the past. They will continue to bring each night to a close by handing out lyrics to newcomers and singing the group's typical closing songs in unison:

> Come sing our samba with us
> It's samba *de roda de bamba*[18]
> People come from everywhere

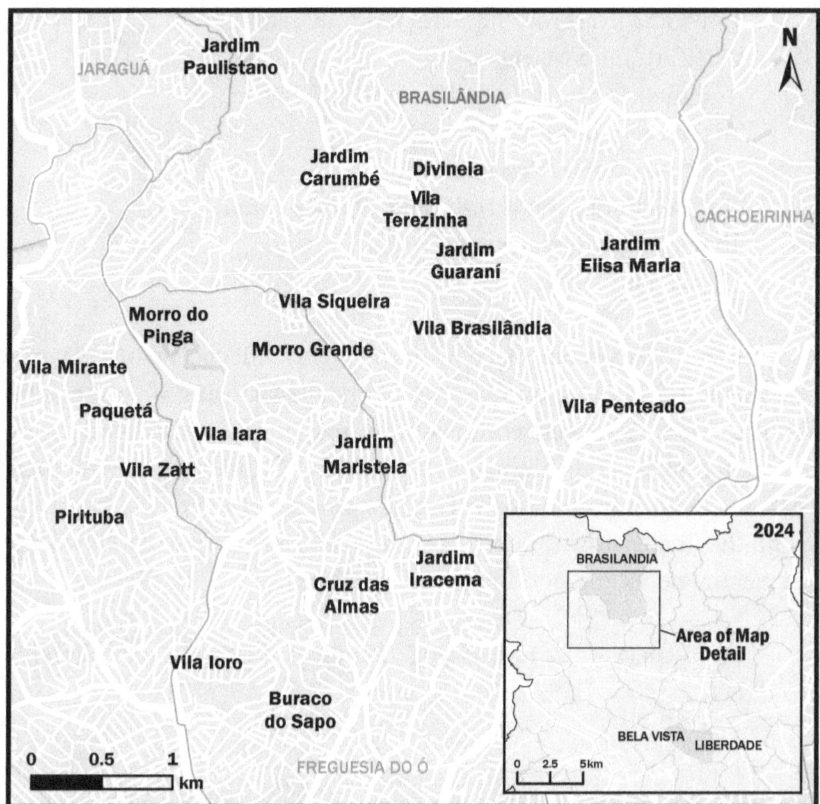

MAP E.1 · Lyrical map of Samba do Congo's song "Nossa Quebrada." Data sources: GeoSampa; OpenStreetMap (Light Gray Canvas) © OpenStreetMap contributors, Microsoft, Facebook, Google, Esri Community Maps contributors, map layer by Esri. Map by Andrew G. Britt.

The pace will quicken as the group arrives at the last two verses: a lyrical map (map E.1) of the many places—neighborhoods, *loteamentos*, favelas—that today comprise the Brasilândia district.

> There are folks from Brasilândia and Divineia,
> Pirituba, Jardim Maristela,
> Guarani, Vila Iório and from Paquetá
> You Can't Forget Paulistano and Vila Iara
> Buraco do Sapo, Mirante, and Mangue
> Thank you, Morro Grande
> This is our place

Terezinha, Iraceme, Siqueira, Jardim Carumbé
Vila Zatt, Elisa Maria
And the Morro da Pinga I want to add too
To commemorate
Cruz das Almas, Vila Penteado
Our neighborhood is the cradle of the *bamba*
Thank you, Morro Grande
This is our place

This final "This is our place" (*É nosso lugar*) will cue a pause. Everyone will stand as the group's leader offers a few closing words, maybe about the night's newest compositions, maybe about the importance of making music and singing pasts in and of Brasilândia. He will then beckon a child from the audience to the middle of the circle. They will set up the finale with a spirited "3 . . . 2 . . . 1." The group will follow with the parting notes and booming proclamation:

"*Vem gente de todo lugar!*" (People come from everywhere!)[19]

Notes

INTRODUCTION

1 Filme, "Vou sambar n'outro lugar." All unattributed translations from the Portuguese are mine.
2 This song was first recorded on Barros, *Balbina de Iansã*.
3 Butler, *Freedoms Given*, 74–75; Brunelli et al., *Barra Funda*; Castro, *Bexiga*, 43–44; Azevedo, "A memória músical de Geraldo Filme"; Azevedo, "São Paulo Negra"; Silva, "Debaixo do 'Pogréssio.'" Also see Filme, "Interview," 72. Renata Monteiro Siqueira has recently challenged the conventional wisdom of the Largo da Banana as the early twentieth-century cradle of samba in São Paulo, arguing that it became known as such only in the 1950s, almost contemporaneous to its demolition. She also asserts that it remained a significant site for samba after the construction of the overpass in 1958. See Siqueira, "O viaduto e o samba."
4 Filme, "Interview," 74–75.
5 For three particularly relevant examples, see Caldeira, *City of Walls*; Holston, *Insurgent Citizenship*; and Hagopian, "Paradoxes of Democracy."
6 Leandro Machado, "'Quem a polícia defende? De que lado está?,' questiona autor de foto símbolo da desigualdade no Brasil." BBC *Brasil*, December 4, 2019. https://www.bbc.com/portuguese/brasil-50666148.
7 Three different among many texts that engage with this representation are Vieira, *História do futuro*; Zweig, *Brasilien*; Eakin, *Brazil*.

8 Rolnik, "Territórios Negros," 38; Telles, *Race in Another America*, 212; Machado, "Paisagem revelada," 63.

9 George Reid Andrews examines this process of replacement in the context of the labor market and immigration subsidies in the state of São Paulo. See Andrews, *Blacks and Whites*, 54, 59.

10 Skidmore, *Black into White*; Andrews, *Afro-Latin America*; Domingues, *Uma história não contada*; Lesser, *Immigration, Ethnicity*; Weinstein, *Color of Modernity*.

11 On Paulista exceptionalism, see Weinstein, *Color of Modernity*, esp. 28–53.

12 Indeed, analysts of race in Brazil commonly frame their inquiry in these terms. See, for example, Andrews, *Blacks and Whites*; Alberto, *Terms of Inclusion*; Weinstein, *Color of Modernity*; Vargas, *Denial of Antiblackness*.

13 For example, see Paixão et al., *Relatório anual das desigualdades raciais* from 2007–2008 and 2009–2010.

14 This term is most often attributed to Gilberto Freyre based on the analysis he advanced in his 1933 book *Casa-grande e senzala* (*The Masters and the Slaves*).

15 Notable exceptions in the academic context that explicitly engage with anti-Blackness and space in São Paulo are Rolnik, *A cidade e a lei*; Domingues, *Uma história não contada*; Oliveira, "Segregação urbana e racial"; Alves, *Anti-Black City*.

16 My emphasis on belonging echoes Paulina Alberto's interpretation of Black intellectuals in São Paulo. She argues that, throughout the twentieth century, "they used dominant ideas of racial inclusiveness to place an African racial or cultural heritage at the center of images of the Brazilian nation and to assert their own belonging as African-descended Brazilians within it." Alberto, *Terms of Inclusion*, 17.

17 Alves, *Anti-Black City*.

18 Butler makes a related argument: "São Paulo had no exclusively black neighborhoods. Even though physical spaces were clearly delineated between the residences and social ambits of whites and blacks, the fluidity of those barriers and the proximity of people of different ethnic backgrounds precluded the 'black worlds' found in segregated environments. This combination of factors helped steer some members of São Paulo's Afro-Brazilian community toward the goal of integration." Butler, *Freedoms Given*, 89. Similarly, Paulina Alberto charts how some Black intellectuals in São Paulo, over the mid-twentieth century, appropriated discourses of inclusion—including the "racial democracy" ideology—to contest anti-Blackness and racialized inequality and violence and assert citizenship and belonging.

19 George Reid Andrews advances a related argument about the creation of racialized São Paulo exceptionalism through the lens of labor. See Andrews, *Blacks and Whites*, esp. 88–89.

20 For example: Butler, *Freedoms Given*; Hanchard, *Orpheus and Power*; Domingues, *Uma história não contada*; Alberto, *Terms of Inclusion*; Seigel, *Uneven Encounters*.

21 Alberto's *Terms of Inclusion* follows Black intellectuals in São Paulo, including former FNB members, past the declaration of the New State and into mid-century decades.

22 Hanchard writes that, owing to officials' promotion of the racial democracy ideology, particularly during the military dictatorship, "Afro-Brazilian activists had to couch their language and praxis in indirect, ambiguous, and fragmented forms under the veil of cultural practice." Hanchard, *Orpheus and Power*, 102.

23 In contrast to the circumstances for Brasilândia, readers interested in the histories of Liberdade and Bela Vista/Bexiga can find an extensive secondary literature. For Bela Vista/Bexiga: Marzola, *Bela Vista*; Lucena, *Bairro do Bexiga*; Scarlato, "Bixiga"; Bernardo, *Memória em branco e negro*; Castro, *Bexiga*; Ana Lúcia Duarte Lanna, "O Bexiga"; Schneck, "Bexiga: Cotidiano e trabalho"; Nascimento, "Lembrança eu tenho." For Liberdade: Guimarães, *Liberdade*; Handa, *O imigrante japonês*; Lesser, *Discontented Diaspora*; Kishimoto, "A experiência do cinema"; Nishida, *Diaspora and Identity*.

24 In 2023, a podcast about Nenê da Brasilândia, a supposed leader of illicit trade in Brasilândia, reached the top 10 on podcast charts in Brazil, a reflection of the enduring popular fascination with Brasilândia as a hub of crime.

25 Santos, "Ser essa terra"; Fária, "A luta Guaraní"; Oliveira et al., "Cotidiano, cultura e resistência"; Jennifer Ann Thomas, "Pauliceia indígena: A vida entre aldeias e periferia em São Paulo," *Mongabay*, April 28, 2021, https://brasil.mongabay.com/2021/04/pauliceia-indigena-a-vida-entre-aldeias-e-periferia-em-sao-paulo/.

26 According to the most recent census, São Paulo has 19,777 Indigenous residents, placing it tenth among Brazilian cities. Gabriel Croquer, "Censo do IBGE: São Paulo é a 10ª cidade com mais indígenas no Brasil; veja mapa de territórios delimitados na capital," *Globo*, August 7, 2023, https://g1.globo.com/sp/sao-paulo/noticia/2023/08/07/censo-do-ibge-sao-paulo-e-a-10a-cidade-com-mais-indigenas-no-brasil-veja-mapa-de-territorios-delimitados-na-capital.ghtml.

27 Santos, *Nem tudo era italiano*.

28 Santos, "'Ser essa terra.'"

29 French, *Legalizing Identities*; Miki, *Frontiers of Citizenship*; O'Toole, *Bound Lives*.

30 Defining "orí," Christen Anne Smith explains that the word "literally means head, but it is also a spirit in Afro-Brazilian religious tradition." Smith, "Black Feminist Model," 81. Princeton University Press recently released a new collection of Maria Beatriz Nascimento's writing: *The Dialectic Is in the Sea: The Black Radical Thought of Beatriz Nascimento.*

31 Gerber, *Orí*, 1:12:49–1:14:14.

32 Smith, "Black Feminist Model," 79; Hartman, *Lose Your Mother.*

33 Smith, "Black Feminist Model," 81.

34 That symbolism had a special significance in 1989 when Orí was released: Just a year earlier, Brazil's new constitution established a process by which the descendants of the enslaved who occupied the so-called remnants of *quilombos* could petition for formal recognition of land possession.

35 Elsewhere in *Orí*, Nascimento drew the connection between identity and territory more explicitly: "Recapturing identity through knowledge of the land . . . as a person who has migrated. *Quilombo* is a geographic space where human beings can feel the ocean . . . all of the cosmic energy enters in your body . . . I feel big here. It's a Black thing, but it's a Black thing because of the connection to the land. The black man is the one that knows the land best . . . just like the Dogon people. The Black man, the color of soil . . . the black earth exists. It is that which we fear losing the most."

36 Lefebvre, *Production of Space*; Massey, "Double Articulation"; Massey, "Global Sense of Place"; Soja, *Postmodern Geographies.*

37 I follow other scholars of race, ethnicity, and skin color in Latin America in analyzing ethnicity and race together in the same frame. See, for example, Telles et al., "Pigmentocracies," 39–40n1.

38 Jackson, *Crabgrass Frontier*; Massey and Denton, *American Apartheid*; Adelman and Mele, *Race, Space, and Exclusion*; Rothstein, *Color of Law.*

39 Wilson and Portes, "Immigrant Enclaves"; Portes and Manning, "Immigrant Enclave"; Zhou, "Revisiting Ethnic Entrepreneurship"; Marcuse, "Enclaves Yes, Ghettos No."

40 A pioneering study to do this in another context was Anderson, "Idea of Chinatown." A more recent intervention is Gao-Miles, "Beyond the Ethnic Enclave."

41 Illuminating works that examine constructions of racialized difference on the scale of regions in Brazil include Marcos Chor Maio, "UNESCO and Race Relations"; Weinstein, "Regionalizing Racial Difference"; Weinstein, *Color of Modernity.*

42 On the materialization of identity, see Frers and Meier, *Encountering Urban Places.* Clara Irazábal explores ethnoracialized place-making

via immigrant-themed parks in Curitiba in Irazábal, *City Making and Urban Governance.*

43 They also ask productive questions such as "What social relations and social identities are being re/produced in and through social and physical spaces? How do social relations and spatial processes affect one another?" Neely and Samura, "Social Geographies of Race," 1934, 1947.

44 Three works that make this comparison explicit are Degler, *Neither Black nor White*; Seigel, *Uneven Encounters*; Graham, *Shifting the Meaning.*

45 For a survey of these discourses, see Nascimento, *Racial Democracy in Brazil*; "The Myth of Racial Democracy," in Costa, *Brazilian Empire*; Lesser, *Negotiating National Identity*; Telles, *Race in Another America*; Antônio Sérgio Guimarães, *Racismo e anti-racismo*; Andrews, *Blacks and Whites*; Alberto, *Terms of Inclusion*; Graham, *Shifting the Meaning.*

46 Caldeira, *City of Walls.*

47 This value means that on average, 37 percent of the Black population in São Paulo would need to move to another census tract for there to be an ethnoracial distribution proportionate to the ethnoracial composition of the city as a whole (25 percent Black, 75 percent non-Black in 1980).

48 For more recent figures, see Daniel Mariani, Murilo Roncolato, Ariel Tonglet e Simon Ducroquet, "O que o mapa racial do Brasil revela sobre a segregação no país," *Nexo*, December 16, 2015, https://www.nexojornal.com.br/especial/2015/12/16/O-que-o-mapa-racial-do-Brasil-revela-sobre-a-segrega%C3%A7%C3%A3o-no-pa%C3%ADs.

49 Telles, *Race in Another America*, 203.

50 This argument echoes Keisha Khan-Perry's study of racialized and gendered sociospatial exclusion in the Gamboa de Baixo neighborhood of Salvador. See Khan-Perry, *Black Women.*

51 Telles, *Race in Another America*, 196.

52 Haddad, "Sobre a divisão," cited in Hidalgo, "As divisões territoriais," 28; Dias, *Desenvolvimento urbano.* For the history of the administrative division of land in São Paulo, see "São Paulo," IBGE, accessed May 13, 2017, https://cidades.ibge.gov.br/brasil/sp/sao-paulo/historico.

53 André Marega Pinhel and Rodrigo Fernandes Silva, "The Paradoxes of Ethnoracial Space in São Paulo, 1930s–1980s: Caracterização da distribuição étnico racial da população nos distritos da Bela Vista, Brasilândia e Liberdade," Report, Cambridge, 2021.

54 Paviani, *Brasília, ideologia e realidade*; Holston, *Modernist City*; Scott, *Seeing Like a State*; Perlman, *Myth of Marginality*; Fischer, *Poverty of Rights*; McCann, *Hard Times.*

55 Randolph, "A nova perspectiva"; Miraftab, "Insurgent Planning"; Holston, *Insurgent Citizenship*.

56 Gregory and Geddes, *Toward Spatial Humanities*.

57 Based at Rice University and developed by Farès el-Dahdah and Alida C. Metcalf, imagineRio is a "a searchable atlas that illustrates the social and urban evolution of Rio de Janeiro over its entire history, as it has existed and as it has been imagined." Pauliceia 2.0 is an open-source historical mapping platform focused on São Paulo and produced through a partnership between the Federal University of São Paulo (UNIFESP), the State Archive of São Paulo, the National Institute for Space Research (INPE), and Emory University. The coordinators are Luís Ferla and Karla Donato Fook.

58 WB, interview by author, Brasilândia, São Paulo, August 28, 2016.

59 Nascimento and Pandeiro, "Metrô da Brasilândia."

60 As I discuss in chapter 5, in 1984 a bust of Barbosa was installed along May 13 Street in Bela Vista. Today, Barbosa's likeness is visible in Bexiga's crosswalk lights, and he has a street named after him.

61 Campos, *Adoniran*, 230–31.

CHAPTER ONE. AVENUES AND THE AFTERLIVES OF SLAVERY

1 FR, interview by author, Brasilândia, São Paulo, June 29, 2017.

2 Other significant texts engaged in this project include Bernardo, *Memória em branco e negro*; Castro, *Bexiga*; Domingues, *Uma história não contada*; Santos, *Nem tudo era italiano*.

3 Hartman, *Lose Your Mother*, 6.

4 Patterson, *Slavery and Social Death*.

5 Abdias do Nascimento argued that "the Black masses in Brazil have only one option: to disappear. Whether it be through compulsory miscegenation/assimilation or, when they escape from this, through direct elimination—death pure and simple." Nascimento, *Brazil: Mixture or Massacre?*, 7.

6 Advertisements for Caninha do Ó appeared in early editions of *O Estado de S. Paulo* from the 1870s forward.

7 Morse, *Bandeirantes*; Ferreira, *A epopéia bandeirante*; Russell-Wood, "Rethinking Bandeirismo."

8 Barro, *Nossa Senhora do Ó*, 41.

9 Noelli and Mota, "Índios, jesuítas, bandeirantes."

10 Monteiro, *Negros da terra*, 239n54.

11 Barro, *Nossa Senhora do Ó*, 42.

12 Maços da populaçāo, 1765–1851, APESP, https://www.arquivoestado.sp.gov.br/web/digitalizado/textual/macos_populacao.

13 The exact figure was 49.7 percent. Kuznesof, *Household Economy*, 103.
14 For figures from the province of São Paulo, see Luna and Klein, *Slavery and the Economy*, 49. On the social composition of the city and predominance of women, see Dias, *Power and Everyday Life*, 15–16.
15 Luna and Klein, *Slavery and the Economy*, 161.
16 Luna and Klein, *Slavery and the Economy*, 165.
17 Marcílio, *A cidade de São Paulo*, 146.
18 Maços, APESP.
19 Schorer, *A lavoura canavieira*; Costa, *Da senzala à colônia*, 98–99; Love, *São Paulo*, 6; Dean, *Rio Claro*; Kuznesof, *Household Economy*.
20 "Planta de uma sorte de terra pertencente a Pedro de Oliveira Simões na Freguesia da N. Senhora do Ó," 1895, Mapoteca, AHM; "Terrenos particulares de propriedade de Pedro de Oliveira Simões, terreno próximo aos de Dona Veridiana Prado. Assinado por Luiz Frenckel," FCMSP/Série: Obras Particulares, Freguesia de Nossa Senhora do Ó, 1895, XD23. For more on the Prado's landholdings throughout the state of São Paulo, see Levi, *Prados of São Paulo*, 68–73.
21 Marcílio, *A cidade de São Paulo*, 85.
22 Kidder, *Sketches*, 239–40.
23 Quoted in Barro, *Nossa Senhora do Ó*, 51.
24 Kidder, *Sketches*, 239–40.
25 Dias, *Power and Everyday Life*, 42.
26 Luna and Klein, *Slavery and the Economy*, 29–30.
27 My use of *fugitive* and *fugitivity* echoes the conceptualization of these terms and practices by Fred Moten. See Harney and Moten, *Undercommons*.
28 Barro, *Nossa Senhora do Ó*, 43–44.
29 Barro, *Nossa Senhora do Ó*, 44–45.
30 "Parte da policia: Mogy-Mirim," *Diário de S. Paulo*, May 24, 1867, 2.
31 "Annuncios: Escravo fugido," *Diário de S. Paulo*, June 2, 1869, 3.
32 Freguesia here denotes "parish," and in the sources from this era "Freguesia do Ó" is a commonly used, shortened version of "Freguesia da Nossa Senhora do Ó."
33 "Limeira," *O Estado de S. Paulo*, November 20, 1877, 4.
34 Neither source collection, it should be noted, provides substantial quantitative insight into the frequency or duration of escape.
35 For other examples and broader studies, see Freyre, *O escravo nos anúncios*; Schwarcz, *Retrato*; Dean, *Rio Claro*, 82; Costa, *Da senzala à colônia*, 373; Dean, *Rio Claro*, 82.
36 Dias, *Power and Everyday Life*, 16.
37 Costa, *Da senzala à colônia*, 371–72.
38 Barro, *Nossa Senhora do Ó*, 45.
39 Barro, *Nossa Senhora do Ó*, 45.

40 Kidder, *Sketches*, 259.

41 Costa, *Da senzala à colônia*, 202–16; Marcílio, *A cidade de São Paulo*, 84–90; Dean, *Rio Claro*, 41.

42 "Relatorio apresentado a Assembléa Legilsativa Provincial de S. Paulo na 1.a sessão da décima sexta legislatura no dia 3 de fevereiro de 1866 pelo presidente da mesma provincia, o dr. João da Silva Carrão. S. Paulo, Typ. Imparcial de J.R.A. Marques, 1866," Provincial Presidential Reports (1830–1930): São Paulo, Center for Research Libraries, accessed August 30, 2017, http://www-apps.crl.edu/brazil/provincial/s%C3%A3o_paulo.

43 "Discurso com que o illustrissimo e excellentissimo senhor conselheiro Antonio José Henriques, presidente da provincia de São Paulo, abrio a Assembléa Legislativa Provincial no anno de 1861. S. Paulo, Typ. Imparcial de Joaquim Roberto de Azevedo Marques, 1861," Provincial Presidential Reports (1830–1930): São Paulo, Center for Research Libraries, accessed August 30, 2017, http://www-apps.crl.edu/brazil/provincial/s%C3%A3o_paulo.

44 "Dicionário de Ruas de São Paulo," AHM, accessed June 4, 2018, http://www.dicionarioderuas.prefeitura.sp.gov.br/PaginasPublicas/Introducao.aspx.

45 Maços, 1825 and 1842, APESP.

46 Maço, 1825, APESP. Pedro de Jesus Maria was listed in the *maço* of 1822 as 71, when he and Anna Maria's household consisted of five children ranging in age from two to twenty-six.

47 In his pioneering study of a local coffee region, Stanley Stein found *Congo* among the four most common terms of identification for enslaved Africans in Brazil. Stein, *Vassouras*, 76–77.

48 Schwarcz, *Retrato*, 139.

49 *Correio paulistano*, September 4, 1879, printed in Schwarcz, *Retrato*, 140.

50 DaMatta's intimates at a racialized nature of this division, as well: "As such, it is on the street or in the forest where *malandros* [tricksters], the marginalized, and the spirits live, these entities with whom one never has precise contractual relations." DaMatta, *Carnavais, malandros, e heróis*, 92–104.

51 Dias, *Power and Everyday Life*, 10.

52 Johnson, *Slavery's Metropolis*, 121; Evans, *Congo Square*; Widmer, "Invention of a Memory."

53 From 1804 to 1829 the percentage of owners producing cane alcohol in the city of São Paulo ("Capital Region") decreased from 9 percent to 3 percent, while the percentage of slaves diminished from 14 percent to 9 percent. N. S. do Ó would seem to have maintained its place in what became a more limited market with the development of coffee

agriculture over the nineteenth century. Luna and Klein, *Slavery and Economy*, 51–52, 124.

54 Costa, *Da senzala à colônia*, 101.

55 Sant'Anna, *São Paulo histórico*, 301.

56 Skidmore, *Black into White*; Lesser, *Negotiating National Identity*; Barbara Weinstein, "Regionalizing Racial Difference."

57 Dean characterized the contradiction of plantations in the West Paulista region as "at the same time the most progressive and the most retrograde sector of Brazilian society." Dean, *Rio Claro*, 51.

58 Bassanezi, *São Paulo do passado*, 92.

59 Morse, *From Community*, 122. N. S. do Ó was in fact the only region in the city with negative growth during this period.

60 Dead, *Rio Claro*, 41.

61 Morse, *From Community*, 173.

62 Guimarães, *Rosaura*, cited in Dias, *Power and Everyday Life*, 165.

63 "Planta geral da Capital de São Paulo, Organisada sob a direcção do Dr Gomes Cardim—1897," AHM, ArquiAmigos, accessed June 12, 2018, http://www.arquiamigos.org.br/info/info20/img/1897-download.jpg.

64 Ugo Bonvicini, "Planta da cidade de São Paulo com identificação dos primeiros edifícios públicos. 1893," APESP, accessed June 12, 2018, http://www.arquivoestado.sp.gov.br/site/acervo/repositorio_digital/mapa_carto/BR_APESP_IGC_IGG_CAR_I_S_0289_001_001.

65 Rolnik, *A cidade e a lei*.

66 This phrase appears in both popular and academic contexts, including in book titles such as Somekh and Campos, *A cidade que não pode parar*.

67 *Cidade*, "A Saga da Metrópole," 4, 10–11; Toledo and Kühl, *Prestes Maia*.

68 I use *urbanist* and *urbanism* in English as synonymous with city planner and city planning. For more discussion about the history of the term *urbanismo*, see Villaça, "Uma contribuição." On the growth of São Paulo in this period, see Peixoto-Mehrtens, *Urban Space*, 54.

69 Interview by author with [name withheld], Liberdade, São Paulo, June 14, 2017.

70 Outtes, "Disciplining," 321–22.

71 Morse, *From Community*, 284–85.

72 Maia, *Estudo de um plano*, 186.

73 Maia, *Estudo de um plano*, x–xi.

74 Maia, *Estudo de um plano*, 46. Also see Leme, "São Paulo," 131.

75 Maia, *Estudo de um plano*, x.

76 Luiz de Anhaia Mello, "Problemas de urbanismo: mais uma contribuição para o calçamento," *Revista Polytechnica* 83 (1927), 343–44, quoted in Outtes, "Disciplining," 340. Mello would later argue that "the paving of streets and its financing should be distributed through the adjacent properties and the secondary zone of benefit." Outtes, "Disciplining," 347.

77 Maia, *Estudo de um plano*, 275–76.

78 "Equídade nos melhoramentos municipais," *Correio Paulistano*, February 3, 1942, 5.

79 Fausto, *A Revolução de 1930*; Viscardi, *O teatro das oligarquias*.

80 Here Mello uses *paulista* instead of *paulistano*, despite the reference to *city* planning focused on SAC's works within the city of São Paulo specifically. The slippage in geographic scale seems to reflect the rippling significance that figures like Mello saw in the remaking of the city. Luiz de Anhaia Mello, "A 'Sociedade Amigos da Cidade' e sua função no quadro urbano," *Boletim do Instituto de Engenharia*, 21:115, 263, originally in English, quoted in Outtes, "Disciplining," 303.

81 Leme, "São Paulo," 128.

82 Leme, "São Paulo," 121.

83 José Alfredo O. Vidigal Pontes, "Francisco Prestes Maia: O Político que não Gostava de Política," in *Cidade*, "A Saga da Metrópole," 7.

84 Weinstein, *Color of Modernity*; Woodard, *Place in Politics*.

85 Peixoto-Mehrtens, *Urban Space*, 54.

86 Lesser, *Negotiating National Identity*, 130–33, especially. Also see Costa, *Brazilian Empire*, 204; Williams, *Culture Wars in Brazil*.

87 Wolfe, *Autos and Progress*, 96.

88 "Visita ao sr. Interventor Federal em S. Paulo, dr. Fernando Costa—Palestra do eng. arq. F. Prestes Maia sobre 'Planos de Melhoramentos de São Paulo,'" *Engenharia*, March 1943, xxix–xxx. Silva Freire lamented that Prestes Maia's speech was not transcribed, another indication of the opaque nature of government information in this era.

89 Weinstein, *Color of Modernity*.

90 Toledo and Kuhl, *Prestes Maia*, 227.

91 "Os rumos do governo da cidade de São Paulo," *Correio Paulistano*, June 25, 1939, 41.

92 "As novas avenidas de S. Paulo," *Correio Paulistano*, November 15, 1941, 5.

93 "As atividades do governo Prestes Maia," *Correio Paulistano*, December 7, 1941, 3.

94 The social history of expropriation and demolition has expanded in recent years. See, for example: Reynolds, *Before Eminent Domain*; Ammon, *Bulldozer*; Khan-Perry, *Black Women*; Highsmith, *Demolition Means Progress*; Leu, *Defiant Geogarpies*.

95 For one study that considers expropriation in the context of São Paulo's 1929 flood, see Ferla et al., "A enchente de 1929."

96 Roland Corbisier, "A lei do inquilinato e o conceito cristão de propriedade," *Digesto Economico* 54 (May 1949), quoted in Bon-

duki, *Origens*, 89–90. Also see Ioris, *Transforming Brazil*; "Roland Corbisier," CPDOC, accessed September 15, 2017, http://cpdoc.fgv.br/producao/dossies/AEraVargas2/biografias/roland_corbisier.

97 Mello, "Problemas de urbanismo," quoted in Outtes, "Disciplining," 340.

98 The decree-law was drafted by Francisco Campos, the architect of the Fascist-inspired Constitution of 1937 and minister of justice during the first years of the Estado Novo, along with Carlos Medeiros, who served on a variety of such commissions during Vargas's regime. "Francisco Campos," CPDOC, accessed September 14, 2017, http://cpdoc.fgv.br/producao/dossies/AEraVargas1/biografias/francisco_campos; "Carlos Medeira," CPDOC, accessed September 14, 2017, http://www.fgv.br/cpdoc/acervo/dicionarios/verbete-biografico/carlos-medeiros-silva.

99 Bonduki, *Origens*, 256.

100 Feldman, *Planejamento e zoneamento*, 16.

101 Bonduki, *Origens*, 261; Feldman, *Planejamento e zoneamento*, 18.

102 Silva, "Debaixo do 'Pogréssio,'" 244.

103 Bonduki, *Origens*; Santos, *Metrópole.*

104 Luiz de Anhaia Mello, "Habitação e urbanismo," *Engenharia* 4, no. 37, 2–3, in Outtes, "Disciplining," 358.

105 See, for example, Leme, "São Paulo," 144.

106 Maia, *Os melhoramentos de São Paulo*, 14.

107 Maia, *Os melhoramentos de São Paulo*, 14–15.

108 "Há 50 anos, a começo da grande avenida," *O Estado de S. Paulo*, July 28, 1987.

109 Leme, "São Paulo," 132.

110 "Prestes Maia—Fez / Prestes Maia—Fará," Biblioteca Prestes Maia, Coleção Pretes Maia, 7.

111 "Prestes Maia—Fez / Prestes Maia—Fará," Biblioteca Prestes Maia, Coleção Pretes Maia, 32.

112 Widespread, organized popular participation in the production of urban space in Brazil has led some planning theorists and urban anthropologists to describe these nonstate spatial actors as "insurgent planners." Miraftab, "Insurgent Planning"; Randolph, "A nova perspectiva"; Holston, *Insurgent Citizenship.*

113 For an examination of an earlier history of official treatment of cortiços and their residents, see Chaloub, *Cidade febril.*

114 Outtes, "Disciplining." Morse, *From Community*, 193–94. Teresa Caldeira defines *cortiço* as "a type of tenement occupied by workers who cannot afford to own a home." Caldeira, *City of Walls*, 14. They remain a prominent feature of popular housing in the city of São Paulo.

115 *Progresso* ran from 1928 to at least 1932 and was headed by Lino Guedes and Argentino Celso Wanderley. Alberto, *Terms of Inclusion*, 105–6; Domingues, *A nova abolição*, 35.

116 "Cortiços: Favellas paulistanas," *Progresso* 18, November 24, 1929, 5. Cited in Butler, *Freedoms Given*, 82.

117 Image available in Maia, *Estudo de um plano*, 309.

118 Maia, *Estudo de um plano*, 309.

119 Bonduki, *Origens*, 76.

120 Bonduki, *Origens*, 63.

121 Marzola, *Bela Vista*, 81–84.

122 Schneck, "Bexiga: Cotidiano e trabalho."

123 Other examples taken from interviews with current and former residents can be found in Bernardo, *Memória em branco e negro*, 147; Scarlato, "Estrutura," 118; Barbosa, *Frente Negra Brasileira: Depoimentos.*

124 Maia, *Estudo de um plano*, 22.

125 This is another example (in addition to the *Progresso* article "Cortiços: Favellas paulistanas") of joining *cortiço* and *favela*, two spatial forms typically differentiated in academic literature. The examples reveal the mutability of these categories.

126 "Demolições," *Jornal de Notícias*, September 27, 1951, 2.

127 The full title of the journal was *A Marmita: Um jornal de grande tiragem e grandes tiradas* (The Lunchbox: A journal of great circulation and great tirades).

128 "Entrevistas Deshumanas: Onde o amor cheira mal," *A Martmita*, January 28, 1948, 5.

129 "Entrevistas Deshumanas: Onde o amor cheira mal," *A Martmita*, January 28, 1948, 4.

130 "Demolições," *Jornal de Notícias*, September 27, 1951, 2.

131 Avenida 9 de Julho, folder 319, groups 1–7; and Avenida 23 de Maio, folder 52, groups 1–9, DESAP.

132 Amaral, *Artes plásticas*, 107n21. See also "Ramos de Azevedo mudou imagem de São Paulo," *O Estado de S. Paulo*, June 12, 1998, 21.

133 Ademir Medici, "Domiziano Rossi e sua ligação com São Bernardo," *Diário do Grande abc*, October 11, 2012, http://www.dgabc.com.br/Noticia/313179/domiziano-rossi-e-sua-ligacao-com-sao-bernardo (accessed November 15, 2017). "Vida Social," *O Combate*, October 25, 1921, 1.

134 "Um senhorio de maus bofes," *A Gazeta*, December 17, 1925, 3. Amélia Cohn and Sedi Hirano, "A Gazeta," Fudação Getúlio Vargas, CPDOC, http://www.fgv.br/cpdoc/acervo/dicionarios/verbete-tematico/gazeta-a.

135 Scarlato, "Estrutura," 118–19.

136 Donald Pierson, "Habitações de São Paulo."

137 For a detailed examination of the "Fernandes thesis" about Brazilian race relations, see Andrews, *Blacks and Whites*, 71–81.

138 Fernandes, *O significado*, 89.

139 Lucrécio, "Interview," 37.

140 Alberto, *Terms of Inclusion*, 59.

141 Oliveira, "Segregação urbana," 180.

142 Interview by author with [name withheld], Bela Vista, São Paulo, April 21, 2017.

143 For one version of this foundation myth, see Vianna, *Mystery of Samba*. See also McCann, *Hello*.

144 This interpretation follows Maria Clementina Pereira Cunha, who writes: "Even still, it is necessary to emphasize that an absolute majority of the sambistas that we will encounter in the following pages, the protagonists of this history, is constituted by descendants of slaves. It is impossible to ignore this mark, written into the color of their skins and the memories they learned from their parents and grandparents. This does not mean, however, that samba can be taken in advance as an exclusive manifestation of the 'race' or as a culture unique to these realms—and, much less, as an unequivocal, conflict-free practice." Cunha, *Não tá sopa*, 11.

145 Three prominent academic histories of samba in São Paulo are Britto, *Samba na Cidade de São Paulo*; Von Simson, *Carnaval em branco e negro*; and Silva, "Debaixo do 'Pogréssio.'"

146 Maisonnave, "Girl from Shinjuku," 317.

147 McCann, *Hello*, 42.

148 Marco Aurélio Guimarães Jangada, "O samba segundo São Paulo," *Realidade*, February 1972, 54.

149 Filme, "Interview," 74—75.

150 On Plínio Marcos's album *Em prosa e samba*, the folklorist points to another school, Morro de Perdizes, as founded earlier. Lavapés today is celebrated as the "marco zero" of samba paulistano, including a plaque at the five-point intersection where the school sits in Liberdade. Marcos, *Em Prosa e Samba*.

151 Moraes, "Polifonia na metrópole."

152 Jangada, "O samba," 56.

153 Andrade, "O samba rural paulista," 40.

154 Castro, *Bexiga*, 43–44.

155 Jangada, "O samba," 53. See also note 3 in the introduction to this book.

156 João Antônio, "Águas-Fortes Paulistanas," *O Estado de S. Paulo: Cultura* 337 (1986), 11.

157 "Em vesperas de conclusção o Viaduto Pacaembú," *Correio Paulistano*, January 17, 1942, 3.

158 Silva, *Artes do corpo*, 176.

159 This song was first recorded on Barros, *Balbina de Iansã*.

160 A *cavaquinho* is an instrument similar to a ukulele.

161 Adoniran Barbosa (aka João Rubinato), "Saudosa Maloca," 1951, video of live performance, YouTube, accessed June 13, 2018, https://www.youtube.com/watch?v=801MQjNJvrg.

162 Silva, "Debaixo do 'Pogréssio,'" 187.

163 Raquel Rolnik, "Territórios Negros."

164 For a few examples of this analysis, see Costa, *Brazilian Empire*, 171; Butler, *Freedoms Given*; Scott, "Meaning of Freedom"; Monsma, *A reprodução de racismo*.

165 Williams, *Brazil*, 188.

CHAPTER TWO. SPATIAL PROJECTS OF FORGETTING

A section of chapter 2 was originally published as "Spatial Projects of Forgetting: Razing the Remedies Church and Museum to the Enslaved in São Paulo's 'Black Zone,' 1930s–1940s," *Journal of Latin American Studies* 54, no. 4 (2022): 561–92, https://doi.org/10.1017/S0022216X22000669.

1 Rogério Daflon, "Escavações de obra de drenagem da Zona Portuária encontram restos dos cais da Imperatriz e do. . . ," *O Globo*, January 3, 2011, https://oglobo.globo.com/rio/escavacoes-de-obra-de-drenagem-da-zona-portuaria-encontram-restos-dos-cais-da-imperatriz-do-2816387#ixzz4tzJRWOMB.

2 "The Outstanding Universal Value of the Valongo Wharf Archaeological Site," UNESCO, July 27, 2017, accessed July 4, 2018, http://www.unesco.org/new/en/social-and-human-sciences/themes/slave-route/sv000/news/the_outstanding_universal_value_of_the_valongo_wharf_arch/.

3 Araujo, *Public Memory of Slavery*, 8.

4 My italics. David Amsden, "Building the First Slavery Museum in America," *New York Times Magazine*, February 26, 2015, https://www.nytimes.com/2015/03/01/magazine/building-the-first-slave-museum-in-america.html.

5 Tomich, "Wealth of Empire"; Tomich, *Pelo prisma da escravidão*; Salles and Marquese, *Escravidão e capitalismo histórico*.

6 Andrews, *Blacks and Whites*; Skidmore, *Black into White*; Schwarcz, *O espetáculo das raças*; Domingues, *Uma história não contada*; Lesser, *Immigration, Ethnicity*; Weinstein, *Color of Modernity*.

7 Butler, *Freedoms Given*, 76.

8 Barra Funda was the third neighborhood. Filme founded the samba school Paulistano da Glória, located in the Liberdade district, and

participated for many years in Vai-Vai, a samba school located in Bela Vista. Filme, "Interview," 74–75.

9 Young, *Texture of Memory*; Klein, *History of Forgetting*; Ricoeur, *Memory, History, Forgetting*; Guy Beiner, *Forgetful Remembrance*; Giselle Beiguelman, *Memória da amnesia*.

10 Maia, *Estudo de um plano*, iii.

11 Weinstein, *Color of Modernity*; Woodard, *Place in Politics*, 77–78.

12 Engineers were celebrated participants in the 1932 conflict; see Peixoto-Mehrtens, *Urban Space*, 165. Two years after the conflict, a book was published profiling the engineers who had participated; Morgan, *Os engenheiros*.

13 Morse, *Bandeirantes*; Antonio Celso Ferreira, *A epopéia bandeirante*; Russell-Wood, "Rethinking Bandeirismo."

14 Prado, "Avenida 9 de Julho," 3.

15 Notice how the "native blood" passively "disperses itself" in the emerging Paulista race.

16 Campos, "A vila de São Paulo," 30.

17 Prado, "Avenida 9 de Julho," 4.

18 "Governar é abrir estradas," *O Globo*, August 25, 1928, accessed September 15, 2017, http://acervo.oglobo.globo.com/rio-de-historias/washington-luis-inaugura-primeira-rodovia-asfaltada-do-brasil-8849272.

19 Prado, "Avenida 9 de Julho," 4.

20 The English translation of Cunha's work is *Rebellion in the Backlands*, published in 2010 by the University of Chicago Press. Two contemporary studies of real and imagined geographies and regional identity linked to Brazil's Northeast are Albuquerque, *Invention of Brazilian Northeast*; and Campbell, *Region Out of Place*.

21 For an expansive collection of essays on history and cultural patrimony in the "Valley of Coffee," see Fernandes and Coelho, *História e geografia*. Also see Assunção, "Stanzas and Sticks."

22 Vila Buarque, located just northeast of the historical city center, remains a neighborhood in contemporary São Paulo. Tabatinguera Street exists, though it is not commonly described as a neighborhood.

23 "Factors Diversos: Ao redor do mundo em S. Paulo—A Saracura," *Correio Paulistano*, October 9, 1907, 4.

24 This condition amounts to acute or chronic kidney inflammation.

25 Dias, *Power and Everyday Life*, 103.

26 Dias, *Power and Everyday Life*, 97; Andrews, *Afro-Latin America*, 105.

27 Lucena, *Bairro do Bexiga*, 24, quoted in Nascimento, "Lembrança eu tenho," 32–33. Also see Bruno, *História e tradições*, 738–45.

28 Marzola, *Bela Vista*, 39.

29 Bruno, *História e tradições*, 571.

30 Lévi-Strauss, *Tristes Tropiques*, 99. Though this work was first published in the mid-1950s, Lévi-Strauss's observations of São Paulo were based on his residence in the city in the mid-1930s.

31 She includes Black and Brown individuals in her calculations of Afro-Brazilians. Butler, *Freedoms Given*, 76.

32 The map excluded the northern region of Nossa Senhora do Ó, technically outside the city limits, which also had a sizable population of African descendants. Lowrie, "O elemento negro."

33 Schneck, "Bexiga: Cotidiano e trabalho," 370.

34 Moreno, *Memórias*, 87–88.

35 Jeffrey Lesser has identified commonplace descriptions of Portuguese and their descendants as connected to Africans and their descendants in Brazil. For instance: "For the Portuguese immigrant, the black man, and the donkey, three p's: bread (*pão*) to eat, clothes (*pano*) to wear, and a stick (*pau*) to work with." Lesser, *Immigration, Ethnicity*, 103.

36 Maia, *Estudo de um plano*, 57 (my emphasis).

37 Arthur Saboya, preface to Maia, *Estudo de um plano*, iv. Some observers have seen a continuity between this and earlier planning projects fixated on the center. The mayoral administration of Antônio Prado, for instance, is seen as one of the first coordinated efforts to displace undesirable spaces and bodies. Nascimento, "Entre sambas e rezas," 72.

38 "Os rumos do governo da cidade de São Paulo," *Correio Paulistano*, June 25, 1939, 41 (my emphasis).

39 Avenida 9 de Julho, folder 319, groups 1–7, DESAP.

40 The link between modern, concrete urban forms and aviation would reach its fullest articulation in the design of Brazil's new capital, Brasília, inaugurated in 1960 and whose shape was an airplane. See Holston, *Modernist City*.

41 Quoted in Nascimento, "Entre sambas e rezas," 77.

42 Dias, *Power and Everyday Life*, 5, 10.

43 Morse, *From Community*, 23.

44 Maia, *Os melhoramentos de São Paulo*, 10.

45 Maia, *Estudo de um plano*, 22.

46 Israel Dias Novaes, "A dramática luta de Prestes Maia para rehabilitar São Paulo: Discurso pronunciado da tribuna da assembléia legislativa do estado de São Paulo, sessão de 5 de Dezembro de 1961," Coleção Pretes Maia, Biblioteca Prestes Maia, 11.

47 Quoted in Nascimento, "Entre sambas e rezas," 77.

48 I met Penteado at the Casa da Cultura da Brasilândia in 2016, where he was a special guest for a program of the Samba do Congo group named Afro-Bantu Paulista. I discuss this and other historical and contemporary connections between Brasilândia and Bela Vista in chapters 3 and 4 and the conclusion.

49 The significance of July 9 Avenue and this moment of spatial change in São Paulo is reflected in the fact that Getúlio Vargas's first visit to São Paulo following the 1932 civil war occurred in 1938, for the inauguration of the July 9 Avenue tunnel, an impressive work of engineering that stretched beneath Paulista Avenue. Woodard, "All for São Paulo," 90.

50 This is not necessarily rare for urban centers throughout the Americas. Few studies have addressed the geography of slave markets as explicitly as Walter Johnson's study of New Orleans, *Soul by Soul: Life Inside the Antebellum Slave Market.* Kwesi DeGraft-Hanson explores the "hidden landscape" of a slave market in Savanah, GA, in "Unearthing the Weeping Time: Savannah's Ten Broeck Race Course and 1859 Slave Sale." More recently, The Equal Justice Initiative's Legacy Museum opened on top of a former warehouse for enslaved people in the city of Montgomery, Alabama. See "The Legacy Museum: From Enslavement to Mass Incarceration," accessed June 22, 2018, https://eji.org/legacy-museum.

51 Dias, *Power and Everyday Life*, 73.

52 Machado, *Crime e escravidão*, 173.

53 Tomich, "Wealth of Empire"; Tomich, *Pelo prisma da escravidão*; Salles and Marquese, *Escravidão e capitalismo histórico.*

54 Curtin, *Atlantic Slave Trade*; Klein, *Atlantic Slave Trade*; Lovejoy, "Atlantic Slave Trade"; Eltis, "Transatlantic Slave Trade."

55 Despite being the most active market for the internal trade in enslaved people in the nineteenth century, the province of São Paulo has received substantially less attention than Rio de Janeiro. Slenes's work is an exception, as is Ian Read's recent work. Klein, "Internal Slave Trade"; Slenes, "Demography and Economics"; Frank and Berry, "Slave Market"; Slenes, "Brazilian Internal Slave Trade"; Graham, "Another Middle Passage?"; Read, "Off the Block."

56 Read, "Off the Block," 27.

57 Graham, "Another Middle Passage?," 303.

58 Maria Helena P. T. Machado, "Sendo cativo nas ruas," 25–26.

59 Azevedo, *A cidade de São Paulo*, 3:133.

60 Additional research would help to further illuminate this history. In limited searching, I located two articles from *O Estado de S. Paulo* advertising the sale of captives that reference the Piques Square: one from 1880 listing a specific address on the Piques Bridge, and another from 1875 listing the Piques Paredão (Large Hill), likely signifying the Piques Square itself. See "Escravos," *O Estado de S. Paulo*, June 12, 1875, 3; and "Escravos a venda," *O Estado de S. Paulo*, November 20, 1880, 2. I have also encountered numerous advertisements for the sale of enslaved people in *O Estado de S. Paulo* that list locations elsewhere in the city (most often the addresses of buildings, not public

spaces), suggesting that the traffic and commerce may have been more diffuse. While this research did not reveal as clear a picture as I would have hoped, the popular memories and academic histories discussed throughout this section support, to my eyes, the link between the contemporary Praça da Bandeira and the traffic and commerce of the enslaved in the city.

61 Rolnik, *A cidade e a lei*, 76.

62 Maia, *Os melhoramentos de São Paulo*, 11–12, 25.

63 "O Prefeito, Razões e Desrazões," Interview with Benedito Lima de Toledo by Marcos Faerman in *Cidade*, "A Saga da Metrópole," 38.

64 Maia, *Os melhoramentos de São Paulo*, 11–12, 25.

65 Parecer 109–40 da Comissão da e Educação e Cultura, Sobre o Processo de Lei 74–49, December, 15, 1949.

66 "O transito na Praça da Bandeira," *O Estado de S. Paulo*, May 13, 1948, 21.

67 Lei 3865, April 5, 1950. The place remained "Largo da Memória" on official maps of São Paulo into the 1950s, reflecting the limited effects that official decrees about São Paulo's place-names could have in cartographic practice.

68 Also see images of the Praça da Bandeira in Maia, *Os melhoramentos de São Paulo*, where no flag is visible.

69 Vicente de Azevedo writes that a trip through the state of São Paulo inspired Alves's poems "O navio negreiro" and "Vozes d'África." Azevedo, *O noiva da morte*, 83.

70 Marques, *Ruas e tradições*, 145.

71 Marx, *Making Race and Nation*, 81–82. For compelling episodes on the intersection of flags, religion, and Black identity in Brazil, see Burdick, *Color of Sound*, esp. chap. 3, "The Flags of Jesus and Brazil: Body, History, and Nation in Samba Gospel." Also see Gilroy, *There Ain't No Black*.

72 Brefe, *O museu paulista*; "Afonso d´E. Taunay," Academia Brasileira de Letras, accessed June 2, 2018, http://www.academia.org.br/academicos/afonso-de-taunay.

73 Affonso de E. Taunay, "Heraldica municipal brasileira," *Jornal do Commercio*, April 5, 1931.

74 Skidmore, *Black into White*; Lesser, *Negotiating National Identity*; Weinstein, "Regionalizing Racial Difference."

75 Marques, *Ruas e tradições*.

76 In one of the prefaces to *Ruas e tradições*, Schmidt wrote: "Marques, employee of the Postal Administration. Pensioner with refined habits on Tabatinguera Street. Frequenter of the Brandão, the Acadêmico, and the Guarani! A mystery . . ."

77 Cavalheiro, *Monteiro Lobato*, 245, cited in Bignotto, "Novas perspectivas," 54–55.

78 Bignotto, "Novas perspectivas," 245.

79 An article from *O Estado de S. Paulo* described him as "editor of the Radio Cultura and the author of various *radio-novelas* that achieved great success." "Aniversarios," *O Estado de S. Paulo*, June 24, 1945, 4.

80 Letter from Gabriel Marques to Monteiro Lobato, Biblioteca Monteiro Lobato, Folder 8B, April 18, 1945.

81 Letter from Gabriel Marques to Monteiro Lobato, Biblioteca Monteiro Lobato, Folder 8B, April 18, 1945.

82 Though not a central figure, Lobato appears throughout this book. Chapter 3 recounts a petition by residents in a region of the parish of Nossa Senhora do Ó to change the name of their neighborhood to "Monteiro Lobato Village." Chapter 4 describes the ascription of a racist moniker to the neighborhood of Brasilândia—Macacolândia, or "Monkey-land"—whose purveyor may have drawn inspiration from one of Lobato's stories.

83 "Gabriel Marques," *A Gazeta*, October 8, 1931, 2.

84 "Gabriel Marques," *A Gazeta*, October 8, 1931, 2.

85 A useful contrast can be drawn between Marques's view here and the article about the Trezentos *cortiço* published in the Black newspaper *Progresso* in this same era and discussed in chapter 1.

86 "Os concursos literarios de 1927: Os esquecidos de Deus," *Diário Nacional*, September 5, 1928, 8.

87 Jesus, *Quarto de despejo. Diário Nacional* ran from 1927 to 1932 and was known as the "instrument of action" of the Partído Democrático, a party founded in 1926 to contest the long dominance of the Partido Republicano Paulista. "Diário Nacional," CPDOC, http://cpdoc.fgv.br/sites/default/files/verbetes/primeira-republica/DI%C3%81RIO%20NACIONAL.pdf.

88 "O Canindé tal que se acha . . . O que são as ruas do popular bairro," *Diário Nacional*, April 4, 1928.

89 "Os esquecidos de Deus: A vida apagada de uma classe utilissima," *Diário Nacional*, July 1, 1928.

90 *Taxada di doce*, likely "pan of sweets," may have been a specialty that African descendent captives were known for making. Author Magalhães de Azeredo referred to an enslaved woman making tachada de doce in his *Alma primitiva* (1895), 188. *Cafuné* is a practice of scratching and caressing another person's head, traditionally done by an enslaved person for a member of the enslaver's family. It was associated with pleasure as well as utility. Roger Bastide interpreted that pleasure to its fullest Freudian extent in "Psicanálise do cafuné." Gilberto Freyre discusses the practice in *Masters and the Slaves*, 355, 397. On the "painful scene," see Marques, *Ruas e tradições*, 145–51.

91 Marques, *Ruas e tradições*, 150.

92 Elsewhere, he critiques Prestes Maia, specifically, for his "pickaxes of redevelopment"; see Marques, *Ruas e tradições*, 259.

93 Marques, *Ruas e tradições*, 150 (my emphasis).

94 Marques, *Ruas e tradições*, 28. Marques references here the poem "Antônio Triste" (1946) by Paulo Bomfim, which opens: "Slender like a lamppost on the Avenue / Full of currents and thoughts."

95 Marques, *Ruas e tradições*, 10. In the 1910s Schmidt participated in the founding of a literary collective, Grupo Zumbi, named after the leader of the seventeenth-century Palmares *quilombo*. Today, Schmidt has a municipal library named after him. The library opened in 1966 at the beginning of the former Estrada do Congo, now Elísio Teixeira Leite Avenue, in the Cruz das Almas neighborhood within Brasilândia. Paulillo, *Tradição e modernidade*.

96 In the 1920s and 1930s, this area had a high concentration of Japanese immigrants and their descendants. Fantin, "Os japoneses," 79.

97 Marques, *Ruas e tradições*, 10.

98 A notice for a funerary mass for Gabriel Marques, "Escritor e Jornalista," ran in *O Estado de S. Paulo*, June 6, 1980, 23.

99 Debes, "Gabriel Marques," 6. He explains further that Marques "divided his activities between the tasks of a Post Office functionary, militancy in the press and the cultivation of letters."

100 Debes, "Gabriel Marques," 6.

101 "Martins, Miragaia, Drausio and Camargo" were the four students killed on May 23, 1932, in an anti-Vargas demonstration. The event predated the open conflict that erupted a few weeks later, on July 9, which would become closely associated with the acronym MMDC in memory of the dead students.

102 My italics.

103 Parecer 43/55 da Comissão de Educação e Cultura, Sobre o Processo de Lei N. 229/54, June 6, 1955.

104 Lemos led Oscar Niemeyer's office in São Paulo, participating in the construction of Ibirapuera Park and the Copan building. He was also involved in multiple historic preservation initiatives, including as the first head of CONDEPHAAT. "Homenagem aos 90 anos do arquiteto e urbanista Carlos Lemos," Conselho de Arquitetura e Urbanismo no Brasil, June 18, 2015, http://www.caubr.gov.br/homenagem-aos-90-anos-do-arquiteto-carlos-lemos/.

105 Letter from Carlos Lemos, Tombamento Record, CONDEPHAAT, Process 044, October 20, 1971.

106 "Largo da Memória vai ser reformado," *O Estado de S. Paulo*, January 9, 1972.

107 There was no mention, expectedly, of this history despite a section on the square in Benedito Lima de Toledo and Beatriz Mugayar Kühl, *Prestes Maia*, 236.

108 Nora differentiates sites of memory from sites of history. Separated by the "will to remember," sites of memory "originate with the sense that there is no spontaneous memory, that we must deliberately create archives, maintain anniversaries, organize celebrations, pronounce eulogies, and notarize bills because such activities no longer occur naturally." He continues, "Without commemorative vigilance, history would soon sweep sites of memory away." Nora, "Between Memory and History," 12.

109 He writes that "the more memory comes to rest in its exteriorized forms, the less it is experienced internally. . . . In effect, the initial impulse to memorialize events like the Holocaust may actually spring from an opposite and equal desire to forget them." Young, *Texture of Memory*, 5.

110 "A festa na egreja dos Remédios," *O Estado de S. Paulo*, June 12, 1888, 2; *A Redempção: Folha commeorativa da abolição do captiveiro*, May 13, 1899, 8.

111 "Igreja Nossa Senhora dos Aflitos," Arquidiocese de São Paulo, accessed August 16, 2016, http://www.arquisp.org.br/regiaose/paroquias/mosteiros-igrejas-historicas-oratorios-da-regiao-se/igreja-nossa-senhora-dos-aflitos; Cymbalista, *Cidades dos vivos*, 41. Igreja dos Aflitos from "Além Muros . . . ," by Paula Ester Janovitch, *Revista Cidade*, 126–27.

112 Carlos Frederico Rath, "Planta da Cidade de São Paulo," 1868, AHM, https://www.arquiamigos.org.br/info/info20/i-1868.htm.

113 Fr.do de Albuquerque and Jules Martin, "Mappa da Capital da Cidade de S. Paulo," 1877, AHM, https://www.arquiamigos.org.br/info/info20/i-1877.htm.

114 Moura, *São Paulo de outrora*, 126–36.

115 Osvaldinho Da Cuíca, *História Do Samba Paulista I*.

116 "Estatutos da Confraria de Nossa Senhora do Remédio de São Paulo," 1836, Obras Raras de São Paulo, Biblioteca Mário de Andrade (São Paulo: Na Typographia do Governo, 1836).

117 *A Redempção*, May 13, 1899, 8.

118 Franscisco, "Periodização e práticas antiescravistas." See also Fontes, "A prática abolicionista."

119 Costa, *Da senzala à colônia*, 491–92.

120 Rolnik, "City and the Law," 106.

121 Butler, *Freedoms Given*, 28.

122 The poem itself was printed in *Jornal da Tarde*, May 31, 1881, 2; *Correio Paulistano*, May 6, 1888, 3.

123 Antonio Manuel Bueno de Andrada, "A Abolição em São Paulo," *O Estado de S. Paulo*, May 13, 1918, 3.

124 Brasil Bandecchi, "O Fabuloso Antônio Bento," *O Novo Horizonte*, March 1961, 4.

125 Leite and Cuti, *E disse o velho militante*, 57.

126 Costa, *Da senzala à colônia*, 347.

127 *A Redempção*, May 13, 1899, 7.

128 "Os festejos," *O Estado de S. Paulo*, May 14, 1889, 1.

129 *A Redempção*, July 18, 1897, 3. Also see Fernandes, *A integração do negro*, 80.

130 Leite and Cuti, *E disse o velho militante*, 144.

131 *A Voz da Raça*, April 22, 1933, 4; Leite and Cuti, *E disse o velho militante*, 96.

132 The FNB successfully appealed to Getúlio Vargas, who ordered the Civil Guard to admit Black members. Andrews, *Blacks and Whites*, 150–51.

133 This story came from *O Alvorecer de uma Ideologia*, written by José Correia Leite and published as an annex in Leite and Cuti, *E disse o velho militante*, 290 (emphasis in original).

134 Alberto discusses how close interactions with Italian immigrants and their descendants (including being the target of anti-Black epithets), shaped the racial consciousness of Leite, along with other leading Black intellectual Abdias do Nascimento (who grew up in the São Paulo interior in Franca and lived in the city of São Paulo). Alberto, *Terms of Inclusion*, 162.

135 On anti-immigrant attitudes and xenophobia among leaders of the FNB in São Paulo, see Butler, *Freedoms Given*; Andrews, *Blacks and Whites*; Alberto, *Terms of Inclusion*.

136 On the meanings of Pai-João, see Abreu, "Outras histórias."

137 Moura, *São Paulo de outrora*, 84.

138 Moura, *São Paulo de outrora*, 86.

139 Moura, *São Paulo de outrora*, 89.

140 Andrade, *Cartas de trabalho*, 80.

141 Andrade, *Cartas de trabalho*, 81.

142 Thank you to Dr. Fernando Atique for bringing this source to my attention.

143 "Mário de Andrade, Departamento de Cultura e o IPHAN," May 16, 2018, accessed August 25, 2025, https://prefeitura.sp.gov.br/web/cultura/w/patrimonio_historico/noticias/23275.

144 Maia and Cintra, "Um problema actual." On the communal grave, see Britt, "Spatial Projects of Forgetting," 574.

145 One conto equaled one thousand milreis, the currency of Brazil until 1942. The conversion to US dollars is based on the rate of exchange published in the *New York Times* on March 7, 1939 (1 milreis = 5.90 cents).

146 "A Egreja dos Remédios," *O Estado de S. Paulo*, March 14, 1939, 6.
147 "A Egreja dos Remédios," *O Estado de S. Paulo*, March 14, 1939, 6.
148 My emphasis. "A Egreja dos Remédios," *O Estado de S. Paulo*, March 14, 1939, 6.
149 "A tradicional Egreja dos Remédios vae ser demolida," *Correio Paulistano*, March 19, 1939, 16.
150 "Vai ser ampliada a Praça Sete de Setembro," *Correio Paulistano*, February 26, 1939, 3.
151 "O Edificio do Congresso," *Correio Paulistano*, November 21, 1942, 4.
152 "A Nova Igreja dos Remédios," *O Estado de S. Paulo*, December 7, 1944, 13.
153 Cited in Rolim, "Luis Saia," 199.
154 Nuto Sant'Anna, "Foi quartel-general dos escravos de S. Paulo," *Folha da Noite*, June 9, 1942, 15.
155 Afonso Schmidt, "A Egreja do Bom Ladrão," *O Estado de S. Paulo*, July 14, 1940, 4.
156 Schmidt describes visiting the Remedies church in the article.
157 Schmidt, "A Egreja do Bom Ladrão."
158 Brazil's national currency changed in 1942 from the milreis to the cruzeiro, with 1 milreis equaling 1 cruzeiro. The conversion to USD is based on the rate of exchange published in the *New York Times* on July 7, 1941 (1 cruzeiro = 5.15 cents). "Praça João Mendes," Planta P3270-C2, DESAP, July 4, 1941, retrieved May 15, 2021, from *Pauliceia Esfacelada*, https://pauliceia-esfacelada.com/.
159 "Praça João Mendes," Planta and Patrimonios Historicos da Cidade, *O Estado de S. Paulo*, November 11, 1946, 5.
160 "Praça João Mendes."
161 Andrade, *Obras completas*, 9:136.
162 Ferreira, *O nobre e antigo bairro*, 74.
163 "Igreja dos Remédios: Decreto da autoridade eclesiastica reduzindo o tradicional templo ao uso profano para que possa ser demolido," *O Estado de S. Paulo*, December 6, 1942, 11.
164 Benedito Junqueira (BJ) Duarte, "Depósito Municipal," 1944, Tombo: DC/0003441/A, Acervo da Secretaria Municipal da Cultura.
165 "Patrimonios historicos da cidade," *O Estado de S. Paulo*, November 11, 1946, 5.
166 "A vida administrativa de São Paulo," report by Interventor Federal, Fernando Costa, presented to Getúlio Vargas, 1943, 369 (my emphasis).
167 Biblioteca Prestes Maia, Coleção Pretes Maia.
168 Barbuy et al., *Azulejos*, 9.
169 Ferreira, *O nobre e antigo bairro*, 48.
170 Lelis Vieira, "Templo que desaparece . . . ," *Correio Paulistano*, December 19, 1942, 3.

171 "Patrimonios historicos da cidade," *O Estado de S. Paulo*, November 11, 1946, 5.

172 Luiz de Anhaia Mello, "Habitação e urbanismo," *Engenharia* 4, no. 37, 2–3, cited in Outtes, "Disciplining," 358.

173 Caldeira, *City of Walls*; Holston, *Insurgent Citizenship*; Bonduki, *Origens*.

174 Toledo, "O Prefeito, Razões e Desrazões," 37.

175 Butler, *Freedoms Given*, 78. Also see Monroe, "Brotherhoods of their Own."

176 Maia, *Estudo de um plano*.

177 Amaral, *Os pretos*, cited in Oliveira, "Segregação urbana."

178 Amaral, *Os pretos*, cited in Oliveira, "Segregação urbana," 159.

179 Bicudo, *Estudos raciais*, 75.

180 Azevedo, *Onda Negra, Medo Branco*, 19; Dias, *Power and Everyday Life*, 132; Santos, *Nem tudo era italiano*, 100; Jacino, *Desigualdade racial no Brasil*.

181 This argument aligns with what historian Daryle Williams has described as "an intellectual tradition in postabolition memory politics that worked hard to forget slavery and the presence of Africans in the formation of Brazilian civilization." Williams, *Culture Wars in Brazil*, 174.

182 For a recent work also engaged in analysis of demolitions, race, and space but in Rio de Janeiro, see Leu, *Defiant Geographies*.

183 Carvalho, *Porous City*, 82–91.

184 Anthropologist Julia O'Donnell has analyzed the short story "A cidade branca" (The white city), by Benjamin Costallat, which appeared in the 1923 collection *Cock-tail*. The story centers on the destruction of the Morro do Castelo, a community of more than five thousand mostly non-White residents, in Rio de Janeiro in the early 1920s. Costallat's story envisions the emergence of a "virgin," distinctively Brazilian, distinctively *White* "city of the future" following the demolition of the Morro do Castelo. Costallat's vision echoes anti-Black, racialized rhetoric similar to discourses about urban space in São Paulo. Such visions did not, however, contribute to convincing constructions of Rio de Janeiro as a non-Black or White city. See O'Donnell, "A cidade branca."

CHAPTER THREE. NEIGHBORHOODS OF MIXTURE AND MASSACRE

1 Vila do Congo is listed in the print directory of roads and neighborhoods of São Paulo, *O Mapograf Guia* (São Paulo: On Line Editora, 2015).

2 Barro, *Nossa Senhora do Ó*. See also my discussion in chapter 1.

3 Nascimento, *Racial Democracy in Brazil*; Skidmore, *Black into White*; Telles, *Race in Another America*.

4 The purchase coincided with the establishment of the subdistrict of Brasilândia (sans the "Vila"), which elevated the administrative status of the neighborhood. Lei No. 8.092, February 28, 1964. "Brasilândia: Uma história de amor," *Jornal Interbairros*, 2nd ed., 2000, 21.

5 Nascimento, *Brazil: Mixture or Massacre?*, 2.

6 The first volume published in this collection was about the neighborhood Brás in 1968. One of the most recent, about Itaim Paulista, was published in 2006. All editions have recently been digitized and are available online at http://www.prefeitura.sp.gov.br/cidade/secretarias/cultura/arquivo_historico/publicacoes/index.php?p=8313.

7 Emílio Haddad, "Sobre a divisão," cited in Hidalgo, "As divisões territoriais," 28; Dias, *Desenvolvimento urbano*. For the history of the administrative division of land in São Paulo, see "São Paulo," IBGE, accessed May 13, 2017, https://cidades.ibge.gov.br/brasil/sp/sao-paulo/historico.

8 Paula, *A cidade*; Mayol, "The Neighborhood," in Certeau et al., *Practice*, vol. 2.

9 About the history of this organization, see Leme, "São Paulo."

10 Barbosa, "O loteamento," 145.

11 Barbosa, "O loteamento," 153.

12 Feldman, *Planejamento e zoneamento*, 18.

13 Deák and Schiffer, *O processo de urbanização*; Santos, *Metrópole*; Bonduki, *Habitar São Paulo*.

14 As Bonduki indicates, the shift to *loteamento* development also signaled a change in the housing market from tenancy to individual home ownership. Bonduki, *Origens*, 302. Also see Sachs-Jeantet, *São Paulo*.

15 Azevedo, *A cidade de São Paulo*, 1:226, 1:136. His only mention of Brasilândia by name came in this passage: "The boundary of São Paulo's terrain and the area before the Serra da Cantareira is extremely clear, as one can observe around Vila Brasilândia, three kilometers northwest of Freguesia do Ó."

16 Azevedo, *A cidade de São Paulo*, 4:45–46.

17 Processo 50.235/55, March 12, 1957, CGDP.

18 Comparing Vila Brasilândia to cities of the extreme interior, Silva concluded that the latter were generally better serviced. Silva saw the condition of the neighborhood despite its proximity to the center of São Paulo as particularly unacceptable: "Vila Brasilândia, just a few kilometers from Praça da Sé," he said, "is completely abandoned." 159th Sessão Ordinária da Câmara Municipal, May 6, 1953.

19 159th Sessão Ordinária da Câmara Municipal, May 6, 1953. For the history of the administrative organization of São Paulo's municipal government, see Feldman, *Planejamento e zoneamento*.

20 159th Sessão Ordinária da Câmara Municipal, May 6, 1953.

21 "Uma repasada de olhos na vida de Brasilândia nos seus 37 anos de existência," *Jornal da Brasilândia*, January 1984.

22 Maia, *Estudo de um plano*.

23 See chapter 1, especially sections on the histories of the *cortiços* Trezentos and Navio Parado.

24 LAS, interview by author, Brasilândia, São Paulo, March 7, 2016.

25 Interview by author with [name withheld], Brasilândia, São Paulo, August 8, 2016.

26 "Apaixonado pelo País," *O Estado de S. Paulo*, March 27, 1995.

27 Ferrara, *A imprensa negra paulista*, 67.

28 Leite and Cuti, *E disse o velho militante*, 194. For more on this region, see Caçula, *Casa Verde*.

29 Andrews, *Blacks and Whites*, 149.

30 Butler, *Freedoms Given*; Seigel, *Uneven Encounters*; Alberto, *Terms of Inclusion*.

31 Oliveira, "Segregação urbana," 227.

32 Oliveira, "Segregação urbana," 162.

33 Maia, *Os melhoramentos de São Paulo*, 17. Also see Jorge, *Tietê*.

34 Vasconcellos, *Circular é preciso*, 70–71. Comissão de Estudos do Transporte Coletivo no Município de São Paulo and Companhia Municipal de Transportes Coletivos.

35 Bonduki, *Origens*, 301.

36 Bonduki, *Origens*, 301.

37 Santos, *Metrópole*.

38 "Transporte Coletivo: Cassação de licenças de empresas particulares," *O Estado de S. Paulo*, March 1, 1958, 9.

39 "Transporte Coletivo: Cassação de licenças de empresas particulares," *O Estado de S. Paulo*, March 1, 1958, 9.

40 "Admite a CMTC irregularidades na concessão de linha à TUSA," *O Estado de S. Paulo*, March 9, 1958, 16.

41 Nabil Bonduki characterizes the institution similarly: "Not by accident, the city government never could properly structure the Division (later Department) of Urbanism, a sector responsible for establishing guidelines, approving and inspecting *loteamentos*, in addition to regularizing clandestine *loteamentos*. The sector in charge of *loteamento* approval always had an insufficient number of functionaries, resulting in the extreme slowness of bureaucratic proceedings and in the absence of inspections." Bonduki, *Origens*, 299.

42 Processo 50.235/55, July 23, 1958, CGDP (my italics).

43 Processo 50.235/55, July 23, 1958, CGDP.

44 Processo 50.235/55, November 27, 1959, CGDP.

45 159th Sessão Ordinária da Câmara Municipal, May 6, 1953.

46 For a survey of recent and not-so-recent work on this subject, see Motta, "Classic Works," 121–44.

47 Processo 50.235/55, 1965, CGDP.

48 "Anuário estatístico do Brasil—1965," IBGE, 319, https://biblioteca.ibge.gov.br/visualizacao/periodicos/20/aeb_1965.pdf.

49 Other, so-called clandestine *loteamentos*—those established without city approval—are not included in the map unless they were formalized by urban authorities.

50 RA, conversation with author, São Carlos, São Paulo State, February 10, 2017. The quote is from Sílvia Bessa, "Eu faço casa. Por que não tenho uma de tijolo?," *Diário de Pernambuco*, March 30, 2017, https://www.diariodepernambuco.com.br/noticia/brasil/2017/03/eu-faco-casa-por-que-nao-tenho-uma-de-tijolo.html.

51 "Apaixonado pelo País," *O Estado de S. Paulo*. The article was prompted by the forty-eighth anniversary of the neighborhood's founding. The nostalgic, largely celebratory piece was a product of the 1990s, as well, when Brasilândia had gained widespread infamy as one the most violent and dangerous regions of São Paulo. The neighborhood journal of Vila Brasilândia, *O Jornal da Brasilândia*, recorded other figures: five thousand bricks and two hundred roof tiles. "Uma repasada de olhos na vida de Brasilândia nos seus 37 anos de existência," *O Jornal da Brasilândia*, January 1984.

52 Anthropologist Teresa Caldeira highlights the cumulative, gradual nature of autoconstruction as "a lifetime process in which the workers [homeowners] buy a lot and build either a room or shack at the back of it, move in, and then spend decades expanding and improving the construction, furnishing, and decorating the house." Caldeira, *City of Walls*, 222; Holston, *Insurgent Citizenship*. Caldeira and Holston emphasize autoconstruction as a strategy for making citizenship claims. Caldeira writes, for instance, "Workers simultaneously become property owners, urbanize the outskirts of the metropolitan region, and are politicized" (*City of Walls*, 13). Holston describes autoconstruction as "a domain of symbolic elaboration," and comes close to exploring the relationship to identity when he writes, "This autoconstruction of house, self, and citizen in the periphery is both individual and collective" (*Insurgent Citizenship*, 8, 263).

53 These histories are covered in detail in chapter 1.

54 Though slightly outside the boundaries of the contemporary district of Brasilândia, Cruz das Almas seems to have long comprised part of

the imagined space. For instance, the first neighborhood newspaper, *O Jornal da Brasilândia*, included Cruz das Almas in the region of Brasilândia.

55 Indicação N. 737–56, Atas e Anais da Câmara Municipal de São Paulo, March 5, 1956.

56 My discussion of Lobato in chapter 2 focused especially on his relationship with author Gabriel Marques.

57 "Cruz das Almas," *Jornal Cantareira*, April 22, 2013, accessed August 21, 2016, http://www.cantareira.org/noticias/periferia-brasilandia-cruz-das-almas. I have yet to locate the year or circumstances surrounding the renaming of Manoel José de Almeida Street. Through the mid-1950s, the road was still Cruz das Almas.

58 LS, interview by author, Brasilândia district, São Paulo, July 5, 2016. The qualification "commonly credited" is explained in detail subsequently.

59 Barro, *Nossa Senhora do Ó*, 71.

60 Indicação N. 1037–57, 180 Sessão Ordinária, Atas e Anais da Câmara Municipal de São Paulo, April 30, 1957.

61 "Cruz das Almas," *Jornal Cantareira*.

62 Municipal Decree 4568, January 15, 1960.

63 LS, interview.

64 Azevedo, *A cidade de São Paulo*, 4:45–46.

65 Balbo, *Pavimentação asfáltica*.

66 Morse, *Bandeirantes*; Ferreira, *A epopéia bandeirante*; Russell-Wood, "Rethinking Bandeirismo."

67 *O Estado de S. Paulo*, April 22, 1948, 9.

68 Dias, *Power and Everyday Life*, 11–12.

69 MB, interview by author, Brasilândia district, São Paulo, June 22, 2017.

70 LS, interview.

71 Santos, "Marcas de pé descalço," 29.

72 Terras públicas, Freguesia da Nossa Senhora do Ó, 1855, APESP.

73 See Costa and Gomes, *Religiões negras no Brasil*.

74 *O Estado de S. Paulo*, January 10, 1879.

75 Dated October 19, 1874, and printed in Silva, "Últimos desejos," 186–87.

76 *Correio Paulistano*, January 11, 1906, 7.

77 Processos 187.137/68, 180.308/64, and 107.454/69, CGDP.

78 Processo 50.235/55, CGDP (my italics).

79 "Noticias do Foro," *Diario Nacional*, August 13, 1929, 4.

80 Barro, *Nossa Senhora do Ó*. See chapter 1 for a detailed examination of the fugitive population in the parish.

81 See Fária, "A luta Guaraní," esp. 181–202.

82 LS, interview.

83 Lesser, *Negotiating National Identity*; Lesser, *Immigration, Ethnicity*; Fontes, *Um nordeste em São Paulo*.

84 "Uma repasada de olhos na vida de Brasilândia nos seus 37 anos de existência," *O Jornal da Brasilândia*, January 1984.

85 "Apaixonado pelo País," *O Estado de S. Paulo*.

86 Holston, *Modernist City*.

87 Interview by author with [name withheld], Brasilândia, São Paulo, July 21, 2016. This resident's father was one of the "Candango" workers who helped to build the new capital.

88 "Com 10.000 Habitantes e 3.000 predios, Vila Brasilandia continua sem transportes," *Jornal das Notícias*, October 17, 1948, 5. My italics.

89 In the census of 1890, the population of African descent in the city of São Paulo amounted to 15.6 percent of the total. In N. S. do Ó, however, the figure exceeded 40 percent. Rolnik, *A cidade e a lei*. See chapter 1 for other demographic data from throughout the nineteenth century.

90 "Com 10.000 Habitantes," 5.

91 Wilhelm, *São Paulo Metrópole*, 15.

92 "Uma repasada."

93 "Uma repasada."

94 Santiago, *Distrito da Brasilândia*. Pandeiro is an official ambassador of São Paulo samba.

95 Lesser emphasizes the importance of space to Shindo Renmei, finding that the "society's main goal, which became public in August 1945, following Japan's surrender, was to maintain a permanent Japanized *space* in Brazil through the preservation of language, culture, and religion among Nikkei and the reestablishment of Japanese schools" (Lesser, *Negotiating National Identity*, 138; my italics).

96 Lesser, *Negotiating National Identity*, 130.

97 Lesser, *Immigration, Ethnicity*.

98 Handa, *O imigrante japonês*, 176.

99 Handa, *O imigrante japonês*, 154–56.

100 Fantin, "Os japoneses," 79.

101 Handa, *O imigrante japonês*, 588.

102 "O japonezinho morreu brincando," *O Correio de S. Paulo*, June 13, 1936, 1.

103 Nicolau Sevcenko characterized São Paulo as an "inverted babel" because of the multitude of languages spoken on its streets. Sevcenko, *Orfeu extático*.

104 "A symphonia da metropole," *Correio de S. Paulo*, August 15, 1935, 1.

105 See, for example, Decreto-Lei no 4.166 from March 11, 1942, reprinted in Fantin, "Os japoneses," 82–83. Lesser, *Immigration, Ethnicity*. Also see Campos, *A política da língua*.

106 Sachio Negawa, "The Conde District—Brazil's First Japantown," *Discover Nikkei*, April 27, 2007, http://www.discovernikkei.org/es/journal/2007/4/27/brazil-nihonjinmachi/.

107 Fantin, "Os japoneses," 82; Handa, *O imigrante japonês*, 638. While noting that the evacuation campaign was not as rigorous as a similar order in the port city of Santos, Handa described the uncertainty facing evacuees: "Move, but move where?! The majority did not have money to move, and all were in agony, not knowing what to do."

108 Santiago, *Distrito da Brasilândia.*

109 Lesser, *Negotiating National Identity*, esp. 135–46.

110 M. family, interview with author, Brasilândia, São Paulo, July 21, 2016.

111 In 1953 the first postwar Japanese immigrants arrived at the São Paulo port of Santos. Sakurai, "A imigração dos japoneses," 218.

112 Letter from Kinroku Awazu to Francisco Matarazzo Sobrinho, processo 1629, September 2, 1953, AHM (my italics).

113 Processo 1629, September 23, 1953, AHM.

114 Processo 3781 (1954) and processo 5615 (1955), AHM.

115 Vargas's statement here invokes the archetype of the Brazilian male as the "homen cordial," or "cordial man," discussed most prominently in Sérgio Buarque de Holanda's 1936 *Raizes do Brasil.*

116 "Album do IV Centenário da Fundação de São Paulo," 1.2, 2045, Library of the Museum of Japanese Immigration.

117 Araujo, "Enquistamentos étnicos," 229.

118 Araujo, "Enquistamentos étnicos," 237.

119 Araujo, "Enquistamentos étnicos," 238.

120 Araujo, "Enquistamentos étnicos," 239. He is citing here Bruno Rudolfer, "Novo metodo de representação ecologica," conferencia na Associação dos Geografos de São Paulo, resumida em *Diário Popular*, August 11, 1937.

121 Araujo, "Enquistamentos étnicos," 235.

122 Araujo, "Enquistamentos étnicos," 244.

123 Samuel Lowrie, "O elemento Negro"; "Anexo: Densidade geral da população por quarteirão," *Revista do Arquivo Municipal* 43 (1938).

124 Handa, *O imigrante japonês*, 170. "A Região da Rua Conde de Sarzedas, o Oásis dos Imigrantes Japoneses (1910–1940)."

125 An October 2017 exhibition, aligned with one hundred years after Handa's arrival to Brazil in 1917, celebrated Handa's work. "Exposição: Tomoo Handa, 100 anos de Brasil," Bunkyo, October 6, 2017, https://bunkyo.org.br/br/2017/10/exposicao-tomoo-handa-100-anos-de-brasil-2/. The first book published by the Centro de Estudos Nipo-Brasileiros in 1970 was Handa's *O imigrante japonês: História de sua vida no Brasil.*

126 Unno, "Cartography in Japan," 399–400.
127 Unno, "Cartography in Japan," 349.
128 Seigel, *Uneven Encounters*, 213.
129 "A Mãe Preta e o Vereador," *Folha da Manhã*, September 2, 1953, cited in Lopes, "As representações sociais," 135.
130 As detailed in the previous chapter, during his first term as mayor, Prestes Maia unsuccessfully attempted to secure the demolition of the church in this plaza, the Igreja Nossa Senhora do Rosário dos Homens Pretos, to make way for an urban reform project along with the construction of a monument to Duque de Caxias. Amaral, *Os pretos*, 132.
131 Alberto, "A Mãe Preta," 377–402. The winner of the contest to design the statue was Júlio Guerra, a local sculptor who would go on to design a monument to *bandeirante* Borba Gato a short few years later. Janovitch, "Borba Gato."
132 Seigel, *Uneven Encounters*, 212.
133 Alberto, "A Mãe Preta."
134 Pulquéria Albuquerque, interview by author, Brasilândia, São Paulo, June 6, 2016, and August 16, 2016.
135 Albuquerque, interview by author.
136 Silva, *Orixás da metrópole*, 83.
137 Prandi, *Herdeiras do axé*, 172–73. Interview conducted on August 25, 1987. Bracketed sections are from the original.
138 Silvio de Oxumaré, "Os primeiros Candomblés de São Paulo—Manaundê, pioneira da zona norte de São Paulo," *Revista Orixás, Candomblé e Umbanda* 2:8, 44, quoted in Santos, "Nos domínios de Exu," 125.
139 Oxumaré, "Os primeiros Candomblés," quoted in Santos, "Nos domínios de Exu," 125.
140 Oxumaré, "Os primeiros Candomblés," quoted in Santos, "Nos domínios de Exu," 125.
141 The "likely" here derives from analysis of aerial photographs from the VASP aerial photography project (1952–1957), which shows the creek side of Rua Ruiva (where the *terreiro* was established) empty. A separate map source, from Geoportal Memória Paulista, http://www.geoportal.com.br/memoriapaulista, with aerial photography from 1958 similarly shows the site as empty.
142 Folha 124, processo 50.235/55, November 19, 1957, CGDP. Presumably these are the lots on the south side of Ruiva Street, which appear on the map from 1954.
143 Oxumaré, "Os primeiros Candomblés," 44, quoted in Santos, "Nos domínios de Exu," 125.
144 Albuquerque, interview.
145 Evangelista, "Fundando um axé."

146 Albuquerque, interview.

147 Oxumaré, "Os primeiros Candomblés," 44, quoted in Santos, "Nos domínios de Exu," 125.

148 Oxumaré, "Os primeiros Candomblés, 44, quoted in Santos, "Nos domínios de Exu," 125.

149 Prandi, *Os Candomblês de São Paulo*, 21.

150 Teresinha Bernardo, *Memória em branco e negro: olhares sobre São Paulo* (São Paulo: EDUC, 1998), 51.

151 Bernardo, *Memória em branco e negro*, 51–52.

152 Bernardo, *Memória em branco e negro*, 70.

153 Lei No. 8.092, February 28, 1964.

154 "Brasilândia: Uma história de amor," *Jornal Interbairros*, 2nd ed., 2000, 21. The amount was noted as 32,000 cruzeiros.

155 "Editorial Imigração Japonesa," *Jornal Folha Carioca*, June 30, 1953, in *Revista de Imigração e Colonização* XIII, 168, in Sakurai, "A imigração dos japoneses," 212.

156 Azevedo, *A cidade de São Paulo*, 1:19.

157 Azevedo, *A cidade de São Paulo*, 1:19.

158 Maio, "UNESCO and Race Relations," 131.

159 Alberto, *Terms of Inclusion*, 182–84, 217.

CHAPTER FOUR. BELONGING-AS-BEING

1 Loitero and Ripol, "Hino do Samba do Congo."

2 One of the most active of these initiatives was led by Renato Dias and named Kolombolo Diá Piratininga in 2002. Located in the Vila Madalena neighborhood, the organization sponsored weekly samba gatherings, historical and cultural research, and a suite of media production related to African-descendent and especially Bantu culture.

3 Rio, *Religions in Rio*; Moura, *Tia Ciata*; Velloso, "As tias baianas"; Carvalho, *Porous City*, 82–91. Also see Gomes, "Para além da casa." There is an expansive academic literature stretching to the nineteenth century that has participated in the elaboration and critical analysis of this spatial identity. Key authors in a less recent bibliography include Nina Rodriques, Manuel Querino, Pierre Verger, E. Franklin Frazier, Ruth Landes, Donald Pierson, Roger Bastide, and Edison Carneiro. More recent works include Matory, *Black Atlantic Religion*; Butler, "Africa in the Reinvention"; Romo, *Brazil's Living Museum*; Pinho, *Reinvenções da África*. John F. Collins examines the notion of Salvador and, more specifically, the Pelourinho/Maciel neighborhoods, as the "cradle" and "heart" of Africa in *Revolt of the Saints*; Smith, *Afro-Paradise*.

4 Rosa, "Além da invisibilidade."

5 Rolnik, "Territórios Negros," 38. I have located two other uses of this term in published literature: Telles, *Race in Another America*, 212; Machado, "Paisagem revelada," 63.

6 Telles, *Race in Another America*, 212.

7 On the history of Guaianases, see Silva, "Negros em Guaianases."

8 Nascimento, *Racial Democracy in Brazil*; Skidmore, *Black into White*; Edward E. Telles, *Race in Another America*.

9 Mira cites the paid circulation (including subscriptions and newsstands) of *Veja* in 1972 as 97,000 and in 1976 as 215,000. Maria Celeste Mira, "O leitor," 147.

10 By the 1990s, *Veja*'s circulation would rank fourth among major global magazines behind *Time*, *Newsweek*, and *U.S. News and World Report*. See Rocha, "A escola na mídia."

11 Mira details *Veja's* appeal to university students and professional class, in particular. See Mira, "O leitor," esp. 135–36, 145. Also relevant to this section's discussion of "integration" is the way that *Veja*'s editors framed their ambitions for the publication in the first edition: "Brazil can no longer be the old archipelago separated by distance, by geographic space, by ignorance, by the prejudices and the regionalisms: it needs information in order to choose a new path." Cited in Mira, "O leitor," 120.

12 "Vivendo sem água," *Veja*, August 6, 1975, 51 (my emphasis).

13 Feldman, *Planejamento e zoneamento*; Ioris, *Transforming Brazil*; Sachs-Jeantet, *São Paulo*.

14 Kowarick and Bonduki, "Espaço urbano," 151.

15 The exact numbers are 175.7 km² to 742.2 km². Santos, *Metrópole*, 24.

16 Villaça, "Uma contribuição"; Rubens de Mattos Pereira, "Planejamento Local Integrado," *Folha de S. Paulo*, suplemento especial "Grande São Paulo, Desafio do Ano 2000," September–October 1967, 375; Mentone, "Plano metropolitano." Also see Feldman, *Planejamento e zoneamento*, 216.

17 Sachs-Jeantet, *São Paulo*, 71.

18 The exact figures are: 1950 (19,329), 1960 (49,743), 1970 (114,855). IBGE., archived at https://web.archive.org/web/20221014121943/https://smul.prefeitura.sp.gov.br/historico_demografico/tabelas/pop_dist.php.

19 *Cidade*, "A Saga da Metrópole," 4, 10–11; Toledo and Kühl, *Prestes Maia*; Peixoto-Mehrtens, *Urban Space*; Outtes, "Disciplining"; Maia, *Estudo de um plano*; Maia, *Os melhoramentos de São Paulo*; Leme, "ReVisão do Plano de Avenida"; Bonduki, *Origens*.

20 The creation of the PUB was coordinated by the Grupo Executivo de Planejamento, or GEP, a division of the city created to introduce,

institutionalize, and implement new planning concepts in the Prefeitura. See Feldman, *Planejamento e zoneamento*, 212–13, 233; Caldeira, *City of Walls*, 404n27.

21 Somekh and Campos, *A cidade*, 114.

22 Somekh and Campos, *A cidade*, 114; Feldman, *Planejamento e zoneamento*, 212–16, 237–42; Deák, "À busca das categorias."

23 Feldman, *Planejamento e zoneamento*, 22, 243. Also see Villaça, "Uma contribuição," 213; Somekh and Campos, *A cidade*, 108–18.

24 "O Prefeito, Razões e Desrazões," interview with Benedito Lima de Toledo by Marcos Faerman, in *Cidade* "A Saga da Metrópole," 39.

25 Kowarick and Bonduki, "Espaço urbano," 159.

26 Plano de Urbanização, Prefeitura Municipal de São Paulo, Processo 2598, Projeto de Lei No. 54, May 27, 1968.

27 Interview by author with [name withheld], Brasilândia, São Paulo, August 8, 2016.

28 "Mais luz para evitar crimes," *O Estado de S. Paulo*, August 17, 1967, 21.

29 Cardoso and Singer, *O milagre brasileiro*; Baer, *Brazilian Economy*; Thomas Skidmore, *Politics of Military Rule*; Wolfe, *Autos and Progress*; Fontes, *Um nordeste em São Paulo*.

30 "Grande São Paulo: O desafio do ano 2000; Pobre cidade grande," *Folha de S. Paulo*, September 1967, Série Realidade Brasileira, 289.

31 Banco Nacional de Habitação; Companhia Metropolitana de Habitação de São Paulo.

32 Sachs-Jeantet, *São Paulo*, 21–22.

33 Interview by author with [name withheld], Brasilândia, São Paulo, August 1, 2016.

34 Sachs-Jeantet, *São Paulo*, 76–77. Also see Bonduki, *Origens*, 299, for midcentury efforts to curb irregular *loteamentos*.

35 Sachs-Jeantet, *São Paulo*, 76–77. The concrete actions of the law included steps taken against fraudulent developers (*loteadores*); a census of irregular *loteamentos*; the shift of responsibility to district administrations to uphold the law; a mechanism to halt the construction of a *loteamento* if it did not obey norms; and public illumination for streets that local residents had constructed by themselves. The law stipulated that the legal authorization of a *loteamento* required confirmation of the construction of infrastructure by, and on the dime of, the developer.

36 Sachs-Jeantet, *São Paulo*, 78.

37 Processo 50.235/55, CGDP, Prefeitura de São Paulo. Also see chapter 3.

38 Machado, "Paisagem revelada."

39 QV, interview by author, Brasilândia, São Paulo, June 8, 2016.

40 Carolina Maria de Jesus, *Quatro de despejo*, 1960. The book was subsequently published in English as *Child of the Dark: The Diary of Carolina Maria de Jesus* in 1962.

41 This use of "stain" paralleled the discourse about *cortiços*, or tenements, described in chapter 1. "Um Ano de Administração—1961: Entrevista pelo prefeito Francisco Prestes Maia," Prefeitura de São Paulo, 1962, 34, Biblioteca Prestes Maia.

42 Bonduki, *Origens*, 272.

43 Santos, *Metrópole*, 54.

44 Taschner, "Depois da queda."

45 "Grande São Paulo," 290.

46 "Favelas em São Paulo: Caracterização Físico-Espacial," 1989, SEHAB/HABI, Prefeitura do Município de São Paulo, 3.0348, Habitação, e. 1, 34.

47 "Programa Bairro Legal—Brasilândia," 2002, SEHAB/HABI, Prefeitura do Município de São Paulo, 3.0220, Perfil Socioeconômico, e. 1.

48 "Favelas em São Paulo," 58–59.

49 Freguesia do Ó Regional Administration report from 1970, cited in Barro, *Nossa Senhora do Ó*, 81.

50 Kowarick and Bonduki, "Espaço urbano," 165. For more on the conditions of São Paulo's periphery in this era, see Caldeira, *City of Walls*, esp. 228–30, and Santos, *Metrópole*, 52–67.

51 "A refavela sem BNH: O início," *Jornal da Brasilândia*, March 1984. Similar organizations were founded throughout the city of São Paulo and beyond. Collective infrastructure and housing construction in Brasilândia also took place outside this organizational framework. In 1983, for instance, property owners along a street in the region's Jardim Guarani *loteamento* would permit, and themselves physically participate in, the construction of a favela in an area originally dedicated for public use (but unbuilt and vacant). The local newspaper recounted the "uncommon" collective building effort (*mutirão de construção*), contrasting the collaborative relationship with what were typically more tense dynamics between property owners and favela settlers. See "Nova favela no Jd. Guarani," *Jornal da Brasilândia*, August 1983, 5.

52 In 1980 the municipal government launched its regularization effort for the whole city with a pilot program centered on four *loteamentos* in Brasilândia. See "Plano para regularizar os lotes clandestinos," *O Estado de S. Paulo*, July 8, 1980, 19.

53 Processo 0.045.580, CGDP, Prefeitura de São Paulo.

54 "Salvaterra: Uma favela pertinho do céu," *Jornal da Brasilândia*, May 1982, 8.

55 Kucinski, *Jornalistas e revolucionários*; Sousa, "O jornal *Movimento*."

56 "Freguesia do Ó, imagens do início do século," *O Estado de S. Paulo*, January 14, 1979.

57 One of the most famous, perhaps, was Noite Illustrada, a composer who penned songs with other notable sambistas in Rio de Janeiro.

LN, interview by author, Brasilândia, São Paulo, July 10, 2016. See chapter 1 for more on the dislocation caused indirectly and directly by avenues projects in the city center.

58 G1 São Paulo, "Rosas de Ouro é campeã do Carnaval de SP," March 4, 2025, https://g1.globo.com/sp/sao-paulo/carnaval/2025/noticia/2025/03/04/rosas-de-ouro-e-campea-do-carnaval-de-sp.ghtml.

59 Caçula, *Casa Verde*.

60 "Rosas de Ouro," Liga de São Paulo, accessed June 17, 2018, http://ligasp.com.br/escolas-de-samba/rosas-de-ouro; "Rosas de Ouro comemora os 43 anos da sua fundação," *Freguesia News*, October 23, 2014, http://freguesianews.com.br/?opc=meio_variedades&id_noti=3907.

61 *Jornal da Brasilândia* 1, no. 2 (June 1982).

62 WB, interview by author, Brasilândia, São Paulo, June 22, 2017. Also see Antunes, "Avaliação de projetos sociais," 60.

63 CF, interviews by author, Brasilândia, São Paulo, July 12 and July 19, 2016; HP, interview by author, Brasilândia, São Paulo, July 22, 2016. On this subject, see also Conti, "A memória do samba," 139–40, 171–72, 179, 200–201, 204.

64 Marco Aurélio Guimarães Jangada, "O samba segundo São Paulo," *Realidade*, February 1972, 56. *Realidade* was modeled after *Life* magazine. Mira, "O leitor," 30.

65 Machado, "Paisagem revelada," 63.

66 Interview by author with [name withheld], Brasilândia, São Paulo, São Paulo, June 22, 2017.

67 Bastide, "Catimbó," 146–59. Also see Hale, "Catimbó," 135–36.

68 Andrews, *Blacks and Whites*, 225; Alberto, "When Rio Was Black," 20. Alberto writes, for example: "Under the military dictatorship that began in 1964, ideologies of *brasilidade* and racial democracy took on an even more totalizing, indeed suffocating character. The military government sought to enforce the image of a racially harmonious, Africanized Brazil at home and abroad, while preempting the development of homegrown or U.S.- or African-inspired, racially oppositional politics. These objectives led them to emphasize Brazil's Africanness in terms of a folkloric, ancient, and depoliticized African presence, heavily mediated by cultural and racial mixture and contained by processes of nationalization."

69 PSO, interview by author, Brasilândia, São Paulo, August 3, 2016.

70 PSO, interview. BS, interview by author, August 15, 2016; MB, interview by author, Brasilândia, São Paulo. June 17, 2017. Also see interviews in Santiago, *Distrito da Brasilândia*.

71 PSO, interview.

72 Athayde and Meirelles, *Um país chamado favela*; Perlman, "Myth of Marginality Revisited." For further discussion of asphalt and this binary, see Sheriff, *Dreaming Equality*, and Khan-Perry, *Black Women*.

73 PSO, interview.

74 Somekh, *A cidade vertical.*

75 Hosokawa, "Dancing in the Tomb," 68.

76 "Carnaval 1973—Rosas de Ouro," *Acervo Virtual do Carnaval de SP*, accessed September 5, 2025, https://www.carnavalpaulistano.com.br/a_escola_carnaval_dados.asp?rg_carnaval=403.

77 Metcalf, *Go-Betweens*, esp. 80–86.

78 Ulrich, "Guilherme de Almeida e a construção da identidade paulista."

79 "Carnaval 1975—Rosas de Ouro," *Acervo Virtual do Carnaval de SP*, accessed September 5, 2025, https://www.carnavalpaulistano.com.br/a_escola_carnaval_dados.asp?rg_carnaval=405.

80 *Jornal da Brasilândia* 1, no. 2 (June 1982).

81 Interview by author with [name withheld]; José Augusto de Oliveira, "Rosas de Ouro," *Jornal da Brasilândia*, May 1982, 7.

82 Interviews by author with [names withheld]; Robson Fernandjes, "Rosas toca a ferida da escravidão," *O Estado de S. Paulo: Estadão Zona Norte*, February 17, 2006.

83 Silva, *Centro de cultura.*

84 Andrews, *Blacks and Whites*, 191.

85 Butler, *Freedoms Given*, 87.

86 The figure was twenty-seven deaths, corresponding to a rate of 10.2 per 100,000 residents, in the period stretching from July 2016 to June 2017.

87 "Mapa da Morte: Mapa da morte em SP vai da Suécia até o México; locais dos crimes se repetem," *Folha de S. Paulo*, October 12, 2017.

88 Johan Galtung coined "structural violence" in the 1969 article "Violence, Peace and Peace Research." Anthropologist Katherine Hirschfeld published a review essay in 2017 of the term and its (mis) uses for the field of global and public health, most notably concerning Paul Farmer's "Anthropology of Structural Violence." Hirschfeld, "Rethinking 'Structural Violence.'" For a more empirical and contemporary study of place, race, and violence, see Breunlin and Regis, "Putting the Ninth Ward."

89 Caldeira focuses on discourses about crime in the late 1970s and early 1980s, arguing that, paradoxically, exaggerated perceptions of crime exacerbated segregation and inequality at a moment of political opening in the course of Brazil's redemocratization. Caldeira, *City of Walls*.

90 HP, interview; CF, interview.

91 Caldeira, *City of Walls*; Fontes, "Trabalhadores e associativismo urbano."

92 "Mais luz para evitar crimes."

93 "Mais luz para evitar crimes."

94 "Esquadrão: Mais uma baixa," *Veja*, June 6, 1973, 28; and "Decretada a prisão de policial," *O Estado de S. Paulo*, August 4, 1972.

95 "O Esquadrão, consequência?" *O Estado de S. Paulo*, April 26, 1970.

96 "Franco-Atiradores," *Veja*, November 10, 1971, 34.

97 "Terrorista é morto a tiros," *O Estado de S. Paulo*, January 20, 1972. For more information about Torigoi, Japanese-Brazilian involvement in antidictatorship activities, and ethnic militancy, see Lesser, *Discontented Diaspora*, 76, 90.

98 Magalhães, *Marighella*.

99 The street naming occurred by decree of the São Paulo city council in 1992. Other streets were named in honor of Steve Biko and Patrice Lumumba. Decree 31.230, February 13, 1992.

100 One notable print precursor in Brazil was *Vida Policial*, a weekly published in Rio de Janeiro between 1925 and 1927. See Caulfield, "Getting into Trouble"; Shizuno, "A Revista *Vida Policial*."

101 Gomes cited in Costa, "A justiça," 28.

102 Costa, "A justiça," 30. Macumba here references African-descendent spiritual practices.

103 "Lua Nova," SciELO Brazil, accessed June 6, 2018, http://www.scielo.br/revistas/ln/paboutj.htm.

104 José Wilson, "O crime pelo rádio," *Lua Nova: Revista de Cultura e Política* 1, no. 3 (December 1984).

105 A taste of Gomes's style can be ascertained by watching his appearance as a detective-journalist in the semifictional, feature-length film *O outro lado do crime* (The other side of crime), from 1978.

106 Wilson, "O crime pelo rádio," 80.

107 Wilson, "O crime pelo rádio," 83.

108 Wilson, "O crime pelo rádio," 81.

109 Wanda Jorge, "Srs. saudosistas, liguem o rádio," *Jornal da República*, September 25, 1979, 13.

110 Costa, "A justiça," 41.

111 Costa, "A justiça," 79.

112 "Ouça, o Rádio está no ar," de Azeni Passos, *Diário Popular*, June 20, 1977, 12.

113 Oliveira, "Segregação urbana," 151.

114 Interview by author with [name withheld]; LN, interview.

115 CP, interview by author, Brasilândia, São Paulo, May 7, 2016.

116 Interview by author with [name withheld], Brasilândia, São Paulo, August 8, 2016.

117 Lobato is discussed in chapter 2 concerning his relationship with Gabriel Marques and in chapter 3 regarding a popular petition to rename the Cruz das Almas neighborhood "Vila Monteiro Lobato."

118 "Anno escolar de 1929: Livros escolares approvados e adoptados pela Directoria Gera da Instrucção Pública de São Paulo," *O Estado de S. Paulo*, January 31, 1928, 5.

119 Schwartz, *Slaves, Peasants, and Rebels.*

120 Freitas, *República de Palmares*, 20–21.

121 Alberto, *Terms of Inclusion*, 68.

122 The author's racial discourse has generated legal cases and popular debates about race in Brazil in the recent past, especially around figures like Tia Nastácia, who, in *Caçadas de Pedrinho*, Lobato termed a "charcoal monkey." See Júnior et al., "Monteiro Lobato"; and Habib, "Eis o mundo encantado."

123 "Monteiro Lobato, que Jeca Tatu inventou," *O Estado de S. Paulo*, July 9, 1972, 20.

124 Degler, *Neither Black nor White*, 122.

125 For example: Tracy Devine Guzmán writes that during the War of the Triple Alliance, Paraguayans "obsessively disdained the Brazilians as an empire of 'black stinking monkeys' and 'black dirty pigs'" (*Native and National*, 74). I use "common sense" here in reference to Stuart Hall's reading of Antonio Gramsci: Despite being "usually 'disjointed and episodic,' fragmentary and contradictory," common sense is the second and all-important "floor" on which ideology contends for efficacy, "the terrain of conceptions and categories on which the practical consciousness of the masses of the people is actually formed." Hall, "Gramsci's Relevance," 431.

126 CF, interview.

127 Degler, *Neither Black nor White*, 122.

128 Geographer Jason Henderson, for example, has recorded a nickname cited commonly in public discourse about the city of Atlanta's transportation system, officially named the Metropolitan Atlanta Rapid Transit Authority, or MARTA. He writes, "Since it was established in the 1960s . . . [MARTA] was jokingly referred to as 'Moving Africans Rapidly Through Atlanta.'" See Henderson, "Secessionist Automobility," 298.

129 Oliveira, "Segregação urbana," 152.

130 CF, interview; LN, interview.

131 Oliveira, "Segregação urbana," 152.

132 Lab Cidade, "Narradores do Jardim Paraná."

133 "Só socialismo resolverá a questão racial," *Jornal da Brasilândia*, 1982, 5.

134 While Mahin is often described as a principal protagonist in the 1835 revolt, historians have debated whether her participation is a sociohistorical fact or contemporary construction. In what is the most meaningful source testifying to her participation in 1830s revolts—in addition to her very existence, which some historians doubt—her son identified her as being involved in the Sabinada uprising of 1837–1838.

For an entry into the debate, see Reis, *Slave Rebellion in Brazil*; and Lima, "Desvendando Luíza Mahin."

135 Indicação 1810, Câmara Municipal de São Paulo, November 7, 1966. The degree curiously and incorrectly identified Vagliengo as the "author of the *loteamento*" of Brasilândia.

136 hooks, *Feminist Theory*, xvi (my emphasis).

137 Further echoes can be found in the conclusion of Keisha Khan-Perry's *Black Women Against the Land Grab*, titled "Above the Asphalt: From the Margins to the Center of Black Diasporic Politics." Her analysis of Black women's fight for racial justice and the right to the city in twenty-first-century Salvador also resonate deeply with the earlier histories chronicled in this book: "The restructuring of cities has come with a monumental price for poor blacks, as it exacerbates existing problems of violence, poverty, and social abandonment. The struggle against this global problem must be intensified. In response to these violent acts of urban displacement, the black struggle for the human right to housing has increased. Demolition and land expulsion are among the most important human rights issues facing blacks today." Khan-Perry, *Black Women*, loc. 2940.

CHAPTER FIVE. PRODUCING ETHNORACIAL INFRASTRUCTURES

1 In his autobiographical *My Life*, Clinton described the trip (his first to South America) as follows: "I traveled to Venezuela, Brazil, and Argentina to express the importance of Latin America to America's future and to keep pushing the idea of a free trade area covering all the Americas" (766).

2 National Security Council, Speechwriting Office, and Antony Blinken, "Brazil—Speech to Business Leaders 10/15/97," Clinton Digital Library, https://clinton.presidentiallibraries.us/items/show/9732.

3 Recall that São Paulo sambista Geraldo Filme had described Barra Funda, along with Liberdade and Bela Vista, as part of São Paulo's early and mid-twentieth-century "Black zone."

4 Seminal work on ethnic enclaves include Wilson and Portes, "Immigrant Enclaves"; Portes and Manning, "Immigrant Enclave"; Zhou, "Revisiting Ethnic Entrepreneurship"; Marcuse, "Enclaves Yes, Ghettos No."

5 The spelling of *Bexiga* with two *i*'s itself reflected efforts to assert the neighborhood's distinct Italian identity. I repeat that spelling convention when the cited written source utilizes it. Otherwise, I refer to the neighborhood as Bexiga and the broader district as Bela Vista.

6 Santos, *Metrópole*; Caldeira, *City of Walls*; Sachs-Jeantet, *São Paulo*.

7 On the multiple views of Japanese-Brazilians—from "model minority" to "yellow peril"—see Lesser, *Discontented Diaspora*, xx, xxix. On changing constructions of whiteness in Brazil, see Lesser, *Negotiating National Identity*. For a compelling revisionist work on the discourse of "Italian" São Paulo, see Santos, *Nem tudo era italiano*.

8 André Marega Pinhel and Rodrigo Fernandes Silva, "The Paradoxes of Ethnoracial Space in São Paulo, 1930s–1980s: Caracterização da distribuição étnico racial da população nos distritos da Bela Vista, Brasilândia e Liberdade," Report, Cambridge, 2021.

9 Guimarães, "Como trabalhar"; Daniel, *Race and Multiraciality*.

10 Pinhel and Silva, "The Paradoxes"; Paixão, *Desenvolvimento humano*.

11 For more, see Lesser, *Negotiating National Identity*; Lesser, *Discontented Diaspora*.

12 This is an especially important note given that Japanese immigrant descendants are often still identified as "Japanese" (as opposed to Japanese-Brazilian, say) even multiple generations after their ancestor settled in Brazil.

13 Interview by author with [name withheld], Liberdade, São Paulo, June 14, 2017.

14 Into the following decades municipal officials and planners would author other plans for the "reurbanization" of parts of Liberdade, indicating the continued perception among authorities and residents that it needed fixing. See "Reurbanização Praça da Liberdade," SP-Urbanismo Archive, tombo 2208; "Sujeira encobre beleza oriental da Liberdade," *O Estado de S. Paulo*, September 17, 1992, 3; and Empresa Municipal de Urbanização, "Boulevard Liberdade," 1993, SP-Urbanismo Archive, tombo 2210.

15 Handa, *O imigrante japonês*, 176; Sachio Negawa, "The Conde District—Brazil's First Japantown," *Discover Nikkei*, April 27, 2007, http://www.discovernikkei.org/es/journal/2007/4/27/brazil-nihonjinmachi/. Chapter 3 includes early depictions of the "Japanese" neighborhood in the popular press, as in: "Masasuk Sato is a Japanese who resides on Conde de Sarzedas Street, right in the middle of the Japanese neighorhood." "O japonezinho morreu brincando," *O Correio de S. Paulo*, June 13, 1936, 1. Guilherme de Almeida also depicted Conde de Sarzedas in one of his articles about São Paulo's ethnic enclaves, later collected as *Cosmópolis: (São Paulo/29) oito reportagens*.

16 Lesser, *Negotiating National Identity*, esp. 130–33. Also see Costa, *Brazilian Empire*, 204; Williams, *Culture Wars in Brazil*.

17 Kishimoto, "A experiência do cinema," 38; Nishida, *Diaspora and Identity*, 27. Lesser describes other episodes of forced displacement in Belém do Pará, Recife, and Álvares Machado. See Lesser, *Negotiating National Identity*, 135.

18 Sachio Negawa, "Chapter 6: The Formation and Development of Bairro Oriental: The Birth of Cine Niterói and Bunkyô," *Discover Nikkei*, September 6, 2007, https://discovernikkei.org/en/journal/2007/8/9/brazil-nihonjinmachi/.

19 For more on cinema in São Paulo, see Simões, *Salas de cinema*; Suk, "Becoming Modern." About cinema and Japanese films, also see Lesser, *Discontented Diaspora*.

20 Kishimoto, "A experiência do cinema," 20.

21 Lesser, *Discontented Diaspora*, 29–30.

22 "O bairro da Liberdade," ACAL, accessed April 2, 2018, http://www.feiraliberdade.com.br/o-bairro-da-liberdade.html.

23 Negawa, "Chapter 6."

24 Kishimoto, "A experiência do cinema," 20. "Cine Niterói: a retomada do bairro japonês."

25 Negawa, "Chapter 6."

26 "Na Liberdade, um mundo de sons e cores: Antigo reduto de japoneses, o bairro hoje é um pedaço do Oriente, onde convivem também chineses, coreanos e vietnamitas," *Folha de S. Paulo*, September 4, 1982.

27 Câmara Municipal de São Paulo, Projeto da Lei 0357/2017.

28 Kishimoto, "A experiência do cinema," 38.

29 Vila Brasilândia's wooden cinema was substantially more modest than Cine Niterói in Liberdade. In February 1953, engineers from the city conducted an examination of forty-eight cinemas throughout São Paulo and closed Brasilândia's for its lack of safety precautions. "Examinados 48 cinemas," *O Estado de S. Paulo*, February 17, 1953. An article from the month following indicated that the examination had expanded to include all of the city's 160 cinemas, of which six (including Brasilândia) had been deemed unsafe.

30 Urban planners and municipal officials had discussed building a subway system since the 1920s; however, only in the 1960s did they begin to pursue the project seriously. The decades-long efforts to realize Prestes Maia's Avenues Plan in the city may have siphoned financial resources and political capital from efforts to construct a metro system. "Após 6 anos de obras, Metrô de São Paulo, o primeiro do país, é inaugurado em 1974," Acervo: *O Globo*, June 5, 2014, http://acervo.oglobo.globo.com/em-destaque/apos-6-anos-de-obras-metro-de-sao-paulo-primeiro-do-pais-inaugurado-em-1974-12730229.

31 Celso Leite Ribeiro, "Quinze quilometros de metrô na administração do P. Maia," *O Estado de S. Paulo*, June 24, 1962, 20. Remarkably, Prestes Maia argued in the mainstream press that the metro "will cost almost nothing, or perhaps, will end up a bit more than the City Government will have to expend to construct the May 23 Avenue."

32 "Após 6 anos."
33 Williams, *Brazil*, 191–92.
34 "Parecer Conjunto No. 72/73 das Comissões de Urbanismo, Obras e Serviços Municipais e de Finanças e Orçamento sôbre o Projeto de Lei Nº 188/73," Câmara Municipal de São Paulo, 1973, archived at https://www.saopaulo.sp.leg.br/atividade-legislativa/legislacao-municipal-biblioteca/.
35 Roberto Camargo, "A Liberdade inicia sua transformação," *O Estado de S. Paulo*, June 2, 1974.
36 Camargo, "A Liberdade."
37 São Paulo (Cidade), *Inventário geral do patrimônio ambiental e cultural: Liberdade*, 47.
38 Kishimoto, "A experiência do cinema," 24.
39 "Parecer Conjunto No. 72/73 das Comissões de Urbanismo, Obras e Serviços Municipais e de Finanças e Orçamento sôbre o Projeto de Lei Nº 188/73," Câmara Municipal de São Paulo, 1973, archived at https://www.saopaulo.sp.leg.br/atividade-legislativa/legislacao-municipal-biblioteca/.
40 Parecer No. 151/73 da Comissão de Justiça e Redação sobre of Projeto de Lei, November 27, 1973.
41 Projeto da Lei 188/1973, processo 172.937/73.
42 On Maluf's biography and Syrian-Lebanese ethnicity in Brazil, see Karam, *Another Arabesque*.
43 "História da Liberdade: Um 'Gaijin' criou o bairro oriental," *Diário Nippak*, August 20, 1993.
44 "Liberdade: O coração oriental da cidade," *Diário de S. Paulo*, November 6, 1974.
45 On "Oriental characteristics," see Câmara Municipal de São Paulo, 49ª Sessão Ordinária, June 27, 1969, in *Diário Oficial do Estado de São Paulo*, July 2, 1969, 57–58; on the November 1969 decree, see Decreto 8.476, "Dispõe sôbre a construção e reconstrução de passeios no bairro da Liberdade, na chamada zona oriental," November 4, 1969.
46 There is some deviation from this official term in both primary source material from the 1970s and contemporary scholarship. For example, a 1974 article in *Diário de S. Paulo* explained: "Next Saturday, Mayor Miguel Colasuonno and various other city officials will go to Liberdade to inaugurate the 'little Japan,' the name that the neighborhood is already known by, at the moment when the work of decoration is concluding" ("Liberdade: O coração oriental da cidade"). For an example in the secondary literature, see Negawa, who consistently describes the neighborhood as a "Japan Town." These deviations reflect the tension between distinct constructions of the neighborhood's identity.

47 "História da Liberdade."
48 Guimarães, *Liberdade*, 105–10.
49 "Na Liberdade, um mundo de sons e cores."
50 "História da Liberdade."
51 "Liberdade: O coração oriental da cidade."
52 "Uma destas cenas não combina com o nosso bairro oriental: Proposta—redecorar a estação Liberdade. À moda oriental," *Jornal da Tarde*, August 23, 1976, Liberdade Neighborhood File, Arquivo Histórico Municipal.
53 Câmara Municipal de São Paulo, 49ª Sessão Ordinária, June 27, 1969, in *Diário Oficial do Estado de São Paulo*, July 2, 1969, 57–58.
54 "Liberdade, um bairro oriental," *Diário de S. Paulo*, November 4, 1974.
55 "Ao ascender das luzes surgiu o Bairro Oriental," *Diário de S. Paulo*, November 10, 1974.
56 *Veja*, November 20, 1974, 120.
57 Cited in Caldeira, *City of Walls*, 228.
58 Interview by author with [name withheld], Liberdade, São Paulo, June 14, 2017.
59 "O bairro oriental," *Veja*, January 1973, 40–41.
60 "A Liberdade inicia a sua transformação," *O Estado de S. Paulo*, June 2, 1974.
61 Saito, *A presença japonesa*, 117.
62 Saito, *A presença japonesa*, 117.
63 Saito, *A presença japonesa*, 121.
64 Saito, *A presença japonesa*, 121.
65 Saito, *A presença japonesa*, 121.
66 Saito, *A presença japonesa*, 122.
67 Saito, *A presença japonesa*, 122.
68 Saito, *A presença japonesa*, 122.
69 Projeto de lei N.o 236–78, December 18, 1978.
70 "Princípes japoneses chegam amanhã," *Diário Popular*, June 16, 1978.
71 "Finalmente, na Liberdade, nasce o 'Bairro Oriental," *Folha de S. Paulo*, November 7, 1974.
72 Handa, *Nossa Liberdade*, 13, AHM.
73 "Na Liberdade, um mundo de sons e cores."
74 See Hosokawa, "Dancing in the Tomb."
75 "The Race War That Flopped," *Ebony*, July 1946, 3–9, cited in Jenks, "Home," 107.
76 Jenks, "Home," 23. Also see Smith, "Identities"; Yokota, "From Little Tokyo."
77 Lavapés today is celebrated as the "marco zero" of samba paulistano with a plaque at the five-point intersection where the school sits in the Liberdade district.

78 "São Paulo Antigo e São Paulo Moderno," Lavapés enredo, 1969.
79 Chapter 2 describes these histories in detail.
80 Processo 20125/76, CONDEPHAAT.
81 William Cardoso, "Escavação expõe ossadas de um século e meio em antigo cemitério no centro de SP," *Folha de S. Paulo*, December 6, 2018, https://www1.folha.uol.com.br/cotidiano/2018/12/escavacao-expoe-ossadas-de-um-seculo-e-meio-em-antigo-cemiterio-no-centro-de-sp.shtml.
82 "Covas sanciona lei que cria memorial em terreno na Liberdade onde ossadas do tempo da escravidão foram encontradas," *Globo São Paulo*, January 30, 2020, https://g1.globo.com/sp/sao-paulo/noticia/2020/01/30/covas-sanciona-lei-que-cria-memorial-em-terreno-na-liberdade-onde-ossadas-do-tempo-da-escravidao-foram-encontradas.ghtml.
83 For instance, a monument to Zumbi dos Palmares was erected at Praça Antonio Prado, the original site of the Rosary church, in 2016. In 2020, a monument to the architect-artisan and freed African descendant Tebas was constructed at Praça Clóvis Beviláqua, east of the Praça da Sé.
84 Jehá, *Bexiga: Ano Zero.*
85 Antônio Rodrigues Porto, *História urbanística*, 172, quoted in Nascimento, "Entre sambas e rezas," 87.
86 "Bexiga: O que resta é sòmente saudade," *O Estado de S. Paulo*, January 24, 1971, Arquivo Histórico Municipal.
87 An article from the year following heralded "o velho Bexiga" as "a part of the city reborn." The piece described the neighborhood as "almost a favela," which had been "threatened to death by viaducts, avenues and real estate speculation" Paulo Sergio Markun, "O velho Bexiga: Uma parte da cidade que renasce," *O Estado de S. Paulo*, February 19, 1972.
88 Scarlato, "Bixiga," 29–30.
89 Outtes, "Disciplining."
90 "Bexiga: o que resta é sòmente saudade." The article also noted that of the two hundred property owners whose lots were expropriated by the city, just 10 percent had received payment from the City.
91 Oliveira, "Segregação urbana," 119.
92 Silvio Sayão, "O bairro que se transforma," *Diário de S. Paulo*, June 3, 1973, Bela Vista Neighborhood History File, AHM.
93 Sayão, "O bairro que se transforma."
94 Scarlato, "Bixiga," 30. Elsewhere, Scarlato used the same language of the 1971 film cited at the introduction of this section: "From the period that we called 'year zero,' in which all of those transformations happened, the landscape of way of life in Bexiga began to change. In parallel to the demolitions and the implantation of expressways, the verticalization of the neighborhood began" (32).

95 Nascimento, "Entre sambas e rezas," 87.
96 Oliveira, "Segregação urbana," 119.
97 Nascimento, "Entre sambas e rezas," 87–88.
98 Nascimento, "Entre sambas e rezas," 89.
99 I have not found sources that explain how many individuals relocated to the region in this era as a result of the resettlement program. For more, see Miriam Nicolau Ferrara, "A imprensa negra paulista," 13, 49, cited in Gisele Matos Chaves, "A imprensa negra através do jornal A Voz da Raça: Uma São Paulo de negros para negros," 2016, Universidade de São Paulo, http://lemad.fflch.usp.br/sites/lemad.fflch.usp.br/files/2018-04/a_imprensa_negra_atraves_do_jornal_voz_da_raca.pdf.
100 "Bexiga: O que resta é sòmente saudade."
101 Sayão, "O bairro que se transforma."
102 "Pintando o Bexiga," *Folha de S. Paulo*, September 23, 1992.
103 "O Bexiga vai à luta: O velho enclave boêmio quer ser bairro independente para preservar suas tradições," *Veja*, March 31, 1982.
104 Maria Indes de Carmargo, "A Treze de Maio, de volta aos anos 20," *Jornal da Tarde*, September 9, 1982.
105 Carmargo, "A Treze de Maio." Puglisi recommended that "the project to restore the neighborhood" include "small signs" with the names of former residents and brief biographies.
106 "Restuarada, rua lembrará Bexiga do início do século," *Folha de S. Paulo*, August 5, 1982. Sources indicate the secretary of culture spent between fifteen and twenty-five million cruzeiros to restore the exteriors of around fifty properties.
107 Maria Helena Passos, "O Bexiga revigorado," *Isto é São Paulo*, December 15, 1982, 36.
108 Walter Taverna, interview by author, Bela Vista, São Paulo, February 5, 2017.
109 "Benvidos ao centro turístico italiano da Bela Vista / Promoção: SODEPRO—Prefeitura—Paulistur."
110 As discussed in chapter 3, São Paulo's neighborhoods have no formal definition. For more, see Emílio Haddad, "Sobre o estudo," cited in Hidalgo, "As divisões territoriais," 28; Dias, *Desenvolvimento urbano*. For the history of the administrative division of land in São Paulo, see "São Paulo," IBGE, accessed May 13, 2017, https://cidades.ibge.gov.br/brasil/sp/sao-paulo/historico.
111 Letter from Walter Taverna to Reynaldo de Barros, September 25, 1981, correspondence between SODEPRO e Prefeitura Municipal de São Paulo, SP-Urbanismo Archive.
112 Scarlato, "Bixiga," 32.
113 Letter from Walter Taverna, President, SODEPRO, to Domingos Mantelli Filho, President of Paulistur, December 1, 1980, Folder of

correspondence between SODEPRO e Prefeitura Municipal de São Paulo, SP-Urbanismo Archive.

114 "Bela Vista poderá ter um Centro Turístico Italiano," *Folha da Tarde—LUX Jornal*, January 6, 1981, correspondence between SODEPRO e Prefeitura Municipal de São Paulo, SP-Urbanismo Archive.

115 Projeto da Lei 0200–1974, 33–34. For more on the history of zoning in São Paulo, see Feldman, *Planejamento e zoneamento*.

116 Letter from Paulo Julio Valentino Bruna, October 16, 1982, correspondence between SODEPRO e Prefeitura Municipal de São Paulo, SP-Urbanismo Archive.

117 Italo Bangnoli, "A introdução das tradições italianas no Bexiga," *Jornal da Bela Vista*, February 22, 1986.

118 Scarlato, "Estrutura," 118.

119 Figure covers 1872–1972 and is from Lesser, *Immigration, Ethnicity*, 15. For more on Italian immigration, see Alvim, *Brava Gente!*; Cenni, *Italianos no Brasil*; Carneiro et al., *História do trabalho*.

120 "Alckmin discursa em assinatura de decreto para preparativos do Ano da Itália no Brasil," March 5, 2011, accessed August 15, 2017, http://www.saopaulo.sp.gov.br/discursos/alckmin-discursa-em-assinatura-de-decreto-para-preparativos-do-ano-da-italia-no-brasil.

121 Marzola, *Bela Vista*, 75.

122 Marzola, *Bela Vista*, 76.

123 Luigi Biondi points to the early twentieth century for the consolidation of a shared "Italian" identity in São Paulo. Bondi, "Imigração Italiana e movimento operário em São Paulo: Um balanço historiográfico," in Carneiro et al., *História do trabalho*, 73.

124 "Bela Vista: Plano de Reurbanização," Architect Vera Lucia de A. S. Kitazato, October 1984, SP-Urbanismo Archive.

125 Marzola, *Bela Vista*, 78.

126 "Pesquisa revela presença de grande número de Nordestinos no Bexiga," *Jornal da Bela Vista*, November 16, 1983. "Fora Baianos Sujos." On *nordestino* as a euphemism for Black individuals, see Caldeira, *City of Walls*, esp. 88–89. In his thesis on African-descendent culture in Bexiga, Nascimento similarly noted the in-migration of Northeasterners, with interviewees noting that "today the population of the neighborhood is more Northeastern than black or Italian." Nascimento, "Entre sambas e rezas," 84, 87–89, 92.

127 Scarlato, "Bixiga," 30, 31.

128 Caldeira, *City of Walls*, 32–33.

129 "Pesquisa revela presença . . ." *Jornal da Bela Vista*.

130 Italo Bagnoli, "O Bexiga de antigamente," *Jornal da Bela Vista*, January 17, 1983.

131 Bagnoli, "O Bexiga de antigamente."

132 Jehá, *Bexiga: Ano Zero.*

133 Scarlato, "Estrutura,"121.

134 Scarlato, "Estrutura,"121.

135 Caldeira, *City of Walls*, esp. 31.

136 Scarlato, "Estrutura."

137 This discourse is most striking, perhaps, given that some sources romanticize "Italian" *cortiços* while simultaneously disparaging those established by Northeasterners. For example, Scarlato, "Estrutura," 124.

138 d'Alambert and Fernandes, "Bela Vista," 154.

139 "O Bexiga vai à luta: O velho enclave boêmio quer ser bairro independente para preservar suas tradições," *Veja*, March 31, 1982, 54. In years following Northeastern migrants would also come to occupy a central role in Liberdade's restaurants, including, as Leo Nishihata writes, as the majority of local sushi chefs. Leo Nishihata, "Sushi oxente," in Ogawa, *100 anos*, 86–91.

140 "O Bexiga vai à luta," 56.

141 Sebastião Marinho and Andorinha (José Saturnino dos Santos), "Cada prédio em São Paulo construído tem o sal do suor do nordestino," accessed June 13, 2018, http://www.letrasdemusicas.fm/francis-lopes/cada-predio-em-sao-paulo-construido-tem-o-sal-do-suor-do-nordestino.

142 UCRAN—União dos Cantadores, Repentistas e Apologistas do Nordeste, accessed March 31, 2018, http://www.ucran.com.br/. Though part of the district of Liberdade, this area does not comprise part of the *bairro oriental.*

143 This line references the *terra roxa*, or purple soil, of São Paulo.

144 Teresa Caldeira exams anti-Northeasterner sentiment in the São Paulo neighborhood Moóca. See *City of Walls.*

145 "O Bexiga vai à luta."

146 Ernani Silva Bruno, "Bixiga, de italianos e negros," *Folha de S. Paulo*, December 12, 1983.

147 Ernani Silva Bruno, "Bexiga, um bairro de várias influências," *Folha de S. Paulo*, January 29, 1982.

148 Resolução No. 22/2002, Conselho Municipal de Preservação do Patrimônio Histórico, Cultural e Ambiental da Cidade de São Paulo.

149 Scarlato, "Estrutura," 118.

150 Taverna quoted in "Patrimônio: Conpresp determina tombamento de 906 imóveis na Bela Vista," *O Estado de S. Paulo*, December 17, 2002.

151 d'Alambert and Fernandes, "Bela Vista," 159. My italics.

152 Former São Paulo Mayor João Doria attended the inauguration of the bust as the head of São Paulo's tourism agency. "No Bixiga, um busto lembrando Adoniran," *Jornal da Tarde*, August 8, 1983.

153 On the materialization of identity, see Frers and Meier, *Encountering Urban Places.* Clara Irazábal also examines ethnicized place-making via immigrant-themed parks in Curitiba. See Irazábal, *City Making and Urban Governance.*

154 Pedro Venceslau, "Doria quer revitalizar e mudar nome do bairro para 'Bom Retiro Little Seul,'" *O Estado de S. Paulo*, April 11, 2017.

155 For two interesting recent works about place-making, see Pemberton and Phillimore, "Migrant Place-Making"; Musterd et al., *Place-Making and Policies.* For a local example from São Paulo, see Sandler, "Place and Process."

EPILOGUE

1 Filme, "Tradição (vai no Bexiga para ver)."

2 Vai-Vai was originally founded as a *cordão* and remained as such until the 1970s, when it became a samba school.

3 Prandi, *Os Candomblês de São Paulo*, 21.

4 Priscila Mengue, "Vai-Vai fecha acordo e deixará sede no Bixiga para construção de estação do metrô," *CNN Brasil*, September 23, 2021, https://www.cnnbrasil.com.br/entretenimento/vai-vai-fecha-acordo-e-deixara-sede-cinquentenaria-no-bixiga/.

5 Daniel Mello, "Ação judicial busca preservação de sítio arqueológico quilombola em SP," *Agência Brasil—São Paulo*, February 9, 2023, https://agenciabrasil.ebc.com.br/geral/noticia/2023–02/movimento-entra-com-acao-por-preservacao-de-sitio-arqueologico-em-sp.

6 "Geraldo Filme ganha escultura na Praça David Raw nesta quinta," São Paulo Municipal Government, April 18, 2022, https://capital.sp.gov.br/web/cultura/w/noticias/31161.

7 "Inaugurada em São Paulo a estátua de Tebas, arquiteto escravizado no século XVIII," *ArchDaily Brasil*, November 26, 2020, https://www.archdaily.com.br/br/952117/inaugurada-em-sao-paulo-a-estatua-de-tebas-arquiteto-escravizado-no-seculo-xviii.

8 Filme conducted research at the Curia Metropolitana and in other archives to chart the history of Tebas. Filme, "Interview," 75.

9 Marcel Lopes, "Carolina de Jesus, Geraldo Filme e outras personalidades negras ganharão estátuas na cidade de SP," *O Globo*, August 17, 2021, https://g1.globo.com/sp/sao-paulo/noticia/2021/08/17/carolina-de-jesus-geraldo-filme-e-outras-personalidades-negras-irao-ganhar-estatuas-na-cidade-de-sp.ghtml.

10 William Cardoso, "Escavação expõe ossadas de um século e meio em antigo cemitério no centro de SP," *Folha de S. Paulo*, December 6, 2018, https://www1.folha.uol.com.br/cotidiano/2018/12/escavacao

-expoe-ossadas-de-um-seculo-e-meio-em-antigo-cemiterio-no-centro-de-sp.shtml.

11 "Luminárias japonesas são retiradas de rua na Liberdade a pedido de movimento negro e indígena," *Folha de S.Paulo*, November 2024, https://www1.folha.uol.com.br/cotidiano/2024/11/luminarias-japonesas-sao-retiradas-de-rua-na-liberdade-a-pedido-de-movimento-negro-e-indigena.shtml.

12 "Geraldo Filme ganha escultura," Municipal Secretary of Culture, April 18, 2022, https://prefeitura.sp.gov.br/web/cultura/w/noticias/31161 (my emphasis).

13 Cited in Guimarães and Macedo, "*Diário Trabalhista*."

14 Girlei Luiza Miranda, "Gigi: Nascida para bater," interview by Museu da Pessoa, October 10, 2017, https://museudapessoa.org/historia-de-vida/gigi-nascida-para-bater/; Marina Rossi, "A força do tambor feminino," *El País Brasil*, March 8, 2015,https://brasil.elpais.com/brasil/2015/03/06/politica/1425665356_175973.html.

15 George Rein Andrews discusses historical and contemporary celebrations of May 13 in *Blacks and Whites*, 224–33.

16 Nádia Garcia, "Lavagem da Escadaria do Bexiga e da Rua 13 de Maio é realizado pelo grupo Ilú Obá de Min no dia da Abolição," *Portal do Bixiga*, May 19, 2016, https://www.portaldobixiga.com.br/lavagem-da-escadaria-do-bixiga-e-da-rua-13-de-maio-e-realizada-pelo-grupo-ilu-oba-de-min-no-dia-da-abolicao-da-escravatura/.

17 "SP prevê 'esplanada oriental' na Liberdade," *Estadão Conteúdo*, December 29, 2022, https://www.istoedinheiro.com.br/sp-preve-esplanada-oriental-na-liberdade/.

18 *Roda* signifies in the round, e.g., gathered in a circle. *Bamba* translates roughly to "expert."

19 The version that the group sings at gatherings combines the anthem with another song, titled "Nossa Quebrada." Loteiro and Ripol, "Hino do Samba do Congo"; Ripol and Bonfim, "Nossa quebrada."

Bibliography

PRINCIPAL ARCHIVES CONSULTED

A Folha de S. Paulo
A Rede da Memória Virtual Brasileira—Hermoteca Digital
Arquivo Histórico Municipal da Cidade de São Paulo (AHM)
Arquivo Público do Estado de São Paulo (APESP)
Biblioteca da Câmara Municipal da Cidade de São Paulo
Biblioteca da Sociedade Brasileira de Cultura Japonesa e de Assistência Social (Bunkyo)
Biblioteca Monteiro Lobato, São Paulo
Biblioteca Prestes Maia, São Paulo
Centro de Pesquisa e Documentação de História Contemporânea do Brasil (CPDOC), Fundação Getúlio Vargas, Rio de Janeiro
Conselho de Defesa do Patromônio Histórico, Arqueológico, Artístico e Turístico do Estado de São Paulo (CONDEPHAAT)
Conselho Municipal de Preservação do Patrimônio Histórico, Cultural e Ambiental da Cidade de São Paulo (CONPRESP)
Coordenação de Gestão Documental (CGDP), Prefeitura Municipal da Cidade de São Paulo
Departamento de Desapropriações (DESAP), Prefeitura Municipal da Cidade de São Paulo
Empresa Paulista de Planejamento Urbano (EMPLASA), São Paulo
Grupo Técnico de Informatização dos Cadastros e de Desenvolvimento de Sistemas (GINFO), São Paulo
Instituto Brasileiro de Geografia e Estatística (IBGE)

Instituto do Patrimônio Histórico e Artístico Nacional (IPHAN), São Paulo
Museu da Pessoa, São Paulo
O Estado de S. Paulo
O Globo
SEHAB/HABI, Prefeitura Municipal da Cidade de São Paulo
SP-Urbanismo, Prefeitura Municipal da Cidade de São Paulo

SECONDARY SOURCES

Abreu, Martha. "Outras histórias de Pai João: Conflitos raciais, protesto escravo e irreverência sexual no poesía popular, 1880–1950." *Afro-Ásia* 31 (2004): 235–76.

Adelman, Robert M., and Christopher Mele, eds. *Race, Space, and Exclusion: Segregation and Beyond in Metropolitan America*. New York: Routledge, 2015.

Aja, Alan A. *Miami's Forgotten Cubans: Race, Racialization, and the Miami Afro-Cuban Experience*. New York: Palgrave Macmillan, 2016.

Alberto, Paulina L. "A Mãe Preta entre sentimento, ciência e mito: Intelectuais negros e as metáforas cambiantes de inclusão racial, 1920–1980." In *Políticas da Raça: Experiências e legados da abolição e da pós-emancipação no Brasil*, edited by Flávio Gomes and Petrônio Domingues. São Paulo: Selo Negro, 2014.

Alberto, Paulina L. *Terms of Inclusion: Black Intellectuals in Twentieth-Century Brazil*. Chapel Hill: University of North Carolina Press, 2011.

Alberto, Paulina L. "When Rio Was Black: Soul Music, National Culture, and the Politics of Racial Comparison in 1970s Brazil." *Hispanic American Historical Review* 89, no.1 (2009): 3–39.

Albuquerque, Durval Muniz de, Jr. *The Invention of the Brazilian Northeast*. Durham, NC: Duke University Press, 2014.

Almandoz Marte, Arturo. *Planning Latin America's Capital Cities, 1850–1950*. London: Routledge, 2002.

Almeida, Guilherme de. *Cosmópolis: (São Paulo/29) oito reportagens*. São Paulo: Companhia Editora Nacional, 1962.

Alves, Jaime A. *The Anti-Black City Police Terror and Black Urban Life in Brazil*. Minneapolis: University of Minnesota Press, 2018.

Alves, Jaime A. "From Necropolis to Blackpolis: Necropolitical Governance and Black Spatial Praxis in São Paulo, Brazil." *Antipode* 46, no. 2 (2014): 323–39.

Alvim, Zuleika M. F. *Brava Gente! Os italianos em São Paulo*. São Paulo: Editora Brasiliense, 1986.

Amaral, Aracy A. *Artes plásticas na Semana de 22*. 5th ed. São Paulo: Editora 34, 1998.

Amaral, Raul Joviano do. *Os pretos do Rosário de São Paulo: Subsídios históricos*. São Paulo: João Scortecci Editora, 1991.

Ammon, Francesca Russello. *Bulldozer: Demolition and Clearance of the Postwar Landscape*. New Haven, CT: Yale University Press, 2016.

Amos, H. William. "Chinatown by Numbers: Defining an Ethnic Space by Empirical Linguistic Landscape." *Linguistic Landscape* 2, no. 2 (2016): 127–56.

Anderson, Kay J. "The Idea of Chinatown: The Power of Place and Institutional Practice in the Making of a Racial Category." *Annals of the Association of American Geographers* 77, no. 4 (1987): 580–98.

Andrade, Mario de. *Cartas de trabalho: Correspondência com Rodrigo Mello Franco de Andrade (1936–1945)*. Brasília: SPHAN, 1981.

Andrade, Mario de. "O samba rural paulista." *Revista do Arquivo Municipal* 4, no. 41 (November 1937): 38–116.

Andrade, Oswald de. *Obras completas*. Vol. 9, *Um homen sem profissão*. Rio de Janeiro: Civilização Brasileira, 1976.

Andrews, George Reid. *Afro-Latin America, 1800–2000*. Oxford: Oxford University Press, 2004.

Andrews, George Reid. *Blacks and Whites in São Paulo, Brazil, 1888–1988*. Madison: University of Wisconsin Press, 1991.

Antunes, André Luís de Araújo. "Avaliação de projetos sociais: Um estudo de caso do projeto social 'Samba se aprende na escola' da Sociedade Rosas de Ouro." Undergraduate thesis, Federal University of Santa Catarina, 2008.

Araujo, Ana Lucia. *Public Memory of Slavery: Victims and Perpetrators in the South Atlantic*. Amherst, NY: Cambria, 2010.

Araújo, Oscar Egídio de. "Enquistamentos étnicos." *Revista do Arquivo Municipal* 65 (March 1940): 227–46.

Arruda, Maria Arminda do Nascimento. *Metrópole e cultura: São Paulo no meio do século XX*. Bauru: EDUSC, 2001.

Assunção, Matthias Röhrig. "Stanzas and Sticks: Poetic and Physical Challenges in the Afro-Brazilian Culture of the Paraíba Valley, Rio de Janeiro." *History Workshop Journal* 77, no. 1 (April 2014): 103–36.

Athayde, Celso, and Renato Meirelles. *Um país chamado favela*. São Paulo: Gente, 2014.

Azeredo, Magalhães de. *Alma primitiva*. Rio de Janeiro: Cunha e Irmão, 1895.

Azevedo, Amailton Magno. "A memória músical de Geraldo Filme: Os sambas e as micros-áfricas em São Paulo." PhD diss., Pontifícia Universidade Católica de São Paulo, 2006.

Azevedo, Amailton Magno. "São Paulo Negra: Geraldo Filme e a geografia do samba paulista." *Revista da Associação Brasileira de Pesquisadores/as Negros/as (ABPN)* 6, no. 13 (June 2014).

Azevedo, Arolodo de. *A cidade de São Paulo: Estudos de geografia urbana*. 4 vols. São Paulo: Companhia Editora Nacional, 1958.

Azevedo, Célia Maria Marinho. *Onda negra, medo branco: O negro no imaginário das elites, século XIX*. Rio de Janeiro: Paz e Terra, 1987.

Azevedo, Vicente de. *O noiva da morte*. São Paulo: Clube do Livro, 1970.

Baer, Werner. *The Brazilian Economy: Growth and Development*. 7th ed. Boulder, CO: Lynne Rienner, 2008.

Balbo, José Tadeu. *Pavimentação asfáltica: Materiais, projeto, e restauração*. São Paulo: Oficina de Textos, 2007.

Barbosa, Márcio, ed. *Frente negra brasileira: Depoimentos: Projeto de dinamização de espaços literários afro-brasileiros*. São Paulo: Quilombhoje, 1998.

Barbosa, Synesio Cunha. "O loteamento em São Paulo." *Revista do Arquivo Municipal* 82 (March/April 1942): 143–54.

Barbuy, Heloisa, Paulo César Garcez Marins, Anicleide Zequini, and Aline Antunes Zanatta. *Azulejos: Preservação, exposição, conhecimento*. Itu, São Paulo: Museu Republicano "Convenção de Itu," 2012. https://sites.usp.br/mri/wp-content/uploads/sites/836/2020/12/Azulejos.pdf.

Barro, Máximo. *Nossa Senhora do Ó: História de Bairros de São Paulo*. Prefeitura de São Paulo, 1977.

Barros, Plínio Marcos. *Balbina de Iansã—trilha sonora da peça teatral*. São Paulo: Fermata, 1971, compact disc.

Barros, Plínio Marcos. *Em prosa e samba: Nas quebradas do Mundaréu*. Warner Music Brasil, 2011, compact disc. Originally released in 1974.

Bassanezi, Maria Sílvia C., ed. *São Paulo do passado: Dados demográficos—1886*. Campinas: Núcleo de Estudos de População, Universidade Estadual de Campinas, 1999. https://www.nepo.unicamp.br/publicacoes/censos/1886.pdf.

Bastide, Roger. "Catimbó." In *Encantaria brasileira: O livro dos mestres, caboclos e encantados*, edited by J. Reginaldo Prandi. Rio de Janeiro: Pallas, 2004.

Bastide, Roger. "Psicanálise do cafuné." *Revista do Arquivo Municipal* 6, no. 70 (1940): 118–30.

Beiguelman, Giselle. *Memória da amnésia: Políticas de esquecimento*. São Paulo: SESC São Paulo, 2019.

Beiner, Guy. *Forgetful Remembrance: Social Forgetting and Vernacular Historiography of a Rebellion in Ulster*. Oxford: Oxford University Press, 2018.

Bernardo, Teresinha. *Memória em branco e negro: Olhares sobre São Paulo*. São Paulo: EDUC, 1998.

Bessone, Magali. "Racial or Spatial Categorisations? A Focus on the French Setting." *Theoria: A Journal of Social and Political Theory* 60, no. 137 (2013): 48–67.

Bicudo, Virgínia Leone. *Estudos raciais de pretos e multos em São Paulo*. São Paulo: Editora Sociologia e Política, 2010.

Bignotto, Cilza Carla. "Novas perspectivas sobre as práticas editoriais de Monteiro Lobato (1918–1925)." PhD diss., UNCAMP, 2007.

Bondi, Luigi. "Imigração Italiana e movimento operário em São Paulo: Um balanço historiográfico." In *História do trabalho e gistórias da imigração: Trabalhadores Italianos e sindicatos no Brásil (séculos XIX e XX)*, edited by Carneiro, Maria Luiza Tucci, Federico Croci, and Emilio Franzina, 23–48. São Paulo: EDUSP, 2010.

Bonduki, Nabil. *Habitar São Paulo: Reflexões sobre a gestão urbana*. São Paulo: Estação Liberdade, 2000.

Bonduki, Nabil. *Origens da habitação social no Brasil: Arquitetura moderna, lei do inquilinato e difusão da casa própria*. 7th ed. São Paulo: Estação Liberdade, 2013.

Botão, Renato Ubirajara Dos Santos. "Para além da Nagocracia: A (Re) Africanização do Candomblé Nação Angola-Congo Em São Paulo." Master's thesis, UNESP, 2007.

Bourdieu, Pierre, and Loïc Wacquant. "On the Cunning of Imperialist Reason." *Theory, Culture and Society* 16, no. 1 (1999): 41–58.

Brefe, Ana Claudia Fonseca. *O museu paulista: Affonso de Taunay e a memória nacional, 1917–1945*. São Paulo: Editora UNESP, 2005.

Breunlin, Rachel, and Helen A. Regis. "Putting the Ninth Ward on the Map: Race, Place, and Transformation in Desire, New Orleans." *American Anthropologist* 108, no. 4 (December 2006): 744–64.

Britt, Andrew G. "Spatial Projects of Forgetting: Razing the Remedies Church and Museum to the Enslaved in São Paulo's 'Black Zone,' 1930s–1940s." *Journal of Latin American Studies* 54, no. 4 (2022): 561–92. https://doi.org/10.1017/S0022216X22000669.

Britto, Iêda Marques. *Samba na Cidade de São Paulo, 1900–1930: Um exercício de resistência cultural*. São Paulo: FFLCH-USP, 1986.

Brubaker, Rogers, and Frederick Cooper. "Beyond 'Identity.'" *Theory and Society* 29, no. 1 (2000): 1–47.

Brunelli, Aideli S. Urbani, Ana Paula Karruz, Dilze Onilda de Lima, et al. *Barra Funda*. Prefeitura Municipal da Cidade de São Paulo, 2006.

Brunn, Stanley D. "Reading and Mapping America's Changing Ethnic Geomorphologies and Palimpsest Geographies." In *Multicultural Geographies: The Changing Racial/Ethnic Patterns of the United States*, edited by John W. Frazier and Florence M. Margai. Albany: State University of New York Press, 2010.

Bruno, Ernani Silva. *História e tradições da Cidade de São Paulo*. Rio de Janeiro: Livraria José Olympio Editôra, 1954.

Butler, Kim D. "Africa in the Reinvention of Nineteenth-Century Afro-Bahian Identity." In *Rethinking the African Diaspora: The Making of a Black Atlantic World in the Bight of Benin and Brazil*, edited by Kristin Mann and Edna G. Bay. London: F. Class, 2001.

Butler, Kim D. *Freedoms Given, Freedoms Won: Afro-Brazilians in Post-Abolition São Paulo and Salvador*. New Brunswick, NJ: Rutgers University Press, 1988.

Burdick, John. *The Color of Sound: Race, Religion, and Music in Brazil*. New York: New York University Press, 2013.

Caçula, Tadeu. *Casa Verde: Uma pequena África paulistana*. São Paulo: LiberArts, 2020.

Caldeira, Teresa. *City of Walls: Crime, Segregation, and Citizenship in São Paulo*. Berkeley: University of California Press, 2000.

Campbell, Courtney J. *Region Out of Place: The Brazilian Northeast and the World, 1924–1968*. Pittsburgh, PA: University of Pittsburgh Press, 2022.

Campos, Candido Malta. *Os rumos da cidade: Urbanismo e modernização em São Paulo*. São Paulo: Editora SENAC, 2000.

Campos, Celso de, Jr. *Adoniran: Uma biografia*. São Paulo: Editora Globo, 2003.

Campos, Cristina de, Fernando Atique, and George Dantas. *Profissionais, práticas e representações da construção da cidade e do território*. Sao Pauo: Alameda, 2013.

Campos, Cynthia Machado. *A política da língua na era Vargas: Proibição do falar alemão e resistências no sul do Brasil*. Campinas: UNICAMP, 2006.

Campos, Eudes. "A vila de São Paulo do Campo e seus caminhas." *Revista do Arquivo Municipal* 204 (2006): 11–34.

Cardoso, Fernando Henrique, and Paul Singer. *O milagre brasileiro: Causas e conseqüências*. Caderno Cebrap no. 6 (1972).

Carril, Lourdes. *Quilombo, favela e periferia: A longa busca da cidadania*. São Paulo: Annablume, 2006.

Carvalho, Bruno. *Porous City: A Cultural History of Rio de Janeiro*. Liverpool: Liverpool University Press, 2013.

Castro, Márcio Sampaio de. *Bexiga: Um bairro afro-italiano*. São Paulo: Annablume, 2008.

Caulfield, Sueann. "Getting into Trouble: Dishonest Women, Modern Girls, and Women-Men in the Conceptual Language of *Vida Policial*." *Signs* 19, no. 1 (Fall 1993): 146–76.

Cavalheiro, Edgard. *Monteiro Lobato: Vida e obra*. São Paulo: Editora Brasiliense, 1962.

Cenni, Franco. *Italianos no Brasil: "Andiamo in 'Merica."* São Paulo: EDUSP, 2002.

Certeau, Michel de. *The Practice of Everyday Life*. Berkeley: University of California Press, 1984.

Certeau, Michel de, Luce Giard, and Pierre Mayol. *The Practice of Everyday Life*. Vol. 2, *Living and Cooking*. Minneapolis: University of Minnesota Press, 1998.

Chaloub, Sidney. *Cidade febril: Cortiços e epidemias na Corte Imperial.* São Paulo: Companhia das Letras, 1996.

Cidade. "A Saga da Metrópole e seu inventor: Cem anos de Prestes Maia." *Revista do Departamento do Patrimônio Histórico/Secretaria Municipal da Cultura* 3 (1996).

Clinton, Bill. *My Life.* New York: Vintage, 2004.

Collins, John F. *Revolt of the Saints: Memory and Redemption in the Twilight of Brazilian Racial Democracy.* Durham, NC: Duke University Press, 2015.

Connerton, Paul. *How Modernity Forgets.* Cambridge: Cambridge University Press, 2009.

Conti, Lígia Nassif. "A memória do samba na capital do trabalho: Os sambistas paulistanos e a construção de uma singularidade para o samba de São Paulo (1968–1991)." PhD diss., USP, 2015.

Costa, Emilia Viotti da. *The Brazilian Empire: Myths and Histories.* Chapel Hill: University of North Carolina Press, 2000.

Costa, Emilia Viotti da. *Da senzala à colonia.* 4th ed. São Paulo: Editora UNESP, 2006.

Costa, Geraldo Magela, and Jupira Gomes de Mendonça. *Planejamento urbano no Brasil: Trajetória, avanços e perspectivas.* Belo Horizonte: Editora C/Arte, 2008.

Costa, Maria Tereza Paulinho da. "A justiça em ondas médias: O programa Gil Gomes." Master's thesis, UNICAMP, 1989.

Costa, Valéria Gomes, and Flávio Gomes. *Religiões negras no Brasil: Da escravidão à pós emancipação.* São Paulo: Selo Negro, 2016.

Craib, Raymond B. *Cartographic Mexico: A History of State Fixations and Fugitive Landscapes.* Durham, NC: Duke University Press, 2004.

Cunha, Euclides da. *Rebellion in the Backlands.* Translated by Samuel Putnam. Chicago: University of Chicago Press, 2010. Originally published in Portuguese in 1902.

Cunha, Maria Clementina Pereira. *"Não tá sopa": Samba e sambistas no Rio de Janeiro, de 1890 a 1930.* Campinas: UNICAMP, 2016.

Curtin, Phillip D. *The Atlantic Slave Trade: A Census.* Madison: University of Wisconsin Press, 1969.

Curtis, Carey, John L. Renne, and Luca Bertolini. *Transit Oriented Development: Making it Happen.* New York: Routledge, 2016.

Cymbalista, Renato. *Cidades dos vivos: Arquitetura e atitudes perante a morte nos cemitérios do estado de São Paulo.* São Paulo: Annablume, 2002.

d'Alambert, Clara Correia, and Paulo Cesar Gaioto Fernandes. "Bela Vista: A preservação e odesafio da renovação de um bairro paulistano." *Revista do Arquivo Municipal* 204 (2006), 151–68.

DaMatta, Roberto. *Carnavais, malandros, e heróis: Para uma sociologia do dilema brasileiro.* Rio de Janeiro: Rocco, 1997.

Daniel, G. Reginald. *Race and Multiraciality in Brazil and the United States: Converging Paths?* University Park: Pennsylvania State University Press, 2006.

Deák, Csaba. "À busca das categorias da produção do espaço." Concurso de Livre Docência, FAU-USP, 2001.

Deák, Csaba, and Sueli Ramos Schiffer, eds. *O processo de urbanização no Brasil*. 2nd ed. São Paulo: EDUSP, 2015.

Dean, Warren. *The Industrialization of São Paulo, 1890–1945*. Austin: University of Texas Press, 1969.

Dean, Warren. *Rio Claro: A Brazilian Plantation System, 1820–1920*. Stanford, CA: Stanford University Press, 1976.

Debes, Célio. "Gabriel Marques, um injustiçados lidador das letras." *Suplemento cultural: Revista apm (Associação Paulista de Medicina)* 175 (November 2006): 175–79.

Degler, Carl. *Neither Black nor White: Slavery and Race Relations in Brazil and the United States*. Madison: University of Wisconsin Press, 1986.

DeGraft-Hanson, Kwesi. "Unearthing the Weeping Time: Savannah's Ten Broeck Race Course and 1859 Slave Sale." *Southern Spaces*, February 18, 2010. https://southernspaces.org/2010/unearthing-weeping-time-savannahs-ten-broeck-race-course-and-1859-slave-sale.

Dias, Márcia Lúcia Rebello Pinho. *Desenvolvimento urbano e habitação popular em São Paulo: 1870–1914*. São Paulo: Nobel, 1989.

Dias, Maria Odila Silva. *Power and Everyday Life: The Lives of Working Women in Nineteenth-Century Brazil*. New Brunswick, NJ: Rutgers University Press, 1995.

Dittmar, Hank, and Gloria Ohland, eds. *The New Transit Town: Best Practices in Transit-Oriented Development*. Washington, DC: Island Press, 2003.

Domingues, Petrônio. *A nova abolição*. São Paulo: Grupo Editorial Summus, 2008.

Domingues, Petrônio. *Uma história não contada: Negro, racismo, e branqueamento em São Paulo no pós-abolição*. São Paulo: Editora SENAC, 2004.

Domingues, Petrônio. "Um 'templo de luz': Frente Negra Brasileira (1931–1937) e a questão da educação." *Revista Brasileira de Educação* 13, no. 39 (2008): 517–96.

Drescher, Seymour. *From Slavery to Freedom: Comparative Studies in the Rise and Fall of Atlantic Slavery*. London: Macmillan, 1999.

Eakin, Marshall C. *Brazil: The Once and Future Country*. New York: Palgrave Macmillan, 1998.

Eltis, David. "The Nineteenth-Century Transatlantic Slave Trade: An Annual Time Series of Imports into the Americas Broken Down by Region." *Hispanic American Historical Review* 67, no. 1 (February 1987): 109–38.

Evangelista, Daniele Ferreira. "Fundando um axé: Reflexões sobre o processo de construção de um terreiro de candomblé." *Religião e Sociedade* 35, no. 1 (2015). https://doi.org/10.1590/0100-85872015v35n1cap03.
Evans, Freddi Williams. *Congo Square: African Roots in New Orleans.* Lafayette: University of Louisiana at Lafayette Press, 2011.
Fanon, Frantz. *The Wretched of the Earth.* Translated by Richard Philcox. New York: Grove, 2005. First published in French in 1961.
Fantin, Jader Tadeu. "Os japoneses no bairro da Liberdade—SP na primeira metade do século XX." Master's thesis, FAU-USP, 2013.
Fária, Camila Salles de. "A luta Guaraní pela terra na métropole paulistana: Contradições entre a propriedade privada capitalista e a approiação indígena." PhD diss., USP, 2015.
Farmer, Paul. "Anthropology of Structural Violence." *Current Anthropology* 45, no. 3 (2004): 305–25.
Fausto, Boris. *A Revolução de 1930: Historiografia e história.* São Paulo: Editôra Brasiliense, 1970.
Feldman, Sarah. *Planejamento e zoneamento: São Paulo, 1947–1972.* São Paulo: EDUSP, 2005.
Fernandes, Florestan. *A integração do negro na sociedade de classes.* São Paulo: Dominus Ed., 1965.
Fernandes, Florestan. *O significado do protesto negro.* São Paulo: Cortez Editora, 1989.
Fernandes, Florestan, and Roger Bastide. *Relacões raciais entre brancos e negros em São Paulo.* São Paulo: Anhembi, 1955.
Fernandes, Neusa, and Olinio Gomes P. Coelho, eds. *História e geografia do Vale do Paraíba.* Vassouras: Instituto Histórico e Geográfico de Vassouras, 2013.
Ferrara, Miriam Nicolau. *A imprensa negra paulista (1915–1963).* São Paulo: FFLCH/USP, 1986.
Ferreira, Antonio Celso. *A epopéia bandeirante: Letrados, instituições, invenção histórica (1870–1940).* São Paulo: Editora UNESP, 2002.
Ferreira, Barros. *O nobre e antigo bairro da Sé.* São Paulo: Secretaria de educação e cultura, 2017.
Filme, Geraldo. "Interview." In *A música brasileira por seus intérpretes,* 69–83. São Paulo: SESC, 2000.
Filme, Geraldo. "Tradição (vai no Bexiga para ver)." *Geraldo Filme: Memória Eldorado.* Eldorado, 2003, compact disc. Originally released in 1980.
Filme, Geraldo. "Último sambista." Recorded by Germano Mathias. *História do Samba Paulista I.* CPC-UMES, 1999, compact disc.
Filme, Geraldo. "Vou sambar n'outro lugar." *Em Prosa e Samba: Nas Quebradas do Mundaréu.* Warner Music Brasil, 2011, compact disc. Originally released in 1974.

Fischer, Brodwyn M. *A Poverty of Rights: Citizenship and Inequality in Twentieth-Century Rio de Janeiro*. Stanford, CA: Stanford University Press, 2008.

Fischer, Brodwyn M., Bryan McCann, and Javier Auyero, eds. *Cities from Scratch: Poverty and Informality in Urban Latin America*. Durham, NC: Duke University Press, 2014.

Fontes, Alice. "A prática abolicionista em São Paulo: Os caifases (1882–1888)." Master's thesis, USP, 1976.

Fontes, Paulo. *Migration and the Making of Industrial São Paulo*. Durham, NC: Duke University Press, 2016.

Fontes, Paulo. "Trabalhadores e associativismo urbano no governo Jânio Quadros em São Paulo (1953–1954)." *Revista Brasileira de História* 33, no. 66 (2013): 71–94.

Fontes, Paulo. *Um nordeste em São Paulo: Trabalhadores migrantes em são Miguel Paulista (1945–66)*. Rio de Janeiro: Editora FGV, 2008.

Frank, Zephyr, and Whitney Berry. "The Slave Market in Rio de Janeiro Circa 1869: Context, Movement and Social Experience." *Journal of Latin American Geography* 9, no. 3 (2010): 85–110.

Franscisco, Renata Ribeiro. "Periodização e práticas antiescravistas na Cidade de São Paulo (1850–1871)." *Sankofa. Revista de História da África e de Estudos da Diáspora Africana* 6, no. 12 (December 2013): 39–58.

Frazier, John W., ed. *Multicultural Geographies: The Changing Racial/Ethnic Patterns of the United States*. Albany: State University of New York Press, 2010.

Freitas, Décio. *República de Palmares: Pesquisa e comentários em documentos históricos do século XVII*. Maceió-Alagoas: EDUFAL, 2004.

French, Jan Hoffman. *Legalizing Identities: Becoming Black or Indian in Brazil's Northeast*. Chapel Hill: University of North Carolina Press, 2009.

French, John D. *The Brazilian Workers' ABC: Class Conflict and Alliances in Modern São Paulo*. Chapel Hill: University of North Carolina Press, 1992.

Frers, Lars, and Lars Meier, eds. *Encountering Urban Places: Visual and Material Performances in the City*. Burlington, VT: Ashgate, 2007.

Freyre, Gilberto. *The Masters and the Slaves*. Translated by Samuel Putnam. Berkeley: University of California Press, 1986. Originally published in Portuguese in 1933.

Freyre, Gilberto. *O escravo nos anúncios de jornais brasileiros do século XIX*. São Paulo: Nacional, 1979.

Galtung, Johan. "Violence, Peace and Peace Research," *Journal of Peace Research* 6, no. 3 (1969): 167–91.

Gao-Miles, Linling. "Beyond the Ethnic Enclave: Interethnicity and Trans-Spatiality in an Australian Suburb." *City and Society* 29, no. 1 (2017): 82–103.

Gerber, Raquel, dir. *Orí*. Written by Beatriz Nascimento. Versatil Home Video, 1989. Third World Newsreel, 2008.

Gilroy, Paul. *The Black Atlantic: Modernity and Double Consciousness*. Cambridge, MA: Harvard University Press, 1995.

Gilroy, Paul. *"There Ain't No Black in the Union Jack": The Cultural Politics of Race and Nation*. Chicago: University of Chicago Press, 1991.

Gomes, Tiago de Melo. "Para além da casa da Tia Ciata: Outras experiências no universo cultural carioca, 1830–1930." *Afro-Ásia*, no. 29/30 (2003): 175–98.

Gomez, Michael A. *Exchanging Our Country Marks: The Transformation of African Identities in the Colonial and Antebellum South*. Chapel Hill: University of North Carolina Press, 1998.

Gouvêa, José Paulo Neves. "Cidade do mapa: Produção do espaço através de suas representações." Master's thesis, USP, 2010.

Graden, Dale T. *From Slavery to Freedom in Brazil: Bahia, 1835–1900*. Albuquerque: University of New Mexico Press, 2006.

Graham, Jessica Lynn. *Shifting the Meaning of Democracy: Race, Politics, and Culture in the United States and Brazil*. Berkeley: University of California Press, 2019.

Graham, Richard. "Another Middle Passage? The Internal Slave Trade in Brazil." In *The Chattel Principle: Internal Slave Trades in the Americas*, edited by Walter Johnson. New Haven, CT: Yale University Press, 2005.

Gregory, Ian N., and Alistair Geddes, eds. *Toward Spatial Humanities: Historical GIS and Spatial History*. Bloomington: Indiana University Press, 2014.

Guimarães, Antônio Sérgio. "Como trabalhar com 'raça' em sociologia." *Educação e Pesquisa* 29, no. 1 (2003): 93–107.

Guimarães, Antônio Sérgio. *Racismo e anti-racismo no Brasil*. São Paulo: Editora 34, 1999.

Guimarães, Antonio Sérgio, and Márcio Macedo. "*Diário Trabalhista* e democracia racial negra dos anos 1940." *Dados* 51, no. 1 (2008): 143–82.

Guimarães, Bernardo. *Rosaura, a enjeitada*. Rio de Janeiro: Garnier, 1914.

Guimarães, Lais de Barros Monteiro. *Liberdade*. São Paulo: Prefeitura do Município de São Paulo, Secretaria Municipal de Cultura, 1978.

Guzmán, Tracy Devine. *Native and National in Brazil: Indigeneity After Independence*. Chapel Hill: University of North Carolina Press, 2013.

Habib, Paula Arantes Botelho Brigli. "Eis o mundo encantado que Monteiro Lobato criou: Raça, eugenia e nação." Master's thesis, UNICAMP, 2003.

Haddad, Emílio. "Sobre o estudo da divisão da cidade em zonas homogêneas." PhD diss., FAU-USP, 1987.

Hagopian, Frances. "Paradoxes of Democracy and Citizenship in Brazil." *Latin American Research Review* 46, no. 3 (2011): 216–27.

Hale, Lindsay. "Catimbó." In *African-American Religious Cultures*, edited by Anthony P. Binn. Santa Barbara, CA: ABC-CLIO, 2009.

Hall, Stuart. "Gramsci's Relevance for the Study of Race and Ethnicity." In *Stuart Hall: Critical Dialogues in Cultural Studies*, edited by Kuan-Hsing Chen and David Morley. New York: Routledge, 1996.

Hanchard, Michael. *Orpheus and Power: The Movimento Negro of Rio de Janeiro and São Paulo, Brazil, 1945–1988*. Princeton, NJ: Princeton University Press, 1998.

Handa, Tomoo. *O imigrante japonês: História de sua vida no Brasil*. São Paulo: T. A. Queiroz, Centro de Estudos Nipo-Brasileiros, 1987.

Harley, J. Brian. "Maps, Knowledge, and Power." In *Geographic Thought: A Praxis Perspective*, edited by George Henderson and Marvin Waterstone. New York: Routledge, 2008.

Harney, Stefano, and Fred Moten. *The Undercommons: Fugitive Planning and Black Study*. Wivenhoe, NY: Minor Compositions, 2013.

Hartman, Saidiya. *Lose Your Mother: Journeys Along the Atlantic Slave Route*. New York: Farrar, Straus and Giroux, 2007.

Harvey, David. *Cosmopolitanism and the Geographies of Freedom*. New York: Columbia University Press, 2009.

Harvey, David. *Social Justice and the City*. Athens: University of Georgia Press, 2009.

Henderson, Jason. "Secessionist Automobility: Racism, Anti-Urbanism, and the Politics of Automobility in Atlanta, Georgia." *International Journal of Urban and Regional Research* 30, no. 2 (2006): 293–307.

Hernandez, Felipe, Peter Kellett, and Lea K. Allen, eds. *Rethinking the Informal City: Critical Perspectives from Latin America*. Oxford: Berghahn, 2012.

Hertzman, Marc A. *Making Samba: A New History of Race and Music in Brazil*. Durham, NC: Duke University Press, 2013.

Hidalgo, Bruno Dantas. "As divisões territoriais do Município de São Paulo: Uma proposta de classificação por meio da análise dos Distritos." Undergraduate thesis (TCC), USP, 2003.

Highsmith, Andrew R. *Demolition Means Progress: Flint, Michigan, and the Fate of the American Metropolis*. Chicago: University of Chicago Press, 2016.

Hirschfeld, Katherine. "Rethinking 'Structural Violence.'" *Society* 54 (2017): 156–62.

Holston, James. *Insurgent Citizenship: Disjunctions of Democracy and Modernity in Brazil*. Princeton, NJ: Princeton University Press, 2008.

Holston, James. *The Modernist City: An Anthropological Critique of Brasília*. Chicago: University of Chicago Press, 2000.

hooks, bell. *Feminist Theory: From Margin to Center*. 2nd ed. Cambridge, MA: South End Press, 2000. First edition published in 1984.

Hosokawa, Shuhei. "Dancing in the Tomb of Samba: Japanese-Brazilian Presence/Absence in the São Paulo Carnival." In *Diasporas and Interculturalism in Asian Performing Arts: Translating Traditions*, edited by Hae-kyung Um. New York: Routledge Curzon, 2005.

Huchzermeyer, Marie. *Unlawful Occupation: Informal Settlements and Urban Policy in South Africa and Brazil*. Trenton, NJ: Africa World Press, 2004.

Ianni, Octávio. *Industrialização e desenvolvimento social no Brasil*. Rio de Janeiro: Editôra Civilização Brasileira, 1963.

Ianni, Octávio. *Raças e classes sociais no Brasil*. Rio de Janiero: Civilização Brasileira, 1972.

Ioris, Rafael R. *Transforming Brazil: A History of National Development in the Postwar Era*. New York: Routledge, 2014.

Irazábal, Clara. *City Making and Urban Governance in the Americas: Curitiba and Portland*. Aldershot, UK: Ashgate, 2005.

Jacino, Ramatis. *Desigualdade racial no Brasil: Causas e consequências*. São Paulo: ÌMÓ Editora, 2019.

Jackson, Kenneth T. *Crabgrass Frontier: The Suburbanization of the United States*. Oxford: Oxford University Press, 1987.

Janovitch, Paula Ester. "Além muros . . ." *Cidade: Revista do Departamento do Patrimônio Histórico/Secretaria Municipal da Cultura* 3 (1996).

Janovitch, Paula Ester. "Borba Gato: A estátua mais cafona e polêmica da cidade." *Demonumenta*. Accessed August 27, 2025. http://demonumenta.fau.usp.br/borba-gato/.

Jehá, Regina, dir. *Bexiga: Ano Zero*. Lauper Filmes, 1971. Filmoteca da Emplasa. Posted November 26, 2014, by Emplasa, YouTube, https://youtu.be/Ee5xRCsbsSE?si=hlGJcpU9goeD6pFJ.

Jenks, Hillary. "'Home Is Little Tokyo': Race, Community, and Memory in Twentieth-Century Los Angeles." PhD diss., University of Southern California, 2008.

Jesus, Carolina Maria de. *Quarto de despejo: Diário de uma favelada*. São Paulo: Ática, 2014. Originally published in 1960.

Johnson, Rashauna. *Slavery's Metropolis: Unfree Labor in New Orleans During the Age of Revolutions*. Cambridge: Cambridge University Press, 2016.

Johnson, Walter. *Soul by Soul: Life Inside the Antebellum Slave Market*. Cambridge, MA: Harvard University Press, 1999.

Jorge, Janes. *Tietê, o rio que a cidade perdeu: São Paulo 1890–1940*. São Paulo: Alameda, 2006.

Júnior, João Feres, Leonardo Fernandes Nascimento, and Zena Winona Eisenberg. "Monteiro Lobato e o politicamente correto." *Dados* 56, no. 1 (2013): 69–108.

Karam, John Tokif. *Another Arabesque: Syrian-Lebanese Ethnicity in Neoliberal Brazil*. Philadelphia: Temple University Press, 2007.

Khan-Perry, Keisha. *Black Women Against the Land Grab: The Fight for Racial Justice in Brazil*. Minneapolis: University of Minnesota Press, 2013. Kindle edition.

Kidder, Daniel P. *Sketches of Residence and Travels in Brazil, Embracing Historical and Geographical Notices of the Empire and Its Several Provinces*. Vol. 1. Philadelphia: Sorin and Ball; London: Wiley and Putnam, 1845.

Kishimoto, Alexandre. "A experiência do cinema japonês no bairro da Liberdade." Master's thesis, Universidade de São Paulo, 2009.

Klein, Herbert S. *The Atlantic Slave Trade*. Cambridge: Cambridge University Press, 1999.

Klein, Herbert S. "The Internal Slave Trade in Nineteenth-Century Brazil: A Study of Slave Importations into Rio de Janeiro in 1852." *Hispanic American Historical Review* 51, no. 4 (1971): 567–85.

Klein, Misha. *Kosher Feijoada and Other Paradoxes of Jewish Life in São Paulo*. Gainesville: University Press of Florida, 2012.

Klein, Norman M. *The History of Forgetting: Los Angeles and the Erasure of Memory*. London: Verso, 2008.

Knowles, Caroline. *Race and Social Analysis*. London: Sage, 2003.

Kowarick, Lúcio, and Nabil Bonduki. "Espaço urbano e espaço político: Do populismo à redemocratização." In *As lutas sociais e a cidade: São Paulo, passado e presente*, edited by Clara Ant and Lúcio Kowarick. São Paulo: Paz e Terra, 1988.

Kucinski, Bernardo. *Jornalistas e revolucionários: Nos tempos da imprensa alternativa*. São Paulo: EDUSP, 2003.

Kuznesof, Elizabeth Anne. *Household Economy and Urban Development: São Paulo, 1765 to 1836*. Boulder, CO: Westview, 1986.

Lab Cidade. "Narradores do Jardim Paraná." Do Morro Produções, 2011. https://www.youtube.com/watch?v=ByQyVXSyUWk.

La Cava, Gloria. *Italians in Brazil: The Post-WWII Experience*. New York: Peter Lang, 1999.

Lanna, Ana Lúcia Duarte. "O Bexiga e os italianos em São Paulo." In *São Paulo, os estrangeiros e a construção das cidades*, edited by Ana Lúcia Duarte Lanna, Fernanda Arêas Peixoto, José Tavares Correia de Lira, and Maria Ruth Amaral de Samaio. São Paulo: Alameda, 2011.

Lefebvre, Henri. *The Production of Space*. Translated by Donald Nicholson-Smith. Malden, MA: Blackwell, 1991. Originally published in French in 1974.

Leite, José Correia, and Cuti. *. . . E disse o velho militante*. São Paulo: Secretaria Municipal de Cultura, 1992.

Leme, Maria Cristina da Silva. "ReVisão do Plano de Avenida: Estudo sobre o planejamento urbano em São Paulo, 1930." PhD diss., FAU-USP, 1990.

Leme, Maria Cristina da Silva. "São Paulo: Conflitos e consensus para construção da metrópole: 1930–1945." In *Urbanismo na era Vargas: A transformação das cidades brasileiras*, edited by Vera Rezende. Niterói: Editora da UFF, 2012.

Leme, Maria Cristina da Silva. "Transforming the Modern Latin American City: Robert Moses and the International Basic Economic Corporation." *Planning Perspectives* 25, no. 4 (2010): 515–28.

Leme, Maria Cristina da Silva, ed. *Urbanismo no Brasil: 1895–1965*. São Paulo: Studio Nobel, 1999.

Lesser, Jeffrey. *A Discontented Diaspora: Japanese Brazilians and the Meanings of Ethnic Militancy, 1960–1980*. Durham, NC: Duke University Press, 2007.

Lesser, Jeffrey. *Immigration, Ethnicity, and National Identity in Brazil, 1808 to the Present*. Cambridge: Cambridge University Press, 2013.

Lesser, Jeffrey. *Negotiating National Identity: Immigrants, Minorities, and the Struggle for Ethnicity in Brazil*. Durham, NC: Duke University Press, 1999.

Leu, Lorraine. *Defiant Geographies: Race and Urban Space in 1920s Rio de Janeiro*. Pittsburgh, PA: University of Pittsburgh Press, 2020.

Levi, Darrell E. *The Prados of São Paulo, Brazil: An Elite Family and Social Change, 1840–1930*. Athens: University of Georgia Press, 1987.

Levine, Robert M. *O regime de Vargas: Os anos críticos, 1934–1938*. Rio de Janeiro: Nova Fronteira, 1980.

Lévi-Strauss, Claude. *Tristes Tropiques*. Translated by John Weightman and Doreen Weightman. New York: Penguin, 2012. Originally published in French in 1955.

Lima, Dulcilei da Conceição. "Desvendando Luíza Mahin: Um mito libertário no cerne do feminismo negro." Master's thesis, Universidade Presbiteriana Mackenzie, 2011.

Lin, Jan. *The Power of Urban Ethnic Places: Cultural Heritage and Community Life*. New York: Routledge, 2011.

Loitero, Wagner, and Fernando Ripol. "Hino do Samba do Congo." *Samba do Congo: Nossa Quebrada*. Self-released, 2016, compact disc.

Lopes, Maria Aparecida de Oliveira. "As representações sociais da mãe negra na Cidade de São Paulo (1945–1978)." *Patrimônio e Memória* 3, no. 2 (2007): 124–46.

Lou, Jackie Jia. *The Linguistic Landscape of Chinatown: A Sociolinguistic Ethnography*. Bristol: Multilingual Matters, 2016.

Love, Joseph. *São Paulo in the Brazilian Federation, 1889–1937*. Stanford, CA: Stanford University Press, 1980.

Lovejoy, Paul E. "The Volume of the Atlantic Slave Trade: A Synthesis." *Journal of African History* 23, no. 4 (1982): 473–501.

Lowrie, Samuel. "O elemento Negro na população de São Pauo." *Revista do Arquivo Municipal* 48 (1938): 5–57.

Luca, Tania Regina de. *São Paulo no século XX*. São Paulo: Organização Poiesis Social de Cultura, 2011.

Lucena, Célia Toledo. *Bairro do Bexiga: A sobrevivência cultural.* São Paulo: Brasiliense, 1984.

Lucrécio, Francisco. "Interview." In *Frente Negra Brasileira: Depoimentos: Projeto de dinamização de espaços literários afro-brasileiros*, edited by Márcio Barbosa, 35–64. São Paulo: Quilombhoje, 1998.

Luna, Francisco Vidal, and Herbert S. Klein. *Slavery and the Economy of São Paulo, 1750–1850.* Stanford, CA: Stanford University Press, 2003.

Machado, Angileli Cecilia Maria de Morais. "Paisagem revelada no cotidiano da periferia: Distrito de Brasilândia, Zona Norte do Município de São Paulo." Master's thesis, Universidade de São Paulo, 2007.

Machado, Maria Helena P. T. *Crime e escravidão: Trabalho, luta e resistência nas Lavouras Paulistas (1930–1888).* São Paulo: EDUSP, 2014.

Machado, Maria Helena P. T. "Sendo cativo nas ruas: A escravidão urbana na Cidade de São Paulo." In *História da Cidade de São Paulo*, edited by Paula Porta. São Paulo: Paz e Terra, 2004.

Magalhães, Mário. *Marighella: O guerrilheiro que incendiou o mundo.* São Paulo: Companhia das Letras, 2012.

Maia, Francisco Prestes. *Estudo de um plano de avenidas para a cidade de São Paulo.* São Paulo: Companhia Melhoramentos de São Paulo, 1930.

Maia, Francisco Prestes. *Os melhoramentos de São Paulo.* São Paulo: Imprensa Oficial do Estado de São Paulo, 1945.

Maia, Francisco Prestes, and João Florence d'Ulhôa Cintra. "Um problema actual: Os grandes melhoramentos de São Paulo." *Boletim do Instituto de Engenharia* 6, no. 25, (1924): 56–60, 91–94, 121–32, 225–32.

Maio, Marcos Chor. "UNESCO and the Study of Race Relations in Brazil: Regional or National Issue?" *Latin American Research Review* 36, no. 2 (2001): 118–36.

Maio, Marcos Chor, and Rosemary Galli. "Florestan Fernandes, Oracy Nogueira, and the UNESCO Project on Race Relations in São Paulo." *Latin American Perspectives* 38, no. 3 (May 2011): 136–49.

Maisonnave, Fabiano. "The Girl from Shinjuku." In *Global Latin America: Into the Twenty-First Century*, edited by Jeffrey Lesser and Matthew Gutmann. Berkeley: University of California Press, 2016.

Marcílio, Maria Luiza. *A Cidade de São Paulo: Povoamento e população, 1750–1850*, 2nd ed. São Paulo: EDUSP, 2014.

Marcuse, Peter. "Enclaves Yes, Ghettos No: Segregation and the State." In *Desegregating the City: Ghettos, Enclaves, and Inequality*, edited by David Varady. New York: State University of New York Press, 2005.

Marques, Gabriel. *Ruas e tradições de São Paulo: Uma história em cada rua.* São Paulo: Conselho Estadual de Cultura, 1966.

Marx, Anthony W. *Making Race and Nation: Comparison of South Africa, the United States, and Brazil.* Cambridge: Cambridge University Press, 1998.

Marzola, Nádia. *Bela Vista: História de bairros de São Paulo*. 2nd ed. São Paulo: Prefeitura da Cidade de São Paulo, 1985.

Massey, Doreen. "Double Articulation: A Place in the World." In *Displacements: Cultural Identities in Question*, edited by Angelika Bammer. Bloomington: Indiana University Press, 1994.

Massey, Doreen. *For Space*. London: Sage, 2005.

Massey, Doreen. "A Global Sense of Place." In *The Cultural Geography Reader*, edited by Timothy Oakes and Patricia Price. New York: Routledge, 2008.

Massey, Douglas, and Nancy Denton. *American Apartheid: Segregation and the Making of the Underclass*. Cambridge, MA: Harvard University Press, 1990.

Matory, J. Lorand. *Black Atlantic Religion: Tradition, Transnationalism, and Matriarchy in the Afro-Brazilian Candomblé*. Princeton, NJ: Princeton University Press, 2005.

McCann, Bryan. *Hard Times in the Marvelous City: From Dictatorship to Democracy in the Favelas of Rio de Janeiro*. Durham, NC: Duke University Press, 2014.

McCann, Bryan. *Hello, Hello Brazil: Popular Music in the Making of Modern Brazil*. Durham, NC: Duke University Press, 2004.

Meade, Teresa A. *"Civilizing" Rio: Reform and Resistance in a Brazilian City, 1889–1930*. University Park: Pennsylvania State University Press, 1997.

Medina, Cremilda, ed. *Ó freguesia, quantas histórias*. São Paulo: USP/ECA, 2000.

Mentone, Renato Lagos. "Plano metropolitano de desenvolvimento integrado da Grande São Paulo/PMDI-GSP, 1970: Da expectativa ao desconhecimento." Master's thesis, FAU USP, 2015.

Metcalf, Alida C. *Go-Betweens and the Colonization of Brazil: 1500–1600*. Austin: University of Texas Press, 2006.

Miki, Yuko. *Frontiers of Citizenship: A Black and Indigenous History of Postcolonial Brazil*. Cambridge: Cambridge University Press, 2018.

Mira, Maria Celeste. "O leitor e a banca de revistas: O caso de Editora Abril." PhD diss., UNICAMP, 1997.

Miraftab, Faranak. "Insurgent Planning: Situating Radical Planning in the Global South." *Planning Theory* 8, no. 1 (2009): 32–50.

Monroe, Alicia. "Brotherhoods of Their Own: Black Confraternities and Civic Leadership in São Paulo, Brazil, 1850–1920." PhD diss., Emory University, 2014.

Monsma, Karl. *A reprodução de racismo: Fazendeiros, negros e imigrantes no oeste paulista, 1880–1914*. São Carlos: EdUFSCar, 2016.

Monteiro, John Manuel. *Negros da terra: Indíos e bandeirantes nas origins de São Paulo*. São Paulo: Companhia das Letras, 1994.

Moraes, José Geraldo Vinci de. "Polifonia na metrópole: História e música popular em São Paulo." *Tempo* 10 (2000): 39–62.

Moreno, Júlio. *Memórias de Armandinho do Bexiga*. São Paulo: Editora SENAC, 1996.

Morgan, Arthur. *Os engenheiros de São Paulo em 1932: Pela lei e pela ordem*. São Paulo: N.p., 1934.

Morse, Richard. *The Bandeirantes: The Historical Role of Brazilian Pathfinders*. New York: Alfred A. Knopf, 1965.

Morse, Richard. *From Community to Metropolis: A Biography of São Paulo, Brazil*. Gainesville: University of Florida Press, 1958.

Motta, Márcia Maria Menendes. "Classic Works of Brazil's New Rural History: Feudalism and the Latifundio in the Interpretations of the Left (1940/1964)." *Historia Critica* 51 (September–December 2013): 121–44.

Moura, Paulo Cursino de. *São Paulo de outrora: Evocações da metrópole*. São Paulo: Editora Comp. Melhoramentos de S. Paulo, 1932.

Moura, Roberto. *Tia Ciata e a Pequena África no Rio de Janeiro*. Rio de Janeiro: Prefeitura da Cidade do Rio de Janeiro, Secretaria Municipal de Cultura, 1995.

Musterd, Sako, Zoltán Kovács, and Zoltn Kovcs, eds. *Place-Making and Policies for Competitive Cities*. West Sussex, UK: Wiley-Blackwell, 2013.

Nascimento, Abdias do. *Brazil: Mixture or Massacre? Essays on the Genocide of a Black People*. 2nd ed. Dover, MA: Majority Press, 1989.

Nascimento, Abdias do. *Racial Democracy in Brazil, Myth or Reality? A Dossier of Brazilian Racism*. Ibadan, Nigeria: Sketch, 1977.

Nascimento, Larissa. "Entre sambas e rezas: Vivências, negociações e ressignificações da cultura afro-brasileira no Bexiga." Master's thesis, Federal University of São Carlos, 2014.

Nascimento, Larissa. "'Lembrança eu tenho da Saracura': Notas sobre a população negra e as reconfigurações urbanas no bairro do Bexiga." *Intratextos* 6, no. 1 (2014): 25–50.

Nascimento, Luz, and Luiz do Pandeiro. "Metrô da Brasilândia." On *Luz nascimento*. Angel Artes Produções Artísticas, 2013, compact disc.

Nascimento, Maria Beatriz. *The Dialectic Is in the Sea: The Black Radical Thought of Beatriz Nascimento*. Edited by Christen A. Smith, Bethânia N. F. Gomes, and Archie Davies. Princeton, NJ: Princeton University Press, 2023.

Neely, Brooke, and Michelle Samura. "Social Geographies of Race: Connecting Race and Space." *Ethnic and Racial Studies* 34, no. 11 (2011): 1933–52.

Nelson, Jennifer. *Razing Africville: A Geography of Racism*. Toronto: University of Toronto Press, 2009.

Nightingale, Carl H. *Segregation: A Global History of Divided Cities*. Chicago: University of Chicago Press, 2012.

Nishida, Mieko. *Diaspora and Identity: Japanese Brazilians in Brazil and Japan.* Honolulu: University of Hawai'i Press, 2018.

Noelli, Francisco, and Lúcio Mota. "Índios, jesuítas, bandeirantes e espanhóis no Guairá dos séculos XVI e XVII." *Revista GeoNotas* 3, no. 3 (1999).

Nogueira, Oracy. "Preconceito racial de marca e preconceito racial de origem: Sugestão de um quadro de referência para a interpretação do material sobre relações raciais no Brasil." XXXI Congresso Internacional de Americanistas, 1954. Reprinted in *Tempo Social, revista de sociologia da usp* 19, no. 1 (November 2006): 287–308.

Nora, Pierre. "Between Memory and History: Les Lieux de Mémoire." *Representations* 26 (Spring 1989): 7–24.

O'Donnell, Júlia. "A cidade branca: Benjamim Costallat e o Rio de Janeiro dos anos 1920." *História Social* 22/23 (July 2003): 117–41.

O'Dougherty, Maureen. *Consumption Intensified: The Politics of Middle-Class Daily Life in Brazil.* Durham, NC: Duke University Press, 2002.

Ogawa, Alfredo, ed. *100 anos da imigração japonesa: As surpreendentes histórias do povo que ajudou a mudar o Brasil.* São Paulo: Editora Abril, 2008.

Oliveira, André Côrtes de. "Quem é a 'Gente Negra Nacional'? Frente Negra Brasileira e *A Voz da Raça* (1933–1937)." Master's thesis, UNICAMP, 2006.

Oliveira, Reinaldo José de. "Segregação urbana e racial na Cidade de São Paulo: As periferias de Brasilândia, Cidade Tiradentes e Jardim Ângela." PhD diss., PUC-SP, 2000.

Oliveira, Reinaldo José de. *Territorialidade negra e segregação racial na Cidade de São Paulo.* São Paulo: Alameda Casa Editorial, 2016.

Oliveira, Robson da Silva, Maria Aparecida Papali, and Cilene Gomes. "Cotidiano, cultura e resistência: Terra Indígena Guarani do Pico do Jaraguá-SP." *Cadernos do ceom* 34, no. 54 (June 2021): 242–57.

Omi, Michael, and Howard Winant. *Racial Formation in the United States: From the 1960s to the 1990s.* New York: Routledge, 1994.

Osvaldinho da Cuíca. *História do Samba Paulista I.* CPC-UMES, 1999, compact disc.

O'Toole, Rachel Sarah. *Bound Lives: Africans Indians and the Making of Race in Colonial Peru.* Pittsburgh, PA: University of Pittsburgh Press, 2012.

Outtes, Joel. "Disciplining Society Through the City: The Birth of *Urbanismo* (City Planning) in Brazil, 1916–1941." PhD thesis, Oxford University, 2000.

Owensby, Brian P. *Intimate Ironies: Modernity and the Making of Middle-Class Lives in Brazil.* Stanford, CA: Stanford University Press, 1999.

Paixão, Marcelo J. P. *Desenvolvimento humano e relações raciais.* Rio de Janeiro: Lamparina, 2003.

Paixão, Marcelo, and Luiz M. Carvano. *Relatório anual das desigualdades raciais no Brasil, 2007–2008*. São Paulo: Garamond, 2008.

Paixão, Marcelo, Irene Rossetto, Fabiana Montovanele, and Luiz M. Carvano, eds. *Relatório anual das desigualdades raciais no Brasil, 2009–2010*. Rio de Janeiro: Editora Garamond Ltda, 2010.

Passos, Maria Lucia Perrone de Faro. *Desenhando Sao Paulo: Mapas e literatura, 1877–1954*. São Paulo: Editora Senac, 2008.

Patterson, Orlando. *Slavery and Social Death: A Comparative Study*. Cambridge, MA: Harvard University Press, 2018. Originally published in 1982.

Paula, Zueleide Casagrande de. *A cidade e os jardins: Jardim América, de projeto urbano a monumento patrimonial (1915–1986)*. São Paulo: Editora UNESP, 2008.

Paulillo, Maria Célia Rua de Almeida. *Tradição e modernidade: Afonso Schmidt e a literatura paulista, 1906–1928*. São Paulo: Annablume, 2002.

Paviani, Aldo. *Brasília, ideologia e realidade: Espaco urbano em questao*. Brasilia: Universidade de Brasilia, 2010.

Peixoto-Mehrtens, Cristina. *Urban Space and National Identity in Early Twentieth Century São Paulo, Brazil: Crafting Modernity*. New York: Palgrave Macmillan, 2010.

Pemberton, Simon, and Jenny Phillimore. "Migrant Place-Making in Super-Diverse Neighbourhoods: Moving Beyond Ethno-National Approaches." *Urban Studies* 55, no. 4 (2018): 733–50.

Pendall, Rolf, Juliet Gainsborough, Kate Lowe, and Mai Nguyen. "Bringing Equity to Transit Oriented Development: Stations, Systems, and Regional Resilience." In *Urban and Regional Policy and Its Effects: Building Resilient Regions*, edited by Margaret Weir, Nancy Pindus, Howard Wial, and Harold Wolman. Washington, DC: Brookings Institution Press, 2012.

Perlman, Janice. "The Myth of Marginality Revisited." In *Becoming Global and the New Poverty of Cities*, edited by Lisa M. Hanley, Blair A Ruble, and Joseph S. Tulchin. Washington, DC: Woodrow Wilson International Center for Scholars, 2005.

Perlman, Janice. *The Myth of Marginality: Urban Poverty and Politics in Rio de Janeiro*. Berkeley: University of California Press, 1980.

Pierson, Donald. "Habitações de São Paulo: Estudo comparativo." *Revista do Arquivo Municipal* 81 (January–Febrary 1942): 199–238.

Pinho, Patricia de Santana. *Reinvenções da África na Bahia*. São Paulo: Editora Annablume, 2004.

Portes, Alejandro, and Robert D. Manning. "The Immigrant Enclave: Theory and Empirical Examples." In *The Urban Sociology Reader*, edited by Jan Lin and Christopher Mele. New York: Routledge, 2005.

Porto, Antônio Rodrigues. *História urbanística da Cidade de São Paulo (1554 a 1988)*. São Paulo: Carthago e Forte, 1992.

Prado, Fábio da Silva. "Avenida 9 de Julho." *Revista do Arquivo Municipal* 2, no. 14 (July 1935): 3–5.
Prandi, Reginaldo. *Herdeiras do axé: Sociologia das religiões afro-brasileiras.* São Paulo: Editora Hucitec, 1996.
Prandi, Reginaldo. *Os Candomblês de São Paulo: A velha magia na metrópole nova.* São Paulo: HUCITEC, 1991.
Quintão, Antonia Aparecida. *Irmandades negras: Outro espaço de luta e resistência, São Paulo: 1870–1890.* São Paulo: Annablume, 2002.
Ramos Schiffer, Sueli. "Economic Restructuring and Urban Segregation in São Paulo." In *Of States and Cities: The Partitioning of Urban Space,* edited by Peter Marcuse and Ronald van Kempen. Oxford: Oxford University Press, 2012.
Randolph, Ranier. "A nova perspectiva do planejamento subversivo e suas (possiveis) implicacoes para a formacao do planejador urbano e regional: O caso brasileiro." *Scripta Nova (Barcelona)* 12 (2008): 98–110.
Read, Ian. "Off the Block but Within the Neighborhood: The Local Slave Trade in São Paulo." *Slavery and Abolition* 33, no. 1 (2012): 21–42.
Reis, João José. *Slave Rebellion in Brazil: The Muslim Uprising of 1835 in Bahia.* Baltimore, MD: Johns Hopkins University Press, 1995.
Reynolds, Susan. *Before Eminent Domain: Toward a History of Expropriation of Land for the Common Good.* Chapel Hill: University of North Carolina Press, 2010.
Ricoeur, Paul. *Memory, History, Forgetting.* Chicago: University of Chicago Press, 2006.
Rio, João do. *Religions in Rio.* Translated by Ana Lessa-Schmidt. Hanover, CT: New London Librarium, 2015. Originally published in Portuguese in 1904.
Rio, Vicente del, and William J. Siembieda, eds. *Contemporary Urbanism in Brazil: Beyond Brasília.* Gainesville: University Press of Florida, 2009.
Ripol, Fernando, and Márcio Bonfim. "Nossa quebrada." *Samba do Congo: Nossa quebrada.* Self-released, 2016, compact disc.
Rocha, Cristine Maria Famer. "A escola na mídia: Nada fora do controle." PhD diss., UF-Rio Grande do Sul, 2005.
Rodrigues, Gustavo Partezani. *Vias públicas: Tipo e construção em São Paulo (1898–1945).* São Paulo: Imprensa Oficial, 2010.
Rogers, Thomas D. *The Deepest Wounds: A Labor and Environmental History of Sugar in Northeast Brazil.* Chapel Hill: University of North Carolina Press, 2010.
Rolim, Mariana de Souza. "Luis Saia e a idéia de patrimônio." Master's thesis, Universidade Presbiteriana Mackenzie, 2006.
Rolnik, Raquel. *A cidade e a lei: Legislação, política urbana e territórios na Cidade de São Paulo.* São Paulo: FAPESP/Studio Nobel, 1997.

Rolnik, Raquel. "The City and the Law: Legislation, Urban Policy, and Territories in the City of Sao Paulo (1886–1936)." PhD diss., New York University, 1995.

Rolnik, Raquel. "Territórios Negros nas Cidades Brasileiras: Etnicidade e Cidade em São Paulo e Rio de Janeiro." *Estudos Afro-Asiáticos* 17 (1989): 29–41.

Rolph-Trouillot, Michel. *Silencing the Past: Power and the Production of History*. Boston: Beacon, 1995.

Romo, Anadelia A. *Brazil's Living Museum: Race, Reform, and Tradition in Bahia*. Chapel Hill: University of North Carolina Press, 2010.

Rosa, Marcus Vinicius de Freitas. "Além da invisibilidade: História social do racismo em Porto Alegre durante o pós-abolição (1884–1918)." PhD diss., UNICAMP, 2014.

Rothstein, Richard. *The Color of Law: A Forgotten History of How Our Government Segregated America*. New York: Liveright, 2017.

Russell-Wood, A. J. R. "Rethinking Bandeirismo in Colonial Brazil." *The Americas* 61, no. 3 (2005): 353–71.

Sá, Bassan Gomes de, ed. *200 Anos de Paróquia*. São Paulo: Arquidiocese de São Paulo, 1996.

Sachs-Jeantet, Céline. *São Paulo: Políticas públicas e habitação popular*. São Paulo: EDUSP, 1990.

Saito, Hiroshi, ed. *A presença japonesa no Brasil*. São Paulo: T. A. Queiroz, 1980.

Sakurai, Célia. "A imigração dos japoneses para o brasil no pós-guerra (1950–1980)." In *Cem anos da imigração japonesa: História, memória e arte*, edited by Francisco Hashimoto, Janete Leiko Tanno, and Monica Setuyo Okamoto. São Paulo: UNESP, 2008, 189–239.

Salles, Ricardo, and Rafael de Bivar Marquese. *Escravidão e capitalismo histórico no século XIX: Cuba, Brasil, Estados Unidos*. Rio de Janeiro: Civilização Brasileira, 2016.

Sandercock, Leonine, ed. *Making the Invisible Visible: A Multicultural Planning History*. Berkeley: University of California Press, 1998.

Sandler, Daniela. "Place and Process: Culture, Urban Planning, and Social Exclusion in São Paulo." *Social Identities* 13, no. 4 (2007): 471–93.

Sant'Anna, Nuto. *São Paulo histórico: Aspectos, lendas e costumes*. São Paulo: Departamento da Cultura, 1944.

Santiago, Daniel Solá, dir. *Distrito da Brasilândia e suas histórias*. DSS Produções, 2006. Posted May 2, 2013, by Jefferson Russel, YouTube, https://www.youtube.com/watch?v=yrYdzoa78Tw.

Santos, Carlos José Ferreira dos. *Nem tudo era italiano: São Paulo e Pobreza, 1890–1915*. São Paulo: Annablume, 1998.

Santos, Carlos José Ferreira dos. "'Ser essa terra: São Paulo cidade indígena': Exposição no memorial da resistência trata da (re)existência dos povos originários na capital Paulista." *Espaço Ameríndio* 14, no. 1 (2020): 118.

Santos, Fábio A., J. Jorge, Luis Ferla, et al. "A enchente de 1929 na Cidade de São Paulo: Memória, história, e novas abordagens de pesquisa." *Revista do Arquivo Geral da Cidade do Rio de Janeiro* 8 (2014): 149–66.

Santos, Irinéia Maria Franco dos. "Nos domínios de Exu e Xangô o Axé nunca se quebra: Transformações históricas em religões Afro-Brasileiras, São Paulo e Maceió, 1970–2000." PhD diss., USP, 2012.

Santos, Milton. *Metrópole corporativa fragmentada.* São Paulo: EDUSP, 1978.

Santos, Sandra. "Marcas de pé descalço." In *Ó freguesia, quantas histórias,* edited by Cremilda Medina. São Paulo: ECA/USP, 2000.

Scarlato, Francisco Capuano. "Bixiga: Uma ideologia geográfica." *Boletim Paulista de Geografia* 67 (1989): 27–36.

Scarlato, Francisco Capuano. "Estrutura e sobrevivência dos cortiços no bairro do Bexiga." *Revista do Departamento de Geografia* 9 (1995): 117–27.

Schneck, Sheila. "Bexiga: Cotidiano e trabalho em suas interfaces com a cidade (1906–1931)." PhD diss., Universidade de São Paulo, 2016.

Schorer, Maria Thereza. *A lavoura canavieira em São Paulo: Expansão e declínio (1765–1861).* São Paulo: Difusão Européia do Livro, 1968.

Schwarcz, Lilia Moritz. *O espetáculo das raças: Cientistas, instituições e questão racial no Brasil, 1870–1930.* São Paulo: Cia. Das Letras, 1993.

Schwarcz, Lilia Moritz. *Retrato em branco e negro: Jornais, escravos e cidadãos em São Paulo no final do século XIX.* São Paulo: Companhia das Letras, 2001.

Schwartz, Stuart B. *Slaves, Peasants, and Rebels: Reconsidering Brazilian Slavery.* Urbana: University of Illinois Press, 1995.

Schwartz, Stuart B. *Sugar Plantations in the Formation of Brazilian Society: Bahia, 1550–1835.* Cambridge: Cambridge University Press, 1985.

Scott, James. *Seeing Like a State: How Certain Schemes to Improve the Human Condition Have Failed.* New Haven, CT: Yale University Press, 1998.

Scott, Rebecca J. "Exploring the Meaning of Freedom: Postemancipation Societies in Comparative Perspective." In *The Abolition of Slavery in Brazil,* edited by Rebecca J. Scott and George Andrews. Durham, NC: Duke University Press, 1988.

Secretaria Municipal de Cultura, São Paulo (Cidade). *Inventário geral do patrimônio ambiental e cultural: Liberdade,* edited by Leila Regina Diégoli, et al. São Paulo: Departamento do Patrimônio Histórico, 1987. Cadernos do IGEPAC-SP, 2.

Seigel, Micol. *Uneven Encounters: Making Race and Nation in Brazil and the United States.* Durham, NC: Duke University Press, 2009.

Sereza, Haroldo Ceravolo. "Florestan Fernandes." In *Intérpretes do Brasil: Clássicos, rebeldes e renegados,* edited by Luiz Bernardo Pericás and Lincoln Secco. São Paulo: Biotempo, 2015. Kindle Edition.

Sevcenko, Nicolau. "A cidade metástasis e o urbanismo inflacionário: Incursões na entropia paulista." *Revista usp* 63 (September/November 2004): 16–35.

Sevcenko, Nicolau. *Orfeu extático na metrópole: São Paulo, sociedade e cultura nos frementes anos 20*. São Paulo: Companhia das Letras, 1992.

Sheriff, Robin E. *Dreaming Equality: Color, Race, and Racism in Urban Brazil*. New Brunswick, NJ: Rutgers University Press, 2001.

Shih, Shu-Mei. "Comparative Racialization: An Introduction." PMLA 123, no. 5 (2008): 1347–62.

Shizuno, Elena Camargo. "A revista *Vida Policial* (1925–1927): Mistérios e dramas em contos e folhetins." PhD diss., UF-Paraná, 2011.

Silva, Joana Maria Ferreira da. *Centro de cultura e arte negra—cecan: Retratos do Brasil negro*. São Paulo: Selo Negro, 2012.

Silva, Marcos Virgílio da. *Debaixo do "Pogréssio": Sambistas e urbanização paulistana nas décadas de 1950 e 1960*. São Paulo: Alameda/FAPESP, 2018.

Silva, Marcos Virgílio da. "Debaixo do 'Pogréssio': Urbanização, cultura, e experiência popular em João Rubinato e outros Sambistas Paulistanos (1951–1969)." PhD diss., USP, 2011.

Silva, Maria Nilza da. *Nem para todos é a cidade: Segregação urbana e racial em São Paulo*. Brasília: Ministério da Cultura, Fundação Cultural Palmares, 2006.

Silva, Patrícia Garcia Ernando da. "Últimos desejos e promessas da liberdade: Os processos de alforrias em São Paulo (1850–1888)." Master's thesis, USP, 2010.

Silva, Sheila Alice Gomes da. "Negros em Guaianases: Cultura e memória." PhD diss., PUC-SP, 2015.

Silva, Vagner Gonçalves da. *Artes do corpo*. São Paulo: Selo Negro Edições, 2004.

Silva, Vagner Gonçalves da. *Orixás da metrópole*. Petrópolis: Vozes, 1995.

Simões, Inimá. *Salas de cinema em São Paulo*. São Paulo: Secretaria Municipal de Cultura de São Paulo, 1990.

Siqueira, Renata Monteiro. "O Largo da Banana e a presença negra em São Paulo." *Anais do museu paulista* 28 (2020): 1–33.

Siqueira, Renata Monteiro. *O viaduto e o samba: O Largo da Banana, urbanização e relações raciais em São Paulo*. PhD diss., Universidade de São Paulo, Faculdade de Arquitetura e Urbanismo, 2021.

Skidmore, Thomas. *Black into White: Race and Nationality in Brazilian Thought*. Durham, NC: Duke University Press, 1993.

Skidmore, Thomas. *The Politics of Military Rule in Brazil, 1964–85*. Oxford: Oxford University Press, 1988.

Slenes, Robert. "The Brazilian Internal Slave Trade, 1850–1888: Regional Economies, Slave Experience, and the Politics of a Peculiar Market Ian Read." In *The Chattel Principle: Internal Slave Trades in the Americas*, edited by Walter Johnson. New Haven, CT: Yale University Press, 2005.

Slenes, Robert. "The Demography and Economics of Brazilian slavery, 1850–1888." PhD diss., Stanford University, 1975.

Smith, Christen Anne. *Afro-Paradise: Blackness, Violence, and Performance in Brazil*. Urbana: University of Illinois Press, 2016.

Smith, Christen Anne. "Towards a Black Feminist Model of Black Atlantic Liberation: Remembering Beatriz Nascimento." *Meridians* 14, no. 2 (2016): 71–87.

Smith, James M. "Identities and Urban Social Spaces in Little Tokyo, Los Angeles: Japanese Americans in Two Ethno-Spiritual Communities." *Geografiska Annaler: Series B, Human Geography* 90, no. 4 (2008): 389–408.

Soja, Edward W. *Postmodern Geographies: The Reassertion of Space in Critical Social Theory*. New York: Verso, 1989.

Soja, Edward W. *Seeking Spatial Justice*. Minneapolis: University of Minnesota Press, 2010.

Somekh, Nadia. *A cidade vertical e o urbanismo modernizador: São Paulo, 1920–1939*. São Paulo: EDUSP, 1997.

Somekh, Nadia, and Candido Malta Campos. *A cidade que não pode parar: Planos urbanísticos de São Paulo no século xx*. São Paulo: Mackpesquisa, 2002.

Sousa, Inara Bezerra Ferreira. "O jornal *Movimento*: A experiência na luta democrática." Master's thesis, Universidade de Brasília, 2014.

Stein, Stanley J. *Vassouras: A Brazilian Coffee County, 1850–1900: The Roles of Planter and Slave in a Plantation Society*. 2nd ed. Princeton, NJ: Princeton University Press, 1985.

Stepan, Nancy. *"The Hour of Eugenics": Race, Gender, and Nation in Latin America*. Ithaca, NY: Cornell University Press, 1993.

Suk, Lena. "Becoming Modern at the Movies: Gender, Class, and Urban Space in Twentieth Century Brazil." PhD diss., Emory University, 2014.

Taschner, Suzana P. "Depois da queda ou a cidade que virou favela." *Espaço e Debates* 4, no. 12 (1984): 37–65.

Teelucksingh, Cheryl, ed. *Claiming Space: Racialization in Canadian Cities*. Waterloo, ON: Wilfrid Laurier University Press, 2006.

Telles, Edward E. *Race in Another America: The Significance of Skin Color in Brazil*. Princeton, NJ: Princeton University Press, 2004.

Telles, Edward, René D. Flores, and Fernando Urrea-Giraldo. "Pigmentocracies: Educational Inequality, Skin Color and Census Ethnoracial Identification in Eight Latin American Countries." *Research in Social Stratification and Mobility* 40 (June 2015), 39–58.

Toledo, Benedito Lima de, and Beatriz Mugayar Kühl. *Prestes Maia e as origens do urbanismo moderno em São Paulo*. São Paulo: Empresa das Artes Projetos e Edições Artísticas, 1996.

Tomich, Dale. *Pelo prisma da escravidão*. Translated by Antonio de Padua Danesi. São Paulo: EDUSP, 2011.

Tomich, Dale. "The Wealth of Empire: Francisco Arango y Parreño, Political Economy, and the Second Slavery in Cuba." *Comparative Studies in Society and History* 45, no. 1 (January 2003): 4–28.

Tuan, Yi-Fu. *Space and Place: The Perspective of Experience*. Minneapolis: University of Minnesota Press, 1977.

TV Cultura, *Ensaio: Geraldo Filme*. São Paulo: Fundação Padre Anchieta/TV Cultura, 1992. YouTube, accessed August 1, 2022.

Ulrich, Aline. "Guilherme de Almeida e a construção da identidade paulista." Master's thesis, USP, 2007.

Unno, Kaxutaka. "Cartography in Japan." In *History of Cartography: Cartography in the Traditional East and Southeast Asian Societies*, vol. 2, book 2, edited by J. B. Harley and David Woodward. Chicago: University of Chicago Press, 2015.

Valladares, Licia do Prado. *A invenção da favela: Do mito de origem a favela .com*. Rio de Janeiro: Editora FGV, 2005.

Vargas, João Costa. *The Denial of Antiblackness: Multiracial Redemption and Black Suffering*. Minneapolis: University of Minnesota Press, 2019.

Vasconcellos, Eduardo Alcântara de. *Circular é preciso, viver não é preciso: A história do trânsito na cidade de São Paulo*. São Paulo: ANNABLUME, FAPESP, 1999.

Velloso, Mônica Pimenta. "As tias baianas tomam conta do pedaço: Espaço e identidade cultural no Rio de Janeiro." *Estudos Históricos* 3, no. 6 (1990): 207–43.

Vianna, Hermano. *The Mystery of Samba: Popular Music and National Identity in Brazil*. Chapel Hill: University of North Carolina Press, 1995.

Vieira, Antonio. *História do futuro*. Lisbon, 1718; 2nd ed., 1755.

Villaça, Flávio. "Uma contribuição para a história do planejamento urbano no Brasil." In *O processo de urbanização no Brasil*, edited by Csaba Deák and Sueli Ramos Schiffer. São Paulo: EDUSP, 2015.

Viscardi, Cláudia. *O teatro das oligarquias: Uma revisão da "política do café com leite."* Belo Horizonte: Fino Traço, 2012.

Von Simson, Olga Rodrigues de Moraes. *Carnaval em branco e negro: Carnaval popular paulistano, 1914–1988*. Campinas: UNICAMP, 2007.

Weinstein, Barbara. *The Color of Modernity: São Paulo and the Making Race and Nation in Brazil*. Durham, NC: Duke University Press, 2015.

Weinstein, Barbara. "Regionalizing Racial Difference: São Paulo Versus Brazil." In *Race and Nation in Modern Latin America*, edited by Nancy P. Applebaum, Anne S. Macpherson, and Karin Rosemblatt. Chapel Hill: University of North Carolina Press, 2003.

Widmer, Ted. "The Invention of a Memory: Congo Square and African Music in Nineteenth Century New Orleans." In "Stemming the Mississippi."

Special issue, *Revue française d'études américaines* 98, no. 2 (December 2003): 69–78.
Wilhelm, Jorge. *São Paulo Metrópole 65: Subsídios para seu plano diretor.* São Paulo: 1965.
Wilhelm, Jorge. *São Paulo: Uma interpretação*. São Paulo: Editora Senac São Paulo, 2011.
Williams, Daryle. *Culture Wars in Brazil: The First Vargas Regime, 1930–1945.* Durham NC: Duke University Press, 2001.
Williams, Richard J. *Brazil: Modern Architectures in History*. London: Reaktion, 2009.
Wilson, Kenneth, and Alejandro Portes. "Immigrant Enclaves: An Analysis of the Labor Market Experiences of Cubans in Miami." *American Journal of Sociology* 86, no. 2 (September 1980): 295–319.
Winlow, Heather. "Mapping Race and Ethnicity." In *International Encyclopedia of Human Geography*, edited by Rob Kitchin and Nigel Thrift. Amsterdam: Elsevier, 2009.
Wolfe, Joel. *Autos and Progress: The Brazilian Search for Modernity*. Oxford: Oxford University Press, 2010.
Woodard, James. "'All for São Paulo, All for Brazil': Vargas, the Paulistas, and the Historiography of Twentieth-Century Brazil." In *Vargas and Brazil: New Perspectives*, edited by Jens R. Hentschke. New York: Palgrave Macmillan, 2006.
Woodard, James. *A Place in Politics: São Paulo, Brazil, from Seigneurial Republicanism to Regionalist Revolt*. Durham, NC: Duke University Press, 2009.
Yiftachel, Oren, and Haim Yacobi. "Urban Ethnocracy: Ethnicization and the Production of Space in an Israeli 'Mixed City.'" *Environment and Planning D: Society and Space* 21, no. 6 (2003): 673–93.
Yokota, K. A. "From Little Tokyo to Bronzeville and Back: Ethnic Communities in Transition." Master's thesis, University of California, Los Angeles, 1996.
Young, James E. *The Texture of Memory: Holocaust Memorials and Meaning.* New Haven, CT: Yale University Press, 1993.
Zhou, Min. "Revisiting Ethnic Entrepreneurship: Convergencies, Controversies, and Conceptual Advancements." *International Migration Review* 38, no. 3 (Fall 2004): 1040–74.
Zweig, Stefan. *Brasilien: Ein Land der Zukunft*. Stockholm: Bermann-Fischer, 1941.

Index

Page numbers followed by *f* refer to figures and maps.

www.ingramcontent.com/pod-product-compliance
Lightning Source LLC
LaVergne TN
LVHW041059080826
845145LV00007B/1635

* 9 7 8 1 4 7 8 0 3 2 8 1 6 *

20

"Let's get a move on!" Jamie hollered, snapping her fingers and breaking him from his trance.

Tim exhaled the final draw from his *Marlboro* and crushed it out in the gold ashtray that sat in the middle of the table.

He looked up and saw Jamie smiling at him. Her eyes had that special twinkle to them that he loved so well, and he smiled back.

Placing Buddy on the floor, he followed Jamie to the bedroom, jingling as he scampered along behind her.

Tim went out the back door of the kitchen and headed for the shed. It was an old building with a solid concrete foundation that Ed had painted a light yellow many years ago, although it was faded now. And a concrete ramp was poured at the entrance so that Ed and Vickie could roll the lawn tractor up and down with ease.

The door creaked as Tim slowly opened it and peered inside. His main concern was scoping out any wasps that were flying around or perched on an overhead rafter.

A red wasp had popped him twice one afternoon on his right index finger and forearm, and it felt as if some mighty lumberjack had hit him full force with a ball-peen hammer.

The coast was clear as he entered the building. Cold chills ran up and down his spine as he carefully made his way to the dusty fishing poles that were placed